SCHAUM'S OUTLINE OF

THEORY AND PROBLEMS

of

COLLEGE PHYSICS

SIXTH EDITION

•

BY

DANIEL SCHAUM, B.S.

EDITED BY

CAREL W. van der MERWE, Ph.D.

Professor of Physics
New York University

•

SCHAUM'S OUTLINE SERIES

McGRAW-HILL BOOK COMPANY

New York, St. Louis, San Francisco, Toronto, Sydney

———

Fourth Edition, October 1942
Twenty-two Reprintings

———

Fifth Edition, June 1946
Ninety-seven Reprintings

———

Sixth Edition, March 1961
Reprinted

May, June, July, September, October, December 1961
January, February, March, May 1962
June, July, September, October, November 1962
January, February, April, June, July 1963
September, October, November, December 1963
January, February, March, June, July 1964
September, October, November, December 1964
January, February, April, June, July 1965
September, October, November, December 1965
January, February, March, June, July 1966
September, October, November, December 1966
January, February, April, June, August 1967
September, October, November, December 1967
August, September 1968
February 1970

Preface

Lord Kelvin said: *"I often say that when you can measure what you are speaking about, and express it in numbers, you know something about it."* Comprehensive tests indicate definitely that only a small percentage of the subject matter presented in the typical college physics course is ever assimilated by the majority of its students. This book aims to help the student to see clearly the principles of physics and of simple mathematics associated with the problem work of a first year course in college physics.

The previous edition of this book has been very favorably received and adopted as a supplementary problems book by more than five hundred colleges and technical schools. In this sixth edition the scope of the book has been greatly enlarged and most chapters have undergone thorough revision to keep pace with the most recent concepts, methods, and terminology. In mechanics, the English gravitational and mks systems are emphasized, but the cgs system is also used. In electricity, only rationalized mks units are employed. Dimensional units are used throughout in order to stimulate their constant application by the student, and an explanation of the use of units and of dimensions appears in the fifth chapter. Emphasis is placed on the use of the correct number of significant figures in line with scientific and engineering practice. The appendix includes sections on significant figures, trigonometry, exponents, logarithms, and conversion tables.

The author has tried to use both the physical and mathematical methods in giving explanations, using word equations and simple mathematics, instead of mere substitution in a formula. The principles and reasonings affecting the solution of problems are presented directly and in the most simple and familiar terms, and the mathematical deductions stress the significance of the problem as a whole.

The contents are divided into chapters covering duly-recognized areas of theory and study. Each chapter begins with a clear statement of the pertinent definitions, principles, and theorems. This is followed by carefully graded sets of solved and supplementary problems. These are arranged so as to present a natural development of each topic, and they include a wide range of applications in both pure and applied physics. The solved problems serve to illustrate and amplify the theory, provide the repetition of basic principles so vital to effective teaching, and bring into sharp focus those fine points without which the student continually feels himself on unsafe ground. The supplementary problems serve as a complete review of the material of each chapter. This book is in no way a condensation of ordinary text material; it is intended to be a comprehensive problem book.

The author gratefully acknowledges the cooperation and suggestions of many teachers who have been using this book and who have urged him to make such additions and modifications as would better adapt it for college physics courses. Particular thanks are extended to Professor Carel W. van der Merwe of New York University for invaluable assistance and critical review of the entire manuscript.

DANIEL SCHAUM

March, 1961

Contents

MECHANICS

HEAT

ELECTRICITY AND MAGNETISM

Chapter 1

Introduction to Vectors

A SCALAR QUANTITY has only magnitude, *e.g.* time, volume of a body, mass of a body, density of a body, amount of work, amount of money.

Scalars are added by ordinary algebraic methods, *e.g.* 2 sec + 5 sec = 7 sec.

A VECTOR QUANTITY has both magnitude and direction. For example:

1) **Displacement** — an airplane flies a distance of 160 mi in a southerly direction.
2) **Velocity** — a ship sails due east at 20 mi/hr.
3) **Force** — a force of 10 lb acts on a body in a vertically upward direction.

A vector quantity is represented by an arrow drawn to scale. The length of the arrow represents the magnitude of the displacement, velocity, force, etc. The direction of the arrow represents the direction of the displacement, etc.

Vectors are added by geometric methods.

THE RESULTANT of a number of force vectors is that single vector which would have the same effect as all the original vectors together.

THE EQUILIBRANT of a number of vectors is that vector which would balance all the original vectors taken together. It is equal in magnitude but opposite in direction to the resultant.

PARALLELOGRAM METHOD OF VECTOR ADDITION. The resultant of two vectors acting at any angle may be represented by the diagonal of a parallelogram drawn with the two vectors as adjacent sides, and directed away from the origin of the two vectors.

VECTOR POLYGON METHOD OF VECTOR ADDITION. This method of finding the resultant consists in beginning at any convenient point and drawing (to scale) each vector in turn, taking them in any order of succession. The tail end of each vector is attached to the arrow end of the preceding one. The line drawn to complete the triangle or polygon is equal in magnitude to the resultant or equilibrant.

The resultant is represented by the straight line directed from the starting point to the arrow end of the last vector added.

The equilibrant is represented by the same line as the resultant but is oppositely directed, i.e. toward the starting point.

SUBTRACTION OF VECTORS. To subtract vector B from vector A, reverse the direction of vector B and add it vectorially to vector A, i.e. $A - B = A + (-B)$.

A COMPONENT OF A VECTOR is its effective value in any given direction. For example, the horizontal component of a vector is its effective value in a horizontal direction. A vector may be considered as the resultant of two or more component vectors, the vector sum of the components being the original vector. It is customary and most useful to resolve a vector into components along mutually perpendicular directions.

SOLVED PROBLEMS

1. Find the resultant of two forces of 4 lb and 3 lb, acting on a point O at an angle of *a*) 90°, *b*) 60°, with each other. Use the parallelogram method.

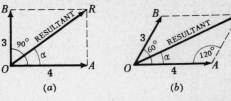

Graphical Solution:

In each case, choosing a suitable scale, draw the vectors OA and OB to represent 4 and 3 lb respectively, at the given angles with each other. Complete the parallelogram by drawing BR parallel to OA, and AR parallel to OB.

The diagonal OR represents in each case the magnitude and direction of the resultant of the two forces.

In *a*), OR is measured by scale and is found to represent 5 lb. Angle α is measured by protractor and is found to be 37°.

In *b*), OR is found to represent 6.1 lb and angle α is 25°.

By Computation:

a) OAR is a right triangle. Then $OR^2 = 4^2 + 3^2 = 25$ and $OR = 5$ lb.

$$\tan \alpha = \frac{AR}{OA} = \frac{3}{4} = 0.75 \quad \text{and} \quad \alpha = \tan^{-1} 0.75 \text{ (i.e., angle whose tangent is 0.75)} = 37°$$

b) $\angle OAR = 120°$. To compute the magnitude of the resultant OR, use the law of cosines.

$$OR^2 = OA^2 + AR^2 - 2(OA)(AR) \cos 120° = 4^2 + 3^2 - 2(4)(3)(-0.5) = 37 \quad \text{and} \quad OR = 6.1 \text{ lb}.$$

To compute angle α, use the law of sines.

$$\frac{\sin \alpha}{AR} = \frac{\sin 120°}{OR} \quad \text{or} \quad \frac{\sin \alpha}{3} = \frac{0.866}{6.1}. \quad \text{Then} \quad \sin \alpha = 0.43 \text{ and } \alpha = \sin^{-1} 0.43 = 25°.$$

Note. $\sin 120° = \sin(180° - 120°) = \sin 60°$, $\cos 120° = -\cos(180° - 120°) = -\cos 60°$.

2. Solve Problem 1 by the vector polygon method.

Graphical Solution:

In each case draw OA to represent the 4 lb force. From A plot $AR = 3$ lb in the direction of the 3 lb force. Draw OR to complete the triangle.

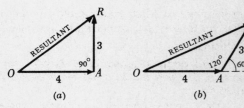

The vector OR is the resultant and is in magnitude equal to 5 lb in (*a*) and 6.1 lb in (*b*).

The computation is exactly the same as in Problem 1.

3. Four coplanar forces act on a body at a point O as shown in Fig.(*a*). Determine graphically their resultant.

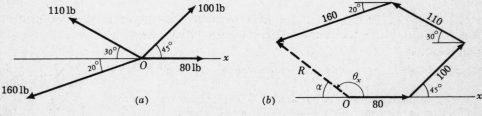

Solution:

Starting from O, the four vectors are plotted in turn, placing the tail end of one vector at the arrow end of the preceding vector, as shown in Fig.(*b*). The directed line R, connecting the tail end of the first vector with the arrow end of the last vector, is the resultant.

R is measured to scale and is found to represent 119 lb. Angle α is measured by protractor and is found to be 37°. Hence the resultant R has a magnitude of 119 lb and is directed 37° above the negative x-axis (or at an angle of $\theta_x = 180° - \alpha = 143°$ with the positive direction of the x-axis).

4. Perform graphically the following vector additions and subtractions, where A, B, and C are vectors. *a*) $A + B$, *b*) $A + B + C$, *c*) $A - B$, *d*) $A + B - C$.

Solution:

   The vector additions and subtractions are shown in Figures $(a) - (d)$ below. In (c), $A - B = A + (-B)$; i.e., to subtract vector B from vector A, reverse the direction of B and add it vectorially to A. Similarly in (d), $A + B - C = A + B + (-C)$, where $-C$ is equal in magnitude but opposite in direction to C.

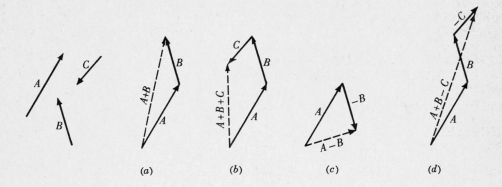

(a)	(b)	(c)	(d)

5. The resultant of two forces at right angles is 100 lb. If one of the forces makes an angle of 30° with the resultant, compute that force.

Solution:

   Draw a rectangle with the diagonal making an angle of 30° with the horizontal and representing 100 lb.

   Or, draw a right triangle with the hypotenuse making an angle of 30° with the horizontal and representing 100 lb.

$$X = 100 \times \cos 30^\circ = 100 \times 0.866 = 86.6 \text{ lb.}$$

6. Two forces at right angles have a resultant of 10 lb. If one of the two forces is 6 lb, compute the other force.

Solution:

   Let Y be the required force. Draw a rectangle with a side representing 6 lb and the diagonal representing 10 lb. Y and 6 lb are at right angles.

   Or, draw a right triangle with the hypotenuse representing 10 lb and one arm representing 6 lb.

$$Y^2 = 10^2 - 6^2 = 100 - 36 = 64 \qquad Y = 8 \text{ lb}$$

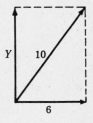 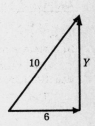

7. A boat travels at 8 mi/hr in still water. At what angle with the shore must the boat be steered to reach a point directly opposite if the velocity of the current is 4 mi/hr?

Graphical Solution:

   Choose a suitable scale. Draw OA to represent the current's velocity, 4 mi/hr.

   Draw ON, an indefinite line perpendicular to OA, to represent the resultant direction of the boat. With A as center and 8 mi/hr as radius describe a circle cutting ON in R.

   Join AR. Complete the parallelogram AB.

   Then OB is the direction of the boat's head, and the required angle DOB is measured to be 60°.

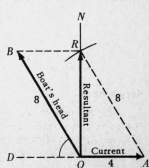

By Computation: $\cos \angle DOB = \cos \angle OAR = 4/8 = 0.5$

   Hence $\angle DOB = \cos^{-1} 0.5 = 60^\circ$.

8. A ship is heading due north at 12 mi/hr but drifts westward with the tide at 5 mi/hr. Determine the magnitude and direction of the resultant velocity of the ship.

Parallelogram Method   Triangle Method

Solution:

The velocity of 12 mi/hr north is added vectorially to the velocity of 5 mi/hr west to give the resultant velocity R of the ship relative to the ground.

Magnitude of $R = \sqrt{5^2 + 12^2} = 13$ mi/hr

The direction of R is such that it makes an angle α whose tangent is $\tan\alpha = 5/12 = 0.42$; hence $\alpha = 23°$.

The resultant velocity is 13 mi/hr in a direction 23° West of North.

9. A motorcyclist is riding north at 50 mi/hr and the wind is blowing westward with a velocity of 30 mi/hr. Determine the apparent wind velocity as observed by the cyclist.

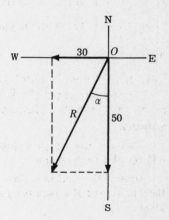

Solution:

When the cyclist is riding north at 50 mi/hr he creates a wind (relative to himself) blowing south at 50 mi/hr which is added vectorially to the west wind of 30 mi/hr to give the resultant velocity R of the air relative to the cyclist.

$R = \sqrt{30^2 + 50^2} = 58$ mi/hr

$\tan\alpha = 30/50 = 0.6$ and $\alpha = 31°$.

The wind seems to blow at 58 mi/hr in a direction 31° W of S.

10. Resolve a force of 1000 lb at 53° with the x-axis into horizontal and vertical components.

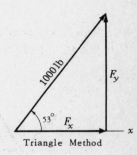

Parallelogram Method   Triangle Method

Solution:

Horizontal component $F_x = 1000 \cos 53°$
$$= 1000(0.6018) = 602 \text{ lb}$$

Vertical component $F_y = 1000 \sin 53°$
$$= 1000(0.7986) = 799 \text{ lb}$$

11. A boy pulls a rope attached to a sled with a force of 20 lb. The rope makes an angle of 30° with the ground. Compute the effective value of the pull tending to move the sled along the ground, and the effective value tending to lift the sled vertically.

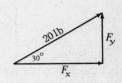

Parallelogram Method   Triangle Method

Solution:

The force tending to move the sled along the ground is the horizontal component F_x. The force tending to lift the sled off the ground is the vertical component F_y.

$$F_x = 20\text{ lb} \times \cos 30° = 20\text{ lb} \times 0.866 = 17.3 \text{ lb}$$
$$F_y = 20\text{ lb} \times \sin 30° = 20\text{ lb} \times 0.500 = 10.0 \text{ lb}$$

12. A block of weight $W = 300\,$lb rests on a smooth board inclined $25°$ with the horizontal.

    a) Find the components of W normal (perpendicular) and parallel to the plane.

    b) What force F_3 parallel to the plane is required to draw the block up the plane?

Solution:

    a) Resolve W into two components, F_1 and F_2, respectively normal and parallel to the plane.

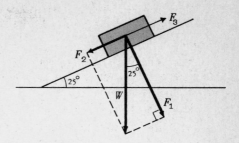

$$F_1 = \text{component of } W \text{ normal to plane}$$
$$= W \cos 25° = 300\,\text{lb} \times 0.9063 = 272\,\text{lb}$$

$$F_2 = \text{component of } W \text{ parallel to plane}$$
$$= W \sin 25° = 300\,\text{lb} \times 0.4226 = 127\,\text{lb down plane}$$

    b) $F_3 = -F_2 = 127\,$lb up the plane

13. What least force F_2 parallel to the plane is required to draw a machine of weight $W = 900\,$lb up a smooth inclined plane 18 ft long to a platform 5 ft above the ground?

Solution:

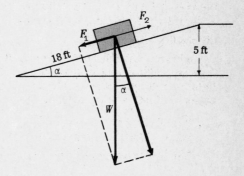

    Resolve the 900 lb weight into two components, normal and parallel to the plane.

    Then $F_1 = 900\,\text{lb} \times \sin \alpha = 900\,\text{lb} \times 5/18 = 250\,$lb down the plane, and the required force $F_2 = -F_1 = 250\,$lb up the plane.

14. Calculate the resultant of the five coplanar forces (19, 15, 16, 11, 12 lb) acting on an object at A, as shown in Fig.(*a*).

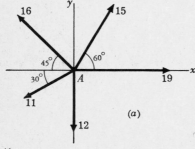

(*a*)

Resolution of 15, 16 and 11 lb forces into
horizontal and vertical components.

Solution:

1) Each force is resolved into horizontal and vertical components. (The force of 19 lb horizontally to the right has no vertical component. The vertically downward force of 12 lb has no horizontal component.)

2) The horizontal components to the right are considered positive, and those to the left negative. The upward vertical components are taken as positive, and those downward as negative.

3) The horizontal components are added separately (algebraically), and the vertical components are added separately (algebraically). This gives two resultant components (ΣF_x and ΣF_y) at right angles. The resultant of ΣF_x and ΣF_y is R.

4) The horizontal and vertical components of the five forces are as follows.

Force	Horizontal Component	Vertical Component
a) 19 lb	19.0	0.0
b) 15 lb	$15 \cos 60° =$ 7.5	$15 \sin 60° =$ 13.0
c) 16 lb	$-16 \cos 45° =$ −11.3	$16 \sin 45° =$ 11.3
d) 11 lb	$-11 \cos 30° =$ − 9.5	$-11 \sin 30° =$ − 5.5
e) 12 lb	0.0	−12.0
	$\Sigma F_x = +$ 5.7 lb	$\Sigma F_y = +$ 6.8 lb

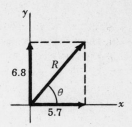

Magnitude of $R = \sqrt{(\Sigma F_x)^2 + (\Sigma F_y)^2} = \sqrt{(5.7)^2 + (6.8)^2} = 8.9$ lb

and $\tan \theta = \dfrac{\Sigma F_y}{\Sigma F_x} = \dfrac{6.8 \text{ lb}}{5.7 \text{ lb}} = 1.2$ from which $\theta = 50°$.

The resultant is 8.9 lb at an angle of 50° with the positive direction of the x-axis.

15. A telescope must be inclined 20.5 seconds of arc with the vertical in order to see a fixed star which is vertically overhead. Due to the earth's orbital motion, the telescope has a speed of 18.5 mi/sec at right angles to the direction of the star. From these facts deduce the speed of light.

Solution:

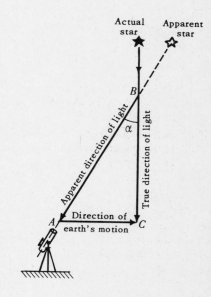

Let c = speed of light, v = speed of telescope. The inclination of the telescope must be such that the time t taken for light to travel a distance BC ($t = BC/c$) equals the time taken by the telescope to travel the distance AC ($t = AC/v$). Then $BC/c = AC/v$ or $AC/BC = \tan \alpha = v/c$ and

$$c = \frac{v}{\tan 20.5''} = \frac{18.5 \text{ mi/sec}}{9.94 \times 10^{-5}} = 1.86 \times 10^5 \text{ mi/sec}$$

This method was used by Bradley in 1728 to determine the speed of light, and 20.5$''$ is called the angle of aberration.

Note. The sines and tangents of very small angles are almost exactly equal numerically to their angles when measured in radians.

$$20.5'' = 20.5'' \times \frac{2\pi \text{ rad}}{360 \text{ deg}} \times \frac{1 \text{ deg}}{3600''} = 9.94 \times 10^{-5} \text{ rad}$$

SUPPLEMENTARY PROBLEMS

16. Two forces, of 80 and 100 lb acting at an angle of 60° with each other, pull on an object. What single pull would replace the given forces?
    Ans. $R = 156$ lb at $\alpha = 34°$ with the 80 lb force

17. Two forces, of 100 lb each and making 120° with each other, pull on an object. Find the single pull that would *a*) replace the given force system, *b*) balance the given force system.
    Ans. *a*) Resultant $R = 100$ lb at 60° with each given force
    b) Equilibrant $E = 100$ lb directed opposite to the resultant

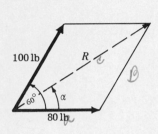

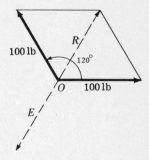

Prob. 16   **Prob. 17**

18. A man walks 50 ft east, 30 ft south, 20 ft west, and 10 ft north. Determine his distance from the starting point.   *Ans.* 36 ft directed 34° south of east

19. Find the vector sum of the following four displacements: 60 ft north; 30 ft west; 40 ft, 60°W of N; 50 ft, 30°W of S. Solve graphically and by the component method.
    Ans. 96.8 ft, 67.7° W of N

20. Given vector A and vector B, and parallelogram $OMPN$. Express the following vectors in terms of A and B: OP, MP, PN, NM.   *Ans.* $OP = A+B$, $MP = B$, $PN = -A$, $NM = -B + A$

21. If CM is a median of triangle ABC, and $CM = \alpha$ and $MB = \beta$, express each of the following directed line segments in terms of vectors α and β: CB, AM, MA, AB, CA.
    Ans. $CB = \alpha + \beta$, $AM = \beta$, $MA = -\beta$, $AB = 2\beta$, $CA = \alpha - \beta$

22. Given vector $A = 80$ ft/sec north and vector $B = 60$ ft/sec east. Find the vector difference $A - B$.
    Ans. 100 ft/sec at $\alpha = 37°$ W of N

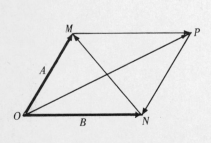

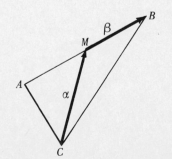

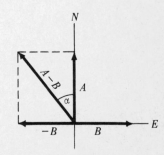

Prob. 20   **Prob. 21**   **Prob. 22**

23. Find graphically the resultant of each of the three coplanar concurrent force systems shown in Fig. (a), (b), (c) below.   *Ans.* (a) 35 lb at $\theta_x = 34°$, (b) 59 lb at $\theta_x = 236°$, (c) 172 lb at $\theta_x = 315°$

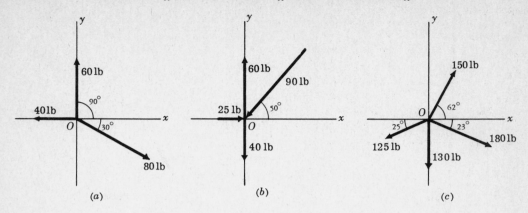

Prob. 23

24. A ship is traveling due east at 10 mi/hr. What must be the speed of a second ship heading in a direction 30° east of north, if it is always due north from the first ship?
Ans. 20 mi/hr

25. From an electric car traveling at 15 mi/hr, a ball is thrown at right angles to the motion of the car and with a speed of 20 ft/sec. What is the speed of the ball (relative to the earth) at the beginning of its flight?
Ans. 29.7 ft/sec

26. A boat, propelled so as to travel with a speed of 500 ft/min in still water, moves directly across a river 2000 ft wide, the river flowing at 300 ft/min. How long will it take the boat to cross the river? Towards what point on the opposite shore is the boat headed when it starts?
Ans. 5 minutes, 1500 feet upstream

27. A stationary soldier sees an enemy tank 500 ft away moving at 44 ft/sec on a line perpendicular to his line of sight. (a) If the speed of the bullet is 1000 ft/sec, at what horizontal angle with his line of sight must he aim the gun to hit the tank? (b) How many feet to one side of the tank must he aim?
Ans. 2.52°, 22 ft

28. Resolve a force of 10 lb into two components at right angles, the line of action of one component making an angle of 45° with the line of action of the 10 lb force. Solve by construction and by computation.
Ans. Each component 7.07 lb

29. Resolve a force of 100 lb into two components at right angles, one component making an angle of 30° with the 100 lb force. Solve by construction and by computation.
Ans. 50 lb, 86.6 lb

30. A telegraph pole is supported by a guy wire which exerts a 250 lb pull on the top of the pole. The guy wire makes an angle of 42° with the pole. Determine the horizontal and vertical components of the pull on the pole.   *Ans.* 167 lb horizontal, 186 lb vertical

31. A horse exerts a force of 300 lb to pull a barge along a canal, using a 50 ft rope. If the barge is kept 10 ft from the canal bank, compute (a) the effective value of the pull tending to move the barge along the canal, and (b) the sideways force which must be exerted by the rudder to keep the barge 10 ft from the bank.
Ans. 294 lb, 60 lb

32. What force parallel to the plane is required to draw a 200 lb box with uniform speed up a smooth 32° incline?
Ans. 106 lb

33. Compute the resultant and equilibrant of the following system of coplanar concurrent forces:
3 lb, 0°; 4 lb, 30°; 4 lb, 150°.
Ans. Resultant = 5 lb at 53°, equilibrant = 5 lb at 233°

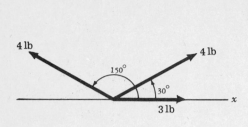

Prob. 33

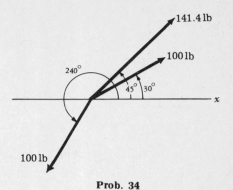

Prob. 34

34. Compute the resultant and equilibrant of the following system of coplanar concurrent forces:
100 lb, 30°; 141.4 lb, 45°; 100 lb, 240°.
Ans. Resultant = 151 lb at 25°, equilibrant = 151 lb at 205°

35. Compute the resultant of the following system of coplanar concurrent forces: Forces of 20, 40, 25, 42 and
12 lb, making angles of 30°, 120°, 180°, 270° and 315° respectively with the positive direction of the *x*-axis.
Ans. 20 lb at 197°

Chapter 2

Equilibrium of a Rigid Body

PARALLEL COPLANAR FORCES

THE MOMENT OF A FORCE, or torque, about an axis is the effectiveness of the force in producing rotation about that axis. It is measured by the product of the force and the perpendicular distance from the axis of rotation to the line of action of the force.

Moment = force × perpendicular distance from axis to action line of force.

When the force is expressed in pounds and the distance in feet, the unit of moment is the pound-foot (lb-ft).

DEFINITION OF EQUILIBRIUM. A body is in **translational equilibrium** if it is at rest, or is moving at constant speed in a straight line. It is in **rotational equilibrium** if it is not rotating, or if it is rotating at constant angular speed about an axis.

A system of forces acting on a body produces equilibrium if, when acting together, the forces have no tendency to produce a change in the body's translatory (straight line) motion, or in its rotary motion.

CONDITIONS FOR EQUILIBRIUM UNDER ACTION OF PARALLEL COPLANAR FORCES.

1) The algebraic sum of the forces acting on the body in any given direction must be zero. This is equivalent to saying that the sum of the upward forces equals the sum of the downward forces, and similarly for those forces along the other directions such as left to right, etc.

   When this condition is satisfied there is no unbalanced force acting on the body, (and therefore the body will have no linear acceleration). In other words, the system of forces will not tend to produce any change in the linear motion of the body.

2) The algebraic sum of the moments of all the forces acting about any axis perpendicular to the plane of the forces must be zero. This is equivalent to saying that the sum of the clockwise moments about any such axis equals the sum of the counterclockwise moments about that axis.

   When this condition is satisfied there is no unbalanced torque or moment acting on the body, (and hence the body will have no angular acceleration). In other words, the system of moments will not tend to produce any change in the angular motion of the body. If it is initially at rest it will not start to rotate, and if it is initially rotating it will maintain the same rate of rotation.

A COUPLE consists of two equal and oppositely directed parallel forces, not in the same straight line. A couple can produce only rotation.

The moment of a couple is equal to the product of one of the forces and the perpendicular distance between them. A couple can be balanced only by another couple of equal moment, in the opposite direction.

THE CENTER OF GRAVITY of a body is the point at which the entire weight of the body may be considered as concentrated, i.e. the line of action of the weight passes through the center of gravity. A single vertically upward force equal to the weight of the body and applied at the center of gravity will keep the body in equilibrium.

SOLVED PROBLEMS

1. Forces of 8, 6, 5, 3, 7, 9 and 4 lb act on a 4 ft by 2 ft rectangle as shown. Determine the algebraic sum of the moments (ΣL) of these forces about an axis *a*) through A, *b*) through B, *c*) through C, *d*) through the center O.

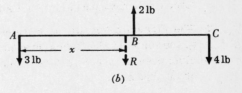

Solution:

Moment = force × perpendicular distance from axis to action line of force.

Consider clockwise moments as negative and counterclockwise moments as positive.

a) $\Sigma L_A = 8\,\text{lb} \times 0\,\text{ft} + 6\,\text{lb} \times 0\,\text{ft} - 5\,\text{lb} \times 2\,\text{ft} - 3\,\text{lb} \times 4\,\text{ft}$
$\qquad\qquad -7\,\text{lb} \times 1\,\text{ft} + 9\,\text{lb} \times 2\,\text{ft} + 4\,\text{lb} \times 2\,\text{ft}$
$\qquad = (0 + 0 - 10 - 12 - 7 + 18 + 8)\,\text{lb-ft} = -3\,\text{lb-ft}$

b) $\Sigma L_B = -8(2) + 6(4) + 5(2) + 3(0) + 7(1) - 9(2) + 4(0) = +7\,\text{lb-ft}$

c) $\Sigma L_C = -8(2) + 6(0) - 5(2) - 3(4) + 7(1) + 9(2) + 4(0) = -13\,\text{lb-ft}$

d) $\Sigma L_O = -8(1) + 6(2) + 5(0) - 3(2) + 7(0) + 9(0) + 4(1) = +2\,\text{lb-ft}$

2. A horizontal weightless rod AC, 10 ft long, is acted upon by three vertical forces as shown in Fig. (*a*).
a) Find the algebraic sum of the forces (ΣF) acting on the rod.
b) Find the algebraic sum of the moments (ΣL) about an axis through each of the following points: A, B, C.
c) Determine completely the resultant R and the equilibrant of the given force system.

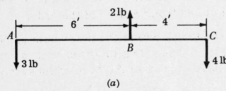 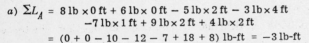

(*a*)   (*b*)

Solution:

a) Consider upward forces positive. Then $\Sigma F = (-3 + 2 - 4)\,\text{lb} = -5\,\text{lb}$ (down).

b) Consider clockwise moments negative and counterclockwise moments positive.

$\qquad \Sigma L_A = 3\,\text{lb} \times 0\,\text{ft} + 2\,\text{lb} \times 6\,\text{ft} - 4\,\text{lb} \times 10\,\text{ft} = -28\,\text{lb-ft}$ (clockwise)

$\qquad \Sigma L_B = +3\,\text{lb} \times 6\,\text{ft} + 2\,\text{lb} \times 0\,\text{ft} - 4\,\text{lb} \times 4\,\text{ft} = +2\,\text{lb-ft}$ (counterclockwise)

$\qquad \Sigma L_C = +3\,\text{lb} \times 10\,\text{ft} - 2\,\text{lb} \times 4\,\text{ft} + 4\,\text{lb} \times 0\,\text{ft} = +22\,\text{lb-ft}$ (counterclockwise)

c) From *a*) the value of resultant $R = \Sigma F = -5\,\text{lb}$ (down). Then from Fig. (*b*),

$\qquad$ moment of R about axis through A = sum of moments of given forces about A (ΣL_A)

$\qquad\qquad\qquad -5\,\text{lb} \times x = -28\,\text{lb-ft}, \qquad$ and $x = 5.6\,\text{ft from } A$.

The resultant R of the given force system is 5 lb down, its line of action being at a perpendicular distance $x = 5.6$ ft from A.

The equilibrant (i.e., the force required to produce equilibrium) is 5 lb *up* at a perpendicular distance $x = 5.6$ ft from A.

3. A weight of 20 lb balances a weight of 36 lb at the extremities of a weightless lever 14 in. long. Compute the lengths of the arms.

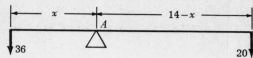

Solution:

Let the lengths of the arms be x and $14-x$, as shown in the adjoining figure.

Since the lever is in equilibrium, the sum of the torques about any axis perpendicular to the plane of the forces is zero. Summing the moments about an axis through A,

$$\Sigma L_A = +36(x) - 20(14-x) = 0 \quad \text{and} \quad x = 5\,\text{in.} \quad \text{The arms are 5 and 9 in.}$$

4. Where must a weight be hung on a pole, of negligible weight, so that the boy at one end supports 1/3 as much as the man at the other end?

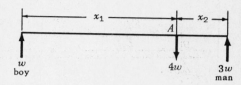

Solution:

Let w = weight supported by boy
       $3w$ = weight supported by man.

Since the pole is in equilibrium, the sum of the torques about any axis perpendicular to the plane of the forces must be zero. Summing moments about A,

$$\Sigma L_A = -w(x_1) + 3w(x_2) = 0 \quad \text{and} \quad x_1 = 3x_2$$

The weight must be at a distance from the boy equal to 3/4 the length of the pole.

5. A uniform rod 10 ft long and weighing 30 lb is supported in a horizontal position on a fulcrum with weights of 40 and 50 lb suspended from its ends. Compute the position of the fulcrum.

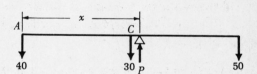

Solution:

Consider the weight of the uniform rod as concentrated at its center C.

Let P = upward force at fulcrum.

Since the rod is in equilibrium, the sum of the vertical forces acting on the rod is zero. Then, considering upward forces positive,

$$\Sigma F = -40 - 30 + P - 50 = 0 \quad \text{and} \quad P = 120\,\text{lb}$$

Since the rod is in equilibrium, the sum of the torques about any axis perpendicular to the plane of the forces is zero. Summing moments about an axis through A,

$$\Sigma L_A = -50(10) + 120(x) - 30(5) + 40(0) = 0 \quad \text{and} \quad x = 5.4\,\text{ft}$$

The fulcrum is 5.4 ft from the 40 lb weight.

6. A uniform rod 10 ft long and weighing 15 lb is supported horizontally by props P and R at distances of 2 and 8 ft from one end. Weights of 25, 10, and 12 lb are attached at distances of 1, 7, and 10 ft respectively from the same end. Find the force on each prop.

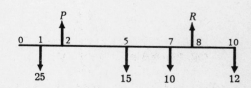

Solution:

Let P and R be the upward reactions of the props. The weight of the uniform rod, 15 lb, is considered as acting at its center.

Summing the moments about an axis through the point at which P acts,

$$\Sigma L_P = 25(1) + P(0) - 15(3) - 10(5) + R(6) - 12(8) = 0 \quad \text{and} \quad R = 27.7\,\text{lb}$$

Summing forces in the vertical direction (upward forces positive),

$$\Sigma F = P + 27.7 - 25 - 15 - 10 - 12 = 0 \quad \text{and} \quad P = 34.3\,\text{lb}$$

The forces on the props at P and R are respectively 34.3 and 27.7 lb down.

7. Determine completely the resultant R of the three forces shown in the figure below.

Solution:

$$R = \Sigma F = -30 - 50 - 20 = -100\,\text{lb (down)}.$$

Let x = perpendicular distance of action line of R from O. Then

moment of R about O = sum of moments of given forces about O

$$-R(x) = -30(4) - 50(10) - 20(15)$$
$$-100x = -920, \quad\text{and}\quad x = 9.2\,\text{ft from } O.$$

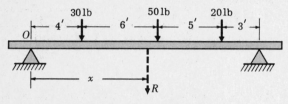

Fig. Problem 7 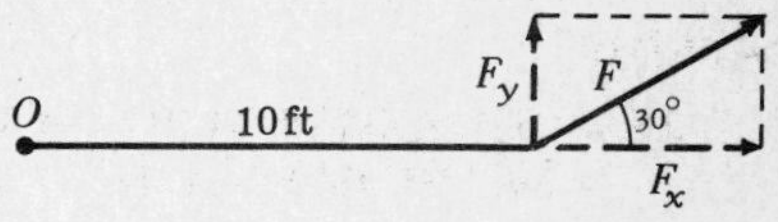   **Fig. Problem 8**

8. In the figure above, find the moment of the force $F = 50\,\text{lb}$ about an axis through O.

Solution:

Replace F by its horizontal and vertical components, F_x and F_y.

The moment of F_x about O is zero, since its action line passes through O. Hence the moment of F about O is equal to the moment of F_y about O, or

$$+F_y(10\,\text{ft}) = +(50\,\text{lb} \times \sin 30^\circ)(10\,\text{ft}) = +250\,\text{lb-ft (counterclockwise)}$$

9. A thin heavy uniform iron rod 16 inches long is bent at the 10 inch mark forming a right-angled L-shaped piece $6'' \times 10''$. The bent rod is hung on a peg at the point of bend. What angle does the 10 inch side make with the vertical when the system is in equilibrium?

Solution:

Summing moments about an axis through P,

$$\Sigma L_P = 6w(x_1) - 10w(x_2) = 0 \quad\text{or}\quad 6w(3\cos\theta) - 10w(5\sin\theta) = 0$$

Then $18\cos\theta = 50\sin\theta$, $\dfrac{\sin\theta}{\cos\theta} = \dfrac{18}{50}$ or $\tan\theta = 0.36$, and $\theta = 20^\circ$.

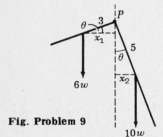

Fig. Problem 9

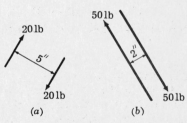

Fig. Problem 10

10. A couple of moment $-100\,\text{in-lb}$ acts in the plane of the paper. Indicate this couple with *a*) 20 lb forces, *b*) 50 lb forces.

Solution:

In *a*) the moment arm is 5 inches, in *b*) it is 2 inches.

In each case the parallel forces may be drawn at any angle. But since the moment of the couple is negative, the direction of rotation must be clockwise. Refer to the figure above.

11. *a*) 1. What is the moment of the couple shown in Fig. (*a*)?

    2. How can this couple be balanced?

    3. What must be the perpendicular distance between the lines of action of a balancing couple of 12 lb?

b) A weightless bar *AB*, 50 in. long, is acted on by forces as shown in Fig. (*b*). Is this bar in equilibrium? If not, what must be applied to produce equilibrium?

Solution:

a) 1. Moment of couple = 9 lb × 4 ft = 36 lb-ft counterclockwise.

    2. By a couple of moment 36 lb-ft clockwise (i.e., − 36 lb-ft).

    3. Perpendicular distance = $\dfrac{\text{moment of couple}}{\text{force}}$ = $\dfrac{36 \text{ lb-ft}}{12 \text{ lb}}$ = 3 ft.

b) The total upward force (6 lb) is equal to the total downward force (2 lb + 4 lb). Hence the first condition of equilibrium is satisfied.

    To determine if the second condition of equilibrium is satisfied, sum the moments about *A*.

$$\Sigma L_A = +6 \text{ lb} \times 10 \text{ in.} - 4 \text{ lb} \times 50 \text{ in.} = -140 \text{ lb-in. (clockwise)}$$

    The effective value of the three forces is a clockwise couple of moment 140 lb-in. Hence the bar is not in equilibrium, since it is caused to rotate by the unbalanced couple. To produce equilibrium an equal and oppositely directed couple, of 140 lb-in counterclockwise, must be applied to the bar. Fig. (*c*) shows the bar in equilibrium by the addition of two 7 lb forces oppositely directed and separated by a distance of 20 in. (7 lb × 20 in. = 140 lb-in.)

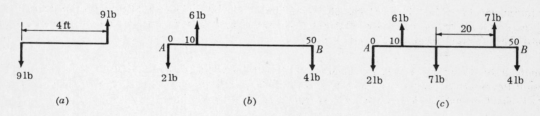

    (*a*)   (*b*)   (*c*)

12. Show that the moment of a couple is independent of the choice of moment center.

Solution:

    As in Fig. (*a*) below, draw a couple with $F_1 = F_2$ in magnitude. Through any moment center *O* between the forces draw line *AB* normal to the action lines of the forces. Then, since counterclockwise moments are considered as positive and $F_1 = F_2$ (in magnitude), we have:

$$\text{Moment of couple about } O = + (F_1 \times OA) + (F_2 \times OB)$$
$$= + F_1(OA + OB) = + F_1 \times AB$$

    As in Fig. (*b*) below, choose a different location for moment center *O* and draw *OAB* normal to the action lines of the forces. Considering clockwise moments as negative, we have:

$$\text{Moment of couple about } O = - (F_1 \times OA) + (F_2 \times OB)$$
$$= + F_1(OB - OA) = + F_1 \times AB, \quad \text{as before.}$$

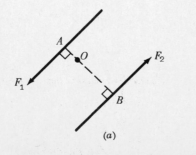

    (*a*)

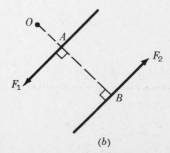

    (*b*)

SUPPLEMENTARY PROBLEMS

13. Forces of 2, 6, 5, 4, 3 and 9 lb act on a 2 ft square as shown below. Determine the sum of the moments of these forces *a*) about *A*, *b*) about the center *C* of the square.

   Ans. *a*) − 6 lb-ft (clockwise), *b*) + 1 lb-ft (counterclockwise)

14. A weightless bar *AB*, 100 in. long, is acted upon by horizontal forces of 8, 4, 2 and 2 lb as shown in the figure below. What is necessary to produce equilibrium?

   Ans. 8 lb to the right at 30 in. above *A*

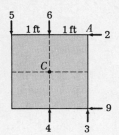

Fig. Problem 13

Fig. Problem 14

15. A uniform bar *AB*, 100 cm long, weighs 60 lb. An upward force of 50 lb is applied to the bar 20 cm from end *A*, and downward forces of 60 and 30 lb act respectively at *A* and *B*. Find the value and location of the equilibrant.   *Ans.* 100 lb up at 50 cm

16. A uniform rod *AB* is 100 cm long and weighs 5 lb. A downward force of 2 lb is applied 20 cm from end *A*, and upward forces of 5, 3, and 8 lb act at end *A*, 60 cm from *A*, and 100 cm from *A* respectively. What is necessary to produce equilibrium?   *Ans.* 9 lb downward at 76.7 cm from *A*

17. Three men carry a uniform timber. One takes hold at one end, and the other two carry by means of a crossbar placed underneath. At what point of timber must the bar be placed so that each man may carry one-third of the weight of the timber?   *Ans.* 1/4 length from free end

18. A bar *AB*, 10 ft long, has its center of gravity 2 ft from end *A* and is to be supported at its extremities. What is the force on supports at *A* and *B*, if the bar weighs 100 lb?

   Ans. 80 lb down at *A*, 20 lb down at *B*

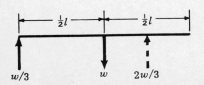

Fig. Problem 15

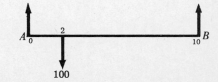

Fig. Problem 16

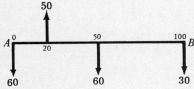

Fig. Problem 17

Fig. Problem 18

19. A uniform scaffold 12 ft long and weighing $w = 100$ lb is supported horizontally by two vertical ropes hung from its ends. Find the tension in each rope when a 180 lb painter stands 4 ft from one end. *Ans.* 170 lb at A, 110 lb at B

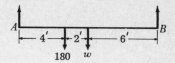

20. A uniform bar AB is 100 cm long and weighs 50 lb. The bar is to be supported at ends A and B. An upward force of 40 lb is applied 80 cm from A. Compute the forces on the supports. *Ans.* Force down at A is 17 lb; force up at B is 7 lb

21. A uniform pole 20 ft long and weighing 30 lb is supported by a boy 3 ft from one end and a man 6 ft from the other end. At what point must a 150 lb weight be attached so that the man supports twice as much as the boy? *Ans.* 7.4 ft from the boy

22. Find the sum of the moments of the forces about an axis a) through A in Fig.(a), b) through B in Fig.(b), and c) through C in Fig.(c). *Ans.* a) $+56$ lb-ft, b) 0 lb-ft, c) -275 lb-ft

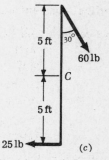

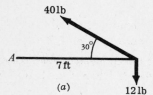 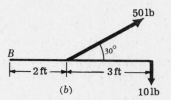

(a)   (b)   (c)

23. Given a couple consisting of forces of magnitude 6 lb and perpendicular distance between the lines of action 10 units. What must be the perpendicular distance between the lines of action of a balancing couple made up of 12 lb forces? What must be the forces of a balancing couple, the lines of action of which are 8 units apart? *Ans.* 5 units, 7.5 lb

24. Weightless bars are acted upon by forces shown in Fig.(a),(b),(c) below. What must be applied to each bar to produce equilibrium?   *Ans.* a) A couple of moment $+30$ lb-ft (counterclockwise)
        b) A couple of moment -28 lb-ft (clockwise)
        c) A couple of moment $+10$ lb-ft (counterclockwise)

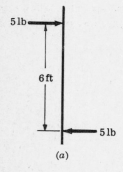 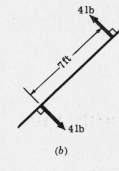 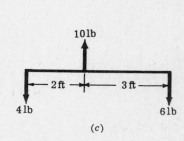

(a)   (b)   (c)

25. A uniform bar 10 ft long and weighing 12 lb is loaded as follows: 10 lb at the left end, 15 lb at 3 ft, 5 lb at 4 ft, 20 lb at 7 ft, and 25 lb at 10 ft, all distances being measured from the left end of the bar. Locate the center of gravity of the loaded bar. *Ans.* 5.9 ft from the left end

26. Man A weighs 150 lb and man B weighs 200 lb. They desire to find the weight and position of the center of gravity of a heavy bar 16 ft long. They put a fulcrum under the bar, and when the man B stands on one end and the fulcrum is 7.5 ft from him, the bar is balanced in a horizontal position. When man A stands on the same end, the fulcrum is 8 ft from him for balance. Draw the two diagrams required and calculate a) the weight of the bar and b) the position of its center of gravity. *Ans.* a) 600 lb, b) 10 ft from the end on which the men stand

Chapter 3

Equilibrium of a Rigid Body

NON-PARALLEL COPLANAR FORCES

CONDITIONS FOR EQUILIBRIUM. The equilibrium of a body under the action of **non-parallel** forces acting in a plane can be reduced to a problem in two sets of **parallel** forces by considering horizontal and vertical components. The methods of Chapter 2 are applied to the horizontal and vertical components separately. The two conditions for equilibrium then become:

1) Forces. The vector sum of all the forces acting on the body is zero. This is equivalent to saying that the algebraic sum of the forces or components of forces acting on the body in any direction is zero. It follows that:

 a) The algebraic sum of the horizontal components is zero, i.e. $\Sigma F_x = 0$.
 b) The algebraic sum of the vertical components is zero,   i.e. $\Sigma F_y = 0$.

  Each force is resolved into horizontal and vertical components, making two systems of parallel forces at right angles to each other. Then $\Sigma F_x = 0$ and $\Sigma F_y = 0$.

2) Moments. The algebraic sum of the moments of all the forces about any axis perpendicular to the plane of the forces is zero (i.e. $\Sigma L = 0$). This is equivalent to saying that the sum of the clockwise moments about any such axis equals the sum of the counterclockwise moments about that axis.

SPECIAL CASE: EQUILIBRIUM UNDER ACTION OF THREE NON-PARALLEL FORCES.
 1) The three forces must lie in a plane.
 2) Their lines of action must intersect in a common point.
 3) The vectors representing them can be arranged to form a closed triangle with sides respectively parallel to the directions and proportional in length to the magnitudes of the forces.

SOLVED PROBLEMS

1. A weight of 100 lb is supported in equilibrium by two ropes, as shown in Fig.(*a*). One rope pulls in a horizontal direction and the other in a direction of 30° with the vertical. Compute the tension in each rope.

Solution by Component Method. Refer to Fig.(*b*) below.

 Let T_1 and T_2 represent the required tensions, and w the 100 lb weight. Resolve T_2 into horizontal component h and vertical component v. (T_1 has no vertical component, and w has no horizontal component.)

 Point O is in equilibrium under the action of forces w, T_1, T_2. Therefore:

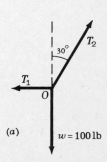

(*a*) $w = 100$ lb

1) $\Sigma F_x = 0$, i.e. algebraic sum of horizontal components is zero; then

$$\Sigma F_x = h - T_1 = 0 \quad \text{or} \quad h = T_1$$

2) $\Sigma F_y = 0$, i.e. algebraic sum of vertical components is zero; then

$$\Sigma F_y = v - w = 0 \quad \text{or} \quad v = w = 100\,\text{lb}$$

$$T_1 = h = v \tan 30° = 100\,\text{lb} \times 0.577 = 57.7\,\text{lb}$$

$$T_2 = \frac{v}{\cos 30°} = \frac{100\,\text{lb}}{0.866} = 115\,\text{lb}$$

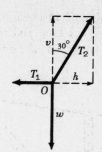

(b) Component Method

Solution by Vector Triangle Method. Refer to Fig.(*c*).

Point O is in equilibrium under the action of the three forces w, T_1, T_2. Hence they form a closed triangle whose sides are parallel to the directions of the forces and proportional to the magnitudes of the forces.

Draw vector w to represent 100 lb, directed vertically downward. From the ends of w draw direction lines parallel to T_1 and T_2. The intersection of these two direction lines determines the force triangle whose sides are respectively proportional to w, T_1, T_2.

$$T_1 = w \tan 30° = 100\,\text{lb} \times 0.577 = 57.7\,\text{lb}$$

$$T_2 = \frac{w}{\cos 30°} = \frac{100\,\text{lb}}{0.866} = 115\,\text{lb}$$

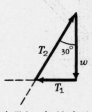

(c) Triangle Method

2. A 600 lb bale is suspended from a pole by means of a 12 ft rod AO hinged at A and a rope OB tied to the pole at B, 9 ft above A. Find the tension T in the rope OB and the push P of the rod AO. Neglect the weight of the rod.

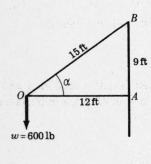

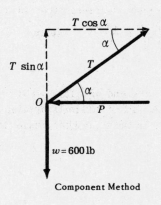

Component Method

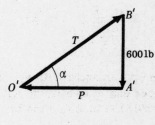

Triangle Method

Solution:

$OB = \sqrt{12^2 + 9^2} = 15\,\text{ft}$. Note that $\sin \alpha = 9/15$, $\cos \alpha = 12/15$.

Component Method

Point O is in equilibrium under the action of forces $T, P, w = 600$ lb. Hence

1) $\Sigma F_y = 0$. Then $T \sin \alpha - w = 0$ or $T(9/15) - 600 = 0$, and $T = 1000\,\text{lb}$.

2) $\Sigma F_x = 0$. Then $T \cos \alpha - P = 0$ or $1000(12/15) - P = 0$, and $P = 800\,\text{lb}$.

Vector Triangle Method

Point O is in equilibrium under the action of the three forces T, P, w. Hence the action lines of the forces form a closed triangle whose sides are parallel to the directions of the forces and proportional to the magnitudes of the forces.

Triangles OAB and $O'A'B'$ are similar since their respective sides are parallel. Then

$$\frac{T}{600\,\text{lb}} = \frac{15\,\text{ft}}{9\,\text{ft}} \quad \text{and} \quad \frac{P}{600\,\text{lb}} = \frac{12\,\text{ft}}{9\,\text{ft}}. \quad \text{Solving,} \quad T = 1000\,\text{lb and } P = 800\,\text{lb}.$$

3. The simplified boom hoist shown carries a load of 900 lb. The mast AC is 9 ft long, and the boom AB is 15 ft long and is hinged at A and held by a cable CB. Find the tension T in the cable and the compression P in the boom AB. Neglect the weight of the boom.

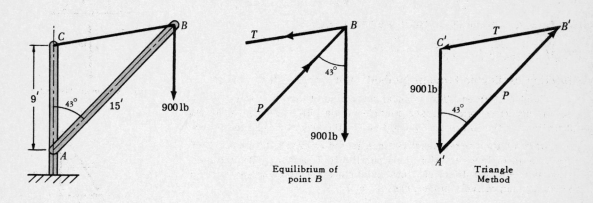

Equilibrium of
point B

Triangle
Method

Solution:

By the cosine law, $(CB)^2 = 9^2 + 15^2 - 2(9)(15)\cos 43°$ from which $CB = 10.4$ ft.

Vector Triangle Method

Point B is in equilibrium under the action of three forces: $T, P, 900$ lb weight. Hence the action lines of the forces form a closed triangle whose sides are parallel to the directions of the forces and proportional to the magnitudes of the forces.

Triangles ABC and $A'B'C'$ are similar since their respective sides are parallel. Then

$$\frac{T}{900 \text{ lb}} = \frac{10.4 \text{ ft}}{9 \text{ ft}} \quad \text{and} \quad \frac{P}{900 \text{ lb}} = \frac{15 \text{ ft}}{9 \text{ ft}}. \quad \text{Solving,} \quad T = 1040 \text{ lb and } P = 1500 \text{ lb.}$$

4. To pull an automobile out of a ditch, one end of a rope AOB is wrapped around a tree at A and the other end is tied to the auto at B. A pull of 100 lb is applied to the center O of the rope and perpendicular to AB. Find the tension T in the rope when angle AOB is 170°.

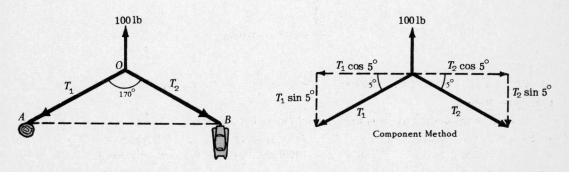

Component Method

Solution by Component Method

Point O is in equilibrium under the action of forces $T_1, T_2, 100$ lb. Hence:

1) $\Sigma F_x = 0$. Then $T_2 \cos 5° - T_1 \cos 5° = 0$ or $T_1 = T_2$ (= tension T in rope).

2) $\Sigma F_y = 0$. Then $100 \text{ lb} - T_1 \sin 5° - T_2 \sin 5° = 0$ or, since $T_1 = T_2 = T$,

$$2T \sin 5° = 100 \text{ lb} \quad \text{and} \quad T = \frac{50 \text{ lb}}{\sin 5°} = \frac{50 \text{ lb}}{0.0872} = 573 \text{ lb.}$$

5. A rope 11 ft long is fastened to two hooks 9 ft apart on a horizontal ceiling. To the rope is attached a 100 lb weight so that the segments of the rope are 7 ft and 4 ft. Determine the tension in each segment.

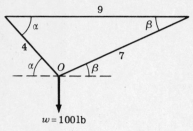
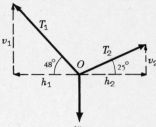

Solution:

Angles α and β are computed by the law of cosines.

$$7^2 = 4^2 + 9^2 - 2(4)(9) \cos \alpha \qquad \cos \alpha = 0.667 \qquad \alpha = 48°$$
$$4^2 = 7^2 + 9^2 - 2(7)(9) \cos \beta \qquad \cos \beta = 0.905 \qquad \beta = 25°$$

Let h_1 and v_1 be respectively the horizontal and vertical components of the tension T_1 in the 4 ft segment, and h_2 and v_2 the horizontal and vertical components of the tension T_2 in the 7 ft segment.

Point O is in equilibrium under the action of forces T_1, T_2, w. Hence:

1) $\Sigma F_x = 0$. Then $h_2 - h_1 = 0$ or $T_2 \cos 25° - T_1 \cos 48° = 0$ from which $T_1 = 1.36\, T_2$.

2) $\Sigma F_y = 0$. Then $v_1 + v_2 - w = 0$ or $T_1 \sin 48° + T_2 \sin 25° - 100\,\text{lb} = 0$.

Substituting $T_1 = 1.36\, T_2$, $1.36 T_2 (0.743) + T_2 (0.423) - 100\,\text{lb} = 0$.

Solving, $T_2 = 70\,\text{lb}$ and $T_1 = 1.36 T_2 = 1.36\,(70) = 95\,\text{lb}$.

6. A weight of 120 lb is applied to the junction C of two rafters of equal length and inclined 70° with each other. The feet of the rafters lie in a horizontal plane and are fastened together by a tie-rod AB. Compute the tension in the tie-rod and the compression in the rafters. Neglect the weight of the truss.

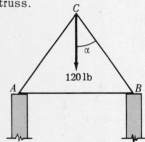
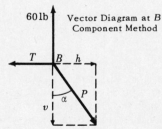
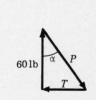

Solution:

Consider the equilibrium of point B. The three forces acting on B are:

1) The rafter pushes B downward and to the right with a force P.
2) The tie-rod pulls B to the left with a force T.
3) The vertical support at B pushes upward on B with a force equal to half the 120 lb weight.

Component Method

Resolve P into horizontal and vertical components, h and v. $(\alpha = 70°/2 = 35°)$

From $\Sigma F_x = 0$, $T = h$. Then $T = h = v \tan \alpha = 60\,\text{lb} \times 0.700 = 42\,\text{lb}$.

From $\Sigma F_y = 0$, $v = 60\,\text{lb}$. Then $P = \dfrac{v}{\cos \alpha} = \dfrac{60\,\text{lb}}{0.819} = 73\,\text{lb}$.

Vector Triangle Method

The 3 forces acting on B (P, T, 60 lb) form a closed triangle whose sides are parallel to the directions of the forces and proportional to the magnitudes of the forces. Then

$$T = 60\,\text{lb} \times \tan 35° = 42\,\text{lb} \qquad \text{and} \qquad P = \frac{60\,\text{lb}}{\cos 35°} = 73\,\text{lb}.$$

7. A ladder AB, 15 ft long and weighing 60 lb, with its center of gravity G 1/3 up, rests with one end A on the rough ground and the other end B 12 ft above the ground and against a smooth vertical wall. Find the reaction R of the wall and the reaction N of the ground.

Solution:

$$AC = \sqrt{15^2 - 12^2} = 9 \text{ ft}, \quad AP = AC/3 = 3 \text{ ft}$$

The three forces acting on the ladder are:

1) Its weight w acting vertically downward through the center of gravity G 1/3 up.

2) The reaction R of the smooth wall which acts perpendicular to the wall and to the left.

3) The reaction N of the rough ground at A, which has a horizontal component h to the right and a vertically upward component v.

The ladder is in equilibrium. Hence:

a) Algebraic sum of moments about any axis is zero. It is advantageous to take moments about an axis through A, since the moments of the unknowns v and h about A are zero (because the lines of action of v and h pass through A). Then

$$\Sigma L_A = R \times 12 \text{ ft} - 60 \text{ lb} \times 3 \text{ ft} = 0 \quad \text{and} \quad R = 15 \text{ lb}$$

b) $\Sigma F_x = h - R = 0$ and $h = R = 15$ lb.

c) $\Sigma F_y = v - w = 0$ and $v = w = 60$ lb.

$N = \sqrt{h^2 + v^2} = \sqrt{15^2 + 60^2} = 62$ lb at an angle OAP with the ground.
$\tan \angle OAP = v/h = 60/15 = 4$ from which $\angle OAP = 76°$.

Note that N, w, and R intersect at a point (special case of three forces).

8. The hinges A and B of a door weighing 80 lb are 10 ft apart and the width of the door is 4 ft. The weight of the door is supported by the upper hinge. Find the forces exerted on the door at the hinges.

Solution:

Consider forces acting on the door. The vertical forces acting are the weight w of the door (acting vertically downward through the center of gravity) and the upward force F_3 which is equal and opposite to w. The horizontal forces acting are F_1 which keeps the door from pulling away from the wall at A, and F_2 which pushes the door away from the wall at B.

The door is in equilibrium. Hence:

1) $\Sigma F_x = F_2 - F_1 = 0$ or $F_2 = F_1$.

2) $\Sigma F_y = F_3 - w = 0$ or $F_3 = w$.

3) Summing moments about A (since the moments of F_1 and F_3 about A are zero), $\Sigma L_A = F_2 \times AB - w \times BD = 0$.

Then from 1) and 3), $F_2 = F_1 = w \times \dfrac{BD}{AB} = 80 \text{ lb} \times \dfrac{2 \text{ ft}}{10 \text{ ft}} = 16$ lb.

$R = \sqrt{F_3^2 + F_1^2} = \sqrt{80^2 + 16^2} = 82$ lb at $\alpha = \tan^{-1}\dfrac{F_3}{F_1} = \tan^{-1} 5 = 79°$.

The upper hinge exerts a force $R = 82$ lb at an angle $\alpha = 79°$. The lower hinge supplies a horizontal force $F_2 = 16$ lb.

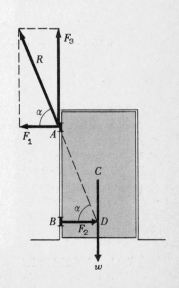

9. A uniform horizontal boom AB, 10 ft long and weighing 40 lb, is pivoted at end A. A 200 lb weight is hung at the other end B. Compute the force required to support the boom at a point C 3 ft from the fulcrum by a rope making an angle of $34°$ with the mast.

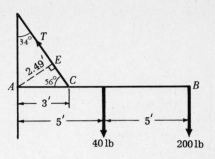

Solution:

$AE = AC \sin 56° = 3 \text{ ft} \times 0.829 = 2.49 \text{ ft}.$

Let T = force required = tension in rope. Take moments about an axis through A.

$\Sigma L_A = T \times 2.49 \text{ ft} - 40 \text{ lb} \times 5 \text{ ft} - 200 \text{ lb} \times 10 \text{ ft} = 0$

from which $T = 884 \text{ lb}.$

10. A uniform derrick boom AB, 12 ft long and weighing 100 lb, is hinged at A to a vertical mast. Its outer end B is connected by a rope BC to the mast and supports a 400 lb load. The boom and rope make angles of $60°$ and $70°$ respectively with the mast. Compute the tension T in the rope and the reaction R on the lower end of the boom.

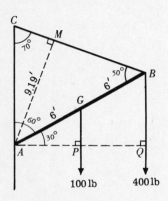

Space Diagram

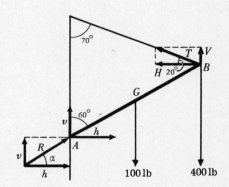

Force Diagram

Solution:

From the Space Diagram,

$\angle ABC = 180° - 70° - 60° = 50°$ $AP = AG \cos 30° = 6 \times 0.866 = 5.20 \text{ ft}$

$AM = AB \sin 50° = 12 \times 0.766 = 9.19 \text{ ft}$ $AQ = AB \cos 30° = 12 \times 0.866 = 10.4 \text{ ft}.$

Refer to the Force Diagram. The forces acting on the boom are:

1) The weight of the boom, 100 lb, acting at its center of gravity G.

2) The load, 400 lb, acting at B.

3) The pull T of the rope, which is resolved into rectangular components H and V.

4) The reaction R of the wall on the boom at A, which has rectangular components h and v.

The boom is in equilibrium. Therefore:

a) Summing moments about an axis through A,

$\Sigma L_A = R \times 0 \text{ ft} + T \times 9.19 \text{ ft} - 100 \text{ lb} \times 5.20 \text{ ft} - 400 \text{ lb} \times 10.4 \text{ ft} = 0$ or $T = 509 \text{ lb}.$

Then $H = T \cos 20° = 478 \text{ lb}$ and $V = T \sin 20° = 174 \text{ lb}.$

b) $\Sigma F_x = h - H = 0$ or $h = H = 478 \text{ lb}.$

c) $\Sigma F_y = v + V - 100 - 400 = 0$, where $V = 174 \text{ lb}$. Then $v = 326 \text{ lb}.$

Reaction $R = \sqrt{h^2 + v^2} = 578 \text{ lb}$ at $\alpha = \tan^{-1} v/h = \tan^{-1} 0.682 = 34°.$

Note that the reaction R is not in line with the boom.

11. A uniform bar AB, 16 ft long and weighing 12 lb, is supported horizontally by cords fastened to its ends. The cord at B makes an angle of 30° with the vertical. A 40 lb weight is suspended from a point on the bar 4 ft from end A. Compute the tension T in the cord supporting the A end, and the angle that the cord makes with the vertical.

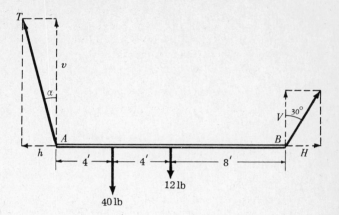

Solution:

Let h and v be respectively the horizontal and vertical components of the tension in the cord at A, and H and V the horizontal and vertical components of the tension in the cord at B.

The bar is in equilibrium. Therefore:

1) Summing moments about an axis through A, $\Sigma L_A = V(16) - 12(8) - 40(4) = 0$ or $V = 16$ lb.

2) $\Sigma F_x = H - h = 0$. Then $h = H = V \tan 30° = 16(0.5774) = 9.24$ lb.

3) $\Sigma F_y = v + V - 40 - 12 = 0$ or $v = 36$ lb.

$\quad T = \sqrt{h^2 + v^2} = \sqrt{(9.24)^2 + (36)^2} = 37.2$ lb at $\alpha = \tan^{-1} h/v = \tan^{-1} 0.257 = 14.4°$.

12. A weightless bar AB, 100 in. long, has five forces applied to it as shown in the diagram below. Determine the magnitude, location and direction of the equilibrant.

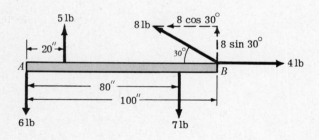
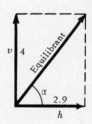

Solution:

In the figure the 8 lb force is resolved into horizontal and vertical components.

Let h = horizontal component of equilibrant, v = vertical component of equilibrant.

Consider that the bar is in equilibrium under the action of the given forces and the equilibrant. Therefore:

1) From $\Sigma F_x = 0$, $4 - 8 \cos 30° + h = 0$ and $h = +2.9$ lb (to the right).

2) From $\Sigma F_y = 0$, $5 + 8 \sin 30° - 6 - 7 + v = 0$ and $v = +4$ lb (up).

3) Let x = horizontal distance of equilibrant from A.

From $\Sigma L_A = 0$, $5 \times 20 - 7 \times 80 + 8 \sin 30° \times 100 + v \times x = 0$ and $x = 15$ in. from A.

Equilibrant $= \sqrt{h^2 + v^2} = 4.9$ lb at an angle $\alpha = \tan^{-1} v/h = \tan^{-1} 1.38 = 54°$.

The equilibrant is 4.9 lb applied 15 in. to the right of A at an angle 54° with the bar.

SUPPLEMENTARY PROBLEMS

13. A 600 lb bale hangs from a steel cable, as shown in Fig.(a) below. (a) Determine the tension T in the cable if the bale is held to one side with a horizontal force of 300 lb. (b) If the cable is 13 ft long, what horizontal force is required to hold the bale a horizontal distance of 5 ft from the vertical line through the point of support?   *Ans.* 671 lb, 250 lb

14. A 64 lb load is attached to the middle of a rope 10 ft long whose ends are fastened to two hooks which are 6 ft apart on the same level. Compute the tension in each segment of the rope. See Fig.(b) below.
Ans. 40 lb in each segment

15. The ends of a rope are fastened to two hooks on a horizontal ceiling. A 100 lb crate is attached to the rope so that the two segments of the rope make angles of 35° and 55° respectively with the horizontal. Compute the tension in each segment. Refer to Fig.(c) below.
Ans. $T_1 = 57.4$ lb, $T_2 = 81.9$ lb

16. The upper end of a uniform beam, 8 ft long and weighing 160 lb, is hinged to a support. To the lower end is attached a rope which extends horizontally and holds the beam at an angle of 40° with the vertical. Determine the tension T in the rope. See Fig.(d) below.
Ans. 67.1 lb

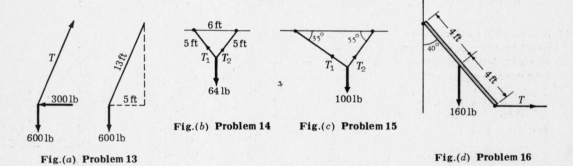

Fig.(a) Problem 13   **Fig.(b) Problem 14**   **Fig.(c) Problem 15**   **Fig.(d) Problem 16**

17. A light rod AB is hinged at one end B and carries an 80 lb load at the other end A, as shown in Fig.(e) below. The rod is held in a horizontal position by a rope which is attached to end A and makes an angle of 50° with the rod. Determine the tension in the rope AC and the push of the rod against the hinge.
Ans. tension, 104 lb; push, 67.1 lb

18. Refer to Fig.(f) below. A uniform steel bar AB weighing 100 lb is hinged at one end B and is held in a horizontal position by a wire which is attached to end A and makes an angle of 34° with the bar. Determine the tension in the wire AC and the reaction of the hinge.
Ans. tension, 89.4 lb; hinge reaction, 89.4 lb directed 34° with the horizontal

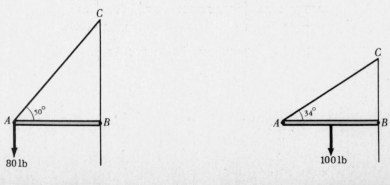

Fig.(e) Problem 17   **Fig.(f) Problem 18**

19. The foot of a ladder rests against a vertical wall and on a horizontal floor, as shown in adjoining Fig.(*g*). The top of the ladder is supported from the wall by a horizontal rope 30 ft long. The ladder is 50 ft long, weighs 100 lb with its center of gravity 20 ft from the foot, and a 150 lb man is 10 ft from the top. Determine the tension in the rope.   *Ans.* 120 lb

20. A 100 lb load is applied to the junction C of two rafters, AC and BC, which make angles of 60° and 30° respectively with the horizontal plane upon which the feet of the rafters rest, as shown in adjoining Fig.(*h*). The feet of the rafters are fastened together by a tie-rod. Determine the compression in each rafter, the tension in the tie-rod, and the downward force on each support. Neglect the weight of the truss.
Ans. 50 lb in longer, 86.6 lb in shorter; 43.3 lb; 25 lb and 75 lb

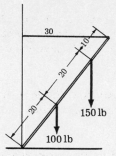
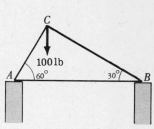

Fig.(*g*) Problem 19   **Fig.(*h*) Problem 20**

21. The hinges of a door weighing 20 lb are 12 ft apart, and the door is 3 ft wide. The weight of the door is supported by the upper hinge. Determine the forces exerted on the door at the hinges.
Ans. Horizontal reaction at lower hinge is 2.5 lb; resultant force at upper hinge is 20.1 lb.

22. A horizontal uniform boom AB, 4 ft long and weighing 10 lb, is supporting a weight of 20 lb, as shown in adjoining diagrams (*a*) and (*b*). In each case, compute the
    1) tension in tie-rod,
    2) compression of boom,
    3) hinge reaction components.
Ans. (*a*) *1*) 33.3 lb
        2) 26.7 lb
        3) *V* comp. +10 lb, *H* comp. +26.7 lb
    (*b*) *1*) 41.6 lb
        2) 25.0 lb
        3) *V* comp. −3.3 lb, *H* comp. +25.0 lb

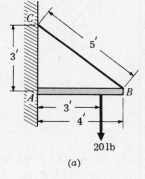
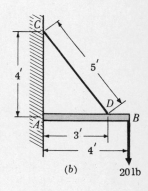

(*a*)   (*b*)

23. Determine completely the resultant of the four forces shown in the diagram below.
Ans. 833 lb down at 9.12 ft horizontal distance from left support.

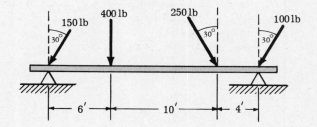

Chapter 4

Uniformly Accelerated Motion

SPEED AND VELOCITY. The average speed $\bar{v}$ of a body which travels a distance s in time t is defined by

$$\bar{v} = \frac{s}{t} \tag{1}$$

from which
$$s = \bar{v}t \tag{2}$$

Speed is a scalar quantity which specifies the magnitude, or numerical value, of the rate of motion without reference to the direction of motion. **Velocity** is a vector quantity whose magnitude is identical with speed and which has direction associated with this speed. The velocity of a body is changing if it changes in speed, or in direction of motion, or in both.

Any unit of linear speed $= \dfrac{\text{a unit of length}}{\text{a unit of time}}$. Hence three units of linear speed are the meter per second (m/sec), the foot per second (ft/sec), and the mile per hour (mi/hr).

Note. Symbols and abbreviations for unit terms need not be punctuated by a period mark except when the abbreviation resembles another word, e.g., in. for inch.

ACCELERATION is the time rate of change of velocity. It is a vector quantity.

Assume that the velocity of a body increases or decreases uniformly and that it has an initial velocity v_O and at the end of a time interval t it has a final velocity v. Then its acceleration a is constant and is given by

$$a = \frac{v - v_O}{t} = \frac{\text{change in velocity}}{\text{elapsed time}} \tag{3}$$

from which
$$v = v_O + at \tag{4}$$

Since the acceleration is constant, the average velocity $\bar{v}$ of the body is

$$\bar{v} = \frac{v_O + v}{2} \tag{5}$$

and the distance s it covers in time t is $s = \bar{v}t$ or

$$s = \frac{v_O + v}{2}t \tag{6}$$

Substituting $v = v_O + at$ from (4) into (6), $\quad s = \dfrac{v_O + v}{2}t = \dfrac{v_O + (v_O + at)}{2}t \quad$ or

$$s = v_Ot + \tfrac{1}{2}at^2 \tag{7}$$

From (3), $t = \dfrac{v - v_O}{a}$; substituting into (6), $s = (\dfrac{v_O + v}{2})(\dfrac{v - v_O}{a}) = \dfrac{v^2 - v_O^2}{2a}$ or

$$v^2 = v_O^2 + 2as \qquad\qquad (8)$$

When the body starts from rest the initial velocity $v_O = 0$ and equations (4), (7), (8) become respectively

$$v = at, \qquad s = \tfrac{1}{2}at^2, \qquad v^2 = 2as \qquad\qquad \text{when } v_O = 0.$$

ACCELERATION DUE TO GRAVITY (g). The acceleration of a freely falling body (air resistance neglected) is constant for any one place, and varies but slightly over the earth's surface. Its approximate value is

$$g = 32 \text{ ft/sec}^2 = 9.8 \text{ m/sec}^2$$

The equations for motion with constant acceleration may be applied to freely falling bodies by substituting g for a.

SOLVED PROBLEMS

1. A body moves from rest with constant acceleration of 8 meters per sec per sec. Find a) the instantaneous speed v at the end of 5 sec, b) the average speed $\overline{v}$ for the 5 sec interval, c) the distance s covered in 5 sec from rest.

Solution:

a) $v = v_O + at = 0 + 8 \text{ m/sec}^2 \times 5 \text{ sec} = 40 \text{ m/sec}$

b) $\overline{v} = \tfrac{1}{2}(v_O + v) = \tfrac{1}{2}(0 + 40) \text{ m/sec} = 20 \text{ m/sec}$

c) $s = v_O t + \tfrac{1}{2}at^2 = 0 + \tfrac{1}{2}(8 \text{ m/sec}^2)(5 \text{ sec})^2 = 100 \text{ m}$ or $s = \overline{v}t = 20 \text{ m/sec} \times 5 \text{ sec} = 100 \text{ m}$

2. A truck's speed increases uniformly from 15 mi/hr to 60 mi/hr in 20 sec. Determine a) the average speed $\overline{v}$ in mi/hr and in ft/sec, b) the acceleration a in mi/hr/sec and in ft/sec/sec, c) the distance s in ft traveled during this period.

Solution:

$$15 \frac{\text{mi}}{\text{hr}} = 15 \frac{\text{mi}}{\text{hr}} \times \frac{5280 \text{ ft}}{1 \text{ mi}} \times \frac{1 \text{ hr}}{3600 \text{ sec}} = 22 \frac{\text{ft}}{\text{sec}}, \qquad 60 \frac{\text{mi}}{\text{hr}} = 88 \frac{\text{ft}}{\text{sec}}$$

a) $\overline{v} = \tfrac{1}{2}(v_O + v) = \tfrac{1}{2}(15 + 60) \text{ mi/hr} = 37.5 \text{ mi/hr}$
$= \tfrac{1}{2}(22 + 88) \text{ ft/sec} = 55 \text{ ft/sec}$

b) $a = \dfrac{v - v_O}{t} = \dfrac{(60 - 15) \text{ mi/hr}}{20 \text{ sec}} = 2.25 \dfrac{\text{mi/hr}}{\text{sec}}$

$= \dfrac{(88 - 22) \text{ ft/sec}}{20 \text{ sec}} = 3.30 \dfrac{\text{ft/sec}}{\text{sec}}$

c) $s = \overline{v}t = 55 \text{ ft/sec} \times 20 \text{ sec} = 1100 \text{ ft}$

3. A sled starting from rest slides down an inclined plane with uniform acceleration and travels 9 meters in 3 sec. In what time from rest will it acquire a velocity of 24 meters per sec down the plane?

Solution:

To find a: from $s = \frac{1}{2}at^2$, $\quad a = \frac{2s}{t^2} = \frac{2(9\,\mathrm{m})}{(3\,\mathrm{sec})^2} = 2$ m/sec^2 down the plane.

To find v: from $a = \frac{v - v_0}{t}$, $\quad t = \frac{v - v_0}{a} = \frac{(24 - 0)\ \mathrm{m/sec}}{2\ \mathrm{m/sec}^2} = 12$ sec.

4. A bus traveling at 50 ft/sec is increasing its speed at the rate of 4 ft/sec each sec. *a*) Find the distance covered in 6 sec. *b*) If its speed is decreasing at the rate of 4 ft/sec each sec, find the distance traversed in 6 sec and the time it takes to come to rest.

Solution:

a) $s = v_0 t + \frac{1}{2}at^2$

$\quad = 50$ ft/sec $\times$ 6 sec $+ \frac{1}{2}(4\,\mathrm{ft/sec}^2)(6\,\mathrm{sec})^2 = 300$ ft $+ 72$ ft $= 372$ ft

b) Here the acceleration is negative and $a = -4$ ft/sec^2.

$s = v_0 t + \frac{1}{2}at^2$

$\quad = 50$ ft/sec $\times$ 6 sec $+ \frac{1}{2}(-4\,\mathrm{ft/sec}^2)(6\,\mathrm{sec})^2 = 300$ ft $- 72$ ft $= 228$ ft

The bus stops when $v = 0$. From $v = v_0 + at$, $\quad 0 = 50$ ft/sec $+ (-4\,\mathrm{ft/sec}^2)t \quad$ and $\quad t = 12.5$ sec.

5. When an auto is touring at 45 mi/hr the brakes are applied and it slows down uniformly to 15 mi/hr in 5 sec. Determine *a*) the acceleration and *b*) the distance s covered during the fifth second.

Solution:

a) $a = \frac{v - v_0}{t} = \frac{(22 - 66)\ \mathrm{ft/sec}}{5\ \mathrm{sec}} = -8.8$ ft/sec^2

b) $s = $ distance covered in 5 sec $-$ distance covered in 4 sec

$\quad = (v_0 t_5 + \frac{1}{2}at_5^2) - (v_0 t_4 + \frac{1}{2}at_4^2)$

$\quad = v_0(t_5 - t_4) + \frac{1}{2}a(t_5^2 - t_4^2)$

$\quad = 66$ ft/sec $\times (5 - 4)$ sec $+ \frac{1}{2}(-8.8\,\mathrm{ft/sec}^2)(5^2 - 4^2)$ sec$^2 = 26.4$ ft

6. The velocity of a train is reduced uniformly from 35 ft/sec to 15 ft/sec while traveling a distance of 500 ft. *a*) Compute the acceleration. *b*) How much farther will it travel before coming to rest, assuming the same acceleration?

Solution:

a) $\qquad v^2 = v_0^2 + 2as$

$(15\ \mathrm{ft/sec})^2 = (35\ \mathrm{ft/sec})^2 + 2a(500\ \mathrm{ft}) \qquad\qquad a = -1$ ft/sec^2

b) Here the initial velocity $v_0 = 15$ ft/sec and the final velocity $v = 0$.

$\qquad v^2 = v_0^2 + 2as$

$\qquad 0 = (15\ \mathrm{ft/sec})^2 + 2(-1\ \mathrm{ft/sec}^2)s \qquad\qquad s = 112$ ft

7. A steel ball dropped from a tower strikes the ground in 3 sec. Find the velocity v with which the ball strikes the ground and the height s of the tower.

Solution:

The acceleration of a freely falling body is 32 ft/sec^2.

$v = v_0 + gt = 0 + 32\ \mathrm{ft/sec}^2 \times 3\ \mathrm{sec} = 96$ ft/sec

$s = v_0 t + \frac{1}{2}gt^2 = 0t + \frac{1}{2}(32\ \mathrm{ft/sec}^2)(3\ \mathrm{sec})^2 = 144$ ft

8. A pebble is thrown vertically down from a bridge with initial velocity 30 ft/sec and strikes the water in 2 sec. Find the velocity v with which the pebble strikes and the height s of the bridge.

Solution:

$$v = v_0 + gt = 30 \text{ ft/sec} + 32 \text{ ft/sec}^2 \times 2 \text{ sec} = 94 \text{ ft/sec}$$

$$s = v_0 t + \tfrac{1}{2}gt^2 = 30 \text{ ft/sec} \times 2 \text{ sec} + \tfrac{1}{2}(32 \text{ ft/sec}^2)(2 \text{ sec})^2 = 124 \text{ ft}$$

9. A body falls freely from rest for 6 sec. Find the distance s traveled in the last 2 sec.

Solution:

$$s = \text{distance fallen in 6 sec} - \text{distance fallen in 4 sec}$$

$$= \tfrac{1}{2}gt_6^2 - \tfrac{1}{2}gt_4^2 = \tfrac{1}{2}g(t_6^2 - t_4^2) = \tfrac{1}{2}(32 \text{ ft/sec}^2)(6^2 - 4^2)\sec^2 = 320 \text{ ft}$$

10. From what height must water fall from a dam to strike the turbine wheel with a speed of 120 ft/sec?

Solution:

$$v^2 = v_0^2 + 2gs, \qquad (120 \text{ ft/sec})^2 = 0 + 2(32 \text{ ft/sec}^2)s, \qquad s = 225 \text{ ft}$$

11. An antiaircraft shell is fired vertically upward with a muzzle velocity of 1600 ft/sec. Compute
a) the maximum height it can reach,
b) the time taken to reach this height,
c) the instantaneous velocities at the ends of 40 and 60 sec.
d) When will its height be 30,000 ft? Neglect air resistance.

Solution:

At the highest point the shell has lost all its initial velocity and $v = 0$.

a) $v^2 = v_0^2 + 2gs, \qquad 0 = (1600 \text{ ft/sec})^2 + 2(-32 \text{ ft/sec}^2)s \qquad$ and $\qquad s = 40{,}000 \text{ ft}$

b) $v = v_0 + gt, \qquad 0 = 1600 \text{ ft/sec} + (-32 \text{ ft/sec}^2)t \qquad$ and $\qquad t = 50 \text{ sec}$

c) At $t = 40$ sec: $\quad v = v_0 + gt = 1600 \text{ ft/sec} + (-32 \text{ ft/sec}^2)(40 \text{ sec}) = +320 \text{ ft/sec (up)}$

   At $t = 60$ sec: $\quad v = v_0 + gt = 1600 \text{ ft/sec} + (-32 \text{ ft/sec}^2)(60 \text{ sec}) = -320 \text{ ft/sec (down)}$

d) $s = v_0 t + \tfrac{1}{2}gt^2, \qquad 30{,}000 = 1600t + \tfrac{1}{2}(-32)t^2 \quad$ or $\quad 16t^2 - 1600t + 30{,}000 = 0.$

   Then $\quad t^2 - 100t + 1875 = 0, \quad (t - 25)(t - 75) = 0, \quad t = 25$ and 75 sec.

   At $t = 25$ sec the shell is at a height of 30,000 ft and is ascending, and at the end of 75 sec it is at the same height but is falling.

12. A ball thrown vertically upward returns to the starting point in 4 sec. Find its initial speed.

Solution:

Take the upward direction as positive; then $g = -32 \text{ ft/sec}^2$ (down).

At $t = 4$ sec it is at its initial position, i.e. the displacement $s = 0$ ft.

$$s = v_0 t + \tfrac{1}{2}gt^2, \qquad 0 = v_0(4 \text{ sec}) + \tfrac{1}{2}(-32 \text{ ft/sec}^2)(4 \text{ sec})^2, \qquad \text{and} \qquad v_0 = 64 \text{ ft/sec}$$

13. A bomb is dropped from a balloon which is 875 ft above the ground and ascending at 40 ft/sec. Find *a*) the maximum height reached, *b*) the position and velocity of the bomb 5 sec after being dropped, *c*) the time taken to hit the ground.

Solution:

Let the origin be at the point where the bomb is released, i.e. 875 ft above the ground.

Take the upward direction as positive; then $v_O = +40$ ft/sec, $g = -32$ ft/sec^2.

a) At the highest point $v = 0$.

$$v^2 = v_O^2 + 2gs, \qquad 0 = (40)^2 + 2(-32)s, \qquad s = +25 \text{ ft (above the origin).}$$

Hence the maximum height above the ground $= 875$ ft $+ 25$ ft $= 900$ ft.

b) $s = v_O t + \frac{1}{2}gt^2 = 40(5) + \frac{1}{2}(-32)5^2 = -200$ ft (below the origin).

$\qquad v = v_O + gt = 40 + (-32)5 = -120$ ft/sec (down).

The bomb is 200 ft below the origin, or $875 - 200 = 675$ ft above the ground, and has a downward velocity of 120 ft/sec.

c) When the bomb hits the ground its displacement $s = -875$ ft (below the origin).

$$s = v_O t + \frac{1}{2}gt^2, \qquad -875 = 40t + \frac{1}{2}(-32)t^2 \quad \text{or} \quad -875 = 40t - 16t^2.$$

Then $16t^2 - 40t - 875 = 0$, $(4t - 35)(4t + 25) = 0$, and the required time is $t = 35/4 = 8.75$ sec.

14. A body slides down a frictionless incline which makes an angle of 30° with the horizontal. Compute the velocity v after sliding 8 meters from rest, and the time t it takes to slide the 8 meters.

Solution:

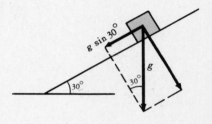

The acceleration due to gravity may be resolved into two components, parallel and perpendicular to the plane. The component parallel to the plane is $g \sin 30°$, and this component causes the acceleration $g \sin 30°$ which is used in place of a in the equations for accelerated motion. (The component perpendicular to the incline has no effect on the motion.)

Let the downward direction along the slope be positive.

$$v = \sqrt{2as} = \sqrt{2(g \sin 30°)s} = \sqrt{2(9.8 \text{ m/sec}^2 \times \tfrac{1}{2})(8 \text{ m})} = 8.85 \text{ m/sec}$$

$$t = \frac{\text{distance}}{\text{average speed}} = \frac{8 \text{ m}}{\frac{1}{2}(0 + 8.85) \text{ m/sec}} = 1.81 \text{ sec}$$

15. A body is projected up a smooth 30° incline with a velocity of 40 m/sec measured along the slope. Determine *a*) the time it takes to return to the starting point and *b*) the distance it moves along the slope before reaching its highest point.

Solution:

a) Let upward direction along the slope be positive. When the body returns to the starting point the displacement $s = 0$. Then

$$s = v_O t + \frac{1}{2}at^2 = v_O t + \frac{1}{2}(g \sin 30°)t^2$$

$$0 = 40 \text{ m/sec} \times t + \frac{1}{2}(-9.8 \text{ m/sec}^2 \times \tfrac{1}{2})t^2, \qquad t = 16.3 \text{ sec}$$

b) At the highest point (greatest distance) the velocity is zero, since at that point the body has lost all its initial velocity and is about to return down the plane.

$$v^2 = v_O^2 + 2as = v_O^2 + 2(g \sin 30°)s$$

$$0 = (40 \text{ m/sec})^2 + 2(-9.8 \text{ m/sec}^2 \times \tfrac{1}{2})s, \qquad s = 163 \text{ m}$$

16. A cannon ball is fired horizontally with a velocity of 1000 ft/sec from the top of a cliff 256 ft high. *a*) In what time *t* will it strike the plain at the foot of the cliff? *b*) At what distance *x* from the foot of the cliff will it strike? *c*) With what velocity *v* will it strike?

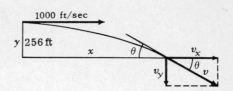

Solution:

The vertical and horizontal velocities are independent of each other.

a) Consider the vertical motion alone. Since the initial vertical velocity is zero,

$$y = \tfrac{1}{2}gt^2, \qquad 256 \text{ ft} = \tfrac{1}{2}(32 \text{ ft/sec}^2)t^2, \qquad t = 4 \text{ sec}.$$

b) Consider the horizontal motion alone.

$$x = \text{horizontal speed} \times t = 1000 \text{ ft/sec} \times 4 \text{ sec} = 4000 \text{ ft}.$$

c) Vertical velocity v_y at 4 sec $= gt = 32 \text{ ft/sec}^2 \times 4 \text{ sec} = 128 \text{ ft/sec}$.

Horizontal velocity v_x at 4 sec $= 1000 \text{ ft/sec}$.

Final resultant velocity $v = \sqrt{(1000 \text{ ft/sec})^2 + (128 \text{ ft/sec})^2} = 1008 \text{ ft/sec}$.

Angle θ which v makes with the horizontal $= \tan^{-1}\dfrac{128}{1000} = \tan^{-1} 0.128 = 7.3°$.

17. An airplane, flying horizontally 3600 ft above the ground and at 120 mi/hr, drops a bomb on a target on the ground. Determine the acute angle between the vertical and the line joining the airplane and target at the instant when the bomb is released.

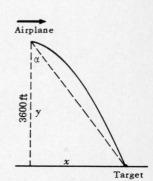

Solution:

The bomb falls with vertical acceleration $g = 32 \text{ ft/sec}^2$ and at the same time moves horizontally at 120 mi/hr $= 176 \text{ ft/sec}$.

Consider the vertical motion alone. Let $t =$ time it takes bomb to hit ground. Then

$$y = \tfrac{1}{2}gt^2, \qquad 3600 \text{ ft} = \tfrac{1}{2}(32 \text{ ft/sec}^2)t^2, \qquad t = 15 \text{ sec}.$$

Consider the horizontal motion alone. The horizontal distance x traveled by the bomb in 15 sec is
$x = 176 \text{ ft/sec} \times 15 \text{ sec} = 2640 \text{ ft}$.

Thus $\tan \alpha = \dfrac{x}{y} = \dfrac{2640 \text{ ft}}{3600 \text{ ft}} = 0.733$ and $\alpha = 36.3°$.

18. A projectile is fired with initial velocity of $v = 1000$ ft/sec at an angle $30°$ with the horizontal. At what distance x from the gun will the projectile strike the ground?

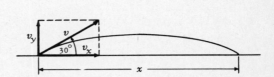

Solution:

Resolve the initial velocity v into rectangular components v_x and v_y. Then

$$v_x = v \cos 30° = 866 \text{ ft/sec} \qquad \text{and} \qquad v_y = v \sin 30° = 500 \text{ ft/sec}.$$

Let $s_y =$ vertical displacement, $t =$ time it takes projectile to return to ground.

To find t, consider the vertical motion alone and let the upward direction be positive (i.e., $v_y = +500$ ft/sec, $g = -32$ ft/sec^2). At the end of its flight the projectile is at its initial level (on the ground) and $s_y = 0$. Then

$$s_y = v_y t + \tfrac{1}{2}gt^2, \qquad 0 = (500 \text{ ft/sec})t + \tfrac{1}{2}(-32 \text{ ft/sec}^2)t^2 \quad \text{and} \quad t = 31.2 \text{ sec}.$$

Considering the horizontal motion alone, $x = v_x t = 866 \text{ ft/sec} \times 31.2 \text{ sec} = 27,000 \text{ ft}$.

19. *a)* Find the range x of a gun which fires a shell with a muzzle velocity v at an angle of elevation θ.

b) Find the angle of elevation θ of a gun which fires a shell with a muzzle velocity of 1200 ft/sec at a target on the same level but 5000 yards distant.

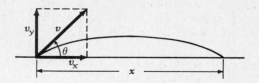

Solution:

a) Let t = time it takes shell to hit target. Then $x = v_x t$ or $t = x/v_x$.

Consider the vertical motion alone and let the upward direction be positive. When the shell strikes the target,

$$\text{vertical displacement} = 0 = v_y t - \tfrac{1}{2}gt^2 \quad \text{or} \quad t = 2v_y/g .$$

Then $t = \dfrac{x}{v_x} = \dfrac{2v_y}{g}$ and $x = \dfrac{2v_x v_y}{g} = \dfrac{2(v\cos\theta)(v\sin\theta)}{g} = \dfrac{v^2 \sin 2\theta}{g}$

since $2\sin\theta\cos\theta = \sin 2\theta$.

The maximum range corresponds to $\theta = 45^\circ$, since 2θ has a maximum value 1 when $2\theta = 90^\circ$ or $\theta = 45^\circ$.

b) From $x = \dfrac{v^2 \sin 2\theta}{g}$, $\sin 2\theta = \dfrac{gx}{v^2} = \dfrac{32(15,000)}{(1200)^2} = 0.333$, $2\theta = \sin^{-1} 0.333 = 19.5^\circ$ and $\theta = 9.7^\circ$.

SUPPLEMENTARY PROBLEMS

20. A bus travels 225 mi in 5 hr. Find the average speed in mi/hr and in ft/sec.
Ans. 45 mi/hr, 66 ft/sec

21. An auto travels at the rate 25 mi/hr for 4 minutes, then at 50 mi/hr for 8 minutes, and finally at 20 mi/hr for 2 minutes. Find *a)* the total distance covered in miles and *b)* the average speed in mi/min, in mi/hr, and in ft/sec during the 12 minutes. *Ans.* 9 mi, 9/14 mi/min, 38.6 mi/hr, 56.6 ft/sec

22. A body with initial speed 10 ft/sec moves with a constant acceleration of 2 ft per sec per sec. Find

a) the speed acquired in 1 minute due to the acceleration,   *Ans. a)* 120 ft/sec

b) the speed at the end of 1 minute,   *Ans. b)* 130 ft/sec

c) the average speed for the 1 minute interval,   *Ans. c)* 70 ft/sec

d) the distance traveled in 1 minute.   *Ans. d)* 4200 ft

23. A body with initial velocity 8 m/sec moves with constant acceleration and travels 640 m in 40 sec. Find

a) the average velocity for the 40 sec interval,   *Ans. a)* 16 m/sec

b) the final velocity,   *Ans. b)* 24 m/sec

c) the velocity acquired in the given time,   *Ans. c)* 16 m/sec

d) the acceleration.   *Ans. d)* 0.4 m/sec^2

24. Convert the following accelerations to ft/sec/sec.

a) 1800 ft/sec/min   *Ans. a)* 30 ft/sec^2 *d)* 1800 ft/sec/hr   *Ans. d)* 0.5 ft/sec^2

b) 1800 ft/min/sec   *Ans. b)* 30 ft/sec^2 *e)* 1800 ft/min/hr   *Ans. e)* 0.0083 ft/sec^2

c) 1800 ft/min/min   *Ans. c)* 0.5 ft/sec^2 *f)* 15 mi/hr/sec   *Ans. f)* 22 ft/sec^2

25. A truck moves from rest with constant acceleration 5 m/sec^2. Calculate the speed acquired and the distance covered in 4 sec from rest. *Ans.* 20 m/sec, 40 m

26. A box slides down an inclined plane with uniform acceleration and attains a velocity of 27 ft/sec in 3 sec from rest. Find the velocity acquired and the distance moved in 6 sec from rest.
Ans. 54 ft/sec down the plane, 162 ft

27. A car has uniformly accelerated motion and starting from rest has a velocity of 80 ft/sec after traveling 250 ft. Find its acceleration.   *Ans.* 12.8 ft/sec^2

28. A projectile is fired with a muzzle velocity of 600 m/sec. If the length of barrel is 150 cm, find the average acceleration in the barrel.   *Ans.* 1.2×10^5 m/sec/sec

29. An automobile's velocity increases uniformly from 20 ft/sec to 60 ft/sec while covering 200 ft. Find the acceleration and the time taken.   *Ans.* 8 ft/sec^2, 5 sec

30. Before leaving the ground, an airplane traveling with constant acceleration makes a run on a field of 1800 ft in 12 sec from rest. Determine
a) the acceleration,   *Ans. a*) 25 ft/sec^2
b) the speed with which it leaves the ground,   *Ans. b*) 300 ft/sec
c) the distances traveled during the first and twelfth seconds.   *Ans. c*) 12.5 ft, 287.5 ft

31. A train running at 60 mi/hr is stopped with uniform retardation in 44 sec by the application of the brakes. Find the acceleration and the distance traveled before coming to rest.
Ans. -2 ft/sec^2, 1936 ft

32. A body is moving at 40 ft/sec and its speed is decreasing uniformly at the rate of 5 ft/sec per sec. Determine
a) its speed at the end of 6 sec,   *Ans. a*) 10 ft/sec
b) its average speed during the 6 sec,   *Ans. b*) 25 ft/sec
c) the distance passed over in the 6 sec.   *Ans. c*) 150 ft

33. A body falls freely from rest. Find
a) its acceleration,   *Ans. a*) 32 ft/sec^2
b) the distance it falls in 3 sec,   *Ans. b*) 144 ft
c) its speed after falling 256 ft,   *Ans. c*) 128 ft/sec
d) the time required to attain a speed of 80 ft/sec,   *Ans. d*) 2.5 sec
e) the time in which it falls through 900 ft.   *Ans. e*) 7.5 sec

34. A marble dropped from a bridge strikes the water in 5 sec. Calculate the speed with which it strikes and the height of the bridge.   *Ans.* 160 ft/sec, 400 ft

35. A stone is thrown vertically downward with initial speed 8 ft/sec from a height 80 ft. Find the time it takes to strike the ground and the speed with which it strikes.   *Ans.* 2 sec, 72 ft/sec

36. The hammer of a pile driver strikes the pile with a speed of 24 ft/sec. From what height above the top of the pile did it fall? Neglect air and guide resistance.   *Ans.* 9 ft

37. A baseball is thrown vertically upward with a speed, as it leaves the hand, of 96 ft/sec. *a*) How long will it rise? *b*) How high will it rise? *c*) How long after it leaves the hand will it return to the starting point? *d*) When will its speed be 80 ft/sec?   *Ans.* 3 sec, 144 ft, 6 sec, 0.5 sec and 5.5 sec

38. A bomb dropped from a balloon reaches the ground in 20 sec. Determine the height of the balloon
a) if it is at rest in the air, *b*) if it is ascending with a speed of 160 ft/sec when the bomb is dropped.
Ans. 6400 ft, 3200 ft

39. A stone is projected vertically upward with a speed of 80 ft/sec from a tower 224 ft high. Find the maximum height attained and the speed with which it strikes the ground.
Ans. 324 ft, 144 ft/sec

40. A package moving upward in an elevator at a uniform rate of 10 ft/sec falls off and strikes the bottom of the shaft in 2 sec. *a*) How long will it take the package to reach its maximum height? *b*) How far above the bottom of the shaft was the package when it fell off and *c*) $\frac{1}{4}$ sec after falling off the elevator?
Ans. *a*) 5/16 sec, *b*) 44 ft, *c*) 45.5 ft

41. A block slides down a frictionless inclined plane which makes an angle of 22° with the horizontal. Find *a*) the acceleration, *b*) the time taken to slide 54 ft down the plane starting from rest.
Ans. 12 ft/sec², 3 sec

42. A box slides down a smooth inclined plane 100 ft long and 36 ft high. Find its speed at the bottom of the plane if it starts from rest at the top. Compare this with the speed gained by a body in falling freely from rest through 36 ft. *Ans.* 48 ft/sec; 48 ft/sec

43. A body, projected upward at an angle of 30° with the horizontal, has an initial speed of 128 ft/sec. In how many seconds will it reach the ground? How far from the point of projection will it strike? At what angle with the horizontal will it strike? *Ans.* 4 sec, 443 ft, 30°

44. A body is projected downward at an angle of 30° with the horizontal with an initial speed of 128 ft/sec from the top of a cliff 512 ft high. In what time will it strike the ground? How far from the foot of the cliff will it strike the ground? At what angle with the horizontal will it strike?
Ans. 4 sec, 443 ft, 60°

45. A cannon on a level plain is aimed 50° above the horizontal and a shell is fired with a muzzle velocity of 1200 ft/sec toward a vertical cliff 3200 ft away. How far above the bottom does the shell strike the side wall of the cliff? *Ans.* 3540 ft

46. A World Series batter hits a home run ball with a velocity of 132 ft/sec at an angle of 26° above the horizontal. A fielder who has a reach of 7 ft above the ground is backed up against the bleacher wall which is 386 ft from home plate. The ball was 3 ft above the ground when it was hit. How high above the fielder's glove does the ball pass? *Ans.* 15 ft above the fielder's glove

47. A high-jumper whose center of gravity is 3.5 ft above the ground has been clearing 6.0 ft using a Western Roll in which the take-off velocity is at an angle of 60° with the horizontal. With what speed must he take off? How far back from the bar must he take off? *Ans.* 14.6 ft/sec, 2.89 ft

48. Prove that a gun will shoot three times as high when its angle of elevation is 60° as when it is 30°, but will carry the same horizontal distance.

Chapter 5

Force

A FORCE is a push or pull exerted on a body. It is a vector quantity, having magnitude and direction.

If an unbalanced force acts on a body, the body accelerates in the direction of the force. Conversely, if a body is accelerating, there must be an unbalanced force acting on it in the direction of the acceleration. The unbalanced force acting on a body is proportional to the product of the mass and of the acceleration produced by the unbalanced force.

NEWTON'S LAWS OF MOTION.

1. A body will maintain its state of rest or of uniform motion (at constant speed) along a straight line unless compelled by some unbalanced force to change that state. In other words, a body accelerates only if an unbalanced force acts on it.

2. An unbalanced force F acting on a body produces in it an acceleration a which is in the direction of the force and directly proportional to the force, and inversely proportional to the mass m of the body.

    In mathematical terms, this law states that $ka = \dfrac{F}{m}$ or $F = kma$, where k is a proportionality constant. If suitable units are chosen so that $k = 1$, then $F = ma$.

3. To every action, or force, there is an equal and opposite reaction, or force. In other words, if a body exerts a force on a second body, then the second body exerts a numerically equal and oppositely directed force on the first body. These two forces, although equal and oppositely directed, do not balance each other, since both are not exerted on the same body.

UNITS OF FORCE. In the equation $F = kma$, it is desirable to make $k = 1$, i.e. to have units of mass, acceleration and force such that $F = ma$. To do this we specify two fundamental units and derive the third unit from these two.

   (*1*) In the **meter-kilogram-second** or **mks absolute system**, the fundamental mass unit chosen is the kilogram and the acceleration unit is the m/sec^2. The corresponding derived force unit, called the **newton** (nt), is that unbalanced force which will produce an acceleration of 1 m/sec^2 in a mass of 1 kg.

   (*2*) In the **centimeter-gram-second** or **cgs absolute system**, the fundamental mass unit is the gram and the acceleration unit is the cm/sec^2. The corresponding derived force unit, called the **dyne**, is that unbalanced force which will produce an acceleration of 1 cm/sec^2 in a mass of 1 gram.

   (*3*) In the **English gravitational system**, the fundamental force unit is the **pound** and the acceleration unit is the ft/sec^2. The corresponding derived mass unit, called the **slug**, is that mass which when acted on by a 1 lb force acquires an acceleration of 1 ft/sec^2.

35

Thus the following indicate three consistent sets of units that may be used with the equation $F = ma$ $(F = kma$ with $k = 1)$:

Mks system: F (newtons) $= m$ (kilograms) $\times a$ (m/sec^2)

Cgs system: F (dynes) $= m$ (grams) $\times a$ (cm/sec^2)

English system: F (pounds) $= m$ (slugs) $\times a$ (ft/sec^2)

MASS AND WEIGHT. The mass m of a body refers to its inertia, while the weight w of a body is the pull or force due to gravity acting on the body and varies with location. Weight w is a force whose direction is approximately toward the center of the earth.

If a body of mass m is allowed to fall freely, the resultant force acting on it is its weight w, and its acceleration is that due to gravity, g. Then in any consistent system of units the equation $F = ma$ becomes

$$w = mg$$

Thus w (newtons) $= m$ (kilograms) $\times g$ (m/sec^2)

w (dynes) $= m$ (grams) $\times g$ (cm/sec^2)

w (pounds) $= m$ (slugs) $\times g$ (ft/sec^2)

It follows that $m = w/g$. For example, if a body weighs 64 lb at a place where $g = 32\,\text{ft/sec}^2$, its mass is $m = \dfrac{w}{g} = \dfrac{64\,\text{lb}}{32\,\text{ft/sec}^2} = 2$ slugs. If a body weighs 49 newtons at a place where $g = 9.8\,\text{m/sec}^2$, its mass $m = \dfrac{w}{g} = \dfrac{49\,\text{newtons}}{9.8\,\text{m/sec}^2} = 5\,\text{kg}$.

LAW OF UNIVERSAL GRAVITATION. The force of attraction between two masses m and m' separated by a distance r, G being the constant of gravitation, is

$$\text{Force} = G\,\frac{mm'}{r^2}$$

When m and m' are expressed in kilograms and r in meters, the force will be given in newtons if $G = 6.67 \times 10^{-11}\,\text{nt-m}^2/\text{kg}^2$.

FORCE OF FRICTION, or merely **friction**, is a tangential force on a body which opposes any tendency for its surface to move relative to another surface. Tangential forces are parallel to the surfaces which are in contact.

Kinetic or **sliding friction** is the tangential force between two surfaces when one surface is sliding over another.

Static friction is the tangential force between two surfaces when the two surfaces are not sliding relative to each other. The tangential force between two surfaces just before one surface begins to slide over the other is called the **maximum force of static friction**.

COEFFICIENT OF KINETIC OR SLIDING FRICTION (μ_k) between two solid surfaces is the ratio of the force necessary to move one surface over the other with uniform velocity to the normal force pressing the two surfaces together. The coefficient of sliding friction is a ratio of two forces; hence it is a pure number, having no unit.

$$\mu_k = \frac{\text{force required to balance kinetic friction}}{\text{normal force pressing the two surfaces together}} = \frac{f_k}{N}$$

Force of kinetic friction $= \mu_k \times$ normal force pressing the two surfaces together

$$f_k = \mu_k N$$

COEFFICIENT OF STATIC FRICTION (μ_s) is the ratio of the maximum force of static friction to the normal force pressing the two surfaces together. The coefficient of static friction is greater than that of kinetic friction.

$$\mu_s = \frac{\text{maximum force of static friction}}{\text{normal force pressing the two surfaces together}} = \frac{f_s}{N}$$

Maximum force of static friction $= \mu_s \times$ normal force pressing surfaces together

$$f_s = \mu_s N$$

GENERAL CONSIDERATIONS IN SOLVING PROBLEMS

IN ANY SYSTEM OF UNITS a single equation must have all the terms of it alike in physical significance, and numerical equality must be supplemented by physical equality. It is obvious that we cannot equate or add area to volume, just as we cannot add cows to trees. For example, in the equation $v = v_0 + at$ for motion with constant acceleration a starting with initial velocity v_0, all terms are in terms of velocities, since $at = \frac{\text{velocity}}{\text{time}} \times \text{time} = \text{velocity}$. As another example, in the equation $s = v_0 t + \frac{1}{2}at^2$ for motion with constant acceleration a starting with initial velocity v_0, all the terms are in terms of distance, since $v_0 t = \frac{\text{distance}}{\text{time}} \times \text{time} = \text{distance}$, and $at^2 = \frac{\text{distance}}{\text{time}^2} \times \text{time}^2 = \text{distance}$. This helps us to check equations, because all terms must have the same dimensions.

It is also obvious that the same system of units must be used consistently throughout the solution of a problem. Thus in the equation $s = v_0 t + \frac{1}{2}at^2$, if s is in meters, then v_0 must be in m/sec, t in sec, and a in m/sec^2; if s is in ft, then v_0 must be in ft/sec, t in sec, and a in ft/sec^2.

DIMENSIONAL FORMULAS. The dimensions of all mechanical quantities may be expressed in terms of the fundamental dimensions of length L, mass M, and time T. Thus a velocity has the dimensions L/T or $[LT^{-1}]$, as it is usually written, since a velocity is made up of a length divided by an amount of time; an acceleration has the dimensions L/T^2 or $[LT^{-2}]$; a force, being a mass multiplied by an acceleration, has the dimensions $[MLT^{-2}]$; a volume has the dimensions $[L^3]$. This method of distinguishing physical quantities is helpful in checking equations, since every equation must have the same dimensions on both sides. For example, in the equation $s = v_0 t + \frac{1}{2}at^2$, $L = [LT^{-1}][T] + [LT^{-2}][T^2]$ or $L = L + L$.

MATHEMATICAL OPERATIONS WITH UNITS. In every mathematical operation the unit terms (e.g., lb, cm, ft^3, mi/hr, m/sec^2) must be carried along with the numbers and must undergo the same mathematical operations as the numbers. It is as foolish to separate the number of a measure from its unit as it is to separate the laboratory reagent bottles from their labels. The unit is a necessary part of the quantity, as the x *in* $2x$.

Quantities cannot be added or subtracted directly unless they have the same units as well as the same dimensions. For example, if we are to add algebraically 5 in. (length) with 8 cm (length), we must first convert in. to cm or cm to in. However, any number of quantities can be combined in multiplication or division, in which the units as well as the numbers obey the algebraic laws of squaring, cancellation, etc. Thus:

(1) $6\,m^2 + 2\,m^2 = 8\,m^2$ $(m^2 + m^2 = m^2)$

(2) $5\,cm \times 2\,cm^2 = 10\,cm^3$ $(cm \times cm^2 = cm^3)$

(3) $2\,m^3 \times 1500\,kg/m^3 = 3000\,kg$ $(m^3 \times \frac{kg}{m^3} = kg)$

(4) $2\,sec \times 3\,ft/sec^2 = 6\,ft/sec$ $(sec \times \frac{ft}{sec^2} = \frac{ft}{sec})$

(5) $\dfrac{15\,g}{3\,g/cm^3} = 5\,cm^3$ $(\dfrac{g}{g/cm^3} = g \times \dfrac{cm^3}{g} = cm^3)$

ORDER OF MAGNITUDE. An important characteristic of an answer to any practical problem is the correct order of magnitude. This is the proper location of the decimal point or, in the use of the exponential notation, the assignment of the proper power of 10. If this is wrong, though all else is very exact, the answer is worthless, often costly. Thus the first problem discipline is getting, by visual inspection, the correct order of magnitude. Only after this are slide rules and log tables justified for obtaining an accurate numerical solution.

Consider the multiplication: $.0518 \times 122\,lb = 6.32\,lb$. Visual inspection shows that .0518 is a little more than 1/20, and 1/20 of 122 is a little more than 6. Hence the answer should be a little more than 6 lb, which it is. If the answer were given incorrectly as 63.2 lb or 0.632 lb, visual inspection or mental checking of the result would indicate that the decimal point had been misplaced.

The use of powers of 10 in making the check for the order of magnitude is often very helpful. For example, evaluate $\dfrac{(980)(1000)(96.8)}{(.00264)(.0196)}$ to three significant figures. The slide rule gives 183 for the significant figures. For the order of magnitude, we have $\dfrac{(10^3)(10^3)(10^2)}{(2\frac{1}{2} \times 10^{-3})(2 \times 10^{-2})} = \dfrac{10^8}{5 \times 10^{-5}} = 2 \times 10^{12}$. Hence the answer is 1.83×10^{12}.

SOLVED PROBLEMS

1. Find the weight w of a body whose mass m is (a) 1 kilogram, (b) 1 gram, (c) 1 slug.

Solution:

The weight of a body is the pull or force due to gravity acting on the body. Weight is a force whose direction is approximately toward the center of the earth.

(a) In mks units, $w = mg = 1\,kg \times 9.8\,m/sec^2 = 9.8$ newtons

In cgs units, $w = mg = 1000\,g \times 980\,cm/sec^2 = 980,000$ dynes

(b) In mks units, $w = mg = .001\,kg \times 9.8\,m/sec^2 = .0098$ newtons

In cgs units, $w = mg = 1\,g \times 980\,cm/sec^2 = 980$ dynes

(c) In English units, $w = mg = 1\,slug \times 32\,ft/sec^2 = 32\,lb$

2. Find the mass m of a body whose weight w is (a) 19.6 newtons, (b) 1960 dynes, (c) 96 lb.

Solution:

(a) In mks units, $\qquad m = \dfrac{w}{g} = \dfrac{19.6 \text{ newtons}}{9.8 \text{ m/sec}^2} = 2 \text{ kg}$

(b) In cgs units, $\qquad m = \dfrac{w}{g} = \dfrac{1960 \text{ dynes}}{980 \text{ cm/sec}^2} = 2 \text{ g}$

(c) In English units, $\quad m = \dfrac{w}{g} = \dfrac{96 \text{ lb}}{32 \text{ ft/sec}^2} = 3 \text{ slugs}$

3. A body of mass 2 kg is acted upon by a force of (a) 6 newtons, (b) 8000 dynes. Find the acceleration in each case.

Solution:

(a) In mks units, $\quad F = ma \quad$ or $\quad a = \dfrac{F}{m} = \dfrac{6 \text{ newtons}}{2 \text{ kg}} = 3 \text{ m/sec}^2$

(b) In cgs units, $\quad F = ma \quad$ or $\quad a = \dfrac{F}{m} = \dfrac{8000 \text{ dynes}}{2000 \text{ g}} = 4 \text{ cm/sec}^2$

4. Find the force required to give a block weighing 12 lb an acceleration 8 ft/sec^2.

Solution:

$$F = ma = \frac{w}{g}a = \frac{12 \text{ lb}}{32 \text{ ft/sec}^2} \times 8 \text{ ft/sec}^2 = 3 \text{ lb}$$

Note that $m = w/g$ is the mass of the body in **slugs**.

5. A force acts on a 5 kg mass and reduces its velocity from 7 to 3 m/sec in 2 sec. Find the force (a) in newtons, (b) in dynes.

Solution:

(a) In mks units: $\quad F = ma = m \times \dfrac{v_t - v_0}{t} = 5 \text{ kg} \times \dfrac{(3-7) \text{ m/sec}}{2 \text{ sec}} = -10 \text{ newtons}$

The minus sign indicates that the (retarding) force is directed opposite to the motion.

(b) In cgs units: $\quad F = ma = m \times \dfrac{v_t - v_0}{t} = 5000 \text{ g} \times \dfrac{(300-700) \text{ cm/sec}}{2 \text{ sec}} = -10^6 \text{ dynes}$

6. A 2000 lb automobile is speeding at 60 mi/hr (88 ft/sec). Determine the retarding force of the brakes required to stop it in 220 ft on a level road.

Solution:

To compute the negative acceleration required:

$$v_t^2 - v_0^2 = 2as, \qquad (0 \text{ ft/sec})^2 - (88 \text{ ft/sec})^2 = 2a(220 \text{ ft}), \qquad a = -17.6 \text{ ft/sec}^2$$

$$F = ma = 2000/32 \text{ slugs} \times 17.6 \text{ ft/sec}^2 = 1100 \text{ lb}$$

7. A 10 ton engine pulls a 50 ton train on a level track and gives it an acceleration $a_1 = 4$ ft/sec^2. What acceleration (a_2) would the engine give a 20 ton train when exerting the same force?

Solution:

When pulling 50 ton train, weight moved $w_1 = (10 + 50)$ tons $= 60$ tons.
When pulling 20 ton train, weight moved $w_2 = (10 + 20)$ tons $= 30$ tons.

Accelerations caused by a given force vary inversely as the masses acted upon. Then

$$\frac{a_2}{a_1} = \frac{m_1}{m_2} = \frac{w_1/g}{w_2/g} \quad \text{or} \quad \frac{a_2}{a_1} = \frac{w_1}{w_2}, \qquad \frac{a_2}{4 \text{ ft/sec}^2} = \frac{60 \text{ tons}}{30 \text{ tons}}, \qquad a_2 = 8 \text{ ft/sec}^2$$

8. A 50 lb bale hangs at the end of a rope. Find the acceleration of the bale if the tension in the rope is (*a*) 50 lb, (*b*) 40 lb, (*c*) 75 lb.

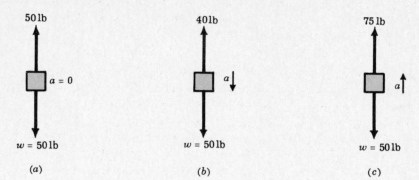

Solution:

In each case the two forces acting *on the bale* are (1) its weight acting downward and (2) the tension in the rope acting upward. The acceleration is in the direction of the unbalanced force.

(*a*) Here the upward tension balances the downward weight. Hence the unbalanced force is (50 − 50) = 0 lb and the body has no acceleration.

(*b*) Since the weight is larger than the tension, the net force is directed downward.

$$\text{Unbalanced force downward} = \text{mass} \times \text{downward acceleration of bale}$$
$$\text{weight} - \text{tension} = ma$$
$$50\,\text{lb} - 40\,\text{lb} = 50/32\ \text{slugs} \times a \qquad\qquad a = 6.4\,\text{ft/sec}^2\ \text{down}$$

(*c*) Since the tension is larger than the weight, the net force is directed upward.

$$\text{Unbalanced force upward} = \text{mass} \times \text{upward acceleration of bale}$$
$$\text{tension} - \text{weight} = ma$$
$$75\,\text{lb} - 50\,\text{lb} = 50/32\ \text{slugs} \times a \qquad\qquad a = 16\,\text{ft/sec}^2\ \text{up}$$

9. A 6400 lb car starts down a mine shaft with an acceleration of 4 ft/sec^2. Determine the tension T in the cable during start.

Solution:

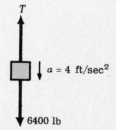

Since the car has a downward acceleration, the net force on the car is directed downward.

$$\text{Unbalanced force downward} = \text{mass} \times \text{downward acceleration of car}$$
$$6400\,\text{lb} - T = 6400/32\ \text{slugs} \times 4\,\text{ft/sec}^2$$
$$T = 5600\,\text{lb}$$

10. A 2 kg mass hangs at the end of a wire. Find the tension T in the wire if the acceleration is (*a*) 5 m/sec^2 up, (*b*) 5 m/sec^2 down.

Solution:

The weight of the 2 kg mass is $w = mg = 2\,\text{kg} \times 9.8\,\text{m/sec}^2$
$$= 19.6\ \text{newtons}.$$

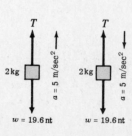

(*a*) Since the acceleration is upward, the net force is directed upward.

$$\text{Unbalanced force upward} = \text{mass} \times \text{upward acceleration of mass}$$
$$T - 19.6\ \text{newtons} = 2\,\text{kg} \times 5\,\text{m/sec}^2$$
$$T = 29.6\ \text{newtons}$$

(*b*) Since the acceleration is downward, the net force is directed downward.

$$\text{Unbalanced force downward} = \text{mass} \times \text{downward acceleration of mass}$$
$$19.6\ \text{newtons} - T = 2\,\text{kg} \times 5\,\text{m/sec}^2$$
$$T = 9.6\ \text{newtons}$$

11. Determine the force that a 200 lb man exerts on the floor of an elevator when it (*a*) is at rest, (*b*) rises with constant velocity 4 ft/sec, (*c*) descends with constant velocity 4 ft/sec, (*d*) rises with constant acceleration 4 ft/sec^2, (*e*) descends with constant acceleration 4 ft/sec^2.

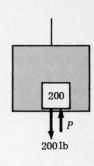

Solution:

By Newton's Third Law, the force that the man exerts downward on the floor of the elevator equals the force with which the elevator floor pushes upward on the man. In this problem we are given the *man's* weight; hence we consider forces *acting on the man*.

(*a*), (*b*), (*c*). If the man is at rest or is raised or lowered with constant velocity, the upward push of the floor is equal in magnitude to the weight of the man, 200 lb. Since there is no acceleration, there can be no unbalanced force.

(*d*) Since the acceleration is upward, the net force is directed upward.

Unbalanced force upward on man = mass × upward acceleration of man
upward push P of floor − weight of man = ma
$$P - 200\,\text{lb} = 200/32 \text{ slugs} \times 4\,\text{ft/sec}^2 \qquad P = 225\,\text{lb}$$

(*e*) Since the acceleration is downward, the net force is directed downward.

Unbalanced force downward on man = mass × downward acceleration of man
weight of man − upward push P of floor = ma
$$200\,\text{lb} - P = 200/32 \text{ slugs} \times 4\,\text{ft/sec}^2 \qquad P = 175\,\text{lb}$$

12. Compute the least acceleration with which a man weighing 200 lb can slide down a rope which can sustain a weight of 150 lb.

Solution:

Least unbalanced force downward on man = mass × least downward acceleration of man
weight of man − max. tension in rope = ma
$$200\,\text{lb} - 150\,\text{lb} = 200/32 \text{ slugs} \times a \qquad a = 8\,\text{ft/sec}^2 \text{ down}$$

13. A cord passing over a pulley has a 7 kg mass tied on one end and a 9 kg mass on the other. Determine the acceleration and the tension in the cord. Neglect friction.

Solution:

The weight of the 7 kg mass is $w = mg = 7(9.8)$ newtons.

Since the cord is continuous, the tension is the same in both parts.

(*a*) Consider the forces acting on the 7 kg mass alone.

Unbalanced force upward on 7 kg mass = mass × its upward acceleration
$$T - 7(9.8) \text{ newtons} = 7\,\text{kg} \times a \qquad (1)$$

(*b*) Consider the forces acting on the 9 kg mass alone.

Unbalanced force downward on 9 kg mass = mass × its downward acceleration
$$9(9.8) \text{ newtons} - T = 9\,\text{kg} \times a \qquad (2)$$

Add equations (*1*) and (*2*) and obtain $2(9.8) = 16a$ from which $a = 1.22\,\text{m/sec}^2$.

Substitute $a = 1.22\,\text{m/sec}^2$ in equation (*1*) or (*2*) to get $T = 77.1$ newtons.

Another Method. Consider the forces acting on the entire system.

Unbalanced force on entire system = mass × acceleration of system
$$(9 \times 9.8 - 7 \times 9.8) \text{ newtons} = (9 + 7)\,\text{kg} \times a$$
$$a = 1.22\,\text{m/sec}^2$$

Then, to find T subsitute $a = 1.22\,\text{m/sec}^2$ in either (*1*) or (*2*).

14. A subway train consists of 3 cars, each weighing 15 tons. The first car, acting as engine, pushes backward on the rails with a force of 9600 lb. Friction exerts a backward drag of 200 lb on each car. Find (a) the acceleration of the train, (b) the tension T_1 in the coupling between the first and second cars, (c) the tension T_2 in the coupling between the second and third cars.

Solution:

The rails push forward on the first car with a force of 9600 lb.

(a) Consider the system as a whole.

Net force on the train = mass × acceleration of train

$$9600 \text{ lb} - 3(200) \text{ lb} = 3(15)(2000)/32 \text{ slugs} \times a \qquad a = 3.2 \text{ ft/sec}^2$$

(b) Consider the last two cars together.

Net force on last two cars = mass × acceleration of last two cars

$$T_1 - 2(200) \text{ lb} = 2(15)(2000)/32 \text{ slugs} \times 3.2 \text{ ft/sec}^2 \qquad T_1 = 6400 \text{ lb}$$

(c) Consider the last car only.

Net force on last car = mass × acceleration of last car

$$T_2 - 200 \text{ lb} = 15(2000)/32 \text{ slugs} \times 3.2 \text{ ft/sec}^2 \qquad T_2 = 3200 \text{ lb}$$

15. A 100 lb block rests on a horizontal floor. A minimum horizontal force of 31 lb is required to start it in motion, and a minimum horizontal force of 24 lb will keep the block moving with constant velocity once it has started. (a) Find the coefficient of static friction μ_s and the coefficient of sliding or kinetic friction μ_k. (b) What is the friction force when a horizontal force of 12 lb acts on the block?

Solution:

(a) $\mu_s = \dfrac{31 \text{ lb}}{100 \text{ lb}} = 0.31$ and $\mu_k = \dfrac{24 \text{ lb}}{100 \text{ lb}} = 0.24$

(b) The friction force is 12 lb directed opposite to the applied force; the block remains at rest.

16. A 100 lb block rests on a rough horizontal floor. The coefficient of kinetic friction between block and floor is 0.25. A horizontal force of 40 lb acts on the block for 3 sec. Compute the velocity of the block at the end of the 3 sec.

Solution:

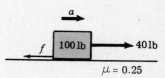

The 40 lb force acts in the direction of motion. The frictional force $f = 0.25 \times 100 \text{ lb} = 25 \text{ lb}$ acts opposite to the motion.

Unbalanced force = ma, $(40 - 25) \text{ lb} = 100/32 \text{ slugs} \times a$, $a = 4.8 \text{ ft/sec}^2$

$$v_t = v_0 + at = 0 + 4.8 \text{ ft/sec}^2 \times 3 \text{ sec} = 14.4 \text{ ft/sec}$$

17. A constant push of 20 lb, applied at an angle of 30° to a 40 lb block which rests on a horizontal surface, gives the block a velocity of 24 ft/sec in 3 sec. Find the coefficient of friction μ.

Solution:

Acceleration of block $= \dfrac{v_t - v_0}{t} = \dfrac{(24 - 0) \text{ ft/sec}}{3 \text{ sec}} = 8 \text{ ft/sec}^2$

Consider the horizontal forces acting:

(1) $F_x = 20 \text{ lb} \times \cos 30° = 17.3 \text{ lb}$ is the effective value of the 20 lb force in balancing the force of friction and in giving the block an acceleration 8 ft/sec².

(2) The force of friction f opposing F_x is

$$f = \mu \times \text{normal force pressing the two surfaces together}$$
$$= \mu \times (40\,\text{lb} + F_y) = \mu(40 + 20\sin 30°)\,\text{lb} = 50\mu\,\text{lb}.$$

Unbalanced horizontal force $=$ mass $\times$ horizontal acceleration
$$F_x - f = 17.3\,\text{lb} - 50\mu\,\text{lb} = 40/32\,\text{slugs} \times 8\,\text{ft/sec}^2 \qquad\qquad \mu = 0.146$$

18. A block rests on a horizontal board. The board is gradually tilted upward and the block just be-gins to slide down the board when the angle of inclination θ_1 is 21°. After the block starts moving, it is found that it will keep sliding at constant speed when the angle of tilt θ_2 is 15°. Find the coefficient of static friction μ_s and the coefficient of sliding or kinetic friction μ_k be-tween the block and the board. See Fig.(a) below.

Solution:

Resolve the weight w of the block into two components:

(1) N, perpendicular to the plane, is the force of the block on the plane.
(2) F, parallel to the plane, is the force tending to move the block down the plane.

The force of friction f, acting up the plane to oppose the motion, balances F since there is no accel-eration.

$$\text{Coefficient of friction} = \frac{\text{friction force}}{\text{normal force}} = \frac{f}{N} = \frac{F}{N} = \tan\theta$$

Then $\mu_s = \tan 21° = 0.38$ and $\mu_k = \tan 15° = 0.26.$

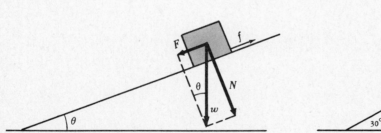

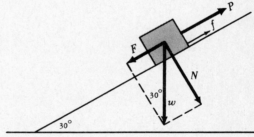

Fig.(a) Problem 18   **Fig.(b) Problem 19**

19. A 100 lb block rests on a rough plane inclined 30° with the horizontal as shown in Fig.(b) above. The coefficient of sliding friction between block and plane is 0.25. What force P parallel to the plane is required to keep the block moving up the plane at constant speed?

Solution:

Resolve the weight $w = 100$ lb of the block into two components: (1) $N = w\cos 30°$ normal to the plane and (2) $F = w\sin 30°$ down the plane.

The friction force $f = \mu N = 0.25\,(w\cos 30°)$ opposes the motion and hence acts *down* the plane.

$$\begin{aligned} P &= \text{force to balance } F + \text{force to balance } f \\ &= w\sin 30° + 0.25\,w\cos 30° \\ &= 50\,\text{lb} + 22\,\text{lb} = 72\,\text{lb} \end{aligned}$$

20. Compute the acceleration of a block sliding down a 30° incline, the coefficient of sliding friction being 0.20.

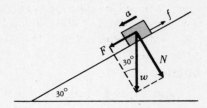

Solution:

The weight w of the block is resolved into components $N = w \cos 30°$ and $F = w \sin 30°$. Here the friction force $f = \mu N = 0.20 \, (w \cos 30°)$ acts up the plane to oppose the motion.

Unbalanced force down the plane $= ma$
$$w \sin 30° - 0.20 \, w \cos 30° = w/32 \text{ slugs} \times a$$
from which $a = 10.5 \, \text{ft/sec}^2$ down plane.

21. (*a*) Find the constant force F required to give the 41 lb block B an upward acceleration of 2 ft/sec². (*b*) What is the tension in the cord? See Fig. (*a*) below.

Solution:

Retarding force of friction on the 55 lb block is $f = 0.20 \times 55 \text{ lb} = 11 \text{ lb}$.
The 55 lb weight is balanced by the upward push of the table.

(*a*)   Unbalanced force acting on system $=$ mass $\times$ acceleration of system
$$F - f - 41 \text{ lb} = F - 11 \text{ lb} - 41 \text{ lb} = (55 + 41)/32 \text{ slugs} \times 2 \text{ ft/sec}^2 \qquad F = 58 \text{ lb}$$

(*b*)   Unbalanced force acting on 41 lb block $=$ mass $\times$ acceleration of 41 lb block
$$T - 41 \text{ lb} = 41/32 \text{ slugs} \times 2 \text{ ft/sec}^2 \qquad T = 43.6 \text{ lb}$$

or Unbalanced force acting on 55 lb block $=$ mass $\times$ acceleration of 55 lb block
$$F - T - f = 58 \text{ lb} - T - 11 \text{ lb} = 55/32 \text{ slugs} \times 2 \text{ ft/sec}^2 \qquad T = 43.6 \text{ lb}$$

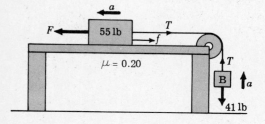

Fig.(*a*) Problem 21

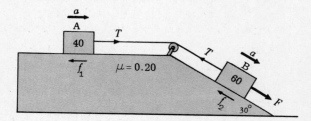

Fig.(*b*) Problem 22

22. In the Fig. (*b*) above, blocks A and B weigh 40 and 60 lb respectively and the coefficient of friction for each surface is 0.20. Find (*a*) the acceleration of the system and (*b*) the tension T in the cord.

Solution:

Resolve the weight of B into two components, parallel and perpendicular to the plane. The component parallel to the plane, $F = 60 \sin 30° = 30 \text{ lb}$, tends to move the block down the plane. The component normal to the plane is $N = 60 \cos 30°$ lb.

Force of friction on A is $f_1 = 0.20 \times 40 \text{ lb} = 8 \text{ lb}$.
Force of friction on B is $f_2 = \mu N = 0.20 \times 60 \cos 30° \text{ lb} = 10.4 \text{ lb}$.

(*a*) Unbalanced force acting on system $=$ mass $\times$ acceleration of system
$$F - f_1 - f_2 = (30 - 8 - 10.4) \text{ lb} = (40 + 60)/32 \text{ slugs} \times a \qquad a = 3.7 \, \text{ft/sec}^2$$

(*b*) Unbalanced force on 40 lb block $=$ mass $\times$ acceleration of 40 lb block
$$T - f_1 = T - 8 \text{ lb} = 40/32 \text{ slugs} \times 3.7 \text{ ft/sec}^2 \qquad T = 12.6 \text{ lb}$$

23. A uniform ladder 20 ft long and weighing 80 lb rests with one end on the rough ground and the other end against a smooth wall. The ladder makes an angle of 60° with the ground, and the coefficient of friction between the ladder and ground is 0.3. How far can a 150 lb man go up the ladder before it begins to slip?

Solution:

The following forces act on the ladder:

(1) The man's weight, acting at s ft from the bottom.
(2) The ladder's weight, acting at its center of gravity.
(3) The friction force f, parallel to the ground.
(4) The upward push of the ground, N.
(5) The push of the wall, P (which is normal to the wall, since the wall is smooth).

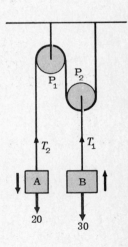

(a) Upward forces = downward forces
$$N = 80\,\text{lb} + 150\,\text{lb} = 230\,\text{lb}$$

Friction force $f = \mu N = 0.3 \times 230\,\text{lb} = 69\,\text{lb}$

(b) Forces toward right = forces toward left
$$P = f = 69\,\text{lb}$$

(c) Take moments about the bottom of the ladder.
Clockwise moments = counterclockwise moments
$$69\,\text{lb} \times 20 \sin 60°\,\text{ft} = 150\,\text{lb} \times s \cos 60° + 80\,\text{lb} \times 10 \cos 60°\,\text{ft} \qquad s = 10.6\,\text{ft}$$

24. In the figure, body A weighs 20 lb and body B weighs 30 lb. A continuous cord attached to A passes over fixed pulley P_1 and under movable pulley P_2. Find the tensions T_1 and T_2 and the acceleration of each body. Neglect friction and the weights of the pulleys and cords.

Solution:

Let a = downward acceleration of A. Then $\frac{1}{2}a$ = upward acceleration of B. (Why?)

(a) $T_2 = \frac{1}{2}T_1$ (1) (Why?)

(b) Net force downward on A = mass × downward acceleration of A
$$20\,\text{lb} - T_2 = 20/32\ \text{slugs} \times a \qquad (2)$$

(c) Net force upward on B = mass × upward acceleration of B
$$T_1 - 30\,\text{lb} = 30/32\ \text{slugs} \times \frac{1}{2}a \qquad (3)$$

Solve simultaneously equations (1), (2), and (3) to obtain
$$a = 5.82\,\text{ft/sec}^2, \quad T_1 = 32.7\,\text{lb}, \quad T_2 = 16.4\,\text{lb}.$$

25. Compute the mass of the earth, assuming it to be a sphere of radius 6.37×10^6 meters.

Solution:

Let m_e = mass of earth, m_b = mass of a body near the earth's surface. The gravitational pull F on the body of mass m_b is $F = m_b g = G\frac{m_b m_e}{r^2}$. Then $g = G\frac{m_e}{r^2}$ and

$$m_e = \frac{gr^2}{G} = \frac{(9.8\,\text{m/sec}^2)(6.37 \times 10^6\,\text{m})^2}{6.67 \times 10^{-11}\ \text{nt-m}^2/\text{kg}^2} = 6.0 \times 10^{24}\,\text{kg}.$$

SUPPLEMENTARY PROBLEMS

26. A given force acts on a 2 kg mass and gives it an acceleration of 3 m/sec². What acceleration is produced by the same force when acting on a mass of (a) 1 kg, (b) 4 kg?
Ans. (a) 6 m/sec², (b) 1.5 m/sec²

27. A given mass acquires an acceleration of 2 ft/sec² when acted upon by a force of 8 lb. What force will give the same mass an acceleration of (a) 1 ft/sec², (b) 10 ft/sec²?   *Ans.* (a) 4 lb, (b) 40 lb

28. Find the weight of a body whose mass is (a) 2 kg, (b) 0.5 g, (c) 2 slugs, (d) 0.5 slugs.
Ans. (a) 19.6 newtons, (b) .0049 newtons or 490 dynes, (c) 64 lb, (d) 16 lb

29. A block hangs at rest from a cord. Find the mass of the block if the tension in the cord is (a) 4.9 newtons, (b) 1.6 lb, (c) 4.9 × 10⁵ dynes.   *Ans.* (a) 0.5 kg, (b) .05 slugs, (c) 0.5 kg

30. Determine the acceleration produced by an unbalanced force (a) of 5 newtons acting on a mass of 2 kg, (b) of 5 dynes acting on a mass of 2 grams, (c) of 5 lb acting on a mass of 2 slugs, (d) of 1 lb acting on a body weighing 32 lb.   *Ans.* (a) 2.5 m/sec², (b) 2.5 cm/sec², (c) 2.5 ft/sec², (d) 1 ft/sec²

31. What constant unbalanced force acting on a body weighing 60 lb will
(a) give it an acceleration of 8 ft/sec²?   *Ans.* 15 lb
(b) give it an acceleration of 96 ft/sec/min?   *Ans.* 3 lb
(c) give it a speed of 24 ft/sec in 6 sec from rest?   *Ans.* 7.5 lb
(d) cause it to move 100 ft in 5 sec from rest?   *Ans.* 15 lb
(e) increase its speed from 16 ft/sec to 48 ft/sec in 4 sec?   *Ans.* 15 lb
(f) change its speed from 64 to 32 ft/sec in passing through a distance of 96 ft?   *Ans.* 30 lb

32. What unbalanced force will produce an acceleration (a) of 2.4 m/sec² in a 4 kg mass, (b) of 80 cm/sec² in a 50 g mass?   *Ans.* (a) 9.6 newtons or 9.6 × 10⁵ dynes, (b) 4 × 10⁻² newtons or 4 × 10³ dynes

33. A mass of 5 kg is acted upon by a steady force of 1 newton. How far will it move from rest in 10 sec?
Ans. 10 meters

34. A 3000 lb automobile speeds at 60 mi/hr. What constant frictional force will bring it to a stop in 5 sec? What distance will it travel in stopping?   *Ans.* 1650 lb, 220 ft

35. A 24 lb body is subjected to a steady force of 6 lb. Find the acceleration and the time taken to move 200 ft from rest.   *Ans.* 8 ft/sec², 7.1 sec

36. A 200 lb crate hangs at the end of a rope. Find its acceleration when the tension in the rope is (a) 250 lb, (b) 160 lb, (c) 200 lb.   *Ans.* (a) 8 ft/sec² up, (b) 6.4 ft/sec² down, (c) 0 ft/sec²

37. An 1800 lb car is drawn vertically up a mine shaft. In starting the car the acceleration is 20 ft/sec². Determine the tension in the cables during start.   *Ans.* 2925 lb

38. A steel cable carries a 3000 lb load which is descending with a speed of 12 ft/sec. It slows down uniformly and comes to a stop in 9 ft. Compute the tension in the cable while slowing down.   *Ans.* 3750 lb

39. What upward force must be exerted on a 100 lb weight to cause it to fall with an acceleration of 10 ft/sec²?
Ans. 69 lb

40. What upward force must be exerted on a 2 kg mass to cause it to rise with an acceleration of 1.6 m/sec²?
Ans. 22.8 newtons

41. A freight elevator weighs 2400 lb. Find the tension in the cables when it (*a*) ascends with an acceleration of 4 ft/sec², (*b*) descends with an acceleration of 4 ft/sec². *Ans.* 2700 lb, 2100 lb

42. A man weighing 160 lb stands on the floor of an elevator which descends with uniform acceleration 1 ft/sec². What force will his feet exert on the floor? What will it be when the elevator is ascending with uniform acceleration 1 ft/sec²? *Ans.* 155 lb, 165 lb

43. The extension of a spring is, within limits, directly proportional to the stretching force. If the scale of a spring balance is marked at a place where $g = 32$ ft/sec², what would a standard 5 lb weight register at a place where $g = 31$ ft/sec²? *Ans.* 4.8 lb

44. A cord passing over a frictionless pulley has a 4 lb weight tied on one end and a 12 lb weight on the other end. Compute the acceleration and the tension in the cord. *Ans.* 16 ft/sec², 6 lb

45. An elevator, starting from rest, accelerates uniformly in an upward direction and travels 3.2 ft in 0.8 sec. A passenger in the elevator is holding a 6 lb package by a string. What is the tension in the string?
Ans. 7.9 lb

46. A 150 lb parachutist falls freely for 5 sec before opening his chute. If the chute opens in 0.8 sec and reduces the jumper's speed to 35 ft/sec, what is the average total force on the ropes of the parachute during this time? Neglect the weight of the parachute. *Ans.* 882 lb

47. A loaded wagon weighing 2000 lb is pulled on a level road by a horse weighing 800 lb. A force of friction of 300 lb acts on the wagon. (*a*) With what force must the horse push (backward) on the ground in order to give the wagon a (forward) velocity of 20 ft/sec in 5 sec, starting from rest? (*b*) How much tension must the rope be able to withstand? *Ans.* 650 lb, 550 lb

48. An inclined plane makes an angle of 30° with the horizontal. Find the constant force, applied parallel to the plane, required to cause an 80 lb box to slide (*a*) up the plane with acceleration 4 ft/sec², (*b*) down the plane with acceleration 4 ft/sec². Neglect friction. *Ans.* (*a*) 50 lb up the plane, (*b*) 30 lb up the plane

49. An inclined plane making an angle of 25° with the horizontal has a pulley at its top. A 20 lb block on the plane is connected to a freely hanging 10 lb block by means of a cord passing over the pulley. Compute the distance the 10 lb block will fall in 2 sec, starting from rest. Neglect friction. *Ans.* 3.3 ft

50. (*a*) What horizontal force is required to slide with uniform motion a 100 lb weight along a horizontal plank, the coefficient of kinetic friction being 0.2? (*b*) If the horizontal force required to slide a 300 lb box with constant velocity along a rough horizontal plank is 60 lb, determine the coefficient of kinetic friction.
Ans. 20 lb, 0.2

51. Determine the force parallel to plane required to support a 200 lb weight on an inclined plane, of height 300 ft and base 400 ft, if the coefficient of friction is 0.25. *Ans.* 80 lb

52. It was found that a force of 80 lb parallel to plane was required to move, with constant velocity, a 100 lb weight up an inclined plane of 30°. Find the coefficient of sliding friction.
Ans. 0.346

53. A metal block is placed on a horizontal oak board. The board is gradually tilted upward and the block just starts to slide when the inclination is 27°. Determine the coefficient of static friction between the block and the board. *Ans.* 0.51

54. A 20 lb block rests on a rough plane which makes an angle of 30° with the horizontal. The coefficient of sliding friction between the block and the plane is 0.15. Compute the force, parallel to the plane, required to cause it just to slide up the plane. *Ans.* slightly more than 12.6 lb

55. A 100 lb body is moved along a horizontal surface, coefficient of friction 0.2, by a cord parallel to the surface and running over a frictionless pulley, the other end of the cord supporting a weight of 25 lb. How far will the body move in 10 sec, starting from rest?   *Ans.* 64 ft

56. A 200 lb sledge is drawn along a rough horizontal plane, coefficient of friction 0.2, by a 100 lb force making an angle of 30° above the plane. How far will the sledge move from rest in 10 sec?
Ans. 453 ft

57. (*a*) What force parallel to plane must be applied to balance a weight of 100 lb on an inclined plane, of height 300 ft and base 400 ft, if the coefficient of friction is 0.3? (*b*) What force is required to keep the above weight moving up the plane at constant velocity? (*c*) If an upward force of 94 lb parallel to plane is applied to the weight, what will happen after the body starts to move? (*d*) How far will the weight move in 10 sec, starting from rest? (*e*) If an upward force of 50 lb parallel to plane is applied, what will occur? (*f*) If an upward force of 26 lb parallel to plane is applied to the weight, what will occur? (*g*) How far will the weight move in 10 sec, starting from rest?
Ans. (*a*) 36 lb, (*b*) 84 lb, (*c*) 3.2 ft/sec^2 up plane, (*d*) 160 ft, (*e*) remains at rest, (*f*) 3.2 ft/sec^2 down plane, (*g*) 160 ft down plane

58. To a 10 lb block on a horizontal table are connected cords which pass over frictionless pulleys at the opposite edges of the table as shown in Fig. (*a*). The cords carry weights of 6 and 9 lb respectively. What speed will the 9 lb weight acquire after falling 3 ft from rest? Coefficient of friction between the table and the 10 lb block is 0.2.   *Ans.* 2.8 ft/sec

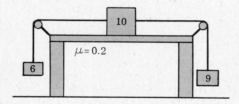

Fig.(*a*) Problem 58

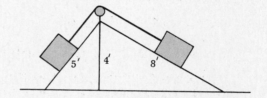

Fig.(*b*) Problem 59

59. Two boards of length 5 ft and 8 ft are hinged together and the hinge supported 4 ft above the ground, thus forming a double inclined plane 13 ft long measured along the slopes. Two blocks of equal weight are placed on the boards and connected by a cord passing over a frictionless pulley at the apex as shown in Fig. (*b*) above. If the coefficient of friction between blocks and boards is 0.3, (*a*) show that the system is in equilibrium. (*b*) If the system is given an initial speed of 3 ft/sec in either direction, compute the distance traveled before coming to rest.
Ans. (*b*) 0.38 ft or 2.01 ft, depending upon the direction of the initial speed.

60. The planets Earth and Mars have diameters 7900 mi and 4200 mi respectively, and the mass of Mars is 0.108 that of Earth. If a body weighs 100 lb on the surface of Earth, what would it weigh on Mars? What is the acceleration due to gravity on Mars?   *Ans.* 38 lb, 12 ft/sec^2

Chapter 6

Work, Energy, Power

WORK. A force does work on a body when it acts against a resisting force to produce **motion** in the body. Work is a scalar quantity.

Consider that a constant external force F acts on a body at an angle θ with the direction of motion and causes it to be displaced a distance s. Then the work W done by the force F on the body is the product of the displacement s and the component of F in the direction of s. Thus

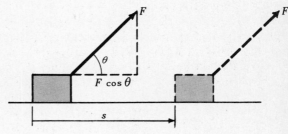

$$W = (F \cos \theta)s$$

If s and F are in the same direction, $\cos \theta = \cos 0° = 1$ and $W = Fs$.

If s and F are in opposite directions, then $\cos \theta = \cos 180° = -1$ and the work is negative. This means that work is done *by* the body. For example, when a car is slowed down by application of the brakes, work is done *by* the car against friction.

UNITS OF WORK. Any unit of work = a unit of force × a unit of length.

One foot-pound (ft-lb) of work is done when a constant force of 1 lb moves a body a distance of 1 ft in the direction of the force.

One newton-meter (nt-m), called **one joule**, is the work done when a constant force of 1 nt moves a body a distance of 1 meter in the direction of the force. Since 1 newton = 0.2248 lb and 1 meter = 3.281 ft,

$$1 \text{ joule} = 1 \text{ newton-meter} = 0.7376 \text{ ft-lb}$$
$$1 \text{ ft-lb} = 1.356 \text{ joules}$$

One dyne-cm, called **one erg**, is the work done when a constant force of 1 dyne moves a body a distance of 1 cm in the direction of the force. Since 1 nt = 10^5 dynes and 1 m = 10^2 cm,

$$1 \text{ joule} = 10^7 \text{ ergs}$$

THE ENERGY of a body is its ability to do work. Since the energy of a body is measured in terms of the work it can do, it has the same units as work. Energy, like work, is a scalar quantity.

POTENTIAL ENERGY (P.E.) of a body is its ability to do work because of its position or state.

> (1) **Absolute Units.** The potential energy of a mass m lifted a vertical distance h, where g is the acceleration due to gravity, is

$$\text{P.E.} = mgh$$

In mks system: P.E. (joules) $= m\,(\text{kg}) \times g\,(\text{m/sec}^2) \times h\,(\text{m})$

In cgs system: P.E. (ergs) $= m\,(\text{grams}) \times g\,(\text{cm/sec}^2) \times h\,(\text{cm})$

Note. Since $mg = w$, we may also write: P.E. $= mgh = wh$.

> (2) **Gravitational Units.** The potential energy of a weight w lifted a vertical distance h is

$$\text{P.E.} = wh$$

In English system: P.E. (ft-lb) $= w\,(\text{lb}) \times h\,(\text{ft})$

KINETIC ENERGY (K.E.) of a body is its ability to do work because of its motion. The K.E. of a mass m moving with a velocity v is

$$\text{K.E.} = \tfrac{1}{2}mv^2$$

In mks system: K.E. (joules) $= \tfrac{1}{2}m\,(\text{kg}) \times v^2\,(\text{m/sec squared})$

In cgs system: K.E. (ergs) $= \tfrac{1}{2}m\,(\text{grams}) \times v^2\,(\text{cm/sec squared})$

In English system: K.E. (ft-lb) $= \tfrac{1}{2}m\,(\text{slugs}) \times v^2\,(\text{ft/sec squared})$

CONSERVATION OF ENERGY. Energy can neither be created nor destroyed, but only transformed from one kind to another. (This implies that mass can, under certain conditions, be regarded as a form of energy. Ordinarily the conversion of mass into energy and vice versa, predicted by the theory of relativity, can be ignored.)

POWER is the time rate of doing work.

$$\text{Average power} = \frac{\text{work done}}{\text{time taken to do this work}}$$

$$= \text{force applied} \times \text{velocity of body to which force is applied}$$

where the velocity of the body is in the direction of the applied force.

UNITS OF POWER. The unit of power in any system is found by dividing the unit of work in that system by the unit of time. Thus two units of power are the joule/sec (or watt) and the ft-lb/sec. Other practical units of power are the kilowatt and the horsepower.

> **1 watt** $=$ 1 joule/sec
>
> **1 kilowatt** (kw) $=$ 1000 watts $=$ 1.34 horsepower
>
> **1 horsepower** (hp) $=$ 550 ft-lb/sec $=$ 33,000 ft-lb/min $=$ 746 watts

Work done $=$ power $\times$ time taken. Hence the total work done in 1 hour, when the rate of doing work is 1 kilowatt, is **1 kilowatt-hour** (kw-hr). The total work done in 1 hour, when the rate of doing work is 1 horsepower, is **1 horsepower-hour** (hp-hr). The kilowatt-hour and the horsepower-hour are units of work.

SOLVED PROBLEMS

1. A block of mass 5 kg is lifted 2 meters in 3 sec. Compute the work done in joules and in ergs.

Solution:

The force required to lift the block (at constant velocity) is equal in magnitude (and opposite in direction) to the weight of the block.

$$\text{Weight of block} = mg = 5\,\text{kg} \times 9.8\,\text{m/sec}^2 = 49\,\text{newtons, in mks units}$$
$$= mg = 5000\,\text{g} \times 980\,\text{cm/sec}^2 = 49 \times 10^5\,\text{dynes, in cgs units}$$

Work = force × distance moved in the direction of the force
$$= 49\,\text{newtons} \times 2\,\text{meters} = 98\,\text{newton-meters or joules, in mks units}$$
$$= 49 \times 10^5\,\text{dynes} \times 200\,\text{cm} = 98 \times 10^7\,\text{dyne-cm or ergs, in cgs units}$$

2. A ladder 16 ft long and weighing 50 lb has its center of gravity 6 ft from the bottom and a 10 lb weight at the top. Compute the work required to raise the ladder from a horizontal position on the ground to a vertical position.

Solution:

Work to raise center of gravity 6 ft	= 50 lb × 6 ft	= 300 ft-lb
Work to raise 10 lb weight 16 ft	= 10 lb × 16 ft	= 160 ft-lb
	Total work	= 460 ft-lb

3. Compute the useful work done by a pump which discharges 600 gallons of linseed oil into a tank 50 ft above the intake. Linseed oil weighs 58.8 lb/ft³. One U.S. gallon = 231 cubic inches.

Solution:

$$\text{Weight of oil} = 600\,\text{gal} \times \frac{231\,\text{in}^3}{1\,\text{gal}} \times \frac{1\,\text{ft}^3}{(12 \times 12 \times 12)\,\text{in}^3} \times \frac{58.8\,\text{lb}}{1\,\text{ft}^3} = 4720\,\text{lb}$$

Note that all the units cancel out, except lb which appears in the result.

$$\text{Work} = 4720\,\text{lb} \times 50\,\text{ft} = 236,000\,\text{ft-lb}$$

4. A sled is drawn a distance of 8 meters along the level ground. The pull in the rope is 75 newtons and the angle between the rope and ground is 28°. Find the work done.

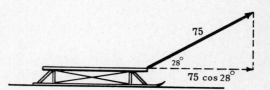

Solution:

The work done by a force is equal to the product of the displacement and the component of the force that is parallel to the displacement.

$$\text{Work} = \text{component of force parallel to displacement} \times \text{displacement}$$
$$= 75 \cos 28°\,\text{nt} \times 8\,\text{m} = 530\,\text{joules}$$

5. A block moves up a 30° inclined plane under the action of certain forces, three of which are shown in the figure below. F_1 is horizontal and equal to 40 lb. F_2 is normal to the plane and equal to

20 lb. F_3 is parallel to the plane and equal to 30 lb. Determine the work done by each of the three forces while the block and point of application of each force move 10 ft up the plane.

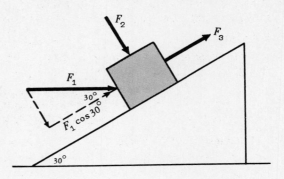

Solution:

The component of F_1 along the path of the point of application is $F_1 \cos 30^\circ = 40\,\text{lb} \times 0.866 = 34.6\,\text{lb}$. Hence the work done by F_1 is $34.6\,\text{lb} \times 10\,\text{ft} = 346\,\text{ft-lb}$.

F_2 does no work, since it has no component along the path.

The component of F_3 in the direction of motion is 30 lb. Hence the work done by $F_3 = 30\,\text{lb} \times 10\,\text{ft} = 300\,\text{ft-lb}$.

6. Within certain limits, the amount a spiral spring is stretched is proportional to the stretching force. A force of 20 lb stretches a spring 5 in. (*a*) How much work is required to stretch the spring 6 in.? (*b*) How much work is done in stretching the spring another inch, i.e. from 6 in. to 7 in.?

Solution:

$$\text{Force required per inch of stretch} = \frac{20\,\text{lb}}{5\,\text{in.}} = 4\,\text{lb/in}$$

(*a*) As the amount of stretch increases, the stretching force increases proportionately. Hence, starting from an unstretched condition, the *average force* is half the maximum force.

Work to stretch 6 in. = average force × distance through which force acts
= $\frac{1}{2}(6\,\text{in.} \times 4\,\text{lb/in.}) \times 6\,\text{in.}$ = 72 in-lb

(*b*) Work to stretch 7 in. = $\frac{1}{2}(7\,\text{in.} \times 4\,\text{lb/in.}) \times 7\,\text{in.}$ = 98 in-lb
Work to stretch from 6 in. to 7 in. = $(98-72)\,\text{in-lb}$ = 26 in-lb

Otherwise: Force to stretch 6 in. = 24 lb; force to stretch 7 in. = 28 lb.
Work to stretch from 6 in. to 7 in. = $\frac{1}{2}(28+24)\,\text{lb} \times 1\,\text{in.}$ = 26 in-lb

7. A 2 kg mass falls 4 meters. Find the potential energy lost in joules and in ergs.

Solution:

In mks units: P.E. (joules) = mgh = $2\,\text{kg} \times 9.8\,\text{m/sec}^2 \times 4\,\text{m}$ = 78.4 joules
In cgs units: P.E. (ergs) = mgh = $2000\,\text{g} \times 980\,\text{cm/sec}^2 \times 400\,\text{cm}$ = 78.4×10^7 ergs

8. A 10 lb body moves with a velocity of 8 ft/sec. Compute its kinetic energy.
Solution:

$$\text{K.E.} = \tfrac{1}{2}mv^2 = \tfrac{1}{2} \times 10/32 \text{ slugs} \times (8\,\text{ft/sec})^2 = 10\,\text{ft-lb}$$

9. A 5 kg body falls freely through a height of 3 meters. Find its kinetic energy in joules when it reaches the ground and show that it equals the potential energy before falling.

Solution:

After falling 3 m, $v^2 = 2gh = 2 \times 9.8\,\text{m/sec}^2 \times 3\,\text{m} = 58.8\,(\text{m/sec})^2$.

K.E. = $\tfrac{1}{2}mv^2$ = $\tfrac{1}{2} \times 5\,\text{kg} \times 58.8\,(\text{m/sec})^2$ = 147 joules
P.E. = mgh = $5\,\text{kg} \times 9.8\,\text{m/sec}^2 \times 3\,\text{m}$ = 147 joules

10. A 40 lb projectile has a velocity of 2000 ft/sec. The shell acquired the velocity in a mortar (barrel) 10 ft long. Determine the average force F against the shell as it was fired.

Solution:

The work expended by the powder on the bullet in the mortar equals the kinetic energy of the moving bullet.

$$\text{Work expended} = \text{kinetic energy gained}$$
$$Fs = \tfrac{1}{2}mv^2$$
$$F \times 10\,\text{ft} = \tfrac{1}{2} \times 40/32\,\text{slugs} \times (2000\,\text{ft/sec})^2$$

Solving, $F = 250,000$ lb.

11. A brick is thrown forward on the ground with a speed of 80 ft/sec. The coefficient of sliding friction between the brick and the ground is 0.25. Compute the time and the distance the brick will travel before coming to rest.

Solution:

Retarding friction force $f = \mu w = 0.25\,w$, where w is the unknown weight of the brick.

$$\text{Kinetic energy lost by brick} = \text{work done against friction force}$$
$$\tfrac{1}{2}(w/32\,\text{slugs})(80\,\text{ft/sec})^2 = 0.25\,w \times s \qquad\qquad s = 400\,\text{ft}$$

$$\text{Time required} = \frac{\text{distance traveled}}{\text{average speed}} = \frac{400\,\text{ft}}{\tfrac{1}{2}(80\,\text{ft/sec})} = 10\,\text{sec.}$$

12. A force F of 16 lb is applied continuously at an angle of 30° to a 100 lb body as shown in Fig.(*a*) below. Compute the velocity of the body after it has moved 20 ft from rest. Neglect friction.

Solution:

$$\text{Work done by the force} = \text{kinetic energy gained by the body}$$
$$(F\cos 30°) \times s = \tfrac{1}{2}mv^2$$
$$(16\,\text{lb} \times \cos 30°) \times 20\,\text{ft} = \tfrac{1}{2} \times 100/32\,\text{slugs} \times v^2$$

Solving, $v = 13.3$ ft/sec.

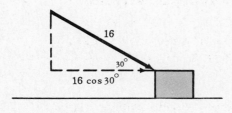

Fig.(*a*) Problem 12

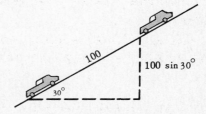

Fig.(*b*) Problem 13

13. A 3200 lb car is coasting down a 30° hill as shown in Fig.(*b*) above. At a time when the car's speed is 40 ft/sec the driver applies the brakes. What force F (parallel to the road) must be applied by the brakes if the car is to stop after traveling 100 ft?

Solution:

$$\text{Work done against friction} = \text{P.E. lost} + \text{K.E. lost}$$
$$F \times 100\,\text{ft} = 3200\,\text{lb} \times (100\,\text{ft} \times \sin 30°) + \tfrac{1}{2} \times 3200/32\,\text{slugs} \times (40\,\text{ft/sec})^2$$

Solving, $F = 2400$ lb.

14. A train starts from rest on top of a 1% grade and runs 4000 ft down the incline under the force due to gravity, and then continues on a level track. The train resistance is assumed constant at 12 lb per ton. Find (a) the speed v at the foot of the grade and (b) the distance s the train moves on the level track before coming to rest.

Solution:

(a) While moving 4000 ft down the slope the train falls 1% × 4000 ft = 40 ft.

$$\text{K.E. gained} = \text{P.E. lost} - \text{work done against friction}$$
$$\tfrac{1}{2}(w/32)v^2 = w \times 40 - (12 \times w/2000) \times 4000 \qquad\qquad v = 32 \text{ ft/sec}$$

Note that w, the weight of the train, may be eliminated from the above equation.

(b) $$\text{K.E. lost} = \text{work done against friction}$$
$$\tfrac{1}{2}(w/32)(32)^2 = (12 \times w/2000)s \qquad\qquad s = 2670 \text{ ft}$$

15. A 120,000 lb train is pulled up a 1% grade by a steady drawbar pull of 800 lb. The train resistance is 8 lb per ton and the initial speed is 30 ft/sec. What distance s up the incline will the train go before its speed is reduced to 20 ft/sec?

Solution:

The train rises 1 ft for every 100 ft up the slope.

$$\text{Initial K.E.} + \text{work by drawbar pull} = \text{final K.E.} + \text{P.E. gained} + \text{work against resistance}$$
$$\tfrac{1}{2}mv_1^2 + 800s = \tfrac{1}{2}mv_2^2 + wh + 8(w/2000) \times s$$
$$\frac{1}{2}\left(\frac{120,000}{32}\right)(30)^2 + 800s = \frac{1}{2}\left(\frac{120,000}{32}\right)(20)^2 + 120,000\left(\frac{s}{100}\right) + 8\left(\frac{120,000}{2000}\right)s$$

Solving, $s = 1070$ ft.

POWER

16. What average power in watts is employed in lifting 50 kg a height of 20 meters in 1 minute?

Solution:

$$\text{Power in watts} = \frac{\text{work in joules}}{\text{time in seconds}} = \frac{\text{force in newtons} \times \text{distance in meters}}{\text{time in seconds}}$$

$$= \frac{(50 \times 9.8) \text{ newtons} \times 20 \text{ meters}}{60 \text{ sec}} = \frac{9800 \text{ joules}}{60 \text{ sec}} = 163 \text{ watts}$$

17. Find the average power used in lifting 5000 lb through a height of 300 ft in 25 sec.

Solution:

$$\text{Power in ft-lb/sec} = \frac{\text{work in ft-lb}}{\text{time in sec}} = \frac{5000 \text{ lb} \times 300 \text{ ft}}{25 \text{ sec}} = 60,000 \text{ ft-lb/sec}$$

$$\text{Power in hp} = 60,000 \text{ ft-lb/sec} \times \frac{1 \text{ hp}}{550 \text{ ft-lb/sec}} = 109 \text{ hp}$$

18. What weight w can a 6 hp engine pull along a level road at 15 mi/hr (22 ft/sec) if the coefficient of friction between the weight and the road is 0.2?

Solution:

The power is expended in working against the friction force $(0.2w)$.

$$\text{Power} = \text{force of friction} \times \text{velocity}$$
$$6 \times 550 \text{ ft-lb/sec} = 0.2w \times 22 \text{ ft/sec} \qquad\qquad w = 750 \text{ lb}$$

19. A motor having an efficiency of 90% operates a crane having an efficiency of 40%. With what steady velocity does the crane lift an 880 lb bale if the power supplied to the motor is 5 kilowatts?

Solution:

Overall efficiency = 40% × 90% = 36%. Useful power = 0.36 × 5 kw = 1.8 kw.

Power output by crane in ft-lb/sec = load lifted × velocity

$$1.8\,\text{kw} \times \frac{1.34\,\text{hp}}{1\,\text{kw}} \times \frac{550\,\text{ft-lb/sec}}{1\,\text{hp}} = 880\,\text{lb} \times v \qquad\qquad v = 1.5\,\text{ft/sec}$$

20. A fireboat engine pumps water from the surface of a river 12 ft below its own level and discharges it through a nozzle of diameter 1.6 in. with a speed of 200 ft/sec. Find the horsepower required assuming (a) no losses, (b) 65% efficiency. Water weighs 62.4 lb/ft³.

Solution:

In 1 sec the pump discharges a cylinder of water of length 200 ft and cross section area $\frac{1}{4}\pi d^2 = \frac{1}{4}(3.14)(1.6/12\,\text{ft})^2 = 0.0140\,\text{ft}^2$. Hence the volume of water discharged per sec = 200 ft × 0.0140 ft² = 2.8 ft³, and the weight of this volume = 2.8 ft³ × 62.4 lb/ft³ = 175 lb.

Work to lift 175 lb water 12 ft = wh = 175 lb × 12 ft = 2100 ft-lb

K.E. of 175 lb water at 200 ft/sec = $\frac{1}{2}mv^2 = \frac{1}{2}(175/32)(200)^2 = 109{,}000$ ft-lb

(a) Power required = $\dfrac{(2100 + 109{,}000)\,\text{ft-lb}}{1\,\text{sec}} \times \dfrac{1\,\text{hp}}{550\,\text{ft-lb/sec}} = 202$ hp

(b) Power required assuming 65% efficiency = 202 hp × 1/0.65 = 311 hp

SUPPLEMENTARY PROBLEMS

21. A force of 3 newtons acts through a distance of 12 meters (parallel to the force). Find the work done in joules and in ergs. *Ans.* 36 joules, 36×10^7 ergs

22. A body of mass 4 kg is raised 1.5 meters. Find the work done. *Ans.* 58.8 joules or 58.8×10^7 ergs

23. A rectangular marble slab, 6 ft 3 in. long, 3 in. thick, and weighing 500 lb lies on a level floor. How much work must be done to set it vertically on end? *Ans.* 1500 ft-lb

24. A uniform steel chain 30 ft long and weighing 4 lb per ft, hangs vertically. Compute the work required to wind it up. *Ans.* 1800 ft-lb

25. Compute the useful work done by an engine which hoists 40 cubic feet of tar a height of 50 ft in 23 sec. Tar weighs 66 lb/ft³. *Ans.* 132,000 ft-lb

26. A pump discharges 100 gallons of water per minute through a large nozzle into a tank 30 ft above the intake. How much useful work is done by the pump in 1 hr? Water weighs 8.34 lb/gal.
Ans. 1.5×10^6 ft-lb

27. An 800 lb bale is pulled up a smooth inclined plane 20 ft long to a platform 5 ft above the ground. Compute the force parallel to the plane and the work done. Neglect friction. *Ans.* 200 lb, 4000 ft-lb

28. A 100,000 lb freight car is pulled 2500 ft up a 1.2% grade at a constant speed of 12 mi/hr. (a) Find the work done against gravity by the drawbar pull. (b) If the train resistance is 8.8 lb per ton, find the total work done. *Ans.* 3.0×10^6 ft-lb, 4.1×10^6 ft-lb

29. A cylindrical tank of diameter 4 ft and height 6 ft is full of water. Compute the work done in pumping the water to a height of 12 ft above the top of the tank. Water weighs 62.4 lb/ft^3. Volume of cylinder = $\pi r^2 h$. *Ans.* 22,500 π ft-lb

30. Find the potential energy gained by a 7 lb weight when lifted 20 ft vertically. *Ans.* 140 ft-lb

31. A 24 lb body moves with velocity 4 ft/sec. Determine its kinetic energy. *Ans.* 6 ft-lb

32. A 4 lb body falls through a vertical distance of 30 ft. Compute the kinetic energy of the body when it reaches the ground and show that it equals the potential energy before falling. *Ans.* 120 ft-lb

33. A 2 kg body is raised a vertical distance of 15 meters. Find the work done on the body and the potential energy gained by the body. *Ans.* 294 joules, 294 joules

34. A 5 gram bullet moves with velocity 600 m/sec. Compute its kinetic energy in joules and in ergs. *Ans.* 9×10^2 joules, 9×10^9 ergs

35. A constant force acts on a mass of 3 kg for 1 minute and gives it a velocity of 2 m/sec. Find the kinetic energy of the mass and the value of the force. *Ans.* 6 joules, 0.1 newton

36. A simple pendulum 1 meter long has a bob of 10 kg. (*a*) How much work in joules will be required to move the pendulum from its vertical position to a horizontal position? (*b*) If the pendulum swings from a horizontal position, what will be the velocity and kinetic energy of the bob at the instant it passes through the lowest position of its path? *Ans.* 98 joules, 4.43 m/sec, 98 joules

37. A horizontal force of 20 lb moves a weight of 50 lb a distance of 100 ft along a rough horizontal plane, coefficient of sliding friction 0.1. How much work is done against the force of friction? How much work is done against the force of gravity? What becomes of the surplus energy? *Ans.* 500 ft-lb, no work, body gains 1500 ft-lb of kinetic energy

38. A 2400 lb car speeding at 60 mi/hr is brought to a stop in a distance of 100 ft. Compute the average braking force used in stopping the car. *Ans.* 2900 lb

39. A 16 lb projectile acquires a velocity of 1800 ft/sec in a mortar 9 ft long. Determine the average force against the shell as it was fired. *Ans.* 90,000 lb

40. A 10 lb weight slides from rest down a rough inclined plane, 100 ft long and inclined 30° with the horizontal, and gains a velocity of 52 ft/sec. Find the work done against friction. *Ans.* 77.5 ft-lb

41. A 4 lb hammer with a horizontal velocity of 20 ft/sec drives a nail 0.1 ft into a board. Compute the approximate average resistance. *Ans.* 250 lb

42. A 4 lb hammer is moving vertically downward at 20 ft/sec when it hits a nail which it drives 0.1 ft into a board. Compute the approximate average resistance. *Ans.* 254 lb

43. An elevator weighing 2 tons rises from rest in the basement to the fourth floor, a distance of 60 ft. As it passes the fourth floor it has a speed of 10 ft/sec. There is a constant frictional force of 100 lb. Calculate the work done by the lifting mechanism. *Ans.* 252,000 ft-lb

44. What constant drawbar pull will give a 500 ton train a speed of 45 mi/hr in 1 mile on a level track, assuming that train resistance is constant at 9 lb per ton? *Ans.* 17,400 lb

45. A loaded freight car weighing 150,000 lb is pulled up a 0.75% grade 4000 ft long by a steady drawbar pull of 1000 lb. The train resistance is 8 lb per ton and the initial speed is 40 ft/sec. Find the speed at the top of the incline. *Ans.* 19 ft/sec

46. Express the kilowatt-hour in the following units of work: joule, erg, foot-pound, horsepower-hour.
   Ans. 3.60×10^6 joules, 3.60×10^{13} ergs, 2.66×10^6 ft-lb, 1.34 hp-hr

47. Calculate the average horsepower required to raise a 300 lb drum to a height of 50 ft in 1 minute.
   Ans. 0.455 hp

48. A system of pulleys is used to lift a 600 lb bale to a height of 20 ft in 30 sec. The efficiency of the system is 75%. Find the average horsepower furnished the system.   *Ans.* 0.97 hp

49. Compute the power output in watts of a machine that lifts a 500 kg crate through a height of 20 meters in 1 minute.   *Ans.* 1630 watts

50. A man pushes downward on a cart with a force of 200 lb. A mule pulls due northward on the cart with a force of 50 lb. If the cart moves due northward on a horizontal roadway with a speed of 11 ft/sec, (a) at what rate does the man do work and (b) at what rate does the mule do work?   *Ans.* 0 hp, 1 hp

51. An engine expends 40 horsepower in pulling a car along a level track at 30 mi/hr. Compute the total air and frictional resistance overcome.   *Ans.* 500 lb

52. A 2200 lb auto travels up a 3% grade at 45 mi/hr. Find the horsepower required, neglecting friction.
   Ans. 7.9 hp

53. Water flows from a reservoir to a turbine 330 ft below. The efficiency of the turbine is 80% and it takes 100 cubic feet of water per minute. Neglecting friction in pipe, compute the horsepower output of the turbine. Water weighs 62.4 lb/ft^3.   *Ans.* 50 hp

54. What weight can a 40 hp engine pull along a level road at 30 mi/hr if the coefficient of friction between the weight and the road is 0.15?   *Ans.* 3330 lb

55. What power must be expended by a man who is dragging a 100 kg log down a hillside at a steady speed of 1 meter/sec, if the hill makes an angle of 20° with the horizontal and the coefficient of friction is 0.9?
   Ans. 494 watts

56. A block is projected up an inclined plane making an angle of 30° with the horizontal at a speed of 40 ft/sec. The coefficient of friction is 0.4. Compute (a) the speed of the block as it returns to its starting point, (b) the time required for the block to ascend and descend the plane.
   Ans. (a) 17 ft/sec, (b) 1.5 + 3.5 = 5 sec

57. A certain coil spring, the unstretched length of which is 5 in., requires a force of 5 lb to stretch it 1 inch. If the spring remains within the elastic limit, what work is required to stretch it from a length of 8 in. to a length of 12 in.?   *Ans.* 100 in-lb

58. An archer pulls back his arrow with a force proportional to the displacement, and must exert a 50 lb force to hold the 1 oz arrow in position ready to shoot. The string of the bow (assumed inextensible) is 5 ft long, and the center of the string is pulled back 1 ft. The mass of the string and bow are negligible. Compute (a) the potential energy stored in the bow, (b) the tension in the string, and (c) the speed with which the arrow leaves the string.   *Ans.* 25 ft-lb, 62.5 lb, 160 ft/sec

Chapter 7

Simple Machines

A MACHINE is any device by which the magnitude, direction or method of application of a force is changed in order to achieve a practical advantage. Examples of simple machines are the lever, inclined plane, pulley, crank and axle, and jackscrew.

PRINCIPLE OF WORK. Work input = useful work output + work done against friction.

This follows from the law of conservation of energy. (In most cases the change in the energy stored in the machine may be neglected, e.g. the kinetic energy of moving parts.)

MECHANICAL ADVANTAGE. The actual mechanical advantage (AMA) of a machine is

$$\text{AMA} \;=\; \text{force ratio} \;=\; \frac{\text{force exerted by machine on load}}{\text{force used to operate machine}}$$

The ideal mechanical advantage (IMA) of a machine is

$$\text{IMA} \;=\; \text{distance ratio} \;=\; \frac{\text{distance moved by force operating machine}}{\text{distance moved by load}}$$

Since friction is always present, AMA is always less than IMA.

EFFICIENCY of a machine $= \dfrac{\text{work output}}{\text{work input}} = \dfrac{\text{power output}}{\text{power input}}$

The efficiency is also the ratio $\dfrac{\text{actual mechanical advantage (AMA)}}{\text{ideal mechanical advantage \quad (IMA)}}$.

SOLVED PROBLEMS

1. A hoisting engine lifts a 500 lb bucket containing 40 ft³ of clay, weighing 125 lb/ft³, a height of 24 ft in 20 sec. The power supplied to the engine is 16 hp. Compute (a) the work output, (b) the power output and power input in ft-lb/sec, (c) the efficiency of the engine and hoist.

   Solution:

   (a) Work output $= (500 + 40 \times 125)\,\text{lb} \times 24\,\text{ft} = 132{,}000\,\text{ft-lb}$

   (b) Power output $= \dfrac{\text{work output}}{\text{time taken}} = \dfrac{132{,}000\,\text{ft-lb}}{20\,\text{sec}} = 6600\,\text{ft-lb/sec}$

   Power input $= 16\,\text{hp} \times \dfrac{550\,\text{ft-lb/sec}}{1\,\text{hp}} = 8800\,\text{ft-lb/sec}$

   (c) Efficiency $= \dfrac{\text{power output}}{\text{power input}} = \dfrac{6600\,\text{ft-lb/sec}}{8800\,\text{ft-lb/sec}} = 0.75 = 75\%$

   $\phantom{\text{Efficiency}} = \dfrac{\text{work output}}{\text{work input}} = \dfrac{132{,}000\,\text{ft-lb}}{8800\,\text{ft-lb/sec} \times 20\,\text{sec}} = 0.75 = 75\%$

2. What power in kilowatts is supplied to a 12 hp motor, having an efficiency of 90%, when it is delivering its full rated output?

Solution:

$$\text{Power input in kilowatts} = \frac{\text{power output}}{\text{efficiency}} = \frac{12 \text{ hp} \times 0.746 \text{ kw/hp}}{0.90} = 9.95 \text{ kw}$$

3. For each of the three levers shown below, determine the downward force F required to lift a load w of 90 lb. Neglect the weights of the levers.

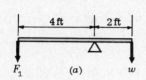 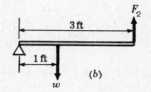 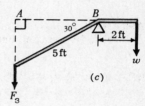

Solution:

In Fig.(c) above, the lever is bent at B, and $AB = 5 \text{ ft} \times \cos 30° = 4.33 \text{ ft}$.
In each case, take moments about the fulcrum.

Clockwise moments = counterclockwise moments

(a)	90 lb × 2 ft = F_1 × 4 ft	F_1 = 45 lb
(b)	90 lb × 1 ft = F_2 × 3 ft	F_2 = 30 lb
(c)	90 lb × 2 ft = F_3 × 4.33 ft	F_3 = 41.6 lb

The ideal mechanical advantages of the three levers are:

(a) IMA $= \dfrac{4 \text{ ft}}{2 \text{ ft}} = 2$ (b) IMA $= \dfrac{3 \text{ ft}}{1 \text{ ft}} = 3$ (c) IMA $= \dfrac{4.33 \text{ ft}}{2 \text{ ft}} = 2.16$

4. Determine the force F required to lift a 100 lb load w with each of the five pulley systems shown below. Neglect friction and the weights of the pulleys.

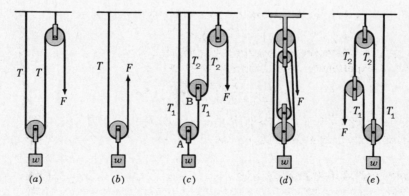

Solution:

(a) Load w is supported by 2 ropes; each rope exerts an upward pull of $T = \frac{1}{2}w$. But $T = F$, as the rope is continuous. Then $F = T = \frac{1}{2}w = \frac{1}{2} \times 100 \text{ lb} = 50 \text{ lb}$.

(b) Here, too, the load is supported by 2 ropes, T and F. Then $F = \frac{1}{2}w = 50 \text{ lb}$.

(c) Let T_1 and T_2 be the tensions in their respective ropes. The pulley A is in equilibrium with the equal forces T_1 and T_1 acting upward, and with w acting downward. Then $w = 2T_1$ or $T_1 = \frac{1}{2}w$.

Consider pulley B: T_1 is balanced by the equal forces T_2 and T_2 acting upward; then $T_1 = 2T_2$ or $T_2 = \frac{1}{2}T_1 = \frac{1}{4}w$. But $F = T_2$, since the rope is continuous; hence $F = T_2 = \frac{1}{4}w = 25 \text{ lb}$.

(d) The same rope passes round all the pulleys; four ropes support the load equally. Then F equals the tension in each of the 4 ropes. $F = \frac{1}{4}w = 25 \text{ lb}$.

(e) The tensions (F, T_1, T_1) in all three parts of the rope passing round the two movable pulleys are equal, as the rope is continuous. Then $F = T_1 = T_1$.

$T_2 = F + T_1 = 2F$, as the upward force T_2 supports the two downward forces F and T_1.

The load is supported by T_1, T_2, T_1. Hence $w = T_1 + T_2 + T_1 = F + 2F + F = 4F$, and $F = 25$ lb.

5. Using a wheel and axle machine, a 400 lb load can be raised by a force of 50 lb applied to the rim of the wheel. The radii of the wheel and axle are 2.5 ft and 3 in. respectively. Determine the actual mechanical advantage, the ideal mechanical advantage, and the efficiency of the machine.

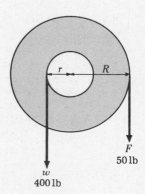

Solution:

$$\text{AMA} = \text{force ratio} = \frac{w}{F} = \frac{400 \text{ lb}}{50 \text{ lb}} = 8.$$

When the wheel is turned through one revolution, F moves a distance $2\pi R$ (equal to the circumference of the wheel) and w moves a distance $2\pi r$.

$$\text{IMA} = \frac{\text{distance moved by } F}{\text{distance moved by } w} = \frac{2\pi R}{2\pi r} = \frac{R}{r} = \frac{30 \text{ in.}}{3 \text{ in.}} = 10$$

Efficiency = AMA/IMA = 8/10 = 0.8 = 80%.

6. An inclined plane is 15 ft long and 3 ft high. (a) What force F parallel to the plane is required to slide a 200 lb box up the plane if friction is neglected? (b) What is the ideal mechanical advantage of the plane? (c) Find the actual mechanical advantage and efficiency if a 64 lb force is required to slide a 200 lb box up the plane.

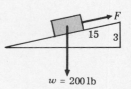

Solution:

(a) When F moves 15 ft up the plane, w is raised 3 ft. Since no work is lost by friction,

$$\text{work input} = \text{work output}$$
$$F \times 15 \text{ ft} = 200 \text{ lb} \times 3 \text{ ft}, \qquad F = 40 \text{ lb}.$$

(b) $\text{IMA} = \dfrac{\text{distance moved by } F}{\text{distance moved by } w} = \dfrac{\text{length of plane}}{\text{height of plane}} = \dfrac{15 \text{ ft}}{3 \text{ ft}} = 5$

(c) $\text{AMA} = \text{force ratio} = \dfrac{w}{F} = \dfrac{200 \text{ lb}}{64 \text{ lb}} = 3.1$

$$\text{Efficiency} = \frac{\text{work output}}{\text{work input}} = \frac{w \times \text{height of plane}}{F \times \text{length of plane}} = \frac{200 \text{ lb} \times 3 \text{ ft}}{64 \text{ lb} \times 15 \text{ ft}} = 0.62 = 62\%$$

Or, efficiency = AMA/IMA = 3.1/5 = 0.62 = 62%.

7. A jackscrew has a lever arm of 18 in. and a pitch of $\frac{1}{4}$ in. If the efficiency is 30%, what force F is required to lift a load w of 2700 lb?

Solution:

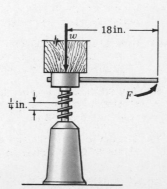

The interval between two consecutive threads is $\frac{1}{4}$ in. Hence the load w is raised $\frac{1}{4}$ in. when the force F acts through the circumference ($2\pi r = 2\pi 18$ in.) of a circle whose radius is the lever arm.

$$\text{Efficiency} = \frac{\text{work output}}{\text{work input}} = \frac{w \times \text{height}}{F \times \text{circumference}}$$

$$0.30 = \frac{2700 \text{ lb} \times \frac{1}{4} \text{ in.}}{F \times 2\pi 18 \text{ in.}} \qquad F = 20 \text{ lb}$$

8. A differential pulley (chain hoist) is shown in the adjacent figure. Two tooth-
ed pulleys of radii $r = 5$ in. and $R = 5\frac{1}{2}$ in. are fastened together and can turn
in the suspended block. A continuous chain passes over the smaller 5 in.
pulley, then around the movable pulley at the bottom, and finally around the
$5\frac{1}{2}$ in. pulley. The operator exerts a downward force F on the chain to lift
load w. (*a*) Determine the ideal mechanical advantage. (*b*) What is the efficiency of the machine if an applied downward force of 50 lb is required to
lift a load of 700 lb?

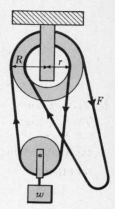

Solution:

(*a*) Consider that the force F moves down a distance sufficient to cause the upper
rigid system of pulleys to make one complete revolution. Then the chain between
the upper and lower pulleys is shortened a distance equal to the circumference
$(2\pi R)$ of the larger pulley and lengthened by a distance equal to the circumference
$(2\pi r)$ of the smaller pulley. Therefore the load is moved up a distance equal to
half the difference between the circumferences, $\frac{1}{2}(2\pi R - 2\pi r)$.

$$\text{IMA} = \frac{\text{distance moved by } F}{\text{distance moved by } w} = \frac{2\pi R}{\frac{1}{2}(2\pi R - 2\pi r)} = \frac{2R}{R - r} = \frac{2 \times 5\frac{1}{2} \text{ in.}}{(5\frac{1}{2} - 5)\text{ in.}} = 22$$

(*b*) When the effort F moves 22 ft, the load is raised 1 ft.

$$\text{Efficiency} = \frac{\text{work output}}{\text{work input}} = \frac{w \times 1 \text{ ft}}{F \times 22 \text{ ft}} = \frac{700 \text{ lb} \times 1 \text{ ft}}{50 \text{ lb} \times 22 \text{ ft}} = 0.64 = 64\%$$

$$= \frac{\text{AMA}}{\text{IMA}} = \frac{700/50}{22} = 0.64 = 64\%$$

SUPPLEMENTARY PROBLEMS

9. A hoist furnished with 120 hp lifts 11,000 lb to a height of 40 ft in
20 sec. Find the efficiency of this machine. *Ans.* 33%

10. What effort is required to raise 300 lb by means of each of the pulley
systems shown in adjoining Fig.(*a*) and (*b*)? *Ans.* 100 lb, 75 lb

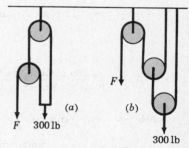

11. With a certain machine the applied force moves 10 ft to raise a load
3 in. Find (*a*) the ideal mechanical advantage, (*b*) the actual mechanical advantage if the efficiency is 60%. What load can be lifted
by an applied force of 50 lb (*c*) if friction is neglected, (*d*) if the
efficiency is 60%? *Ans.* 40, 24, 2000 lb, 1200 lb

12. Using a wheel and axle machine, a force of 30 lb applied to the rim of a wheel can lift a load of 240 lb.
The diameters of the wheel and axle are 3 ft and 4 in. respectively. Determine the actual mechanical advantage, the ideal mechanical advantage, and the efficiency of the machine. *Ans.* 8, 9, 89%

13. A 6 ft crowbar is employed to lift a 400 lb load. What force must the man apply to one end of the crowbar
when a stone (acting as a fulcrum) is placed under the crowbar 8 in. away from the end on which the load
rests? Neglect the weight of the crowbar. *Ans.* 50 lb

14. A jackscrew has an ideal mechanical advantage of 25, and a force of 40 lb is required to lift a load of 300
lb. What is the efficiency of the machine? What load can be lifted by the machine if it is operated by a force
of 60 lb? *Ans.* 30%, 450 lb

15. The screw of a copying press has 5 threads to the inch, and the diameter of the wheel to which the effort is
applied is 20 in. If the efficiency is 40%, what effort will be required to produce a force of 3140 lb on the
plate? *Ans.* 25 lb

16. The diameters of the two upper pulleys of a differential pulley are 10 in. and $9\frac{1}{2}$ in. respectively. If the efficiency of this machine is 45%, what force is required to lift a 900 lb bale? *Ans.* 50 lb

Chapter 8

Impulse and Momentum

MOMENTUM of a body $=$ mass of body $\times$ velocity of body $=$ mv.

Momentum is a vector quantity whose direction is that of its velocity.

Units of momentum are: the slug-ft/sec in the English system, the kg-m/sec in the mks system, and the gram-cm/sec in the cgs system.

IMPULSE $=$ force $\times$ length of time the force acts $=$ Ft.

Impulse is a vector quantity whose direction is that of its force.

Units of impulse are: the lb-sec in the English system, the nt-sec in the mks system, and the dyne-sec in the cgs system.

IMPULSE AND MOMENTUM. The change of momentum produced by an impulse is numerically equal to the impulse. Thus if an unbalanced force F acting for a time t on a body of mass m changes its velocity from an initial value v_o to a final value v_t, then

$$\text{Impulse} = \text{change in momentum}$$
$$Ft = m(v_t - v_o)$$

This equation indicates that the unit of impulse in any system is equal to the corresponding unit of momentum. Thus $1\,\text{lb-sec} = 1\,\text{slug-ft/sec}$ and $1\,\text{nt-sec} = 1\,\text{kg-m/sec}$.

CONSERVATION OF MOMENTUM. In any collision between two or more bodies, the vector sum of the momenta after impact is equal to that before impact. The sum of components of momentum along any given direction remains unaltered during collision.

Thus when two bodies of masses m_1 and m_2 respectively collide,

$$\text{total momentum before impact} = \text{total momentum after impact}$$
or
$$m_1 u_1 + m_2 u_2 = m_1 v_1 + m_2 v_2$$

where u_1, u_2 = velocities of bodies 1 and 2 respectively before impact
v_1, v_2 = velocities of bodies 1 and 2 respectively after impact.

COEFFICIENT OF RESTITUTION. For any direct central impact or collision between two bodies, the coefficient of restitution e is the pure number expressing the ratio of the relative velocity of separation after impact to the relative velocity of approach before impact.

$$e = \frac{v_2 - v_1}{u_1 - u_2}$$

where u_1, u_2 = velocities of bodies 1 and 2 respectively before impact
v_1, v_2 = velocities of bodies 1 and 2 respectively after impact.

For a perfectly elastic collision, $e = 1$. For a completely inelastic collision (the bodies are stuck together), $e = 0$. For all other types of collision e is a number between 0 and 1.

SOLVED PROBLEMS

1. An 8 g bullet is fired horizontally into a 9 kg block of wood which is free to move. The velocity of the block and bullet after impact is 40 cm/sec. Calculate the initial velocity of the bullet.

Solution:

Consider the system (block + bullet). The velocity, and hence the momentum, of the block before impact is zero.

$$\text{Momentum of system before impact} = \text{momentum of system after impact}$$
$$\text{mass} \times \text{velocity of bullet} + 0 = \text{mass} \times \text{velocity of (block + bullet)}$$
$$8\,\text{g} \times v + 0 = (9000 + 8)\,\text{g} \times 40\text{ cm/sec}$$

Solving, $v = 45 \times 10^3$ cm/sec = 450 m/sec.

2. Two inelastic masses of 16 and 4 grams move in opposite directions toward each other with velocities of 30 and 50 cm/sec respectively. Find the resultant velocity v on collision if they are stuck together.

Solution:

Apply the law of conservation of momentum to the system consisting of the two masses.

$$\text{Momentum of system before impact} = \text{momentum of system after impact}$$
$$16\,\text{g} \times 30\text{ cm/sec} - 4\,\text{g} \times 50\text{ cm/sec} = (16 + 4)\,\text{g} \times v \qquad v = 14\text{ cm/sec}$$

3. A 15 g bullet is fired horizontally into a 3 kg block of wood suspended by a long cord, and the bullet remains embedded in the wood. Compute the velocity of the bullet if the impact causes the block to swing 10 cm above its initial level.

Solution:

The velocity V of (block + bullet) just after impact is equal to the velocity which (block + bullet) would acquire in falling freely through a vertical distance of 10 cm.

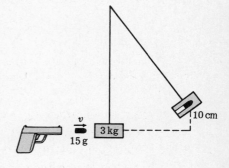

$$V = \sqrt{2gh} = \sqrt{2(9.8\text{ m/sec}^2)(0.10\text{ m})} = 1.4\text{ m/sec}$$

Consider the system (block + bullet). Before impact the block is at rest and hence has zero momentum.

$$\text{Momentum of system before impact} = \text{momentum of system just after impact}$$
$$15\,\text{g} \times v + 0 = (3000 + 15)\,\text{g} \times 1.4\text{ m/sec} \qquad v = 281\text{ m/sec}$$

4. A 0.5 lb ball moving with velocity 38 ft/sec is hit by a bat which causes it to move in a reversed direction with velocity 58 ft/sec. The force of the blow acts on the ball for 0.01 sec. Find the average force F exerted on the ball by the batter.

Solution:

Take the final direction of motion of the ball as positive. Then, initial $v_o = -38$ ft/sec and final $v_t = +58$ ft/sec.

$$Ft = m(v_t - v_o)$$
$$F \times 0.01\text{ sec} = 0.5/32\text{ slugs} \times [58 - (-38)]\text{ ft/sec} \qquad F = 150\text{ lb}$$

5. A 500 lb gun fires a 2 lb projectile with a muzzle velocity of 1600 ft/sec. (*a*) Determine the initial recoil velocity v of the gun. If the recoil is against a constant resisting force of 400 lb, find (*b*) the time in which the gun is brought to rest and (c) the distance it recoils.

Solution:

(a) Consider the system (gun + projectile). The momentum of the system before firing is zero.

Momentum of system after firing = momentum of system before firing

$$2/32 \text{ slugs} \times 1600 \text{ ft/sec} + 500/32 \text{ slugs} \times v = 0 \qquad v = -6.4 \text{ ft/sec}$$

The minus sign indicates that the gun moves in a direction opposite to the projectile.

(b) Impulse in direction of gun's motion = change in momentum in direction of gun's motion

$$Ft = m(v_t - v_0)$$
$$-400 \text{ lb} \times t = 500/32 \text{ slugs} \times (0 - 6.4) \text{ ft/sec} \qquad t = 0.25 \text{ sec}$$

Note that the resisting force F acts in a direction opposite to the gun's motion and hence is negative in the above equation.

(c) Since the resisting force is constant, the gun's motion is uniformly accelerated.

Distance = average velocity × time = $\frac{1}{2}(6.4 + 0)$ ft/sec × 0.25 sec = 0.8 ft

---

6. A 7500 kg truck traveling at 5 m/sec east collides with a 1500 kg car moving at 20 m/sec in a direction 30° south of west. The two vehicles remain tangled together. With what speed and in what direction does the wreckage begin to move?

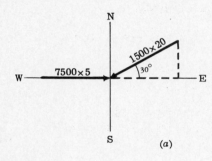

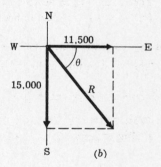

(a) (b)

Solution:

E-W components of momentum

Truck: $+7500 \times 5$ $= +37,500$
Car: $-1500 \times 20 \cos 30° = -26,000$
$+11,500$

N-S components of momentum

Truck: 0
Car: $-1500 \times 20 \sin 30° = -15,000$
$-15,000$

Hence the resultant momentum of the system has a component 11,500 kg-m/sec directed east and a component 15,000 kg-m/sec directed south, as shown in Fig.(b) above.

Resultant moment $R = \sqrt{(11,500)^2 + (-15,000)^2} = 18,900$ kg-m/sec

Speed of system $= \dfrac{\text{momentum of system}}{\text{mass of system}} = \dfrac{18,900 \text{ kg-m/sec}}{(7500 + 1500) \text{ kg}} = 2.1$ m/sec

Direction of R: $\tan \theta = \dfrac{15,000}{11,500} = 1.30$ from which $\theta = 52°$ S of E

---

7. What force is exerted on a stationary flat plate held normal to a jet of water 2 in. in diameter and having a horizontal velocity of 60 ft/sec? After striking, the water is moving parallel to the plate. Water weighs 62.4 lb/ft³.

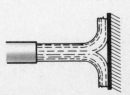

Solution:

Consider what happens during one second. During that second a mass of water, of diameter 2 in. and length 60 ft, strikes the plate and loses all its horizontal velocity of 60 ft/sec upon contact with the plate.

Volume = cross section area × length = $\frac{1}{4}\pi d^2 l$ = $\frac{1}{4}\pi(1/6\ ft)^2 \times 60\ ft$ = 1.31 ft^3

Weight of this volume = 1.31 ft^3 × 62.4 lb/ft^3 = 81.7 lb

Let F = force exerted by the plate on this volume of water. Assume motion to the right as positive.

$$\text{Impulse in horizontal direction} = \text{change in horizontal momentum}$$
$$Ft = m(v_t - v_0)$$
$$F \times 1\ sec = 81.7/32\ slugs \times (0-60)\ ft/sec$$

Solving, $F = -153$ lb, i.e. to the left. Of course, the force of the jet on the plate is also 153 lb but to the right (Newton's Third Law).

8. A 1 lb ball moving at 12 ft/sec collides centrally with a 2 lb ball moving in the opposite direction at 24 ft/sec. Find the velocity of each after impact (a) if the coefficient of restitution is 2/3, (b) if they are stuck together, (c) if the collision is perfectly elastic.

Solution:

(a) Here $m_1 = 1/32$ slug, $u_1 = 12$ ft/sec and $m_2 = 2/32$ slug, $u_2 = -24$ ft/sec.

$$e = \frac{v_2 - v_1}{u_1 - u_2}, \qquad \frac{2}{3} = \frac{v_2 - v_1}{12 - (-24)} \qquad \text{or} \qquad (1)\ \ v_2 - v_1 = 24$$

$$m_1 u_1 + m_2 u_2 = m_1 v_1 + m_2 v_2, \qquad 1(12) + 2(-24) = 1(v_1) + 2(v_2) \qquad \text{or} \qquad (2)\ \ v_1 + 2v_2 = -36$$

Add (1) and (2) to obtain: $3v_2 = -12$, $v_2 = -4$ ft/sec.

Put $v_2 = -4$ in (1) and obtain: $-4 - v_1 = 24$, $v_1 = -28$ ft/sec.

(b) Here $v_1 = v_2 = v$; hence $1(12) + 2(-24) = 1(v) + 2(v)$, $-36 = 3v$ and $v = -12$.

The common final velocity is −12 ft/sec.

(c) Since here $e = 1$, we have $1 = \frac{v_2 - v_1}{12 - (-24)}$ or (1) $v_2 - v_1 = 36$.

From $1(12) + 2(-24) = 1(v_1) + 2(v_2)$ we obtain (2) $v_1 + 2v_2 = -36$.

Adding (1) and (2), $v_2 = 0$ ft/sec. Putting $v_2 = 0$ in (1) or (2), $v_1 = -36$ ft/sec.

9. A ball is dropped from a height of 60 in. above a tile floor and rebounds to a height of 37 in. Find the coefficient of restitution between the ball and the floor.

Solution:

The initial and final velocities of the floor (u_1, v_1) are assumed to be zero.

Since for falling bodies $v = \sqrt{2gh}$, the ball strikes the floor with velocity $u_2 = \sqrt{2g(60)}$ and the rebound velocity is $v_2 = -\sqrt{2g(37)}$, where downward velocities are positive.

$$e = \frac{v_2 - v_1}{u_1 - u_2} = \frac{-\sqrt{2g(37)} - 0}{0 - \sqrt{2g(60)}} = \sqrt{37/60} = 0.79$$

SUPPLEMENTARY PROBLEMS

10. A 10 ton locomotive moving at 2 ft/sec collides with and is coupled to a 40 ton car at rest on the same straight track. Find their common velocity after impact. *Ans.* 0.4 ft/sec

11. An empty coal car weighing 15 tons is coasting on a level track at a constant speed of 16 ft/sec. A load of 5 tons of coal is suddenly dumped (at zero horizontal velocity) into the car from above. What is the new speed of the car and contents? *Ans.* 12 ft/sec

12. Sand drops at the rate of 2000 kg/min from the bottom of a hopper onto a belt conveyor moving horizontally at 250 m/min. Determine the force required to drive the conveyor, neglecting friction. *Ans.* 139 nt

13. Two inelastic bodies of mass 8 and 4 kg move in opposite directions with velocities 11 and 7 m/sec respectively. Compute the resultant velocity on collision if they are stuck together. *Ans.* 5 m/sec

14. A 1200 lb gun mounted on wheels shoots an 8 lb projectile with a muzzle velocity of 1800 ft/sec at an angle of $30°$ with the horizontal. Find the horizontal recoil velocity of the gun. *Ans.* 10.4 ft/sec

15. A 0.4 oz bullet is fired into a 10 lb block of soft wood suspended by a long rope, and the bullet remains embedded in the block. The impact causes the center of gravity of the block to rise 3 in. Find the initial velocity of the bullet. *Ans.* 1600 ft/sec

16. A 6 ton truck traveling north at 15 mi/hr collides with a 4 ton truck traveling west at 45 mi/hr. If the two trucks remain locked together, with what speed and in what direction do they move immediately after the collision? *Ans.* 20.1 mi/hr, in a direction $26.6°$ N of W

17. An 8 lb body is acted upon by an unbalanced force for a period of 4 sec and it gains a velocity of 20 ft/sec. Determine the magnitude of the force. *Ans.* 1.25 lb

18. What average resisting force must act on a 3 kg mass to reduce its speed from 65 to 15 cm/sec in 0.2 sec? *Ans.* 7.5 newtons or 7.5×10^5 dynes

19. A force increases uniformly with time at the rate of 0.4 lb/sec. If its initial value is 7 lb, find the average force and the impulse of the force during the first 5 sec. *Ans.* 8 lb, 40 lb-sec

20. A jet of water from a nozzle 1 inch in diameter has a velocity of 100 ft/sec and strikes a flat plate held normal to the jet and moving away from the jet at 20 ft/sec. (*a*) Compute the force exerted by the jet on the moving plate. (*b*) What is the force if the plate is moving toward the jet at 20 ft/sec? Water weighs 62.4 lb/ft^3. *Ans.* (*a*) 68 lb, (*b*) 153 lb

21. Two 1 kg balls moving in opposite directions at 3 meters/sec collide centrally. Find the velocity of each after impact if (*a*) they are stuck together, (*b*) the collision is perfectly elastic, (*c*) the coefficient of restitution is 1/3. *Ans.* (*a*) 0 m/sec, (*b*) each ball rebounds at 3 m/sec, (*c*) each ball rebounds at 1 m/sec

22. A 9 lb ball moving at 10 ft/sec collides centrally with a stationary 1 lb ball. Determine the velocity of each after impact if (*a*) they are stuck together, (*b*) the collision is perfectly elastic, (*c*) the coefficient of restitution is 0.90. *Ans.* (*a*) 9 ft/sec; (*b*) 9 lb ball at 8 ft/sec, 1 lb ball at 18 ft/sec; (*c*) 9 lb ball at 8.1 ft/sec, 1 lb ball at 17.1 ft/sec

23. A ball is dropped onto a horizontal floor. It reaches a height of 144 cm on the first bounce and 81 cm on the second bounce. Find (*a*) the coefficient of restitution between the ball and the floor, (*b*) the height it attains on the third bounce. *Ans.* 0.75, 45.6 cm

24. Given the impact equations (*1*) $m_1 u_1 + m_2 u_2 = m_1 v_1 + m_2 v_2$ and (*2*) $e = \dfrac{v_2 - v_1}{u_1 - u_2}$.

(*a*) Solve for v_1 and v_2. Hint: Multiply (*2*) by $m_1(u_1 - u_2)$ and add with (*1*).
(*b*) Find expressions for v_1 and v_2 for perfectly elastic impact ($e = 1$).
(*c*) Find expressions for v_1 and v_2 for perfectly elastic impact when $m_1 = m_2$.
(*d*) Find expressions for v_1 and v_2 for completely inelastic impact ($e = 0$).

Ans. (*a*) $v_1 = \dfrac{m_2 u_2(1+e) + u_1(m_1 - em_2)}{m_1 + m_2}$, $v_2 = \dfrac{m_1 u_1(1+e) + u_2(m_2 - em_1)}{m_1 + m_2}$

(*c*) $v_1 = u_2$, $v_2 = u_1$

Chapter 9

Angular Velocity and Acceleration

ANGULAR DISPLACEMENT is usually expressed in degrees, in revolutions, or in radians.

One radian is the angle subtended at the center of a circle by an arc equal in length to the radius. Since circumference = 2π × radius, the angular displacement in 1 revolution is 2π radians.

$$1 \text{ revolution} = 360° = 2\pi \text{ radians}, \quad 1 \text{ radian} = \frac{360°}{2\pi} = \frac{360°}{2 \times 3.14} = 57.3°.$$

Angular displacement in radians = 2π × angular displacement in revolutions.

The radian measure of an angle ($\frac{\text{length of arc}}{\text{length of radius}}$) is a pure number.

ANGULAR VELOCITY (ω) of a body is its time rate of angular displacement about an axis. It is expressed in radians/sec, degrees/sec, revolutions/sec (rps), and revolutions/min (rpm).

If a body describes an angle θ radians in t sec, its average angular speed $\bar{\omega}$ in radians per second (rad/sec) is

$$\bar{\omega} \text{ (rad/sec)} = \frac{\text{angle described (radians)}}{\text{time (sec) required to describe this angle}} = \frac{\theta}{t}$$

Since 1 rev/sec = 2π rad/sec, then ω (rad/sec) = 2π × rev/sec = $2\pi f$, where f is the frequency in rev/sec.

ANGULAR ACCELERATION (α) of a body is the time rate of change of its angular velocity. It is expressed in radians per sec per sec (rad/sec^2).

If the angular velocity of a body changes uniformly from ω_0 to ω_t rad/sec in t sec, then

$$\alpha \text{ (rad/sec}^2) = \frac{\text{change in angular velocity (rad/sec)}}{\text{time (sec) required for this change}} = \frac{\omega_t - \omega_0}{t}$$

RELATION BETWEEN LINEAR AND ANGULAR QUANTITIES.

$s = \theta r$ s = length of the arc, in feet, meters, etc.

r = radius, in feet, meters, etc.

$v = \omega r$ v = linear speed, in ft/sec, m/sec, etc.

$a = \alpha r$ a = linear acceleration, in ft/sec^2, etc.

where θ is in radians, ω in rad/sec, and α in rad/sec^2.

EQUATIONS FOR UNIFORMLY ACCELERATED ANGULAR MOTION are exactly analogous to those for linear motion. If v_O and ω_O denote the initial linear and angular velocities respectively, and v_t and ω_t denote linear and angular velocities after a time t, then

$$v_t = v_O + at \qquad s = v_O t + \tfrac{1}{2}at^2 \qquad v_t^2 = v_O^2 + 2as$$

$$\omega_t = \omega_O + \alpha t \qquad \theta = \omega_O t + \tfrac{1}{2}\alpha t^2 \qquad \omega_t^2 = \omega_O^2 + 2\alpha\theta$$

Starting from rest, $v_O = 0$ and $\omega_O = 0$, and therefore

$$v_t = at \qquad\qquad s = \tfrac{1}{2}at^2 \qquad\qquad v_t^2 = 2as$$

$$\omega_t = \alpha t \qquad\qquad \theta = \tfrac{1}{2}\alpha t^2 \qquad\qquad \omega_t^2 = 2\alpha\theta$$

SOLVED PROBLEMS

1. The bob of a 3 ft pendulum swings through a 9 inch arc. Find the angle θ, in radians and in degrees, through which it swings.

Solution:

$$\theta \text{ in radians } = \frac{s \text{ (length of arc)}}{r \text{ (radius)}} = \frac{9 \text{ in.}}{36 \text{ in.}} = \tfrac{1}{4} \text{ radian}$$

$$\theta \text{ in degrees } = \tfrac{1}{4} \text{ rad} \times \frac{180 \text{ deg}}{\pi \text{ rad}} = 14.3^\circ$$

2. Convert (a) 5 radians to revolutions, (b) 300 revolutions to radians, (c) 720 rpm to rad/sec.

Solution:

(a) $5 \text{ rad} = 5 \text{ rad} \times \dfrac{1 \text{ rev}}{2\pi \text{ rad}} = \dfrac{5}{2\pi} \text{ rev}$ (b) $300 \text{ rev} = 300 \text{ rev} \times \dfrac{2\pi \text{ rad}}{1 \text{ rev}} = 600\pi \text{ rad}$

(c) $720 \dfrac{\text{rev}}{\text{min}} = 720 \dfrac{\text{rev}}{\text{min}} \times \dfrac{1 \text{ min}}{60 \text{ sec}} \times \dfrac{2\pi \text{ rad}}{1 \text{ rev}} = 24\pi \dfrac{\text{rad}}{\text{sec}}$

3. A flywheel makes 300 rpm. Find the angular speed ω of any point on the wheel and the linear speed v of a point 5 ft from the center.

Solution:

Angular speed $\omega = 300 \text{ rpm} = 10\pi \text{ rad/sec}$ is the same for all points of the wheel.
Linear speed v at $r = 5 \text{ ft}$ is $v = \omega r = 10\pi \text{ rad/sec} \times 5 \text{ ft} = 50\pi \text{ ft/sec}$.

4. A point on the rim of a turbine wheel of radius 3 meters moves with linear speed 15 meters per sec. Find the angular speed of the wheel.

Solution:

Angular speed $\omega = v/r = (15 \text{ m/sec})/(3 \text{ m}) = 5 \text{ rad/sec}$ or $5/2\pi$ rev/sec

5. A flywheel is speeded up uniformly to 900 rpm (30π rad/sec) in 15 sec from rest. Find the angular acceleration α in rad/sec^2 and the linear acceleration a of a point 3 ft from the axis.

Solution:

$$\alpha = \frac{\omega_t - \omega_0}{t} = \frac{(30\pi - 0)\ \text{rad/sec}}{15\ \text{sec}} = 2\pi\ \text{rad/sec}^2$$

$$a = \alpha r = 2\pi\ \text{rad/sec}^2 \times 3\ \text{ft} = 6\pi\ \text{ft/sec}^2$$

6. A motor revolving at 1800 rpm slows down uniformly to 1200 rpm in 2 sec. Calculate (*a*) the angular acceleration of the motor and (*b*) the number of revolutions it makes in this time.

Solution:

$$\omega_0 = 1800\ \text{rpm} = 60\pi\ \text{rad/sec}, \quad \omega_t = 1200\ \text{rpm} = 40\pi\ \text{rad/sec}$$

(*a*) $\quad \alpha = \dfrac{\omega_t - \omega_0}{t} = \dfrac{(40\pi - 60\pi)\ \text{rad/sec}}{2\ \text{sec}} = -10\pi\ \text{rad/sec}^2$

(*b*) $\quad \theta = \frac{1}{2}(\omega_0 + \omega_t) \times t = \frac{1}{2}(60\pi + 40\pi)\ \text{rad/sec} \times 2\ \text{sec} = 100\pi\ \text{rad}$ or $50\ \text{rev}$

7. A disk revolves with a constant acceleration of 5 rad/sec^2. How many turns does it make (*a*) in 8 sec from rest, (*b*) during the third second?

Solution:

(*a*) $\theta = \omega_0 t + \frac{1}{2}\alpha t^2 = 0 + \frac{1}{2}(5\ \text{rad/sec}^2)(8\ \text{sec})^2 = 160\ \text{rad}$ or $160/2\pi = 25.5\ \text{rev}$

(*b*) At $t = 2$ sec, $\omega_2 = 5\ \text{rad/sec}^2 \times 2\ \text{sec} = 10\ \text{rad/sec}$; at $t = 3$ sec, $\omega_3 = 15\ \text{rad/sec}$.

$\quad \theta = \frac{1}{2}(\omega_2 + \omega_3) \times t = \frac{1}{2}(10 + 15)\,\text{rad/sec} \times (3 - 2)\,\text{sec} = 12.5\ \text{rad}$ or $12.5/2\pi = 1.99\ \text{rev}$

8. The spindrier of a washing machine revolving at 900 rpm slows down uniformly to 300 rpm while making 50 revolutions. Find (*a*) the angular acceleration and (*b*) the time required to turn through these 50 revolutions.

Solution:

$$\omega_0 = 900\ \text{rpm} = 30\pi\ \text{rad/sec}, \quad \omega_t = 300\ \text{rpm} = 10\pi\ \text{rad/sec}; \quad \theta = 50\ \text{rev} = 100\pi\ \text{rad}.$$

(*a*) $\quad \omega_t^2 = \omega_0^2 + 2\alpha\theta, \quad \alpha = \dfrac{\omega_t^2 - \omega_0^2}{2\theta} = \dfrac{(10\pi\ \text{rad/sec})^2 - (30\pi\ \text{rad/sec})^2}{2 \times 100\pi\ \text{rad}} = -4\pi\ \text{rad/sec}^2$

(*b*) $\quad \theta = \dfrac{\omega_0 + \omega_t}{2} \times t, \quad t = \dfrac{2\theta}{\omega_0 + \omega_t} = \dfrac{2 \times 100\pi\ \text{rad}}{(30\pi + 10\pi)\ \text{rad/sec}} = 5\ \text{sec}$

Or: $\quad \alpha = \dfrac{\omega_t^2 - \omega_0^2}{2\theta} = \dfrac{(5^2 - 15^2)\,(\text{rev/sec})^2}{2 \times 50\ \text{rev}} = -2\ \dfrac{\text{rev}}{\text{sec}^2}, \quad t = \dfrac{2\theta}{\omega_0 + \omega_t} = \dfrac{2 \times 50\ \text{rev}}{(15 + 5)\ \text{rev/sec}} = 5\ \text{sec}$

SUPPLEMENTARY PROBLEMS

9. Convert (a) 50 revolutions to radians, (b) 48π radians to revolutions, (c) 72 rps to radians per sec, (d) 1500 rpm to radians per sec, (e) 7π rad/sec to rpm, (f) 2 rad/sec to deg/sec.
   Ans. (a) 100π rad, (b) 24 rev, (c) 144π rad/sec, (d) 50π rad/sec, (e) 210 rev/min, (f) 114.6 deg/sec

10. Express the angular speed of 40 degrees per sec in (a) revolutions per sec, (b) revolutions per minute, (c) radians per sec.   Ans. 1/9 rps, 60/9 rpm, $2\pi/9$ rad/sec

11. A flywheel makes 480 rpm. Compute the angular speed at any point on the wheel, and the linear speed 3 ft from the center.   Ans. 16π rad/sec, 48π ft/sec

12. Determine the angular speed of a car that rounds a curve of radius 25 ft at 30 mi/hr.
    Ans. 1.76 rad/sec

13. It is desired that the circumferential speed of an emery wheel, of radius 9 in., be 1200 ft/min. Determine the angular speed of the wheel in rev/min and in rad/sec.   Ans. $800/\pi$ rpm, 26.7 rad/sec

14. Through how many radians does a point on the earth's surface move in 6 hours as a result of the earth's rotation? What is the speed, in mi/sec, of a point on the equator? Take the sidereal day = 24 hr, and the equatorial radius = 4000 mi.   Ans. $\pi/2$ rad, 0.29 mi/sec

15. A wheel revolving at 120 rpm increases its speed to 660 rpm in 9 sec. Find the angular acceleration in rev/sec^2 and in rad/sec^2, and the linear acceleration of a point 2.5 ft from the axis.
    Ans. 1 rev/sec^2, 2π rad/sec^2, 5π ft/sec^2

16. The angular speed of a disk decreases uniformly from 12 to 4 rad/sec in 16 sec. Compute the angular acceleration and the number of revolutions made in this time.   Ans. -0.5 rad/sec^2, $64/\pi$ rev

17. How many turns does a flywheel make in 5 sec from rest if it revolves with an angular acceleration of 20 rad/sec^2? How many turns does it make during the fifth second?   Ans. $125/\pi$ rev, $45/\pi$ rev

18. A wheel revolving at 6 rps has an angular acceleration of 4 rad/sec^2. Find the numbers of turns the wheel must make to acquire an angular speed of 26 rps and the time required.
    Ans. 160π rev, 10π sec

19. The spindle of a stirrer rotating at 2100 rpm slows down uniformly to 900 rpm while making 80 revolutions. Compute the angular acceleration of the stirrer and the time required to slow down.
    Ans. -12.5π rad/sec^2, 3.2 sec

Chapter 10

Centripetal and Centrifugal Force

UNIFORM CIRCULAR MOTION. When a body moves with constant **speed** in a circle, it is said to have uniform circular motion.

CENTRIPETAL ACCELERATION. When a body moves with constant **speed** in a circle, the **direction** of the motion is continuously changing; therefore its **velocity** is continuously changing. (Speed is a scalar quantity, having only magnitude; velocity is a vector quantity, having both magnitude and direction.) Hence the body has an acceleration due to the change in the direction of velocity.

The direction of this acceleration is perpendicular to the direction of the velocity, *i.e.* the acceleration is directed toward the center of the circle. (If the direction of the acceleration were not at right angles to that of the velocity, it would have a component in the direction of the velocity, and the magnitude of the velocity, *i.e.* the speed, would not be constant.)

The value of this central (centripetal) acceleration a is

$$a = \frac{\text{(linear speed of body)}^2}{\text{radius of circular path}} = \frac{v^2}{r}$$

Alternative forms are

$$a = \frac{v^2}{r} = \frac{(2\pi r f)^2}{r} = 4\pi^2 f^2 r \quad \text{and} \quad a = \frac{v^2}{r} = \frac{(\omega r)^2}{r} = \omega^2 r$$

where f = angular speed of body in rev/sec, ω = angular speed in rad/sec.

CENTRIPETAL AND CENTRIFUGAL FORCE. To give the body this central acceleration ($a = v^2/r$) an unbalanced force ($F = ma = mv^2/r$), directed toward the center of the circular path, must be exerted on the body. This force is called the **centripetal** or **central** force.

By Newton's Third Law, every action has an equal and opposite reaction. The equal and opposite (radially outward) reaction exerted by the revolving body against this central force is called the **centrifugal force**.

The value of the central force F is

$$F = ma = m\frac{v^2}{r} = 4\pi^2 f^2 r m = m\omega^2 r$$

SOLVED PROBLEMS

1. A 2 lb body is tied to the end of a cord and whirled in a horizontal circle of radius 4 ft at 3 revolutions per sec. (The cord is horizontal, i.e. the attraction due to gravity is neglected.) Determine (a) the linear speed in ft/sec, (b) the acceleration, (c) the pull of the cord on the body, and (d) the pull of the body on the cord. (e) What happens if the cord breaks?

Solution:

(a) $v = 2\pi rf = 2\pi (4\,\text{ft})(3/\text{sec}) = 24\pi$ ft/sec

   or $v = 2\pi rf = (2\pi \times 4)$ ft/rev $\times$ 3 rev/sec $= 24\pi$ ft/sec

(b) $a = v^2/r = (24\pi\ \text{ft/sec})^2/(4\,\text{ft}) = 144\pi^2$ ft/sec^2 toward the center of the circle

(c), (d) $F = ma = m(v^2/r) = (2/32\ \text{slugs})(144\pi^2\ \text{ft/sec}^2) = 9\pi^2$ lb

The pull of the cord on the body is the central or centripetal force. The pull of the body on the cord is the centrifugal force. These two forces are equal in magnitude ($9\pi^2$ lb) and opposite in direction. The centripetal force is directed radially inward, toward the center of the circle; the centrifugal force is directed radially outward.

(e) The body will move along the tangent to the circle at any given instant.

2. What is the maximum speed at which an automobile can round a curve of 80 ft radius on a level road if the coefficient of friction between the tires and the road is 0.30?

Solution:

The central force required to keep the auto in the curved path is supplied by the force of friction between the tires and the road. If w is the weight of the auto, the maximum central force supplied by friction is $0.30w$.

$$\text{Force of friction} = \text{centripetal force}$$
$$0.30w = m(v^2/r) = (w/g)(v^2/r)$$

Then $v^2 = 0.30\,gr$ and $v = \sqrt{0.30\,gr} = \sqrt{0.30\,(32\ \text{ft/sec}^2)(80\ \text{ft})}$
$$= 27.7\ \text{ft/sec}.$$

3. A curve of radius 100 ft is to be banked so that an automobile may make the turn at a speed of 40 ft/sec without depending on friction. What must be the slope of the curve?

Solution:

The two forces acting on the auto at A are:
(1) Its weight $w = mg$ acting vertically downward.
(2) The push P of the track, which is perpendicular to the track.

The resultant of these two forces must be a horizontal force along AC (toward the center C of the path) equal to the centripetal force mv^2/r required to keep the body in its circular path.

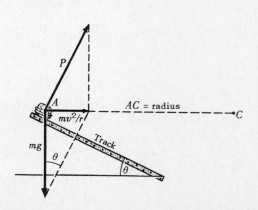

$$\tan\theta = \frac{mv^2/r}{mg} = \frac{v^2}{gr} = \frac{(40)^2}{32 \times 100} = 0.50$$

and θ = angle whose tangent is 0.50 = 26.6°.

4. A ball at B is fastened to one end of a string 24 cm long, and the other end is attached to a fixed point O. The ball describes a horizontal circle of radius CB about a center vertically under O. Find the speed of the ball in its circular path if the string makes an angle of 30° with the vertical.

Solution:

Figure (a).

The two forces acting on the ball are:

(a) its weight, mg

(b) the tension in the string.

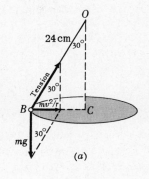
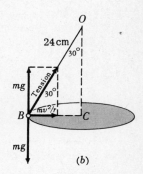

The resultant (ΣF) of these two forces must be a horizontal force along BC (toward C) equal to the centripetal force mv^2/r required to keep the ball in its circular path.

Radius BC = 24 cm × sin 30° = 12 cm

$$\tan 30° = \frac{mv^2/r}{mg} = \frac{v^2}{rg}$$

from which $v = \sqrt{rg \tan 30°} = \sqrt{0.12\,\text{m} \times 9.8\,\text{m/sec}^2 \times 0.5774} = 0.824$ m/sec.

Another Method. See Fig. (b).

The vertical component of the tension balances the weight of the ball (mg). The horizontal component of the tension is equal to the required centripetal force (mv^2/r). The rest of the solution is the same as in the first method.

5. A 2 lb body attached to a cord is whirled in a vertical circle of radius 8 ft. (a) What minimum speed v_t must it have at the top of the circle so that the cord does not slacken? (b) What minimum speed v_b must it have at the bottom of the circle so that the cord will not slacken when the body rounds the top of the circle? (c) Find the tension T_b in the cord when the body is at the bottom of the circle and moving with the critical speed v_b.

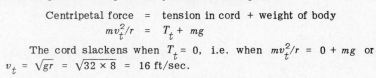

Solution:

(a) Two radially inward forces act on the body at the top: (1) its weight, (2) the tension T_t. The resultant of these two forces is the centripetal force required to keep the body in its circular path.

Centripetal force = tension in cord + weight of body
$$mv_t^2/r = T_t + mg$$

The cord slackens when $T_t = 0$, i.e. when $mv_t^2/r = 0 + mg$ or
$v_t = \sqrt{gr} = \sqrt{32 \times 8} = 16$ ft/sec.

(b) In traveling from bottom to top, the body rises a distance $2r$.

K.E. at bottom = K.E. at top + P.E. at top
$$\tfrac{1}{2}mv_b^2 = \tfrac{1}{2}mv_t^2 + (mg)(2r)$$
$$= \tfrac{1}{2}m(gr) + 2mgr, \quad\text{and}\quad v_b = \sqrt{5gr} = 35.8 \text{ ft/sec}$$

If v_b is less than $\sqrt{5gr}$, v_t will be less than $\sqrt{gr}$ and the cord will be slack at the top.

(c) Centripetal force = tension in cord − weight of body
$$mv_b^2/r = T_b - mg$$

Then $T_b = m(v_b^2/r) + mg = m(5gr/r) + mg = mg(5+1) = 6w = 6(2\,\text{lb}) = 12$ lb.

SUPPLEMENTARY PROBLEMS

6. A mass of 1.5 kg moves in a circle of radius 25 cm at 2 rps. Calculate (a) the linear speed, (b) the acceleration, (c) the centripetal force acting on the body.
Ans. π m/sec, $4\pi^2$ m/sec^2 toward center, $6\pi^2$ newtons or $6\pi^2 \times 10^5$ dynes

7. A 20 lb body moves at 4 rps in a circular path of radius 5 ft. Calculate (a) the linear speed, (b) the acceleration, (c) the centripetal force acting on the body.
Ans. (a) 40π ft/sec, (b) $320\pi^2$ ft/sec^2 toward center, (c) $200\pi^2$ lb

8. Compute the central acceleration of a point on the equator. Take the equatorial radius as 4000 mi and the sidereal day as 24 hr. *Ans.* 0.11 ft/sec^2

9. Determine the force exerted inward on each ball of a governor of a steam engine at the instant that it is describing a circle of 1 ft radius when revolving at 100 rpm, if the ball weighs 3.6 lb. *Ans.* 12.3 lb

10. A 100 ton train rounds a level curve of radius 550 ft at 30 mi/hr. Determine the horizontal force against the rails. *Ans.* 11 tons outward

11. A train rounds a curve of radius 550 ft at 30 mi/hr. What must be the slope of the track so that the force on each rail may be the same? *Ans.* 6.3°

12. An object rests at a point 2 ft from the axis of a horizontal rotary platform which is started from rest and is gradually increasing speed. The coefficient of friction between the object and platform is 0.25. Calculate the angular speed of the platform at which the object is just about to slip. *Ans.* 2 radians/sec

13. A body rests in a pail which is moved in a vertical circle of radius 2 ft. What is the least speed the body must have so as not to fall out when at the top of the path? *Ans.* 8 ft/sec

14. The breaking strength of a string 2 ft long is 17 lb. A 1 lb body is attached to the string and whirled in a vertical circle. Find the maximum number of rps that can be given the body without breaking the string. *Ans.* $8/\pi$ rps

15. A cord 5 ft long is fixed at one end, and to its other end is attached a weight which describes a horizontal circle of radius 3 ft. Compute the angular speed of the cord in radians per sec and in revolutions per minute. *Ans.* 2.8 rad/sec, 27 rpm

16. An automobile goes over the crown of a hill whose roadbed is considered to be the arc of a circle in a vertical plane of radius 120 ft. With what maximum speed may the car travel and not move tangentially off the road? *Ans.* 42 mi/hr

17. The human body can safely stand an acceleration 9 times that due to gravity. With what minimum radius of curvature may a pilot safely turn his plane upward at the end of a dive in which the plane travels at a speed of 480 mi/hr? *Ans.* 1720 ft

18. A 150 lb glider pilot traveling in his glider at 90 mi/hr wishes to turn an inside vertical loop so that when he is upside down at the top of the loop he shall exert an upward force of 50 lb against the seat of the glider. What must be the radius of the loop under these conditions?
Hint: Centripetal force on pilot = force of seat on pilot + his weight. *Ans.* 408 ft

19. A 96 lb boy is swinging on a rope 20 ft long, and at the bottom of each swing he is moving at 30 ft/sec. Calculate the tension in the rope at the bottom of a swing. *Ans.* 231 lb

20. Determine the speed with which the earth would have to rotate on its axis so that a person on the equator would weigh $\frac{3}{4}$ as much as at present. Take the equatorial radius as 4000 miles.

Hint: (1) w (present weight) $= G\dfrac{mM}{r^2} - \dfrac{mv^2}{r}$ (2) $\frac{3}{4}w$ (new weight) $= G\dfrac{mM}{r^2} - \dfrac{mv_1^2}{r}$

where m = mass of man, M = mass of earth, $w = mg$ = present weight of man, v = present speed of earth at equator, v_1 = new speed of earth at equator. *Ans.* 13,100 ft/sec

Chapter 11

Rotation of a Body

TORQUE or **moment of force** is the effectiveness of a force in producing rotation about an axis. It is measured by the product of the force and the perpendicular distance from the axis of rotation to the line of action of the force.

Torque = force × perpendicular distance from axis to line of action of force.

Torque is usually expressed in lb-ft in the engineering system, meter-newtons in the mks system, and cm-dynes in the cgs system.

MOMENT OF INERTIA of a body is a measure of the resistance a body offers to any change in its angular velocity. It is determined by its mass and the distribution of its mass about the axis of rotation. If a body is made up of masses $m_1, m_2, m_3, \ldots$ at respective distances $r_1, r_2, r_3, \ldots$ from an axis, its moment of inertia I about the axis is

$$I = m_1 r_1^2 + m_2 r_2^2 + m_3 r_3^2 + \ldots = \Sigma m r^2$$

The **radius of gyration** of a body is the distance from its axis of rotation to a point at which the total mass of the body might be concentrated without changing its moment of inertia. The moment of inertia I of a body of mass m and radius of gyration k is

$$I = m k^2$$

Moment of inertia is usually expressed in slug-ft^2 in the engineering system, kg-m^2 in the mks system, and g-cm^2 in the cgs system.

TORQUE AND ANGULAR ACCELERATION. An unbalanced torque L, acting on a body of moment of inertia I, produces in it an angular acceleration α given by

$$L = I\alpha$$

$$L(\text{lb-ft}) = I(\text{slug-ft}^2) \times \alpha(\text{rad/sec}^2)$$
$$L(\text{m-nt}) = I(\text{kg-m}^2) \times \alpha(\text{rad/sec}^2)$$
$$L(\text{cm-dyne}) = I(\text{g-cm}^2) \times \alpha(\text{rad/sec}^2)$$

KINETIC ENERGY OF ROTATION of a mass whose moment of inertia about an axis is I, and which is rotating about this axis with angular velocity ω, is

$$\text{K.E.} = \tfrac{1}{2} I \omega^2$$

$$\text{K.E. (ft-lb)} = \tfrac{1}{2} I(\text{slug-ft}^2) \times \omega^2(\text{rad/sec})^2$$
$$\text{K.E. (joules)} = \tfrac{1}{2} I(\text{kg-m}^2) \times \omega^2(\text{rad/sec})^2$$
$$\text{K.E. (ergs)} = \tfrac{1}{2} I(\text{g-cm}^2) \times \omega^2(\text{rad/sec})^2$$

WORK W done on a rotating body by a constant torque equals the product of the torque L and the angular displacement θ.

$$W = L\theta$$

$$W(\text{ft-lb}) = L(\text{lb-ft}) \times \theta(\text{radians})$$
$$W(\text{joules}) = L(\text{m-nt}) \times \theta(\text{radians})$$

POWER P in rotational motion is equal to the product of the torque L and the angular velocity ω with which the torque is applied.

$$P = L\omega$$
$$P\text{(ft-lb/sec)} = L\text{(lb-ft)} \times \omega\text{(rad/sec)}$$
$$P\text{(watts)} = L\text{(m-nt)} \times \omega\text{(rad/sec)}$$

ANGULAR MOMENTUM $= I$(moment of inertia) $\times \omega$(angular velocity in rad/sec).

A rotating body maintains constant angular momentum unless acted upon by an unbalanced external torque.

ANGULAR IMPULSE $= L$(torque) $\times t$(length of time the torque acts).

The change in angular momentum produced by an unbalanced angular impulse is equal to the angular impulse. Thus if an unbalanced torque L acting for a time t on a body of moment inertia I changes its angular velocity from an initial value ω_o to a final value ω_t, then

$$\text{Unbalanced angular impulse} = \text{change in angular momentum}$$
$$Lt = I(\omega_t - \omega_o)$$

ANALOGOUS LINEAR AND ANGULAR QUANTITIES.

Linear displacement	s	is analogous to	Angular displacement	θ
Linear speed	v	" " "	Angular speed	ω
Linear acceleration	a	" " "	Angular acceleration	α
Mass (inertia)	m	" " "	Moment of inertia	I
Force	F	" " "	Torque	L
Linear momentum	mv	" " "	Angular momentum	$I\omega$
Linear impulse	Ft	" " "	Angular impulse	Lt

If, in the equations for linear motion, we replace the linear quantities by the corresponding angular quantities, we get the corresponding equations for angular motion. Thus:

Linear: $F = ma$ K.E. $= \frac{1}{2}mv^2$ Work $= Fs$ Power $= Fv$

Angular: $L = I\alpha$ K.E. $= \frac{1}{2}I\omega^2$ Work $= L\theta$ Power $= L\omega$

MOMENTS OF INERTIA OF SYMMETRICAL BODIES. The following are expressions for the moments of inertia of various symmetrical bodies about an axis through their centers of mass.

$I = mr^2$ for a small mass m at a distance r from the axis of rotation. Also for a *thin ring, hollow cylinder,* or *hoop,* about its own axis, in which all the mass particles can be considered at a distance r from the axis of rotation.

$I = \frac{1}{2}mr^2$ for a *uniform solid cylinder* or *disk,* of any length and of mass m and radius r, about an axis through its center and perpendicular to its face.

$I = \frac{1}{12}ml^2$ for a *thin uniform rod,* of mass m and length l, about a transverse axis through its center.

$I = \frac{1}{12}m(l^2 + b^2)$ for a *uniform rectangular body,* of mass m, length l and width b, about an axis through its center and perpendicular to the bl face.

$I = \frac{2}{5}mr^2$ for a *uniform solid sphere,* of mass m and radius r, about any diameter.

MOMENT OF INERTIA ABOUT A PARALLEL AXIS. The moment of inertia I of a body about an axis parallel to an axis through the center of mass is

$$I = I_G + mh^2$$

where I_G = moment of inertia about an axis through the center of mass
m = total mass of body
h = perpendicular distance between the two parallel axes.

SOLVED PROBLEMS

1. A wheel of radius 3 ft has forces applied to it as shown in the adjoining figure. Find the torque produced by the force of (a) 4 lb, (b) 9 lb, (c) 7 lb, (d) 6 lb.

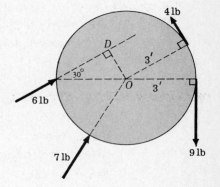

Solution:

In each case the torque is equal to the product of the force and the perpendicular distance from the axis through O to the line of action of the force.

(a) L_4 = 4 lb × 3 ft = 12 lb-ft counterclockwise
(b) L_9 = 9 lb × 3 ft = 27 lb-ft clockwise
(c) L_7 = 7 lb × 0 ft = 0 lb-ft
(d) L_6 = 6 lb × OD = 6 lb × (3 sin 30°) ft = 9 lb-ft clockwise

2. A wheel, of mass 6 kg and radius of gyration 40 cm, is rotating at 300 rpm. Find its moment of inertia and kinetic energy in (a) mks units, (b) cgs units.

Solution:

$$\omega = 300 \text{ rev/min} = 5 \text{ rev/sec} = 5(2\pi) \text{ rad/sec} = 10\pi \text{ rad/sec}$$

(a) $I = mk^2 = (6 \text{ kg})(0.40 \text{ m})^2 = 0.96 \text{ kg-m}^2$
   K.E. $= \frac{1}{2}I\omega^2 = \frac{1}{2}(0.96 \text{ kg-m}^2)(10\pi \text{ rad/sec})^2 = 48\pi^2 \text{ joules}$

(b) $I = mk^2 = (6000 \text{ g})(40 \text{ cm})^2 = 96 \times 10^5 \text{ g-cm}^2$
   K.E. $= \frac{1}{2}I\omega^2 = \frac{1}{2}(96 \times 10^5 \text{ g-cm}^2)(10\pi \text{ rad/sec})^2 = 48\pi^2 \times 10^7 \text{ ergs}$ or $48\pi^2 \text{ joules}$

3. An airplane propeller weighs 144 lb and has a radius of gyration 2 ft. Find its moment of inertia. What unbalanced torque will produce in it an angular acceleration of 25 radians/sec²?

Solution:

$$I = mk^2 = 144/32 \text{ slugs} \times 4 \text{ ft}^2 = 18 \text{ slug-ft}^2$$
$$L = I\alpha = 18 \text{ slug-ft}^2 \times 25 \text{ rad/sec}^2 = 450 \text{ lb-ft}$$

4. A wheel of radius 0.72 ft and moment of inertia 4.8 slug-ft² has a constant force of 10 lb applied tangentially at the rim, as shown in the figure below. Find (a) the angular acceleration α, (b) the angular speed ω after 4 sec from rest, (c) the number of revolutions made in 4 sec from rest. (d) Show that the work done on the wheel in the 4 sec is equal to the kinetic energy of the wheel after 4 sec.

Solution:

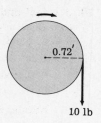

(*a*) Unbalanced torque on wheel = $I\alpha$

$$10\,\text{lb} \times 0.72\,\text{ft} = 4.8\,\text{slug-ft}^2 \times \alpha \qquad \alpha = 1.5\,\text{rad/sec}^2$$

(*b*) $\omega = \omega_0 + \alpha t = 0 + 1.5\,\text{rad/sec}^2 \times 4\,\text{sec} = 6\,\text{rad/sec}$

(*c*) $\theta = \omega_0 t + \tfrac{1}{2}\alpha t^2 = 0 + \tfrac{1}{2}(1.5\,\text{rad/sec}^2)(4\,\text{sec})^2 = 12\,\text{rad} = 12/2\pi\,\text{rev} = 1.91\,\text{rev}$

(*d*) Work $= L\theta = (10\,\text{lb} \times 0.72\,\text{ft})(12\,\text{rad}) = 86.4\,\text{ft-lb}$

  K.E. $= \tfrac{1}{2}I\omega^2 = \tfrac{1}{2}(4.8\,\text{slug-ft}^2)(6\,\text{rad/sec})^2 = 86.4\,\text{ft-lb}$

5. The rotor of a motor has moment of inertia 9 slug-ft^2. What constant unbalanced torque is required to increase its speed from 120 rpm to 420 rpm in 6 sec?

Solution:

Initial $\omega_0 = 120\,\text{rpm} = 2\,\text{rps} = 4\pi\,\text{rad/sec}$; final $\omega = 7\,\text{rps} = 14\pi\,\text{rad/sec}$.

$$L = I\alpha = I \times \frac{\omega - \omega_0}{t} = 9\,\text{slug-ft}^2 \times \frac{(14\pi - 4\pi)\,\text{rad/sec}}{6\,\text{sec}} = 15\pi\,\text{lb-ft}$$

6. An engine flywheel weighs 180 lb and has radius of gyration 2 ft. If it is rotating at 480 rpm, find the steady unbalanced torque required to stop it in 20 sec.

Solution:

$$L = I\alpha = (mk^2)\left(\frac{\omega - \omega_0}{t}\right) = \left(\frac{180}{32} \times 2^2\right)\,\text{slug-ft}^2 \times \frac{(0 - 16\pi)\,\text{rad/sec}}{20\,\text{sec}} = -18\pi\,\text{lb-ft}$$

The negative sign indicates that the (retarding) torque opposes the rotation.

7. A disk has moment of inertia 15 slug-ft^2. Find the work required to increase its speed from 3 to 7 rps.

Solution:

Initial $\omega_0 = 3\,\text{rps} = 6\pi\,\text{rad/sec}$; final $\omega = 7\,\text{rps} = 14\pi\,\text{rad/sec}$.

Work done on wheel $=$ kinetic energy gained by wheel

        $= \tfrac{1}{2}I(\omega^2 - \omega_0^2)$

        $= \tfrac{1}{2} \times 15\,\text{slug-ft}^2 \times (196\pi^2 - 36\pi^2)\,\text{rad}^2/\text{sec}^2 = 1200\pi^2\,\text{ft-lb}$

8. A flywheel has moment of inertia 8.9 slug-ft^2. What constant unbalanced torque L is required to increase its speed from 2 rps to 5 rps in 6 revolutions?

Solution:

$\theta = 6\,\text{rev} = 12\pi\,\text{rad}$. Initial $\omega_0 = 2\,\text{rps} = 4\pi\,\text{rad/sec}$, final $\omega = 5\,\text{rps} = 10\pi\,\text{rad/sec}$.

Work done on wheel $=$ kinetic energy gained by wheel

    $L\theta = \tfrac{1}{2}I(\omega^2 - \omega_0^2)$

$L \times 12\pi\,\text{rad} = \tfrac{1}{2} \times 8.9\,\text{slug-ft}^2 \times (100\pi^2 - 16\pi^2)\,\text{rad}^2/\text{sec}^2 \qquad L = 98\,\text{lb-ft}$

9. A flywheel has moment of inertia 360 slug-ft^2 and weighs 2000 lb. Its shaft has diameter 0.4 in., and the coefficient of friction at the bearing is 0.03. If it is rotating at 150 rpm, how many revolutions will it make before coming to rest?

Solution:

Initial $\omega_0 = 150\,\text{rpm} = 2.5\,\text{rps} = 5\pi\,\text{rad/sec}$; final $\omega = 0\,\text{rad/sec}$.

Work done against force of friction $=$ K.E. lost by wheel

       $L\theta = \tfrac{1}{2}I(\omega^2 - \omega_0^2)$

$-(0.03 \times 2000\,\text{lb})(0.2/12\,\text{ft}) \times \theta = \tfrac{1}{2} \times 360\,\text{slug-ft}^2 \times (0 - 25\pi^2)\,\text{rad}^2/\text{sec}^2$

Solving, $\theta = 4500\pi^2$ radians or 2250π revolutions. The frictional torque opposes the rotation and hence is negative in the above equation.

10. A wheel and axle is caused to rotate about a horizontal axis by means of a 16 lb weight attached to a cord wrapped around an axle of radius 3 inches. The weight falls vertically through 7.2 ft in 6 sec, starting from rest. Determine the moment of inertia of the wheel and axle. (Fig. *a* below)

Solution:

Linear acceleration *a* of 16 lb body:
$$s = v_0 t + \tfrac{1}{2}at^2, \qquad 7.2\,\text{ft} = 0 + \tfrac{1}{2}a(6\,\text{sec})^2, \qquad a = 0.4\,\text{ft/sec}^2$$

Angular acceleration α of wheel and axle:
$$a = \alpha r, \qquad 0.4\,\text{ft/sec}^2 = \alpha(\tfrac{1}{4}\,\text{ft}), \qquad \alpha = 1.6\,\text{rad/sec}^2$$

Unbalanced force on 16 lb body = *ma* of 16 lb body
$$16\,\text{lb} - \text{tension } T \text{ in cord} = 16/32 \text{ slugs} \times 0.4\,\text{ft/sec}^2 \qquad\qquad T = 15.8\,\text{lb}$$

Unbalanced torque on wheel and axle = $I\alpha$ of wheel and axle
$$T \times \tfrac{1}{4}\,\text{ft} = 15.8\,\text{lb} \times \tfrac{1}{4}\,\text{ft} = I \times 1.6\,\text{rad/sec}^2 \qquad\qquad I = 2.47\,\text{slug-ft}^2$$

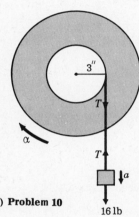

Fig.(*a*) Problem 10

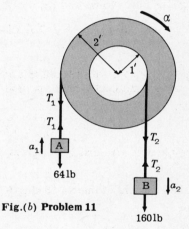

Fig.(*b*) Problem 11

11. The pulley system has moment of inertia 3 slug-ft^2. Block *A* weighs 64 lb and block *B* weighs 160 lb. Find the angular acceleration α of the pulleys and the tensions T_1 and T_2 in the cords when the blocks are released. Refer to Fig.(*b*) above.

Solution:

Since $a = \alpha r$, we have $a_1 = 2\alpha$ and $a_2 = 1\alpha$ numerically.

Unbalanced force on 64 lb weight = mass × acceleration of 64 lb weight
$$T_1 - 64 = (64/32)a_1 = 4\alpha \qquad (1)$$

Unbalanced force on 160 lb weight = mass × acceleration of 160 lb weight
$$160 - T_2 = (160/32)a_2 = 5\alpha \qquad (2)$$

Unbalanced torque on pulley system = moment of inertia × angular acceleration
$$T_2 \times 1 - T_1 \times 2 = 3\alpha \qquad (3)$$

Multiply equation (*1*) by -2 and equation (*2*) by -1 and add to obtain: $T_2 - 2T_1 = 32 - 13\alpha$. Equate the right side of this equation with the right side of (*3*) to get $\alpha = 2\,\text{rad/sec}^2$.

From (*1*), $T_1 = 64 + 4\alpha = 72$ lb. From (*2*), $T_2 = 160 - 5\alpha = 150$ lb.

12. The stiffness of a shaft is such that it requires a torque of 45,000 lb-in per radian of twist. If the twisting moment is proportional to the angle of twist, how much work is required to twist the rod through an angle of $12°$ ($= \pi/15$ radians) from its unstrained position?

Solution:

Maximum torque acting = 45,000 lb-in/rad × $\pi/15$ rad = 3000π lb-in

As the angle of twist increases, the torque increases proportionately. Hence the average torque is half the maximum twisting torque.

Work = average torque × angle = $(\tfrac{1}{2} \times 3000\pi)$ lb-in × $\pi/15$ rad = $100\pi^2$ in-lb

13. A motor runs at 20 rps and supplies a torque of 110 lb-ft. How much power is it delivering?

Solution:

$$\text{Power} = L\omega = 110 \text{ lb-ft} \times (20 \times 2\pi) \text{ rad/sec} = 4400\pi \text{ ft-lb/sec}$$

$$= 4400\pi \text{ ft-lb/sec} \times \frac{1 \text{ hp}}{550 \text{ ft-lb/sec}} = 8\pi \text{ horsepower}$$

14. The driving wheel of a belt drive attached to an electric motor has a diameter of 14 inches and makes 1200 rpm. The tension in the belt is 30 lb on the slack side and 120 lb on the tight side. Find the horsepower transmitted by the belt.

Solution:

$$\text{Torque developed} = (120 - 30) \text{ lb} \times 7/12 \text{ ft} = 52.5 \text{ lb-ft}$$

$$\text{Power} = L\omega = (52.5 \text{ lb-ft})(1200 \times 2\pi \text{ rad/min}) \times \frac{1 \text{ hp}}{33,000 \text{ ft-lb/min}} = 12 \text{ hp}$$

15. A $\frac{3}{4}$ horsepower motor acts for 8 sec on a wheel having moment of inertia 12 slug-ft². Find the angular speed developed in the wheel, assuming no losses.

Solution:

$$\text{Work done by motor in 8 sec} = \text{K.E. of wheel rotating at angular speed } \omega$$
$$\text{power} \times \text{time} = \tfrac{1}{2} I \omega^2$$
$$(\tfrac{3}{4} \times 550) \text{ ft-lb/sec} \times 8 \text{ sec} = \tfrac{1}{2} \times 12 \text{ slug-ft}^2 \times \omega^2 \qquad \omega = 23.5 \text{ rad/sec}$$

16. A 1 kg solid ball rolling on a horizontal surface at 20 meters per second comes to the bottom of an inclined plane which makes an angle of 30° with the horizontal. (*a*) Compute the kinetic energy of the ball when it is at the bottom of the incline. (*b*) How far up the incline will the ball roll? Neglect friction.

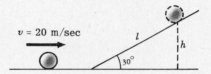

Solution:

(*a*) $\text{Total K.E.} = \text{rotary K.E.} + \text{linear K.E.} \qquad (\omega = v/r)$

$$= \tfrac{1}{2} I \omega^2 + \tfrac{1}{2} m v^2$$

$$= \frac{1}{2} \left(\frac{2}{5} m r^2 \right) \frac{v^2}{r^2} + \frac{1}{2} m v^2 = \frac{7}{10} m v^2 = \frac{7}{10} (1 \text{ kg})(20 \text{ m/sec})^2 = 280 \text{ joules}$$

(*b*) $\text{Total K.E. at bottom} = \text{potential energy at top}$

$$280 \text{ joules} = mgh, \qquad \text{where } h = \text{vertical distance the ball rises}$$
$$= 1 \text{ kg} \times 9.8 \text{ m/sec}^2 \times h \qquad\qquad h = 28.6 \text{ m}$$
$$l = \text{distance up the incline} = h/(\sin 30°) = 28.6/0.5 = 57.2 \text{ m}$$

17. A wheel rolls down a smooth inclined plane 50 ft high. Find its linear speed when it is at the foot of the plane. Assume the weight of the wheel is concentrated at the rim.

Solution:

$$\text{Potential energy lost by wheel} = \text{rotary K.E. gained} + \text{linear K.E. gained by wheel}$$
$$mgh = \tfrac{1}{2} I \omega^2 + \tfrac{1}{2} m v^2$$
$$\text{Since } I = mr^2 \text{ and } \omega = v/r, \quad mgh = \tfrac{1}{2}(mr^2)(v^2/r^2) + \tfrac{1}{2} m v^2 = m v^2$$

$$\text{from which} \quad v = \sqrt{gh} = \sqrt{32 \text{ ft/sec}^2 \times 50 \text{ ft}} = 40 \text{ ft/sec}.$$

18. A thin uniform rod is 2 meters long and has a mass of 543 grams. Find its moment of inertia about a transverse axis through its center.

Solution:

$$I = \frac{ml^2}{12} = \frac{0.543 \text{ kg} \times (2 \text{ m})^2}{12} = 0.181 \text{ kg-m}^2$$

19. Find the radius of gyration k of a solid sphere, diameter 6 ft, rotating about a diameter as an axis.
Solution:

For a solid sphere of radius r rotating about a diameter, $I = \frac{2}{5}mr^2$.

Then $I = mk^2 = \frac{2}{5}mr^2$, $k^2 = \frac{2}{5}r^2$, and $k = r\sqrt{2/5} = 3\,\text{ft} \times \sqrt{0.4} = 1.9\,\text{ft}$.

20. A circular disk has mass 6.5 kg and diameter 80 cm. Compute its moment of inertia (a) about an axis through its center of mass and at right angles to its face, (b) about an axis parallel to the axis through the mass center and passing through its face 18 cm from the circumference.
Solution:

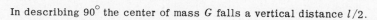

(a) $I_G = \frac{1}{2}mr^2 = \frac{1}{2}(6.5\,\text{kg})(0.4\,\text{m})^2 = 0.52\,\text{kg-m}^2$

(b) $I_A = I_G + mh^2 = 0.52\,\text{kg-m}^2 + (6.5\,\text{kg})(0.22\,\text{m})^2 = 0.83\,\text{kg-m}^2$

21. A thin uniform rod AB of mass m and length l is hinged at one end A to the level floor and stands vertically. If allowed to fall, with what angular speed ω will it strike the floor?
Solution:

The moment of inertia about a transverse axis through one end A is

$$I_A = I_G + mh^2 = \frac{1}{12}ml^2 + m(\frac{l}{2})^2 = \frac{1}{3}ml^2$$

In describing $90°$ the center of mass G falls a vertical distance $l/2$.

Potential energy lost by rod = kinetic energy gained by rod

$$mg(\frac{l}{2}) = \frac{1}{2}(\frac{1}{3}ml^2)(\omega^2 - 0) \qquad \text{from which} \quad \omega = \sqrt{3g/l}$$

SUPPLEMENTARY PROBLEMS

22. A force of 18 lb acts tangentially at the rim of a wheel of diameter 10 in. Determine the torque.
Ans. 7.5 lb-ft

23. A force of 50 lb acts at the rim of a wheel of radius 18 in. at an angle of $30°$ with the spoke. Determine the torque. *Ans.* 37.5 lb-ft

24. Compute the moment of inertia of an 8 kg wheel having a radius of gyration 25 cm. *Ans.* 0.5 kg-meter^2

25. What unbalanced torque will produce an angular acceleration of 3 rad/sec^2 in a 240 lb disk having radius of gyration 2 ft? *Ans.* 90 lb-ft

26. Determine the mean effective torque that must be applied to a 108 lb flywheel, of radius of gyration 16 in., to give it an angular speed of 300 rpm in 10 sec. *Ans.* 6π lb-ft

27. An 80 lb wheel of radius of gyration 2 ft is rotating at 360 rpm. The retarding frictional torque is 4 lb-ft. Compute the time it will take the wheel to come to rest at a uniform rate. *Ans.* 30π sec

28. Compute the kinetic energy of a 9 lb wheel having a radius of gyration 16 inches and rotating at 6 rps. *Ans.* $36\pi^2$ ft-lb

29. A cord 3 meters long is coiled around the axle of a wheel. The cord is pulled with a constant force of 4 kg weight. When the cord leaves the axle, the wheel is rotating at 2 rps. Determine the moment of inertia of the wheel and axle. *Ans.* 1.49 kg-m^2

30. When 100 joules of work is done upon a flywheel, its angular speed increases from 60 rpm to 180 rpm. What is its moment of inertia? *Ans.* 0.633 kg-m^2

31. Calculate the work done in 90 revolutions by a force of 20 lb acting tangentially at the rim of a wheel of radius 8 inches.   *Ans.* 2400π ft-lb

32. A 72 lb wheel, radius of gyration 9 in., is to be given a speed of 10 rps in 25 revolutions from rest. Find the constant unbalanced torque required.   *Ans.* 15.9 lb-ft

33. A 16 lb wheel, radius of gyration 9 in., has a constant force of 2 lb applied (perpendicular to the spoke) 6 inches from the center. Calculate (a) the angular acceleration, (b) the angular speed after 4 sec, (c) the linear speed after 4 sec of a point on the spoke 9 inches from the center, (d) the number of revolutions made in 4 sec, and (e) the work done in 4 sec.
Ans. 3.56 radians/sec^2, 14.2 radians/sec, 10.7 ft/sec, 4.53 revolutions, 28.4 ft-lb

34. An electric motor runs at 900 rpm and delivers 2 hp. How much torque does it deliver?   *Ans.* 11.7 lb-ft

35. Determine the angular speed of a 99 lb wheel, radius of gyration 20 in., when acted upon by a 1 horsepower motor for a period of 4 sec.   *Ans.* 22.6 radians/sec

36. What horsepower is transmitted by a rope which is being wound on a wheel 33 ft in circumference which makes 1 rps, the tension in the rope being 100 lb?   *Ans.* 6 hp

37. The driving side of a belt has 360 lb tension and the slack side has 160 lb tension. The pulley is 3 ft in diameter and makes 300 rpm. It is driving a dynamo having 90% efficiency. How many kilowatts are being delivered by the dynamo?   *Ans.* 11.5 kw

38. A 9 lb pulley is caused to rotate about a horizontal axis by means of a string wrapped around the circumference of the pulley and attached to a 3 lb weight which falls vertically. The diameter of the pulley is 1 ft and its radius of gyration is 4 in. Determine the acceleration of the string. Neglect friction.
Ans. 13.7 ft/sec^2

39. A wheel and axle, having a total moment of inertia 200,000 g-cm^2, is caused to rotate about a horizontal axis by means of an 80 gram weight attached to a cord wrapped around the axle. The radius of the axle is 2 cm. Determine the vertical distance the weight must fall in order to give the wheel a speed of 3 rps starting from rest.   *Ans.* 4.53 m

40. A 10 kg wheel rolls on a horizontal surface at the rate of 4 meters per sec. Compute its total kinetic energy in joules. Assume that the mass is concentrated at the rim.   *Ans.* 160 joules

41. A circular cylinder ($I = \frac{1}{2}mr^2$) rolls down a smooth incline 6 ft high. What is the linear speed of the cylinder when it is at the foot of plane?   *Ans.* 16 ft/sec

42. Compute the moment of inertia of a solid ball, of weight 160 lb and diameter 20 in., about a diameter as an axis.   *Ans.* 1.39 slug-ft^2

43. Compute the radius of gyration of a solid disk, diameter 24 cm, about an axis through its center of mass and at right angles to its face.   *Ans.* 8.49 cm

44. Determine the moment of inertia (a) of a vertical thin hoop, mass 1 kg and diameter 18 cm, about a horizontal axis at its rim; (b) of a solid sphere, mass 2 kg and diameter 10 cm, about an axis tangent to the sphere.
Ans. (a) $I = mr^2 + mr^2 = 2mr^2 = 1.62 \times 10^{-2}$ kg-m^2 (b) $I = 2/5\ mr^2 + mr^2 = 7.00 \times 10^{-3}$ kg-m^2

45. Compute the moment of inertia of a thin uniform rod (yardstick) 3 ft long and weighing 0.60 lb, about a transverse axis (a) through its center, (b) at one end, (c) through the 2 inch mark (16 inches from its center).
Ans. (a) $I = ml^2/12 = 0.0141$ slug-ft^2
(b) $I = ml^2/12 + m(l/2)^2 = 1/3\ ml^2 = 0.0562$ slug-ft^2
(c) $I = ml^2/12 + m(16/12\ \text{ft})^2 = 0.0474$ slug-ft^2

46. A thin uniform rod OA, 3 ft long, is hinged at one end O, as shown in the adjoining figure, so that it can turn in a vertical plane. It is held horizontally and then released. Compute the angular speed of the rod and the linear speed of its free end A at the instant it has described an angle of 60°.
Ans. 5.26 rad/sec^2, 15.8 ft/sec^2

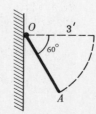

Chapter 12

Simple Harmonic Motion

THE PERIOD T in a SHM is the time occupied in moving from one end of the path to the other end and back again, or the time required for one vibration.

THE FREQUENCY f is the number of vibrations made per second. $f = 1/T$.

THE DISPLACEMENT x is the distance of the vibrating body at any instant from its normal position of rest, i.e. from the center of its path.

The maximum displacement is the **amplitude**.

SIMPLE HARMONIC MOTION (of translation) is periodic oscillating (up and down, or back and forth) motion in a straight line in which

(1) the acceleration of the vibrating body and the restoring force acting on it are always proportional to its displacement from the center of its path and

(2) the acceleration and restoring force are in a direction opposite to the displacement, i.e. toward the center of the path.

REFERENCE CIRCLE. If a point P moves uniformly in a circle, called the reference circle, then the motion of the projection A of the point on the diameter of this circle or on any line in the plane of the circle is simple harmonic motion.

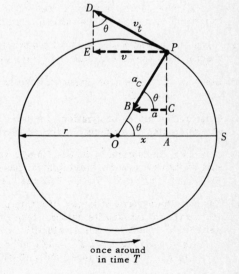

once around
in time T

The **velocity** v of the SHM is the projection of the tangential velocity v_t of P on the diameter. The **acceleration** a of the SHM is the projection on the same diameter of the centripetal acceleration a_c of P. Both motions, of P around the circle and of A along the diameter, have the same period.

VELOCITY AND ACCELERATION IN SHM. To derive expressions for velocity v and acceleration a in SHM, notice that in the adjoining figure right triangles POA, PDE and PBC are similar.

From $\triangle POA$, $\sin \theta = \dfrac{AP}{OP} = \dfrac{\sqrt{r^2 - x^2}}{r}$ and $\cos \theta = \dfrac{OA}{OP} = \dfrac{x}{r}$.

From $\triangle PDE$, $v = v_t \sin \theta$ where $v_t = 2\pi f r = (2\pi/T)r$. Then

$$v = 2\pi f \sqrt{r^2 - x^2} = \frac{2\pi}{T}\sqrt{r^2 - x^2}$$

where r is the amplitude of the SHM (and radius of the reference circle).

From $\triangle PBC$, $a = a_c \cos \theta$ where $a_c = v_t^2/r = 4\pi^2 f^2 r = (4\pi^2/T^2)r$.   Then

$$a = -4\pi^2 f^2 x = -\frac{4\pi^2}{T^2} x$$

where the minus sign indicates that x and a are opposite in direction.

RESTORING FORCE F IN SHM. $F = ma = -m 4\pi^2 f^2 x = -m\dfrac{4\pi^2}{T^2} x$

The force F is proportional to the displacement x but opposite in direction.

FORCE CONSTANT k. $k = -\dfrac{F}{x} = -\dfrac{\text{restoring force}}{\text{displacement from equilibrium position}}$

where k is positive since F and x are opposite in sign.

PERIOD IN SHM. $T = 2\pi \sqrt{-\dfrac{x}{a}}$ since $a = -\dfrac{4\pi^2}{T^2} x$.

Also $T = 2\pi \sqrt{\dfrac{m}{k}}$ since $F = -m 4\pi^2 x/T^2$ gives
$T = 2\pi \sqrt{-mx/F} = 2\pi \sqrt{m/k}$.

Note. Since x and a are opposite in sign, $-x/a$ is positive.

PERIOD OF SIMPLE PENDULUM. $T = 2\pi \sqrt{\dfrac{l}{g}} = 2\pi \sqrt{\dfrac{\text{length of pendulum}}{\text{acceleration due to gravity}}}$

PERIOD OF COMPOUND PENDULUM. $T = 2\pi \sqrt{\dfrac{I}{mgh}}$

where m = mass of compound or physical pendulum,
      I = its moment of inertia about a transverse axis at the point of suspension,
      h = distance of its center of gravity from the point of suspension.

Equating the periods of the simple and compound pendulum, we get

$2\pi \sqrt{\dfrac{l}{g}} = 2\pi \sqrt{\dfrac{I}{mgh}}$ or $\dfrac{l}{g} = \dfrac{I}{mgh}$ or $l = \dfrac{I}{mh}$. Hence a compound pendulum has the same

period as a simple pendulum of such length that $l = I/mh$; this length is called the length of an *equivalent simple pendulum.*

A compound pendulum vibrates as if its mass were concentrated at a single point at a distance l ($= I/mh$) from the axis of suspension. This point is known as the **center of percussion** or **center of oscillation**. If the pendulum is struck at the center of percussion, it rotates about the axis of suspension without jarring it, i.e. without tending to give the axis a motion of translation.

ANGULAR SIMPLE HARMONIC MOTION, or simple harmonic motion of rotation, is periodic, oscillating angular motion in which the restoring **torque** is (*1*) proportional to the angular displacement and (*2*) opposite in direction to the angular displacement. If a body suspended from a vertical wire is twisted about the wire in a horizontal plane and released, it executes rotary (angular) simple harmonic motion.

TORSION CONSTANT K. $K = -\dfrac{L}{\theta} = -\dfrac{\text{restoring torque}}{\text{angle of twist from equilibrium position}}$

where K is positive since L and θ are oppositely directed.

PERIOD OF TORSION PENDULUM. $\quad T \;=\; 2\pi \sqrt{-\dfrac{\theta}{\alpha}} \;=\; 2\pi \sqrt{-\dfrac{\text{angular displacement}}{\text{angular acceleration}}}$

Also $\qquad\qquad\qquad\qquad T \;=\; 2\pi \sqrt{-\dfrac{I}{L/\theta}} \;=\; 2\pi \sqrt{\dfrac{I}{K}}$

where I = moment of inertia of vibrating body about the axis of rotation. The period T is given in seconds *(1)* if I is in slug-ft^2 and K is in lb-ft/radian or *(2)* if I is in kg-m^2 and K is in m-nt/radian.

Note. Since θ and α are opposite in sign, $-\theta/\alpha$ is positive.

As an aid to memory, observe that the equations for a torsion pendulum are identical with those for SHM of translation if the following substitutions are made: replace x, a, m, F, k by θ, α, I, L, K.

SOLVED PROBLEMS

1. A spring makes 12 vibrations in 3 seconds. Find the period T and frequency f of the vibration.

   Solution:

   $$T \;=\; \frac{\text{elapsed time}}{\text{vibrations made}} \;=\; \frac{3\text{ sec}}{12} \;=\; \frac{1}{4}\text{ sec}$$

   $$f \;=\; \frac{\text{vibrations made}}{\text{elapsed time}} \;=\; \frac{12}{3\text{ sec}} \;=\; 4\text{ per sec.} \quad \text{Or, } f = \frac{1}{T} = \frac{1}{\frac{1}{4}\text{ sec}} = 4/\text{sec.}$$

2. A 4 lb steel block vibrates in simple harmonic motion with amplitude $r = 9$ in. and period $T = 3$ sec. Find:

   (a) the frequency f

   (b) its maximum speed and its speed when the displacement $x = 6$ in.

   (c) its maximum acceleration and its acceleration when $x = 6$ in.

   (d) the maximum restoring force acting on it and the restoring force when $x = 5$ in.

   (e) its maximum kinetic energy

   (f) its maximum potential energy

   (g) the total energy of the vibrating block at any position.

   Solution:

   (a) Frequency $f = 1/T = 1/3$ vibration/sec

   (b) Maximum speed occurs at the center of its path, at $x = 0$.

   $$v_{max} \;=\; \frac{2\pi}{T}\sqrt{r^2 - x^2} \;=\; \frac{2\pi}{3\text{ sec}}\sqrt{(\tfrac{3}{4}\text{ ft})^2 - 0} \;=\; 1.57\text{ ft/sec} \quad \text{at } x = 0$$

   $$v_{x\,=\,\frac{1}{2}\text{ ft}} \;=\; \frac{2\pi}{3\text{ sec}}\sqrt{(\tfrac{3}{4}\text{ ft})^2 - (\tfrac{1}{2}\text{ ft})^2} \;=\; 1.17\text{ ft/sec}$$

   (c) Maximum acceleration occurs at maximum displacement, at $x = 9$ in.

   $$a_{max} \;=\; -\frac{4\pi^2}{T^2}x \;=\; \frac{4\pi^2}{(3\text{ sec})^2}(\tfrac{3}{4}\text{ ft}) \;=\; 3.29\text{ ft/sec}^2 \quad \text{toward center of path}$$

   $$a_{x\,=\,\frac{1}{2}\text{ ft}} \;=\; \frac{4\pi^2}{(3\text{ sec})^2}(\tfrac{1}{2}\text{ ft}) \;=\; 2.19\text{ ft/sec}^2 \quad \text{toward center of path}$$

   Otherwise: The acceleration a is proportional to the displacement x, and $a = 3.29$ ft/sec^2 when $x = 9$ in. Hence when $x = 6$ in., $a = 6/9 \times 3.29 = 2.19$ ft/sec^2.

(d) F_{max} = ma_{max} = 4/32 slug × 3.29 ft/sec^2 = 0.41 lb   at x = 9 in.

The restoring force F is proportional to the displacement x, and F = 0.41 lb when x = 9 in. Hence when x = 5 in., F = 5/9 × 0.41 = 0.23 lb.

The restoring force is directed toward the center of the path.

(e) K.E.$_{max}$ = $\frac{1}{2}mv_{max}^2$ = $\frac{1}{2}$(4/32 slug)(1.57 ft/sec)^2 = 0.154 ft-lb   at x = 0

(f) P.E.$_{max}$ = 0.154 ft-lb at ends of path (where speed and K.E. are zero)

Otherwise: The force on the block varies uniformly with x, from 0 lb at x = 0 in. to 0.41 lb at x = 9 in., the average force being $\frac{1}{2}$(0 + 0.41) lb.

$$\text{P.E.}_{max} = \text{work to displace block 9 in. from center of path}$$
$$= \frac{1}{2}(0 + 0.41)\text{lb} \times \frac{3}{4}\text{ft} = 0.154 \text{ ft-lb}$$

(g) 0.154 ft-lb

3. A 5 lb body is suspended by a long and light spiral spring. An added force of 2 lb stretches the spring 4 in. Find (a) the force constant k of the spring and (b) the period of vibration of the 5 lb body if pulled down a little and then released.

Solution:

(a) k = $\dfrac{\text{force } F}{\text{displacement } x}$ = $\dfrac{2\,\text{lb}}{1/3\,\text{ft}}$ = 6 lb/ft   (b) T = $2\pi\sqrt{\dfrac{m}{k}}$ = $2\pi\sqrt{\dfrac{5/32\,\text{slug}}{6\,\text{lb/ft}}}$ = 1.01 sec

4. A long flat steel spring is clamped at the lower end and a 2 kg ball is fastened to the top end. A force of 8 newtons is required to displace the ball 20 cm to one side. Find (a) the force constant k of the spring and (b) the period of vibration of the 2 kg ball when pulled a little to one side and then released. Assume that the ball is executing SHM.

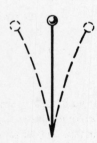

Solution:

(a) k = $\dfrac{\text{force } F}{\text{displacement } x}$ = $\dfrac{8\,\text{newtons}}{0.20\,\text{meter}}$ = 40 newtons/meter

(b) T = $2\pi\sqrt{\dfrac{m}{k}}$ = $2\pi\sqrt{\dfrac{2\,\text{kg}}{40\,\text{newtons/meter}}}$ = 1.40 sec

5. A certain weight when hung on a long and light spiral spring stretches it 6 inches. Determine its period of vibration if pulled down a little and then released.

Solution:

When the weight hangs at rest on the spring, the condition of equilibrium gives: Upward restoring force = weight of mass hung on the spring.

$$k = \frac{\text{upward restoring force}}{\text{downward displacement produced by the stretching force}} = \frac{w\,\text{lb}}{\frac{1}{2}\,\text{ft}} = 2w\ \text{lb/ft}$$

$$T = 2\pi\sqrt{\frac{m}{k}} = 2\pi\sqrt{\frac{w/g}{k}} = 2\pi\sqrt{\frac{w\,\text{lb}}{2w\,\text{lb/ft} \times 32\,\text{ft/sec}^2}} = 0.79\ \text{sec}$$

6. A 40 lb electric motor is mounted on four springs, each having spring constant 15 lb/in. Find the period of the motor when it vibrates vertically.

Solution:

Each spring carries 40/4 lb = 10 lb. T = $2\pi\sqrt{\dfrac{m}{k}}$ = $2\pi\sqrt{\dfrac{10/32\,\text{slug}}{180\,\text{lb/ft}}}$ = 0.26 sec

7. Nine kilograms of mercury is poured into a glass U-tube with uniform bore of 1.2 cm diameter. The mercury oscillates freely up and down about its position of equilibrium. Compute (a) the ratio of the restoring force on the column of mercury to its displacement from equilibrium, and (b) the period of oscillation. One cubic centimeter of mercury has a mass of 13.6 grams. Ignore any effects of surface tension.

Solution:

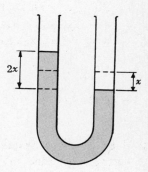

When the mercury column is displaced x cm from its equilibrium position, the restoring force is the weight of a column of mercury $2x$ cm high and 1.2 cm in diameter.

Weight of column of mercury 1 cm high
$$= \tfrac{1}{4}\pi (1.2)^2 \times 0.0136 \times 9.8 \text{ newtons} = 0.151 \text{ newton.}$$

(a) $k = \dfrac{\text{counterclockwise restoring force}}{\text{clockwise displacement}} = \dfrac{2x \text{ cm} \times 0.151 \text{ nt/cm}}{x \text{ cm}}$

$\quad = 0.302 \text{ nt/cm} = 30.2 \text{ newton/meter}$

(b) $T = 2\pi \sqrt{\dfrac{m}{k}} = 2\pi \sqrt{\dfrac{9 \text{ kg}}{30.2 \text{ newton/meter}}} = 3.43 \text{ sec}$

8. Compute the acceleration due to gravity at a place where a simple pendulum, 150 cm long, makes 100 vibrations in 246 sec.

Solution:

$T = (246 \text{ sec})/100 = 2.46 \text{ sec.}$ Squaring $T = 2\pi \sqrt{l/g}$, we obtain $T^2 = 4\pi^2 l/g$.

Then $g = \dfrac{4\pi^2}{T^2} l = \dfrac{4\pi^2}{(2.46 \text{ sec})^2} \times 1.50 \text{ m} = 9.79 \text{ m/sec}^2.$

9. A yardstick vibrates as a compound pendulum about a horizontal axis through the 6-inch mark. (a) Find the period of oscillation. (b) What is the length of the equivalent simple pendulum? (c) About what other point could the yardstick rotate as a compound pendulum and have the same period of vibration?

Solution:

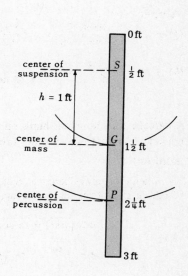

(a) The moment of inertia of the yardstick about a transverse axis through the center of mass G is $I_G = ml^2/12$, where l = length of stick = 3 ft.

Hence the moment of inertia about the center of suspension S is $I_S = I_G + mh^2 = ml^2/12 + mh^2$ where h = distance between S and G = 1 ft. Since $l = 3h$,

$$I_S = 9mh^2/12 + mh^2 = 1.75mh^2$$
$$T = 2\pi \sqrt{\dfrac{I}{mgh}} = 2\pi \sqrt{\dfrac{1.75mh^2}{mgh}} = 2\pi \sqrt{\dfrac{1.75h}{g}}$$
$$= 2\pi \sqrt{\dfrac{1.75 \times 1 \text{ ft}}{32 \text{ ft/sec}^2}} = 1.47 \text{ sec}$$

(b) Length of equivalent simple pendulum $= \dfrac{I_S}{mh} = \dfrac{1.75mh^2}{mh} = 1.75h = 1.75 \text{ ft}$

(c) The center of oscillation P, or the center of percussion P, is at a distance 1.75 ft from the point of suspension S, at the 2.25-ft mark. If the yardstick is suspended about a horizontal axis through P, it will have the same period as when suspended about S.

10. When the balance wheel of a watch is displaced 45° from its equilibrium position it begins to move with angular acceleration 25 rad/sec². Find its frequency f.

Solution:

$$f = \frac{1}{T} = \frac{1}{2\pi}\sqrt{\frac{\alpha}{\theta}} = \frac{1}{2\pi}\sqrt{\frac{25 \text{ rad/sec}^2}{\pi/4 \text{ rad}}} = 0.90 \text{ vibration/sec}$$

11. A steel bar is suspended in a horizontal position by a vertical wire attached to its center. A horizontal couple of moment 5 meter-newtons twists the bar horizontally through an angle of 12°. When the bar is released it oscillates as a torsion pendulum with a period of $\frac{1}{2}$ sec. Determine its moment of inertia.

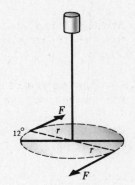

Solution:

Squaring $T = 2\pi\sqrt{\dfrac{I}{L/\theta}}$, we get $T^2 = 4\pi^2\dfrac{I}{L/\theta}$.

Then $I = \dfrac{T^2 L}{4\pi^2\theta} = \dfrac{(\frac{1}{2}\text{ sec})^2 \times 5 \text{ m-nt}}{4\pi^2 \times \pi/15 \text{ rad}} = 0.151 \text{ kg-m}^2$.

SUPPLEMENTARY PROBLEMS

12. A pendulum makes 90 vibrations in 1 minute. Determine the period and the frequency.
 Ans. 0.67 sec, 1.5/sec

13. A mass of 1 kg vibrates up and down along a straight line, 20 cm long, in simple harmonic motion with a period of 4 sec. Determine (a) the amplitude of the vibration, (b) the speed and acceleration of the vibrating body at the midpoint of its path, (c) the speed and acceleration at the upper end of its path, (d) the speed and acceleration when its displacement is 4 cm, (e) the restoring force when it is at the midpoint of its path, (f) the restoring force when it is at the lower end of its path, (g) the restoring force when it is displaced 8 cm below the center of its path.

 Ans. (a) 10 cm   (d) 14.4 cm/sec, π^2 cm/sec²   (g) $0.020\pi^2$ newton
       (b) 5π cm/sec, 0 cm/sec²   (e) 0   or $2000\pi^2$ dynes
       (c) 0 cm/sec, $2.5\pi^2$ cm/sec²   (f) $0.025\pi^2$ newton or $2500\pi^2$ dynes

14. A coiled spring is stretched 4 in. by a load of 3 lb. An 8 lb body is attached to the spring and set into vibration with an amplitude of 5 in. Find (a) the force constant of the spring, (b) the maximum restoring force acting on the vibrating body, (c) the period of vibration, (d) the maximum speed and acceleration of the vibrating body, (e) the speed and acceleration when the displacement is 4 in.

 Ans. (a) 9 lb/ft   (c) $\pi/3$ sec   (e) 3/2 ft/sec, 12 ft/sec²
       (b) 15/4 lb   (d) 5/2 ft/sec at $x = 0$, 15 ft/sec² at $x = 5$ in.

15. A 2.5 kg mass executes simple harmonic motion, making 3 vibrations per sec. Compute the acceleration and the restoring force acting on the body when displaced 5 cm from the center of its path.
 Ans. $1.8\pi^2$ m/sec², $4.5\pi^2$ nt

16. What is the period of a vibrating particle which has an acceleration of 4 ft/sec² when its displacement is 3 inches?   *Ans.* 1.57 sec

17. A 150 gram mass when hung on a long and light spiral spring stretches it 40 cm. Determine its period of vibration if pulled down a little and then released.   *Ans.* 1.27 sec

18. A 9 lb block hangs from a spiral spring of such stiffness that an added weight of 1 lb would stretch it 2 inches farther. Determine its period of vibration if pulled down a little and then released.   *Ans.* 1.36 sec

19. A long and light helical spring is stretched 20 cm when a given mass is hung on it. What is the period of vibration of the mass if pulled down a little and then released?   *Ans.* $2\pi/7$ sec

20. A 2.7 lb weight executes simple harmonic motion with a period of 2.4 sec at the end of a spiral spring. Find the period of oscillation of a 1.2 lb weight attached to the same spring.   *Ans.* 1.6 sec

21. An 8 lb object hangs on a vertical spring and stretches it 4 in., at which position it is in equilibrium. Find the maximum force and the work required to give this system a simple harmonic motion with amplitude (*a*) 3 in., (*b*) 6 in.   *Ans.* (*a*) 6 lb, 9 in-lb; (*b*) 12 lb, 36 in-lb

22. Show that the natural period of vertical oscillation of a load hung on a long and light helical spring is the same as the period of a simple pendulum whose length is equal to the elongation of the spring due to the load.

23. How many half vibrations per minute will a simple pendulum 36 inches long make at a place where g is 32 ft/sec^2?   *Ans.* 62/minute

24. A seconds pendulum beats seconds, its half-period being 1 sec. (*a*) What is the length of a simple seconds pendulum at a place where $g = 980$ cm/sec^2? (*b*) What is the length of a simple pendulum that beats half-seconds, *i.e.* the complete period is 1 sec, at a place where $g = 980$ cm/sec^2?   *Ans.* 99.3 cm, 24.8 cm

25. A hoop, 2 ft in diameter, vibrates as a compound pendulum about a horizontal axis at its rim and perpendicular to its plane. Compute the length of the equivalent simple pendulum.   *Ans.* 2 ft

26. A thin rod, 3 ft long, is suspended about a horizontal axis at one end and swings freely as a compound pendulum. Find (*a*) its period, (*b*) the length of an equivalent simple pendulum, and (*c*) the center of percussion. *Ans.* (*a*) 1.57 sec, (*b*) 2 ft, (*c*) 2 ft from axis of suspension

27. The balance wheel of a watch makes 2 complete vibrations per sec. Determine its maximum angular acceleration when it is turned 15° from its position of rest and then released.   *Ans.* 41.3 radians/sec^2

28. A metal disk has a mass of 2.16 kg and a diameter of 18 cm. It is suspended horizontally (as a torsion pendulum) by a vertical wire attached to its center. A twisting moment of 0.81 meter-newton applied to the wire causes it to turn through an angle of 10°. Determine the period of vibration of the disk when given a small twist and then released.   *Ans.* 0.27 sec

29. A rigid body is suspended by a vertical wire which passes through its center of mass. A horizontal couple of moment 20 lb-ft turns the body through an angle of 15°, and when released it oscillates as a torsion pendulum making 90 vibrations per minute. Compute its moment of inertia about this axis of rotation. *Ans.* 0.86 slug-ft^2

Chapter 13

Elasticity

ELASTICITY is that property by virtue of which a body tends to return to its original size or shape after a deformation and when the deforming forces have been removed.

STRESS is measured by the force applied per unit area which produces or tends to produce deformation in a body. It is expressed in such units as lb/ft^2, nt/m^2, and dynes/cm^2.

$$\text{Stress} = \frac{\text{force}}{\text{area of surface on which force acts}} = \frac{F}{A}$$

STRAIN is the fractional deformation resulting from a stress. It is measured by the ratio of the change in some dimension of the body to the total value of the dimension in which the change occurred. (A strain is a pure number and has no dimensions.) Thus if a wire of initial length l experiences an elongation Δl when a force is applied to the wire, the longitudinal strain is

$$\text{Longitudinal strain} = \frac{\text{change in length}}{\text{initial length}} = \frac{\Delta l}{l}$$

ELASTIC LIMIT is the smallest value of the stress required to produce permanent strain in the body.

HOOKE'S LAW. Within the elastic limit of any body the ratio of the stress to the strain produced is a constant. This constant is called the **modulus of elasticity** of the material of the body.

$$\text{Modulus of elasticity} = \text{stress required to produce unit strain} = \frac{\text{stress}}{\text{strain}}.$$

LENGTH ELASTICITY — YOUNG'S MODULUS Y. Consider that a wire or rod of length l and cross section area A experiences an elongation Δl when a stretching force F is applied to it. Then

$$Y = \frac{\text{longitudinal stress}}{\text{longitudinal strain}} = \frac{F/A}{\Delta l/l} = \frac{Fl}{A \, \Delta l}$$

Y may be expressed in lb/in^2, nt/m^2, or dynes/cm^2.

Y depends only on the material of the wire or rod and not on its dimensions.

VOLUME ELASTICITY — BULK MODULUS B. Consider that a body is subjected to a hydrostatic pressure, the same amount of force acting perpendicularly on each unit of surface area. The shape of the body remains the same but its volume decreases.

Volume stress $= F/A =$ normal force per unit area $=$ pressure increase Δp

$$\text{Volume strain} = \frac{\text{volume decrease } \Delta V}{\text{initial volume } V} = \frac{\Delta V}{V}.$$

$$B = \frac{\text{volume stress}}{\text{volume strain}} = \frac{\Delta p}{\Delta V/V} = \frac{V \, \Delta p}{\Delta V}$$

The reciprocal of the bulk modulus of a substance is called the **compressibility** of the substance.

SHAPE ELASTICITY — SHEAR MODULUS n.

Consider that a pair of e-
qual and opposite tangential
forces F act on a rectangular
block $bcde$, as shown in the
figure. The block is sheared
into the parallelopiped $bc'd'e$,
its end faces bc and ed turning through the small angle ϕ.
The shape of the block is al-
tered but its volume is unchanged.

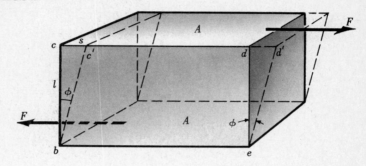

$$\text{Shearing stress} = \frac{\text{tangential force acting}}{\text{area of surface which is being sheared}} = \frac{F}{A}.$$

$$\text{Shearing strain} = \frac{\text{distance sheared}}{\text{distance between the two shearing surfaces}} = \frac{s}{l}.$$

Since s/l is usually very small, this ratio may be considered as equal to the angle of shear ϕ (expressed in radians).

$$n = \frac{\text{shearing stress}}{\text{shearing strain}} = \frac{F/A}{s/l} = \frac{F/A}{\phi} = \frac{F}{A\phi}$$

SOLVED PROBLEMS

1. An elastic rod 12.5 ft long and 0.25 in² in cross section stretches 0.03 in. when a 700 lb weight is hung on it. Find the stress, strain, and Young's modulus Y for the material of the rod.

Solution:

$$\text{Stress} = \frac{F}{A} = \frac{700\,\text{lb}}{0.25\,\text{in}^2} = 2800\,\text{lb/in}^2 \qquad \text{Strain} = \frac{\Delta l}{l} = \frac{0.03\,\text{in.}}{(12.5 \times 12)\,\text{in.}} = 2 \times 10^{-4}$$

$$\text{Young's modulus, } Y = \frac{\text{longitudinal stress}}{\text{longitudinal strain}} = \frac{2800\,\text{lb/in}^2}{2 \times 10^{-4}} = 14 \times 10^{6}\,\text{lb/in}^2$$

2. A solid cylindrical steel column is 11 ft long and 4 in. in diameter. What will be its decrease in length when carrying a load of 80 tons? $Y = 33 \times 10^6$ lb/in².

Solution:

$$\text{Cross section area of column} = \tfrac{1}{4}\pi\,(\text{diameter})^2 = \tfrac{1}{4}(3.14)(4\,\text{in.})^2 = 12.6\,\text{in}^2$$

$$\Delta l = \frac{Fl}{AY} = \frac{(80 \times 2000)\,\text{lb} \times (11 \times 12)\,\text{in.}}{12.6\,\text{in}^2 \times (33 \times 10^6)\,\text{lb/in}^2} = 0.051\,\text{in.}$$

3. The diameter of a brass rod is 6 mm. What force, in dynes, will stretch it by 0.20% of its length? Young's modulus for the brass is 9.0×10^{11} dynes/cm².

Solution:

$$F = \frac{\Delta l}{l}\,AY = 0.0020 \times \tfrac{1}{4}\pi(0.6\,\text{cm})^2 \times (9.0 \times 10^{11}\,\text{dynes/cm}^2) = 5.1 \times 10^8\,\text{dynes}$$

4. The bulk modulus of mercury is 4×10^6 lb/in^2. Compute the volume contraction of 100 in^3 of mercury when subjected to a pressure of 200 lb/in^2.

Solution:

$$\Delta V = \frac{V \Delta p}{B} = \frac{100 \text{ in}^3 \times 200 \text{ lb/in}^2}{4 \times 10^6 \text{ lb/in}^2} = 0.005 \text{ in}^3$$

5. A cube of aluminum, 4 in. on a side, is subjected to a shearing force of 100 tons. The top face of the cube is displaced 0.012 in. with respect to the bottom. Calculate the shearing stress, the shearing strain, and the shear modulus.

Solution:

$$\text{Shearing stress} = \frac{\text{tangential force}}{\text{area of face}} = \frac{(100 \times 2000) \text{lb}}{(4 \text{ in.})^2} = 12,500 \text{ lb/in}^2$$

$$\text{Shearing strain} = \frac{\text{displacement}}{\text{altitude}} = \frac{0.012 \text{ in.}}{4 \text{ in.}} = 0.003$$

$$\text{Shear modulus} = \frac{\text{shearing stress}}{\text{shearing strain}} = \frac{12,500 \text{ lb/in}^2}{0.003} = 4.2 \times 10^6 \text{ lb/in}^2$$

6. An iron ball, of diameter 6.00 in. and weight $w = 31.4$ lb, is suspended from a point 121.00 in. above the floor by an iron wire of unstretched length 114.00 in. The diameter of the wire is 0.036 in. If the ball is set swinging so that its center passes through the lowest point at 16 ft/sec, by how much does it clear the floor? Young's modulus for the iron wire is 27×10^6 lb/in^2.

Solution:

When swinging in arc, at the lowest point: tension $F - w = m(v^2/r)$.

$$\text{Then } F = w + m \frac{v^2}{r} = 31.4 \text{ lb} + \frac{31.4}{32} \text{ slug} \times \frac{(16 \text{ ft/sec})^2}{(114 + 3)/12 \text{ ft}} = 57.2 \text{ lb.}$$

$$\text{Elongation} = \frac{Fl}{AY} = \frac{57.2 \text{ lb} \times 114 \text{ in.}}{\frac{1}{4}\pi(0.036 \text{ in.})^2 \times (27 \times 10^6 \text{ lb/in}^2)} = 0.24 \text{ in.}$$

Hence the ball misses by: 121.00 in. $- (114.00 + 6.00 + 0.24)$ in. $= 0.76$ in.

7. A vertical steel wire, 16 ft long and of 0.0014 in^2 cross section area, has a Young's modulus of 29×10^6 lb/in^2. Compute the period of a 4 lb body attached to the lower end of the wire and executing vertical vibrations.

Solution:

Consider that the wire is stretched x in. from equilibrium position.

Then $Y = Fl/Ax$ or $F = AYx/l$.

$$\text{Force constant } k \text{ of wire is } k = -\frac{\text{restoring force } (-F)}{\text{displacement } (x)} = \frac{AYx/l}{x} = \frac{AY}{l}.$$

$$\text{Period } T = 2\pi\sqrt{\frac{m}{k}} = 2\pi\sqrt{\frac{ml}{AY}} = 2\pi\sqrt{\frac{(4/32 \text{ slug})(16 \text{ ft})}{(0.0014 \text{ in}^2)(29 \times 10^6 \text{ lb/in}^2)}} = 0.044 \text{ sec.}$$

SUPPLEMENTARY PROBLEMS

8. A load of 100 lb is applied to the lower end of a steel rod 3 ft long and 0.2 in. in diameter. How much will the rod stretch? Young's modulus of the steel is 33×10^6 lb/in^2.   *Ans.* 0.0035 in.

9. An iron rod 4 m long and 0.5 cm^2 in cross section stretches 1 mm when a mass of 225 kg is hung on it. Compute the modulus of elasticity of the iron in dynes/cm^2 and in nt/m^2.
    Ans. 17.6×10^{11} dynes/cm^2, 17.6×10^{10} nt/m^2

10. A steel wire, diameter 0.02 in., is 10 ft long. When a load of 10 lb is applied to the wire, it elongates 0.12 in. Determine the modulus of elasticity in tons per square inch.   *Ans.* 1.6×10^4 tons/in^2

11. An elevator is suspended by 3 steel cables each 0.5 in. in diameter. When the floor of the elevator is even with the first floor level of the building, the length of each of the suspending cables is 80 ft. How far below the floor level will the elevator drop when a 1500 lb piece of machinery is pushed on the elevator? Assume that the whole drop is due to stretching of the suspending cables and that Young's modulus of the steel is 27×10^6 lb/in^2.   *Ans.* 0.091 in.

12. Determine the fractional change in volume of a block of glass when subjected to a hydrostatic pressure of 147 lb/in^2. The bulk modulus of the glass is 5×10^5 atmospheres. One atmosphere = 14.7 lb/in^2.
    Ans. 0.00002

13. Compute the volume contraction of a solid copper cube, 4 in. on an edge, when subjected to a hydrostatic pressure of 1000 lb/in^2. The bulk modulus of copper is 3300 tons/in^2.   *Ans.* 0.0097 in^3

14. The compressibility of water is 44×10^{-6} per atmosphere pressure. Find the decrease in volume of 100 cm^3 of water when subjected to 150 atmospheres pressure.   *Ans.* 0.66 cm^3

15. Two parallel and opposite forces, each of 1000 lb, are applied tangentially to opposite faces of a 10 inch cubical block of steel. Find the angle of shear and the relative displacement. The shear modulus of the steel is 12×10^6 lb/in^2.   *Ans.* 8.3×10^{-7} radian, 8.3×10^{-6} in.

Chapter 14

Fluids at Rest

DENSITY ρ of a body $=$ mass per unit volume $= \dfrac{\text{mass of body}}{\text{volume of body}} = \dfrac{m}{V}$.

The density of solids and liquids may be expressed in g/cm^3, kg/m^3, or slugs/ft^3. The density of gases is usually given in g/liter, or g/cm^3.

Density ρ of water at 4°C = 1.000 g/cm^3 = 1000 kg/m^3 = 1.94 slugs/ft^3.

WEIGHT–DENSITY ρg of a body $=$ weight per unit volume $= \dfrac{\text{weight of body } (mg)}{\text{volume of body } (V)} = \dfrac{m}{V}g = \rho g$.

Weight-density ρg of water at 4°C = 62.4 lb/ft^3.

Note. The *density* ρ of water at 4°C = 62.4/32.2 = 1.94 slugs/ft^3.

SPECIFIC GRAVITY (sp gr) of a substance is the ratio of the density of the substance to the density of a substance taken as a standard. Solids and liquids are referred to water as standard, while gases are often referred to air as standard.

$$\text{Sp gr of a body } = \frac{\text{density of body}}{\text{density of water}}$$

$$= \frac{\text{mass of body}}{\text{mass of equal volume water}} = \frac{\text{weight of body}}{\text{weight of equal volume water}}.$$

Specific gravity of water = 1, in any system. The specific gravity of a substance is the same in any system of measures. It is expressed by a pure number without units.

The density and specific gravity of a substance are *numerically* the same when the density is given in g/cm^3, since the density of water is 1 g/cm^3. Thus the specific gravity of aluminum is 2.70; hence its density is 2.70 g/cm^3.

In the mks system, the density of aluminum = 2.70 × density of water
$$= 2.70 \times 1000 \text{ kg/m}^3 = 2700 \text{ kg/m}^3.$$

In the English gravitational system,

(1) density ρ of aluminum = 2.70 × density of water
$$= 2.70 \times 1.94 \text{ slugs/ft}^3 = 5.24 \text{ slugs/ft}^3,$$

(2) weight-density ρg of aluminum = 2.70 × weight-density of water
$$= 2.70 \times 62.4 \text{ lb/ft}^3 = 168 \text{ lb/ft}^3.$$

PRESSURE p = force per unit area $= \dfrac{\text{force } F \text{ acting perpendicular to an area}}{\text{area } A \text{ over which the force is distributed}}$.

$$p = \frac{F}{A}$$

Some units of pressure are the lb/ft^2, lb/in^2, nt/m^2, and dyne/cm^2.

The pressure p due to a column of fluid of height h and density ρ is

$$p = h\rho g$$
$$p\,(\text{lb/ft}^2) = h\,(\text{ft}) \times \rho\,(\text{slugs/ft}^3) \times g\,(32\ \text{ft/sec}^2)$$
$$= h\,(\text{ft}) \times \rho g\,(\text{lb/ft}^3)$$
$$p\,(\text{nt/m}^2) = h\,(\text{m}) \times \rho\,(\text{kg/m}^3) \times g\,(9.8\ \text{m/sec}^2)$$

PASCAL'S PRINCIPLE. When the pressure on any part of a confined fluid (liquid or gas) is changed, the pressure on every other part of the fluid is also changed by the same amount.

ARCHIMEDES' PRINCIPLE. A body wholly or partly immersed in a fluid is buoyed up by a force equal to the weight of the fluid it displaces. In other words, a body immersed in a fluid apparently loses a weight equal to the weight of the displaced fluid. The buoyant force is considered as acting vertically upward through the center of gravity of the displaced fluid. Buoyancy = weight of displaced fluid.

SOLVED PROBLEMS

1. Find the density and specific gravity of gasoline if 51 g occupy 75 cm^3.
   Solution:

   $$\text{Density } \rho = \frac{\text{mass}}{\text{volume}} = \frac{51\,\text{g}}{75\,\text{cm}^3} = 0.68\ \text{g/cm}^3$$

   $$\text{Specific gravity} = \frac{\text{density of gasoline}}{\text{density of water}} = \frac{0.68\ \text{g/cm}^3}{1.00\ \text{g/cm}^3} = 0.68$$

   $$= \frac{\text{mass of 75 cm}^3\text{ gasoline}}{\text{mass of 75 cm}^3\text{ water}} = \frac{51\,\text{g}}{75\,\text{g}} = 0.68$$

   Notice that the density and specific gravity of a substance are numerically the same when the density is expressed in g/cm^3.

2. What volume does 300 g of mercury occupy? Density of mercury is 13.6 g/cm^3.
   Solution:

   $$\text{Volume} = \frac{\text{mass}}{\text{density}} = \frac{300\,\text{g}}{13.6\ \text{g/cm}^3} = 22.1\ \text{cm}^3$$

3. Find the density ρ, the weight-density ρ', and the specific gravity of aluminum if 3.50 ft^3 weighs 588 lb.
   Solution:

   $$\text{Density } \rho = \frac{\text{mass}}{\text{volume}} = \frac{588/32\ \text{slugs}}{3.5\ \text{ft}^3} = 5.25\ \text{slugs/ft}^3$$

   $$\text{Weight-density } \rho' = \frac{\text{weight}}{\text{volume}} = \frac{588\,\text{lb}}{3.5\ \text{ft}^3} = 168\ \text{lb/ft}^3$$

   $$\text{Specific gravity} = \frac{\text{weight-density of aluminum}}{\text{weight-density of water}} = \frac{168\ \text{lb/ft}^3}{62.4\ \text{lb/ft}^3} = 2.7$$

   $$= \frac{\text{weight of 3.5 ft}^3\text{ aluminum}}{\text{weight of 3.5 ft}^3\text{ water}} = \frac{588\,\text{lb}}{3.5 \times 62.4\ \text{lb}} = 2.7$$

   In the English system, (mass) density ρ in slugs/ft^3 is not often used.

4. A can weighs 3 lb when empty, 53 lb when filled with water, and 66 lb when filled with glycerin. Find the specific gravity of glycerin.

Solution:

$$\text{Specific gravity of glycerin} = \frac{\text{weight of glycerin}}{\text{weight of equal volume water}} = \frac{(66-3)\,\text{lb}}{(53-3)\,\text{lb}} = 1.26$$

5. The specific gravity of cast iron is 7.20.
(a) Find its density ρ in g/cm^3 and the mass of $60\,cm^3$ of cast iron.
(b) Find its weight-density ρ' in lb/ft^3 and the weight of $20\,ft^3$ of cast iron.

Solution:

(a) Density ρ of iron $= 7.20 \times \text{density of water} = 7.20 \times 1\,g/cm^3 = 7.20\,g/cm^3$

Mass of $60\,cm^3$ of iron $= 60\,cm^3 \times 7.20\,g/cm^3 = 432\,g$

(b) Weight-density ρ' of iron $= 7.20 \times \text{weight-density of water}$
$$= 7.20 \times 62.4\,lb/ft^3 = 449\,lb/ft^3$$

Weight of $20\,ft^3$ of iron $= 20\,ft^3 \times 449\,lb/ft^3 = 8980\,lb$

6. Determine the volume in gallons of 400 lb of cottonseed oil of specific gravity 0.926. One gallon of water weighs 8.34 lb.

Solution:

$$\text{Weight-density of oil} = 0.926 \times \text{weight-density of water} = 0.926 \times 8.34\,lb/gal$$

$$\text{Volume of oil} = \frac{\text{weight of oil}}{\text{weight-density of oil}} = \frac{400\,lb}{(0.926 \times 8.34)\,lb/gal} = 51.8\,gal$$

7. The mass of a liter of milk is 1032 g. The butterfat which it contains to the extent of 4% by volume has specific gravity 0.865. What is the density of the "fat-free" skimmed milk?

Solution:

Volume of fat in $1000\,cm^3$ milk $= 4\% \times 1000\,cm^3 = 40\,cm^3$

Mass of $40\,cm^3$ fat $= \text{volume} \times \text{density} = 40\,cm^3 \times 0.865\,g/cm^3 = 34.6\,g$

$$\text{Density of skimmed milk} = \frac{\text{mass}}{\text{volume}} = \frac{(1032-34.6)\,g}{(1000-40)\,cm^3} = 1.04\,g/cm^3$$

8. An electrolytic tin-plating process gives a coating 30 millionths of an inch thick. How many square meters can be coated with 1 kilogram of tin, specific gravity 7.3?

Solution:

Thickness of coating $= 30 \times 10^{-6}\,in. = 30 \times 10^{-6}\,in. \times 2.54\,cm/in. = 76.2 \times 10^{-6}\,cm$

Volume of 1 kg tin $= \dfrac{\text{mass}}{\text{density}} = \dfrac{1000\,g}{7.3\,g/cm^3} = 137\,cm^3$

Area of coating $= \dfrac{\text{volume}}{\text{thickness}} = \dfrac{137\,cm^3}{76.2 \times 10^{-6}\,cm} = 1.80 \times 10^6\,cm^2 = 180\,m^2$

9. Find the pressure at the bottom of a vessel 76 cm deep when filled with (a) water, (b) mercury.

Solution:

(a) In mks units: $\quad p = h\rho g = 0.76\,m \times 1000\,kg/m^3 \times 9.8\,m/sec^2 = 7.45 \times 10^3\,nt/m^2$
In cgs units: $\quad p = h\rho g = 76\,cm \times 1\,g/cm^3 \times 980\,cm/sec^2 = 7.45 \times 10^4\,dynes/cm^2$

(b) In mks units: $\quad p = h\rho g = 0.76\,m \times (13.6 \times 1000)\,kg/m^3 \times 9.8\,m/sec^2 = 1.013 \times 10^5\,nt/m^2$
In cgs units: $\quad p = h\rho g = 76\,cm \times 13.6\,g/cm^3 \times 980\,cm/sec^2 = 1.013 \times 10^6\,dynes/cm^2$

19. A piece of alloy weighs 86 lb in air and 73 lb when immersed in water. Find its volume V and specific gravity.

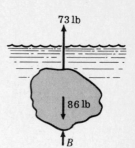

Solution:

$$\text{Buoyant force } B = \text{weight of displaced water}$$
$$86\,\text{lb} - 73\,\text{lb} = 62.4\,\text{lb/ft}^3 \times V \qquad V = 0.208\,\text{ft}^3$$

$$\text{Specific gravity} = \frac{\text{weight of alloy}}{\text{weight of equal volume of water}} = \frac{86\,\text{lb}}{(86 - 73)\,\text{lb}} = 6.6$$

20. A tank containing water rests on a scale and weighs 436.1 lb. Determine the scale reading when a solid rod of diameter 2 in. is held vertically in the water to a depth of 2.5 ft.

Solution:

$$\text{Buoyant force upward on rod} = \text{weight of displaced water}$$
$$= \left[\tfrac{1}{4}\pi(2/12)^2 \times 2.5\right]\text{ft}^3 \times 62.4\,\text{lb/ft}^3 = 3.4\,\text{lb}$$

By Newton's third law, an equal and opposite reacting force of 3.4 lb acts downward on the tank. Hence the scale reading is $(436.1 + 3.4)\,\text{lb} = 439.5\,\text{lb}$.

21. A solid aluminum cylinder, specific gravity 2.7, weighs 67 lb in air and 45 lb when immersed in turpentine. Determine the specific gravity of turpentine.

Solution:

$$\text{Volume of cylinder} = \frac{67\,\text{lb}}{(2.7 \times 62.4)\,\text{lb/ft}^3} = 0.398\,\text{ft}^3$$

$$\text{Buoyant force on cylinder} = \text{weight of displaced turpentine}$$
$$67\,\text{lb} - 45\,\text{lb} = (\text{sp gr} \times 62.4)\,\text{lb/ft}^3 \times 0.398\,\text{ft}^3 \qquad \text{sp gr} = 0.89$$

22. A glass stopper weighs 1.25 oz in air, 0.75 oz in water, and 0.35 oz in sulfuric acid. What is the specific gravity of the acid?

Solution:

$$\text{Sp gr of acid} = \frac{\text{weight of displaced acid}}{\text{weight of equal volume of water}}$$

$$= \frac{\text{loss of weight of stopper in acid}}{\text{loss of weight of stopper in water}} = \frac{(1.25 - 0.35)\,\text{oz}}{(1.25 - 0.75)\,\text{oz}} = 1.8$$

23. A block of oak wood weighs 20 lb in air. A lead sinker weighs 30 lb in water. The sinker is attached to the wood and both together weigh 22 lb in water. Find the specific gravity of the wood.

Solution:

$$\text{Sp gr of wood} = \frac{\text{weight of wood in air}}{\text{weight of an equal volume of water}}$$

$$= \frac{\text{weight of wood in air}}{\text{loss of weight in water}} = \frac{20\,\text{lb}}{(30 + 20 - 22)\,\text{lb}} = 0.71$$

24. A rectangular box open at the top and weighing 6000 lb has base dimensions 10 ft by 8 ft and depth 5 ft.
   (a) How deep y will it sink in fresh water?
   (b) What weight w_B of ballast will cause it to sink to a depth of 3 ft?

Solution:

(a) Since the box floats, buoyant force = weight of box = weight of displaced water.

$$\text{Weight of box} = \text{weight of displaced water}$$
$$6000\,\text{lb} = 62.4\,\text{lb/ft}^3 \times (10\,\text{ft} \times 8\,\text{ft} \times y) \qquad y = 1.20\,\text{ft}$$

(b) Weight of box + ballast = weight of displaced water
$$6000\,\text{lb} + w_B = 62.4\,\text{lb/ft}^3 \times (10 \times 8 \times 3)\,\text{ft}^3 \qquad w_B = 8980\,\text{lb}$$

25. The specific gravity of ice is 0.92. What fraction of the volume of a piece of ice will be submerged when floating in a liquid of specific gravity 1.12?

Solution:

Since the ice floats, the weight of displaced liquid = weight of ice.

Let V_t = total volume of ice, V_S = submerged volume.

$$\text{Weight of ice} = \text{weight of displaced liquid}$$
$$(0.92 \times 62.4)\,\text{lb/ft}^3 \times V_t = (1.12 \times 62.4)\,\text{lb/ft}^3 \times V_S \quad\text{or}\quad V_S/V_t = 0.92/1.12 = 0.82$$

26. A sample of salt solution is 24% salt by weight and has specific gravity 1.18. How many pounds of pure salt are in 1 gallon of the solution? What volume of solution contains 25 lb of pure salt? One gallon of water weighs 8.34 lb.

Solution:

1 gallon of solution weighs (1.18×8.34) lb and contains $0.24(1.18 \times 8.34)$ lb = 2.36 lb salt.

25 lb salt is contained in $\dfrac{25\ \text{lb salt}}{2.36\ \dfrac{\text{lb salt}}{\text{gal solution}}}$ = 10.6 gal solution.

27. A liter flask is filled with two liquids (A and B) of specific gravity 1.4 together. The specific gravity of liquid A is 0.8 and of liquid B 1.8. What volume of each enters the mixture? Assume no volume change on mixing.

Solution:

$$\text{Mass of mixture} = \text{mass of liquid } A + \text{mass of liquid } B$$
$$1000\,\text{cm}^3 \times 1.4\,\text{g/cm}^3 = V \times 0.8\,\text{g/cm}^3 + (1000\,\text{cm}^3 - V) \times 1.8\,\text{g/cm}^3$$

Solving, $V = 400\,\text{cm}^3$ of liquid A; $(1000\,\text{cm}^3 - V) = 600\,\text{cm}^3$ of liquid B.

28. A nugget of gold and quartz has a mass of 100 g. Specific gravity of gold = 19.3, of quartz = 2.6, of nugget = 6.4. Determine the mass of gold in the nugget.

Solution:

Let x = mass of gold in nugget; $(100\,\text{g} - x)$ = mass of quartz in nugget.

$$\text{Volume of nugget} = \text{volume of gold in nugget} + \text{volume of quartz in nugget}$$
$$\frac{100\,\text{g}}{6.4\,\text{g/cm}^3} = \frac{x}{19.3\,\text{g/cm}^3} + \frac{100\,\text{g} - x}{2.6\,\text{g/cm}^3} \qquad \text{Solving,} \ x = 69\,\text{g gold}$$

29. A coal contains 2.4% water. After drying, the moisture-free residue contains 71.0% carbon. Compute the percentage of carbon on the "wet" basis.

Solution:

100 g of "wet" coal contains 2.4 g water and 97.6 g of dry components of which 71% or 0.71×97.6 g = 69.3 g is carbon. Then 100 g of wet coal contains 69.3 g of carbon; hence the percentage of carbon on the "wet" basis is 69.3%.

SUPPLEMENTARY PROBLEMS

30. Find the density and specific gravity of ethyl alcohol if 63.3 g occupy 80.0 cm^3.
Ans. 0.791 g/cm^3, 0.791

31. Determine the volume of 40 kg carbon tetrachloride, sp gr 1.60.   *Ans.* 25 l

32. Determine the weight of 20 cubic feet of aluminum, sp gr 2.70.   *Ans.* 3370 lb

33. A drum holds 200 lb of water or 132 lb of gasoline. Determine (a) the specific gravity of gasoline, (b) the density of gasoline in g/cm^3 and the weight-density in lb/ft^3, and (c) the capacity of the drum in gallons. One gallon of water weighs 8.34 lb.   *Ans.* 0.66, 0.66 g/cm^3, 41.2 lb/ft^3, 24 gal

34. The heaviest solid (osmium) and the lightest room temperature liquid (butane) have specific gravities of 22.5 and 0.6, respectively. Compute the weight-density of osmium in lb/ft^3, and the density of butane in kilograms per liter.   *Ans.* 1400 lb/ft^3, 0.6 kg/l

35. Air weighs about 8 lb per 100 cubic feet. What is its density in g/ft^3, and in grams per liter?
Ans. 36 g/ft^3, 1.3 g/l

36. The lightness of a General Electric plastic foam is illustrated by the fact that a piece 13 × 9.5 × 2.5 in. has a mass of only 350 g. A Du Pont cellulose sponge, 7 × 12 × 2.5 cm, has a mass of 12 g. *Foamglas* is light as balsa, only 10 lb/ft^3, two thirds as heavy as cork. Compute the specific gravity of these synthetics and of cork.
Ans. 0.069, 0.057, 0.16, 0.24

37. What is the density of a steel ball which has diameter 0.750 cm and mass 1.765 g? Volume of a sphere of radius r is $(4/3)\pi r^3$.   *Ans.* 7.99 g/cm^3

38. A piece of capillary tubing was calibrated in the following manner. A thread of mercury, drawn into a 3.247 g clean sample of the tubing, occupied a length of 2.375 cm as observed under a microscope. The mass of the tube with the mercury was 3.489 g. Assuming that the capillary bore is a uniform cylinder, find the diameter of the bore. Density of mercury is 13.60 g/cm^3. Volume of a cylinder of radius r and height h is $\pi r^2 h$.
Ans. 0.98 mm

39. A 1.93 mg piece of gold leaf (sp gr 19.3) can be beaten further into a transparent film covering an area of 14.5 cm^2. (a) What is the volume of 1.93 mg of gold? (b) What is the thickness of the transparent film in angstroms? One angstrom = 10^{-8} cm. (c) If the gold atoms have a diameter of about 5 angstroms, how many atomic layers are contained in this transparent film?
Ans. 10^{-4} cm^3, 690 angstroms, 138 atomic layers

40. In cement mill air there may be as many as 26 million dust particles, specific gravity 3.0, per cubic foot of air. Assuming the particles are spherical with diameter 2 microns, calculate the mass of dust (a) in 1000 ft^3 of mill air, (b) inhaled in each average breath of 30 in^3. One micron = 10^{-4} cm.
Ans. 0.33 g, 5.7×10^{-6} g

41. Determine the ratio of the average pressure on the upper half of one side of a tank filled with grain alcohol to the average pressure on its lower half. The tank has uniform cross section.   *Ans.* 1:3

42. A cubical tank, measuring 10 ft each way, is filled with water. Compute the force on the bottom and the force on a vertical side.   *Ans.* 62,400 lb, 31,200 lb

43. Professor Charles Beebe viewed the "eternal blackness" of 3028 feet below the surface of the ocean through a circular fused quartz window which had an exposed 6 inch diameter. Approximately what load was this window resisting at this depth? Specific gravity of sea water is 1.03.   *Ans.* 38,200 lb

44. A rectangular plate 2 × 3 ft of uniform thickness has a piece removed of 1 ft square, and whose center of area was $\frac{1}{2}$ ft above the lower 3-ft edge. If this plate is immersed vertically with the 3-ft edges parallel to the surface and the upper edge 19 ft below the surface of the water, compute the force on the plate.   *Ans.* 6210 lb

45. A rectangular tank, 30 by 40 cm in plan and 20 cm deep, is filled with water. Find the pressure and the force on the bottom of the tank (a) in mks units, (b) in cgs units.
Ans. (a) 1.96×10^3 nt/m^2, 2.35×10^2 nt; (b) 1.96×10^4 dynes/cm^2, 2.35×10^7 dynes

46. A cubical vessel whose edges are 50 cm is closed at the top. At one side a vertical pipe is let in, the center of the orifice being 30 cm from the bottom. The height of water in the tube above the center of the orifice is 70 cm, and the cross section area of the tube is 100 cm^2. Compute the force on each face, including top and bottom.   *Ans.* 1230 nt on top, 2450 nt on bottom, 1760 nt on vertical face containing opening, 1840 nt on each of other faces

47. Compute the pressure required for a water supply system that will raise water 150 ft vertically.
    Ans. 9360 lb/ft^2 or 65 lb/in^2

48. The area of the piston of a force pump is 7.2 square inches. What force must be applied to raise water 100 ft?
    Ans. 312 lb

49. The diameter of the large piston of a hydraulic press is 2 ft, and the area of the small piston is 1 square inch. If a force of 100 lb is applied to the smaller piston, what is the force exerted by the large piston? What is the pressure in lb/in^2 under each piston?   *Ans.* 45,200 lb, 100 lb/in^2

50. A tank containing oil of specific gravity 0.80 rests on a scale and weighs 320.2 lb. By means of a wire a 6 inch cube of aluminum, sp gr 2.7, is held submerged in the oil. Find (*a*) the tension in the wire and (*b*) the scale reading.   *Ans.* 14.8 lb, 326.4 lb

51. Downward forces of 45 and 15 lb respectively are required to keep a wood block totally immersed in water and in an oil. If the volume of the block is 3 ft^3, find the specific gravity of the oil.   *Ans.* 0.84

52. Determine the acceleration with which an iron ball of specific gravity 7.8 will begin (*a*) to fall under gravity when placed in water, (*b*) to rise when placed in mercury, specific gravity 13.5.
    Ans. (*a*) 27.9 ft/sec^2, (*b*) 23.4 ft/sec^2

53. A 4 inch cube of metal weighs 15.3 lb when immersed in water. Compute its apparent weight when immersed in glycerin, sp gr 1.26.   *Ans.* 14.7 lb

54. A balloon has a capacity of 35,200 ft^3. Find its lifting force when filled with helium gas. Average weight-density of air = 0.0781 lb/ft^3, of helium = 0.0111 lb/ft^3.   *Ans.* 2360 lb

55. A piece of magnalium weighs 0.50 lb in air, 0.30 lb in water, and 0.32 lb in benzene. Determine the specific gravity of magnalium and of benzene.   *Ans.* 2.5, 0.90

56. An alloy spring which may be either bronze (sp gr 8.8) or brass (sp gr 8.4) weighs 0.126 oz in air and 0.111 oz in water. Which is it?   *Ans.* brass

57. What fraction of the volume of a piece of quartz will be submerged when floating in a container of mercury? Specific gravity of quartz 2.65, of mercury 13.6.   *Ans.* 0.195

58. A solid weighs 10 lb in air and 6 lb in a liquid whose specific gravity is 0.8. What is the specific gravity of the solid?   *Ans.* 2

59. A cube of wood floating in water supports a 200 g mass. When the mass is removed the cube rises 2 cm. Determine the size of the cube.   *Ans.* 10 cm on an edge

60. A cork weighs 0.5 oz in air. A sinker weighs 8.6 oz in water. The cork is attached to the sinker and both together weigh 7.1 oz in water. What is the specific gravity of the cork?   *Ans.* 0.25

61. A man and a stone are floating on a raft in a swimming pool which is 30 ft long by 20 ft wide. The stone weighs 75 lb and has specific gravity 2.5. If the man drops the stone overboard, by how much will the water level on the side of the pool change? Neglect the area of the raft.   *Ans.* Fall 0.0144 in.

62. The heights of balancing columns of olive oil and water are 50 cm and 46 cm, respectively. What is the density of olive oil?   *Ans.* 0.92 g/cm^3

63. Battery acid has specific gravity 1.285 and contains 38% H_2SO_4 by weight. How many grams of H_2SO_4 are in a liter of battery acid?   *Ans.* 488 g

64. A clay contains 45% silica and 10% water. What is the percentage of silica in the clay on a dry (water-free) basis?   *Ans.* 50% silica

65. There are available 10 tons of a coal containing 2.5% sulfur, and also supplies of coal containing 0.80% and 1.10% sulfur, respectively. How many tons of each of the latter should be mixed with the original 10 tons to give 20 tons containing 1.7% sulfur?   *Ans.* 6.7 tons of 0.80%, 3.3 tons of 1.10%

Chapter 15

Fluids in Motion

FLOW OR DISCHARGE, Q. When a fluid flows full through a pipe of cross section area A with a velocity v, the **flow** or **discharge** Q is

$$Q = Av$$

where Q is expressed in such units as ft³/sec, m³/sec, cm³/sec.

Note. Q is sometimes called the rate of flow or the discharge rate.

EQUATION OF CONTINUITY. When an incompressible fluid flows full through a pipe of varying cross section area, then

$$Q = A_1 v_1 = A_2 v_2 = \text{constant}$$

where v_1, v_2 are respectively the velocities of the fluid at cross sections A_1, A_2.

BERNOULLI THEOREM for steady flow of a continuous stream of fluid: The sum of the pressure energy, kinetic (velocity) energy and potential (elevation) energy at any point in a stream is equal to the sum of the energies at any other point along the same stream.

$$(1) \qquad p_1\frac{m}{\rho} + \tfrac{1}{2}mv_1^2 + mgh_1 = p_2\frac{m}{\rho} + \tfrac{1}{2}mv_2^2 + mgh_2$$

where m is the mass of fluid considered,
ρ is the density of the fluid,
p_1, v_1 and h_1 are the pressure, speed and height at one point in the stream,
p_2, v_2 and h_2 are the pressure, speed and height at another point.

In the English engineering system, m is expressed in slugs, p in lb/ft², ρ in slugs/ft³, ρg in lb/ft³, $g = 32$ ft/sec², v in ft/sec, and h in ft.

Dividing each term of equation (1) by m/ρ,

$$(2) \qquad p_1 + \tfrac{1}{2}\rho v_1^2 + h_1\rho g = p_2 + \tfrac{1}{2}\rho v_2^2 + h_2\rho g$$

Dividing each term of equation (1) by mg,

$$(3) \qquad \frac{p_1}{\rho g} + \frac{v_1^2}{2g} + h_1 = \frac{p_2}{\rho g} + \frac{v_2^2}{2g} + h_2$$

Note that each term of equation (1) has dimensions of work; each term of (2) has dimensions of pressure; each term of (3) has dimensions of length (height).

VELOCITY OF OUTFLOW of liquid from an orifice $= \sqrt{2gh}$ (Torricelli's Theorem), where h is the height of liquid above the opening, assumed to be constant.

WORK done by a piston in forcing a volume of liquid into a cylinder against an opposing pressure = average pressure × volume.

SOLVED PROBLEMS

1. Oil flows through a 3 inch diameter pipe at an average velocity of 11 ft/sec. What is the flow Q in (a) ft^3/sec, (b) gal/hr? 1 ft^3 = 7.48 gal.

Solution:

$$Q \text{ (ft}^3\text{/sec)} = Av = \tfrac{1}{4}\pi(\tfrac{1}{4} \text{ ft})^2 \times 11 \text{ ft/sec} = 0.540 \text{ ft}^3\text{/sec}$$

$$Q \text{ (gal/hr)} = 0.540 \frac{\text{ft}^3}{\text{sec}} \times \frac{7.48 \text{ gal}}{1 \text{ ft}^3} \times \frac{3600 \text{ sec}}{1 \text{ hr}} = 14{,}500 \text{ gal/hr}$$

2. If the velocity of water in a 6 in. diameter pipe is 5 ft/sec, what is the velocity in a 3 in. diameter pipe which connects with it, both pipes flowing full?

Solution:

Since flow $Q = A_6 v_6 = A_3 v_3$, $(\tfrac{1}{4}\pi d_6^2)v_6 = (\tfrac{1}{4}\pi d_3^2)v_3$ and

$$v_3 = v_6\left(\frac{d_6}{d_3}\right)^2 = 5 \text{ ft/sec} \times \left(\frac{6 \text{ in.}}{3 \text{ in.}}\right)^2 = 20 \text{ ft/sec.}$$

3. What volume of water will escape per minute from a tank through an opening 1 inch in diameter and 16 ft below the level of the water? See Fig. (a) below.

Solution:

Since $p_1 = p_2$ = atmospheric pressure and v_1 is negligible (assumed zero), the Bernoulli equation applied to points 1 and 2 is

$$\tfrac{1}{2}\rho v_1^2 + h_1\rho g = \tfrac{1}{2}\rho v_2^2 + h_2\rho g \quad \text{or} \quad 0 + h_1 g = \tfrac{1}{2}v_2^2 + h_2 g$$

from which $v_2^2 = 2g(h_1 - h_2) = 2gh$ and $v_2 = \sqrt{2gh} = \sqrt{2 \times 32 \text{ ft/sec}^2 \times 16 \text{ ft}} = 32 \text{ ft/sec.}$

$$\text{Flow} = A_2 v_2 = \tfrac{1}{4}\pi(1/12 \text{ ft})^2 \times (32\times60)\text{ ft/min} = 10.5 \text{ ft}^3\text{/min}$$

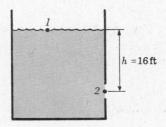

Fig. (a) Problem 3

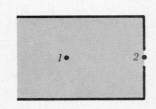

Fig. (b) Problem 4

4. Find the velocity of escape of water through a small opening in a boiler as shown in Fig. (b) above where the pressure is (a) 10^6 nt/m^2 above atmospheric pressure, (b) 50 lb/in^2 above atmospheric pressure.

Solution:

(a) Since $h_1 = h_2$ and v_1 is negligible (assumed zero), the Bernoulli equation applied to points 1 and 2 is

$$p_1 + \tfrac{1}{2}\rho v_1^2 = p_2 + \tfrac{1}{2}\rho v_2^2 \quad \text{or} \quad p_1 + 0 = p_2 + \tfrac{1}{2}\rho v_2^2$$

from which $v_2^2 = \dfrac{2(p_1 - p_2)}{\rho} = \dfrac{2(10^6 \text{ nt/m}^2)}{10^3 \text{ kg/m}^3}$ and $v_2 = 45 \text{ m/sec.}$

Another method. Loss of pressure energy per m^3 water = gain of K.E. per m^3 water

$$\text{pressure difference} \times \text{volume} = \tfrac{1}{2}mv^2$$
$$10^6 \text{ nt/m}^2 \times 1 \text{ m}^3 = \tfrac{1}{2}(10^3 \text{ kg})v^2, \quad v = 45 \text{ m/sec}$$

(b) From (a), $v_2^2 = \dfrac{2(p_1 - p_2)}{\rho} = \dfrac{2(50 \text{ lb/in}^2 \times 144 \text{ in}^2/\text{ft}^2)}{62.4/32 \text{ slugs/ft}^3}$ and $v_2 = 86 \text{ ft/sec.}$

5. Water flows at the rate of 2 ft^3/minute through an opening at the bottom of a tank in which the water is 12 ft deep. Calculate the rate of escape of the water if an added pressure of 8 lb/in^2 is applied to the surface of the water.

Solution:

From the formula $v = \sqrt{2gh}$, the rate of outflow varies directly as the square root of the height of the water above the opening.

Since height of water $h = p/\rho g$, an additional pressure of 8 lb/in^2 = 8 × 144 lb/ft^2 is equivalent to an increased height of $\dfrac{8 \times 144 \text{ lb/ft}^2}{62.4 \text{ lb/ft}^3}$ = 18.5 ft. Then by proportion, letting Q = flow at the increased pressure,

$$\frac{2 \text{ ft}^3/\text{min}}{\sqrt{12 \text{ ft}}} = \frac{Q}{\sqrt{12 \text{ ft} + 18.5 \text{ ft}}} \qquad \text{from which} \qquad Q = 3.19 \text{ ft}^3/\text{min.}$$

6. (a) How much work W is done by a pump in raising 100 ft^3 of water 40 ft and forcing it into a main at a pressure of 20 lb/in^2? (b) How much work is done by a pump in raising 5 m^3 of water 20 m and forcing it into a main at a pressure of 1.5×10^5 nt/m^2?

Solution:

(a) W = work to raise water + work to balance pressure
         = height × weight of 100 ft^3 water + pressure × volume
         = 40 ft × (100 × 62.4) lb + (20 × 144) lb/ft^2 × 100 ft^3 = 5.38×10^5 ft-lb

(b) W = 20 m × (5×10^3 × 9.8) nt + (1.5×10^5) nt/m^2 × 5 m^3 = 1.73×10^6 joules

7. Water from a dam falls on a turbine 100 ft below at the rate of 2000 ft^3/minute. After leaving the turbine wheel the water has a velocity of 30 ft/sec. What is the maximum efficiency of the turbine? What is the maximum horsepower developed?

Solution:

K.E. put into turbine per ft^3 water = potential energy per ft^3 water at top
                        = 62.4 lb × 100 ft = 6240 ft-lb

K.E. per ft^3 water leaving turbine = $\frac{1}{2}mv^2$ = $\frac{1}{2}$(62.4/32 slugs)(30 ft/sec)^2 = 880 ft-lb

Efficiency = $\dfrac{\text{energy input} - \text{energy loss}}{\text{energy input}}$ = $\dfrac{(6240 - 880)\text{ ft-lb}}{6240 \text{ ft-lb}}$ = 0.86 = 86%

Power output = power input × efficiency
              = (2000 × 6240) ft-lb/min × 0.86 × $\dfrac{1 \text{ hp}}{33,000 \text{ ft-lb/min}}$ = 330 hp

8. Determine the maximum height h over which oil of specific gravity 0.80 may be siphoned if the barometer reads 30 in. of mercury. Specific gravity of mercury = 13.6.

Solution:

                Atmospheric pressure = pressure of oil
Height × density of mercury × g = height × density of oil × g
          30 in. × 13.6 g/cm^3 × g = h × 0.80 g/cm^3 × g h = 510 in. = 42.5 ft

9. A horizontal pipe (Section *1*) of diameter 6 in. has a constriction (Section *2*) of diameter 2 in. The velocity of the water in the pipe is 2 ft/sec and the pressure is 15 lb/in^2. Calculate the velocity v_2 and pressure p_2 in the constriction.

Solution:

By the equation of continuity, and since the cross section areas vary as the squares of the diameters,

$$A_1 v_1 = A_2 v_2$$

(6 in.)^2 (2 ft/sec) = (2 in.)$^2 v_2$ and v_2 = 18 ft/sec.

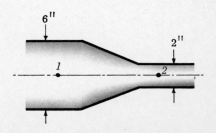

Since the flow is horizontal, $h_1 = h_2$ and the Bernoulli equation reduces to

$$p_1 + \tfrac{1}{2}\rho v_1^2 = p_2 + \tfrac{1}{2}\rho v_2^2 \qquad \text{or} \qquad (B) \quad p_2 = \tfrac{1}{2}\rho(v_1^2 - v_2^2) + p_1$$

where p is in lb/ft^2, ρ in slugs/ft^3, and v in ft/sec. Substituting in (B),

$$p_2 = \tfrac{1}{2}(62.4/32 \text{ slugs/ft}^3) \times (2^2 - 18^2)\text{ft}^2/\text{sec}^2 + 15 \text{ lb/in}^2 \times 144 \text{ in}^2/\text{ft}^2$$
$$= 1850 \text{ lb/ft}^2 = 12.8 \text{ lb/in}^2$$

10. The pipe shown in Fig. (a) below has a diameter of 16 in. at Section 1 and 10 in. at Section 2. The pressure at Section 1 is 24 lb/in^2, and the elevation of point 2 is 20 ft greater than that of point 1. When oil of specific gravity 0.8 flows at the rate of 3 ft^3/sec, find the pressure at Section 2 neglecting energy losses.

Solution:

From $Q = Av$, $\quad v_1 = \dfrac{Q}{A_1} = \dfrac{3 \text{ ft}^3/\text{sec}}{\tfrac{1}{4}\pi(4/3 \text{ ft})^2} = 2.15 \dfrac{\text{ft}}{\text{sec}}$ $\quad$ and $\quad v_2 = \dfrac{Q}{A_2} = 5.49 \dfrac{\text{ft}}{\text{sec}}$.

The Bernoulli equation applied to points 1 and 2 is

$$p_1 + \tfrac{1}{2}\rho v_1^2 + h_1 \rho g = p_2 + \tfrac{1}{2}\rho v_2^2 + h_2 \rho g$$

$$(24 \times 144) \text{ lb/ft}^2 + \tfrac{1}{2}(0.8 \times 62.4/32 \text{ slugs/ft}^3)(2.15 \text{ ft/sec})^2 + 0$$
$$= p_2 + \tfrac{1}{2}(0.8 \times 62.4/32 \text{ slugs/ft}^3)(5.49 \text{ ft/sec})^2 + (20 \text{ ft})(0.8 \times 62.4 \text{ lb/ft}^3)$$

from which $p_2 = 2440 \text{ lb/ft}^2$ $\quad$ or $\quad 2440/144 = 16.9 \text{ lb/in}^2$.

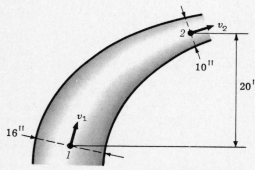

Fig.(a) Problem 10

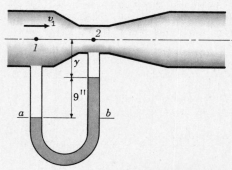

Fig.(b) Problem 11

11. A Venturi meter equipped with a differential mercury manometer is shown in Fig. (b) above. The inlet (Section 1) diameter is 12 in. and the throat (Section 2) diameter is 6 in. Find the ideal flow of water through the meter if the difference in height between the mercury columns is 9 in. Specific gravity of mercury is 13.6.

Solution:

Since $h_1 = h_2$, the Bernoulli equation applied to points 1 and 2 is

$$p_1 + \tfrac{1}{2}\rho v_1^2 = p_2 + \tfrac{1}{2}\rho v_2^2 \qquad \text{or} \qquad (C) \quad p_1 - p_2 = \tfrac{1}{2}\rho(v_2^2 - v_1^2)$$

Now a and b are at the same level in the same liquid (mercury); hence

$$\text{pressure at level } a = \text{pressure at level } b$$
$$p_1 + (0.75 + y)\rho g = p_2 + y\rho g + 0.75 \rho_m g$$

where $\rho = $ density of water and $\rho_m = $ density of mercury,
and $\quad p_1 - p_2 = 0.75(\rho_m g - \rho g) = (0.75 \text{ ft})\left[(13.6 - 1)62.4 \text{ lb/ft}^3\right] = 590 \text{ lb/ft}^2$.

Also, $A_1 v_1 = A_2 v_2$, $\quad \tfrac{1}{4}\pi(1 \text{ ft})^2 v_1 = \tfrac{1}{4}\pi(\tfrac{1}{2} \text{ ft})^2 v_2$ $\quad$ and $\quad v_2 = 4 v_1$.

Substituting in (C), $\quad 590 \text{ lb/ft}^2 = \tfrac{1}{2}(62.4/32 \text{ slugs/ft}^3)(15 v_1^2)$ $\quad$ and $\quad v_1 = 6.35 \text{ ft/sec}$.

Flow $Q = A_1 v_1 = \tfrac{1}{4}\pi(1 \text{ ft})^2 \times 6.35 \text{ ft/sec} = 4.99 \text{ ft}^3/\text{sec}$.

SUPPLEMENTARY PROBLEMS

12. Oil flows through a 4 in. diameter pipe at an average velocity of 10 ft/sec. Find the flow in ft^3/sec, in gal/min, and in barrels/hr. $1 ft^3$ = 7.48 gal, 1 U.S. liquid barrel = 31.5 gal.
Ans. 0.872 ft^3/sec, 391 gal/min, 745 bbl/hr

13. Compute the velocity of water in a pipe having a diameter of 2 in. and delivering 600 ft^3 of water per hour.
Ans. 7.64 ft/sec

14. The velocity of glycerin in a 5 in. diameter pipe is 5.4 ft/sec. Find the velocity in a 3 in. diameter pipe which connects with it, both pipes flowing full. *Ans.* 15 ft/sec

15. Find the kinetic energy of a cubic foot of water moving at 64 ft/sec. *Ans.* 4000 ft-lb

16. A pump of 1 kw output discharges water from a cellar into a street 5 m above. At what rate is the cellar emptied? *Ans.* 20.4 l/sec

17. Determine the work required to pump 5 ft^3 of liquid into a tank where the pressure is 80 lb/in^2.
Ans. 57,600 ft-lb

18. Oil of specific gravity 0.75 flows in a pipeline with a velocity of 5 ft/sec. The pressure at a given cross section is 40 lb/in^2 and the elevation of the center of the section is 16 ft with reference to a given datum plane. Find the pressure energy, velocity (kinetic) energy and potential (elevation) energy per pound of oil.
Ans. 123 ft-lb/lb, 0.391 ft-lb/lb, 16 ft-lb/lb

19. What is the theoretical velocity of outflow of a liquid from a hole which is 25 ft below the surface of the liquid? If the area of the hole is 1 in^2, how much liquid will escape per minute?
Ans. 40 ft/sec, 16.7 ft^3/min

20. Find the flow in liters/sec of liquid through an opening 1 cm^2 in area and 2.5 m below the level of the liquid.
Ans. 0.7 l/sec

21. Calculate the theoretical velocity of efflux of water from an aperture which is 25 ft below the surface of water in a large tank, if an added pressure of 20 lb/in^2 is applied to the surface of the water. *Ans.* 67 ft/sec

22. What horsepower is required to pump 200 ft^3 of water per minute to a height of 25 ft and force it into a main at a pressure of 25 lb/in^2? *Ans.* 31.3 hp

23. A turbine of 75% efficiency uses 550 ft^3 of water per minute from an 80 ft fall. What power, in horsepower and in kilowatts, is developed by the turbine? *Ans.* 62.4 hp, 46.6 kw

24. A pump lifts water at the rate of 0.3 ft^3/sec from a lake through a 2 inch pipe and discharges it into the air at a point 50 ft above the level of the water in the lake. Find (*a*) the velocity of the water at the point of discharge and (*b*) the power delivered by the pump. *Ans.* 13.8 ft/sec, 1.81 hp

25. What is the maximum height over which glycerin, sp gr 1.26, may be siphoned? The barometer reads 76 cm of mercury. *Ans.* 8.2 m

26. Water flows steadily through a horizontal pipe of varying cross section. At one place the pressure is 20 lb/in^2 and the speed is 2 ft/sec. Determine the pressure at another place in the same pipe where the speed is 30 ft/sec. *Ans.* 14 lb/in^2

27. A pipe of varying diameter carries water. At Section *1* the diameter is 8 in. and the pressure is 25 lb/in^2. At Section *2*, which is 14 ft higher than Section *1*, the diameter is 12 in. and the pressure 16 lb/in^2. If the flow is 3 ft^3/sec, find the energy dissipated per pound of water in moving from Section *1* to Section *2*.
Ans. 7.7 ft-lb/lb

28. Kerosene of specific gravity 0.82 flows through a Venturi meter having a throat diameter 4 in. and an entrance diameter 8 in. The drop in pressure between entrance and throat is 600 lb/ft^2. Find the flow in ft^3/sec. *Ans.* 2.47 ft^3/sec

Chapter 16

Surface Tension

SURFACE TENSION σ. A molecule in the interior of a liquid is under attractive forces in all directions, and the vector sum of these forces is zero. But a molecule at the surface of a liquid is acted on by a net inward cohesive force which is perpendicular to the surface. Hence it requires work to move molecules to the surface against this opposing force, and surface molecules have more energy than interior ones.

The surface tension of a liquid is the work that must be done to bring enough molecules from inside the liquid to the surface to form one new unit area of that surface. This work is numerically equal to the tangential contractile force acting across a hypothetical line of unit length on the surface.

In the English gravitational system and in nearly all textbooks on hydraulics, surface tension is expressed in lb/ft. In the mks system, unit surface tension is the nt/m (or joule/m^2). The cgs unit is the dyne/cm (or erg/cm^2).

PRESSURE DUE TO SURFACE TENSION. Surface tension causes the pressure inside a drop of liquid or a bubble filled with gas to be greater than the pressure outside.

(a) In a spherical drop: $p = 2\sigma/r$

(b) In a spherical bubble which is filled with gas: $p = 4\sigma/r$

where σ = surface tension of the liquid, r = radius of drop or bubble
p = pressure inside − pressure outside drop or bubble.

RISE h IN CAPILLARY TUBES. Surface tension causes the rise or fall of a liquid in a capillary tube.

$$h = \frac{2\sigma}{r\rho g} \cos \alpha$$

where σ = surface tension of the liquid, r = radius of the tube
ρ = density of liquid, α = contact angle between liquid and tube.

SOLVED PROBLEMS

1. A horizontal circular loop of wire of diameter 3 in. is lowered into a crude oil sample. The added force (due to surface tension) required to pull the loop out of the liquid is 0.00196 lb. Calculate the surface tension of the crude oil.

Solution:

When the circular wire is pulled out of the liquid, the cylindrical film attached to the wire has an inside and an outside surface. The lines of contact of these surfaces with the wire are two concentric circles of very nearly the same diameter equal to the diameter of the wire loop.

Circumference of loop = π × diameter = 3.14(3/12 ft) = 0.785 ft

Surface tension $\sigma = \dfrac{\text{force}}{\text{total length of line of contact}} = \dfrac{0.00196 \text{ lb}}{2(0.785) \text{ ft}} = 0.00125$ lb/ft

2. A piece of glass tubing of external diameter 4 cm and internal diameter 3.5 cm stands vertically with one end immersed in water. What is the downward pull on the tube due to surface tension? Surface tension of water is 0.074 nt/m.

Solution:

$$\text{Force (nt)} = \text{surface tension (nt/cm)} \times \text{total length of line of contact (cm)}$$
$$= 74 \times 10^{-5} \, \text{nt/cm} \times (4+3.5)\pi \, \text{cm} = 0.0174 \, \text{nt}$$

3. Determine the work in in-lb required to increase the diameter of a spherical soap bubble from 2 in. to 6 in., if the surface tension is 0.0028 lb/ft.

Solution:

The bubble has two surfaces, inside and outside. Surface area of sphere $= 4\pi r^2$.

$$\text{Work (in-lb)} = \text{increase in surface area (in}^2) \times \text{surface tension (lb/in)}$$
$$= 2 \times 4\pi(3^2 - 1^2) \, \text{in}^2 \times 0.0028/12 \, \text{lb/in} = 0.047 \, \text{in-lb}$$

4. Derive the formula giving the relation between the excess pressure p inside a drop of liquid and the surface tension σ.

Solution:

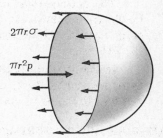

Consider the free body diagram of half of a spherical drop of fluid. The forces exerted on it by the other half of the drop are (1) a force $2\pi r\sigma$ to the left due to surface tension and (2) a force $\pi r^2 p$ to the right due to excess pressure p. Since the half drop is in equilibrium,

$$\text{force to left} = \text{force to right}$$
$$2\pi r\sigma = \pi r^2 p \qquad \text{or} \quad p = 2\sigma/r.$$

5. Compute the pressure (due to surface tension) within a soap bubble of diameter 0.8 in. Surface tension is 0.0024 lb/ft.

Solution:

The film has two surfaces, inside and outside.

$$p = \frac{2\sigma}{r} + \frac{2\sigma}{r} = \frac{4\sigma}{r} = \frac{4 \times 0.0024 \, \text{lb/ft}}{0.4/12 \, \text{ft}} = 0.29 \, \text{lb/ft}^2$$

6. Derive the formula for the height of rise h of liquid in a capillary tube of radius r.

Solution:

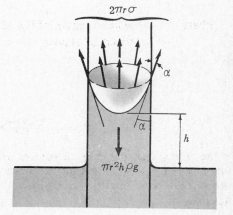

Consider the body of liquid inside the tube and above the outside level. The vertical forces acting on it are:

(1) its weight $= \text{volume} \times \text{weight per unit volume}$
$$= \pi r^2 h \times mg/V = \pi r^2 h \times (m/V)g$$
$$= \pi r^2 h\rho g \quad \text{acting downward,}$$

and (2) the upward component $2\pi r\sigma \cos\alpha$ of the force due to surface tension. For vertical equilibrium,

$$\text{upward force} = \text{downward force}$$
$$2\pi r\sigma \cos\alpha = \pi r^2 h\rho g \qquad \text{or} \quad h = \frac{2\sigma}{r\rho g}\cos\alpha.$$

7. Find the depression of the mercury column in a glass tube of inside diameter 0.4 mm which stands vertically with one end immersed in mercury (sp gr 13.6). The angle of contact is $130°$. Surface tension is 490 dynes/cm. $[\cos 130° = -\cos(180° - 130°)]$.

Solution:

$$h = \frac{2\sigma}{r\rho g}\cos 130° = \frac{2 \times 490 \, \text{dynes/cm}}{0.02 \, \text{cm} \times 13.6 \, \text{g/cm}^3 \times 980 \, \text{cm/sec}^2}(-0.64) = -2.4 \, \text{cm}$$

SUPPLEMENTARY PROBLEMS

8. The surface tension of water at 60°F is 0.00504 lb/ft. Express this value in newtons/meter and in dynes/cm. *Ans.* 0.0735 nt/m, 73.5 dynes/cm

9. A horizontal loop of platinum wire of perimeter 16 cm is lowered into an alcohol sample. The added force (due to surface tension) required to pull the loop out of the liquid is 772 dynes. Find the surface tension of the alcohol. *Ans.* 24 dynes/cm

10. Determine the downward pull (due to surface tension) on a solid glass rod of diameter 1.2 in. when it stands vertically with its lower end submerged in water. Surface tension of water is 0.00504 lb/ft (at 60°F). *Ans.* 0.0016 lb

11. How much work must be done in blowing a spherical soap bubble 8 in. in diameter? The area of a sphere is $4\pi r^2$ and the surface tension of the soap solution is 0.0022 ft-lb/ft^2 or lb/ft. *Ans.* 0.00614 ft-lb

12. Water is converted into a mist consisting of droplets of diameter 12×10^{-5} in. at the rate of 0.1 ft^3/min. Find the power required to form the surfaces of the mist. Surface tension of water is 0.00504 lb/ft. The volume of a sphere of radius r is $(4/3)\pi r^3$. *Ans.* 302 ft-lb/min

13. What is the pressure due to surface tension in a spherical drop of glycerin of diameter 2.8 mm? Surface tension of glycerin is 0.063 nt/m. *Ans.* 90 nt/m^2

14. Calculate the pressure in a small spherical air bubble or cavity of 0.0004 in. radius located in a fresh water lake 15 ft below the surface. The atmospheric pressure is 14.7 lb/in^2 and the surface tension of water is 0.00514 lb/ft (at 40°F). *Ans.* 3360 lb/ft^2

15. How high does water rise in a capillary tube whose inside diameter is 0.008 inch? Surface tension of water is 0.00504 lb/ft. Assume the angle of contact is 0°. *Ans.* 5.8 in.

16. Calculate the surface tension of a liquid which rises 50 cm in a circular tube 0.04 mm in diameter. Density of liquid is 0.8 g/cm^3. Assume the angle of contact is 20°. *Ans.* 0.042 nt/m

Chapter 17

Expansion of Solids and Liquids

CONVERSION OF CENTIGRADE AND FAHRENHEIT. Between the freezing and boiling points of water there are 100 centigrade or 180 fahrenheit intervals. Hence

$$1 \text{ centigrade interval } = \frac{180}{100} = \frac{9}{5} \text{ fahrenheit intervals}$$

$$1 \text{ fahrenheit interval } = \frac{100}{180} = \frac{5}{9} \text{ centigrade interval}$$

But the freezing point of water (at 1 atmosphere pressure) is $0°$ on the centigrade scale and $32°$ on the fahrenheit scale, or $0°C = 32°F$. Then

$$\text{Temperature centigrade } = 5/9 \times (\text{temperature fahrenheit} - 32)$$
$$\text{Temperature fahrenheit } = 9/5 \times \text{temperature centigrade } + 32$$

LINEAR EXPANSION OF SOLIDS. When a substance is subjected to a rise in temperature, its increase in length ($\triangle l$) is very nearly proportional to its initial length and to the rise in temperature ($\triangle t$). If the initial and final lengths are respectively l_1 and l_2, and α is a proportionality constant, then

$$\text{Change in length, } \triangle l = l_2 - l_1 = \alpha l_1 \triangle t$$

$$\text{Final length, } l_2 = l_1 + \alpha l_1 \triangle t = l_1(1 + \alpha \triangle t)$$

where α, called the *coefficient of linear expansion*, depends on the nature of the substance.

From the above equation, $\alpha = \dfrac{\triangle l}{l_1 \triangle t}$. Thus α is the change in length per unit length per degree change in temperature. For example, if a 1.000000 cm length of brass becomes 1.000019 cm long when the temperature is raised $1°C$, the linear expansion coefficient of brass = $\dfrac{0.000019 \text{ cm}}{1.000000 \text{ cm} \times 1°C} = 19 \times 10^{-6} \text{ per } °C.$

VOLUME EXPANSION. If a volume V_1 expands to a volume V_2 when subjected to a rise in temperature $\triangle t$, then

$$\text{Change in volume, } \triangle V = V_2 - V_1 = \beta V_1 \triangle t$$

$$\text{Final volume, } V_2 = V_1 + \beta V_1 \triangle t = V_1(1 + \beta \triangle t)$$

where β = *coefficient of volume expansion* or *cubical expansion coefficient*.

For solids, $\beta = 3 \times$ coefficient of linear expansion = 3α, approximately.

SOLVED PROBLEMS

1. Ethyl alcohol boils at 78.5°C and freezes at −117°C at one atmosphere pressure. Convert these temperatures to the fahrenheit scale.
   Solution:

$$\text{Fahrenheit } = 9/5 \times \text{centigrade } + 32$$
$$\text{Boiling point, } °F = 9/5 \times 78.5 + 32 = 141 + 32 = 173°F$$
$$\text{Freezing point, } °F = 9/5 \times (-117) + 32 = -211 + 32 = -179°F$$

2. Mercury boils at $675°F$ and solidifies at $-38.0°F$ at one atmosphere pressure. Express these temperatures in centigrade units.

Solution:

$$\text{Centigrade} = 5/9 \times (\text{fahrenheit} - 32)$$
$$\text{Boiling point, }°C = 5/9 \times (675 - 32) = 5/9 \times 643 = 357°C$$
$$\text{Solidification point, }°C = 5/9 \times (-38.0 - 32) = 5/9 \times (-70.0) = -38.9°C$$

3. A copper bar is 8 ft long at $15°C$. What is the increase in length when heated to $35°C$? The linear coefficient of expansion of copper is 17×10^{-6} per $°C$.

Solution:

$$\Delta l = \alpha l_1 \Delta t = 17 \times 10^{-6}/°C \times 8\,\text{ft} \times (35 - 15)°C = 0.00272\,\text{ft} = 0.033\,\text{in}.$$

4. A steel plug has a diameter 10.000 cm at $30°C$. At what temperature will it fit exactly into a hole of constant diameter 9.997 cm? Linear expansion coefficient of steel is $11 \times 10^{-6}/°C$.

Solution:

$$\Delta l = l_2 - l_1 = \alpha l_1 \Delta t, \quad (9.997 - 10.000)\,\text{cm} = 11 \times 10^{-6}/°C \times 10.000\,\text{cm} \times \Delta t, \quad \Delta t = -27.3°C.$$
$$\text{Required temperature} = 30°C + (-27.3°C) = 2.7°C$$

5. A steel tape measures the length of a copper rod as 90.00 cm at $10°C$. What would be the reading at $30°C$? Linear expansion coefficients of copper and steel are respectively $\alpha_c = 17 \times 10^{-6}/°C$ and $\alpha_S = 11 \times 10^{-6}/°C$. Assume that the steel tape reads correctly at $10°C$.

Solution:

Apparent expansion of copper rod = expansion of rod − expansion of tape
$$= \alpha_c l_1 \Delta t - \alpha_S l_1 \Delta t = (\alpha_c - \alpha_S) l_1 \Delta t$$
$$= 6 \times 10^{-6}/°C \times 90.00\,\text{cm} \times 20°C = 0.01\,\text{cm}$$

Reading at $30°C$ = 90.00 cm + 0.01 cm = 90.01 cm

6. A glass bulb is filled with 50.00 cm^3 of mercury at $18°C$. What volume (measured at $38°C$) will flow out of the bulb if the temperature is raised to $38°C$? Linear expansion coefficient of the glass is $\alpha_g = 9 \times 10^{-6}/°C$. Volume expansion coefficient of mercury is $\beta_m = 18 \times 10^{-5}/°C$.

Solution:

Volume overflowing = absolute volume expansion of mercury − volume expansion of bulb
$$= \beta_m V_1 \Delta t - 3\alpha_g V_1 \Delta t = (\beta_m - 3\alpha_g) V_1 \Delta t$$
$$= (180 - 3 \times 9) \times 10^{-6}/°C \times 50.00\,\text{cm}^3 \times 20°C = 0.15\,\text{cm}^3$$

7. The density of mercury at $0°C$ is 13.60 g/cm^3, and the coefficient of cubical expansion is 0.000182 per $°C$. Calculate the density of mercury at $50°C$.

Solution:

Let ρ_1 = density of mercury at $0°C$, ρ_2 = density of mercury at $50°C$

V_1 = volume of a mass of mercury at $0°C$, V_2 = volume of same mass at $50°C$.

Since mass of mercury = volume × density = $V_1 \rho_1 = V_2 \rho_2$, we have

$$\rho_2 = \frac{V_1 \rho_1}{V_2} = \frac{V_1 \rho_1}{V_1(1 + \beta \Delta t)} = \frac{\rho_1}{1 + \beta \Delta t} = \frac{13.60\ \text{g/cm}^3}{1 + 0.000182/°C \times 50°C} = 13.48\ \text{g/cm}^3$$

8. The ends of a steel rod exactly 0.2 in^2 in cross section area are held rigidly between two fixed points at a temperature of $30°C$. Determine the pull in the rod when the temperature drops to $20°C$. Young's modulus Y for the steel is 33×10^6 lb/in^2. Coefficient of linear expansion of steel is $11 \times 10^{-6}/°C$.

Solution:

Consider that a rod of length l_1 is free to expand and that the temperature rises from $20°C$ to $30°C$. The elongation of the rod is $\Delta l = \alpha l_1 \Delta t = 11 \times 10^{-6}/^{\circ}C \times l_1 \times (30-20)^{\circ}C = 11 \times 10^{-5} l_1$. The pull F in the rod at $20^{\circ}C$ equals the force required to produce this elongation Δl at constant temperature.

$$Y = \frac{\text{longitudinal stress}}{\text{longitudinal strain}} = \frac{F/A}{\Delta l / l_1} = \frac{F l_1}{A \Delta l}$$

$$F = AY\frac{\Delta l}{l_1} = 0.2\,\text{in}^2 \times 33 \times 10^6\,\text{lb/in}^2 \times \frac{11 \times 10^{-5} l_1}{l_1} = 726\,\text{lb}$$

SUPPLEMENTARY PROBLEMS

9. (a) Reduce $68^{\circ}F$ to C, $5^{\circ}F$ to C, $176^{\circ}F$ to C.   *Ans.* $20^{\circ}C$, $-15^{\circ}C$, $80^{\circ}C$
    (b) Reduce $30^{\circ}C$ to F, $5^{\circ}C$ to F, $-20^{\circ}C$ to F.   *Ans.* $86^{\circ}F$, $41^{\circ}F$, $-4^{\circ}F$

10. Convert $-195.5^{\circ}C$ to F, $-430^{\circ}F$ to C, $1705^{\circ}C$ to F.   *Ans.* $-319.9^{\circ}F$, $-256.7^{\circ}C$, $3101^{\circ}F$

11. At what temperature have the centigrade and fahrenheit readings the same numerical value?   *Ans.* $-40^{\circ}C$

12. The temperature of dry ice (sublimation temperature at normal pressure) is $-109^{\circ}F$. Is this hotter or colder than the temperature of boiling ethane which is $-88^{\circ}C$?   *Ans.* hotter

13. Compute the increase in length of 500 ft of copper wire when its temperature changes from $12^{\circ}C$ to $32^{\circ}C$. The linear coefficient of expansion of copper is $17 \times 10^{-6}/^{\circ}C$.   *Ans.* 0.17 ft

14. A rod 3 ft long is found to have expanded 0.036 inch for a rise of $100^{\circ}F$. What is the coefficient of expansion?   *Ans.* 0.00001 per degree fahrenheit

15. At $15^{\circ}C$, a bare wheel has diameter 30.00 in. and the inside diameter of a steel rim is 29.96 in. To what temperature must the rim be heated so as to slip over the wheel? Coefficient of linear expansion of steel is $11 \times 10^{-6}/^{\circ}C$.   *Ans.* $136^{\circ}C$

16. An iron ball has diameter 6 cm and is 0.010 mm too large to pass through a hole in a brass plate when the ball and plate are at a temperature of $30^{\circ}C$. At what temperature, the same for both ball and plate, will the ball just pass through the hole? The linear coefficient of expansion of iron is $12 \times 10^{-6}/^{\circ}C$, and of brass is $19 \times 10^{-6}/^{\circ}C$.   *Ans.* $54^{\circ}C$

17. (a) An aluminum measuring rod, which is correct at $5^{\circ}C$, measures a certain distance as 88.42 cm at $35^{\circ}C$. Determine the error in measuring the distance due to the expansion of the rod. (b) If this aluminum rod measures a length of steel as 88.42 cm at $35^{\circ}C$, what is the correct length of the steel at $35^{\circ}C$? Coefficient of linear expansion of aluminum is $22 \times 10^{-6}/^{\circ}C$.   *Ans.* 0.06 cm, 88.48 cm

18. Calculate the increase in volume of 100 cm³ of mercury when its temperature changes from $10^{\circ}C$ to $35^{\circ}C$. The volume coefficient of expansion of mercury is $0.00018/^{\circ}C$.   *Ans.* 0.45 cm³

19. The coefficient of linear expansion of glass is $9 \times 10^{-6}/^{\circ}C$. If a specific gravity bottle holds 50.000 cm³ at $15^{\circ}C$, find its capacity at $25^{\circ}C$.   *Ans.* 50.014 cm³

20. Determine the change in volume of a block of cast iron $5 \times 10 \times 6$ in., when the temperature changes from $15^{\circ}C$ to $47^{\circ}C$. Coefficient of linear expansion of cast iron is $0.000010/^{\circ}C$.   *Ans.* 0.29 in³

21. A glass vessel is filled with exactly 1 liter of turpentine at $50^{\circ}F$. What volume of the liquid will overflow if the temperature is raised to $86^{\circ}F$. Linear coefficient of expansion of glass is $9 \times 10^{-6}/^{\circ}C$. Coefficient of cubical expansion of turpentine is $97 \times 10^{-5}/^{\circ}C$.   *Ans.* 19 cm³

22. The density of gold is 19.30 g/cm³ at $20^{\circ}C$, and the coefficient of linear expansion is $14.3 \times 10^{-6}/^{\circ}C$. Compute the density of gold at $90^{\circ}C$.   *Ans.* 19.24 g/cm³

Chapter 18

Expansion of Gases

GAS LAWS. Gases, on account of their greater compressibility and thermal expansivity as compared with liquids and solids, occupy volumes that depend very sensitively on the external variables, pressure and temperature. Special attention must therefore be given to factors influencing the volume of gases.

At sufficiently low pressures and high temperatures, all gases have been found to obey three simple laws. These laws relate the volume of a gas to the pressure and temperature. A gas which obeys these laws is called an **ideal gas** or **perfect gas**. These laws, which are therefore called the ideal gas laws, are described below. They may be applied only to gases which do not undergo a change in chemical complexity when the temperature or pressure is varied.

BOYLE'S LAW. When the temperature is kept constant, the volume of a given mass of an ideal gas varies inversely as the pressure to which it is subjected; therefore the product Pressure × Volume of a given mass of gas remains constant. Thus for a given mass of an ideal gas,

$$(1) \qquad\qquad pV = \text{constant} \qquad\qquad \text{at constant temperature}$$

CHARLES' LAW. The volume of a given mass of an ideal gas kept at constant pressure expands by $1/273$ of its volume at $0°C$ for each $1°C$ rise in temperature. Similarly, it contracts by $1/273$ of its volume at $0°C$ for each $1°C$ drop in temperature, at constant pressure. Thus,

$$(2) \qquad V_t = V_0(1 + \frac{1}{273}t) = \frac{V_0}{273}(273 + t) = k_1 T \qquad \text{at constant pressure}$$

where V_0 = volume at $0°C$, V_t = volume of same mass of gas at $t°C$, $V_0/273 = k_1$ = a constant, and $T = 273 + t$.

GAY-LUSSAC'S LAW. The pressure of a given mass of an ideal gas kept at constant volume increases by $1/273$ of its pressure at $0°C$ for each $1°C$ rise in temperature. Similarly, the pressure decreases by $1/273$ of its pressure at $0°C$ for each $1°C$ it is cooled, at constant volume. Thus,

$$(3) \qquad p_t = p_0(1 + \frac{1}{273}t) = \frac{p_0}{273}(273 + t) = k_2 T \qquad \text{at constant volume}$$

where p_0 = pressure at $0°C$, p_t = pressure of the same mass of gas at $t°C$, $p_0/273 = k_2$ = a constant, and $T = 273 + t$.

KELVIN OR ABSOLUTE THERMODYNAMIC SCALE. Equations (2) and (3) above suggest a new temperature scale in which the value of the degree is the same as the centigrade degree but whose zero point is $-273°C$. This scale is called the **kelvin** ($°K$) or absolute thermodynamic scale.

Kelvin temperature = 273 + centigrade temperature

Thus $0°C = 273°K$, $20°C = 293°K$, $-30°C = 243°K$, $0°K = -273°C$, $300°K = 27°C$.

Now equation (2) indicates that the volume of a gas at constant pressure is proportional to its absolute temperature T, and equation (3) indicates that the pressure of a gas at constant volume is proportional to its absolute temperature T.

114

The temperature −273°C (at which molecules of an ideal gas would cease to move, according to the kinetic theory) is called the **absolute zero of temperature**. In practice all gases, on cooling, liquefy or solidify before −273°C is reached. Absolute zero is defined in terms of the hypothetical gas that would follow the same laws at low temperatures that ideal gases obey at higher temperatures. (Although the exact value for the absolute zero is accepted as − 273.16°C, −273°C is sufficiently accurate for the problems in this book.)

RANKINE OR FAHRENHEIT ABSOLUTE SCALE. In the **rankine** (°R) scale the value of the degree is the same as the fahrenheit degree but the zero point corresponds to 0°K or −273.16°C.

Since $-273.16°C = \frac{9}{5}(-273.16) + 32 = -460°F$, $0°R = -460°F$.

Rankine temperature $=$ 460 + fahrenheit temperature

Thus $0°F = 460°R$, $40°F = 500°R$, $-40°F = 420°R$.

GENERAL GAS LAW for a given mass of gas. Any two of the three gas laws may be combined to obtain

(4) $$\frac{pV}{T} = \text{constant} \qquad \text{for a given mass of gas}$$

This expression indicates that the (pV) energy term increases directly with the absolute temperature T.

It follows that if a given mass of gas is considered under two different conditions of temperature and pressure, we may write

(5) $$\frac{p_1 V_1}{T_1} = \frac{p_2 V_2}{T_2} \qquad \text{for a given mass of gas}$$

Since for a given mass of gas the density ρ varies inversely as the volume, equation (5) may be written

(6) $$\frac{p_1}{\rho_1 T_1} = \frac{p_2}{\rho_2 T_2} \qquad \text{for a given mass of gas}$$

STANDARD PRESSURE is the pressure exerted by a column of mercury exactly 76 cm high at 0°C under standard gravity. This is approximately the average pressure of the atmosphere at sea level and is called **one atmosphere** (1 atm).

1 atmosphere (atm) $=$ 1.013 × 10^5 nt/m^2 $=$ 14.7 lb/in^2

STANDARD CONDITIONS (S.T.P.) denotes a temperature of 0°C (273°K) and a pressure of 1 atmosphere. As both the volume and density of any gas are affected by changes of temperature and pressure, it is customary to reduce all gas volumes to standard conditions for purposes of comparison.

A MOLE (or a gram-mole, or a gram-molecular weight) is the molecular weight of a substance expressed in grams. Thus 1 mole of oxygen is 32 grams of oxygen, since 32 is the molecular weight of oxygen; 4 g of oxygen = 1/8 mole of oxygen.

One mole of any (ideal) **gas** occupies approximately 22.4 liters (22.4 × 10^3 cm^3) at standard conditions (273°K and 1 atm). For example, 32 g (1 mole) of oxygen occupies 22.4 liters at 273°K and 1 atm.

THE UNIVERSAL GAS CONSTANT, or molar gas constant. The general gas law may also be written for one mole of gas

$$pV = RT$$

where R, called the universal gas constant, is the same constant for all gases provided a mole is used. If n moles of gas are considered, then

(7) $$pV = nRT$$

To evaluate R, consider the following:

(a) One mole of a gas occupies 22.4 liters at 1 atm and 273°K.

$$R = \frac{pV}{nT} = \frac{1 \text{ atm} \times 22.4 \, l}{1 \text{ mole} \times 273°K} = 0.0821 \frac{l \text{ atm}}{°K \text{ mole}} = 0.0821 \, l \text{ atm } °K^{-1} \text{ mole}^{-1}$$

(b) Since   1 atm = 1.013×10^5 nt/m², 22.4 l = 0.0224 m³, and 1 m-nt = 1 joule,

$$R = \frac{pV}{nT} = \frac{1.013 \times 10^5 \text{ nt/m}^2 \times 0.0224 \text{ m}^3}{1 \text{ mole} \times 273°K} = 8.31 \frac{\text{joules}}{°K \text{ mole}}$$

DALTON'S LAW OF PARTIAL PRESSURES. The total pressure of a gaseous mixture is equal to the sum of the partial pressures of the components. The partial pressure of a component of a gas mixture is the pressure which the component would exert if it alone occupied the entire volume.

Dalton's law is rigidly accurate only for ideal gases. At pressures of only a few atmospheres or below, gas mixtures may be regarded as ideal gases and this law may be applied in calculations.

KINETIC THEORY OF GASES.

Matter is composed of discrete particles or molecules in continual motion.

The pressure exerted by a gas is due to the bombardment of molecules on the sides of the containing vessel. This pressure is given by

(8) $$p = (1/3)Nm_1v^2 = (1/3)\rho v^2$$

where N = number of molecules per unit volume, m_1 = mass of each molecule
v^2 = average value of the squares of the velocities of the molecules
ρ = density of the gas.

Substituting this value of p in the general gas law $pV = nRT$, and remembering that $\rho V = m$, the mass of gas in the volume V, we get

(9) $$(1/3)mv^2 = nRT$$ or $$(1/2)mv^2 = (3/2)nRT$$

Since v and T are the only variables here, and $(1/2)mv^2$ is the average molecular kinetic energy, we have the important fact that the average molecular kinetic energy varies as the absolute temperature. A change of one centigrade degree in the temperature of any gas of constant mass means that the molecular kinetic energy of that gas changes by 1/273 of its 0°C value.

ROOT-MEAN-SQUARE velocity in a gas is the square root of the average of the squares of the velocities of the molecules. This quantity is found from $p = (1/3)\rho v^2$.

AVOGADRO'S HYPOTHESIS states that equal volumes of all gases under the same conditions of temperature and pressure contain the same number of molecules. This follows from the equation $p = (1/3)Nm_1v^2$, since at the same conditions of temperature and pressure p and m_1v^2 remain fixed; hence N, the number of molecules per unit volume, is the same.

Avogadro's number, 6.02×10^{23}, is the number of molecules in a mole of any substance. The substance may be in the solid, liquid, or gaseous state.

SOLVED PROBLEMS

1. Change (a) $40°C$ and $-5°C$ to the kelvin scale, (b) $220°K$ and $498°K$ to the centigrade scale.

Solution:

(a)

$$\text{Kelvin temperature} = \text{centigrade temperature} + 273$$
$$40°C = x°K = 40 + 273 = 313°K$$
$$-5°C = x°K = -5 + 273 = 268°K$$

(b)

$$\text{Centigrade temperature} = \text{kelvin temperature} - 273$$
$$220°K = x°C = 220 - 273 = -53°C$$
$$498°K = x°C = 498 - 273 = 225°C$$

2. Convert $212°F$ and $-70°F$ to the rankine scale.

Solution:

$$\text{Rankine temperature} = \text{fahrenheit temperature} + 460$$
$$212°F = x°R = 212 + 460 = 672°R$$
$$-70°F = x°R = -70 + 460 = 390°R$$

3. Express $-22°F$ in degrees centigrade and in degrees kelvin.

Solution:

$$\text{Centigrade} = 5/9 \times (°F - 32) = 5/9 \times (-22 - 32) = 5/9 \times (-54) = -30°C$$
$$\text{Kelvin} = 273 + \text{centigrade} = 273 - 30 = 243°K$$

4. A mass of oxygen occupies 20 ft³ at $5°C$ and 760 mm pressure. Determine its volume at $30°C$ and 800 mm pressure.

Solution:

Since the mass of gas is constant, we use the formula

$$\frac{p_1V_1}{T_1} = \frac{p_2V_2}{T_2}. \qquad \frac{760 \text{ mm} \times 20 \text{ ft}^3}{(5+273)°K} = \frac{800 \text{ mm} \times V_2}{(30+273)°K}, \qquad V_2 = 20.7 \text{ ft}^3$$

5. To how many atmospheres pressure must a liter of gas measured at 1 atm and $-20°C$ be subjected to be compressed to $\frac{1}{2}$ liter when the temperature is $40°C$?

Solution:

$$\frac{p_1V_1}{T_1} = \frac{p_2V_2}{T_2}, \qquad \frac{1 \text{ atm} \times 1 \text{ liter}}{(-20+273)°K} = \frac{p_2 \times \frac{1}{2} \text{ liter}}{(40+273)°K}, \qquad p_2 = 2.47 \text{ atm}$$

6. A mass of hydrogen occupies $874 \, ft^3$ at $59°F$ and $19.8 \, lb/in^2$. Find its volume at $-26°F$ and 53.6 lb/in^2.

Solution:

Rankine temperature $(°R)$ = 460 + fahrenheit temperature

$$\frac{p_1 V_1}{T_1} = \frac{p_2 V_2}{T_2}, \qquad \frac{19.8 \, lb\text{-}in^2 \times 874 \, ft^3}{(59+460)°R} = \frac{53.6 \, lb/in^2 \times V_2}{(-26+460)°R}, \qquad V_2 = 270 \, ft^3$$

7. A steel tank contains carbon dioxide at $32°F$ and a pressure of 12 atmospheres. Determine the internal gas pressure when the tank is heated to $212°F$.

Solution:

Since $V_1 = V_2$, the formula $p_1 V_1/T_1 = p_2 V_2/T_2$ becomes

$$\frac{p_1}{T_1} = \frac{p_2}{T_2}, \qquad \frac{12 \, atm}{(32+460)°R} = \frac{p_2}{(212+460)°R}, \qquad p_2 = 16.4 \, atm$$

8. The density of nitrogen is 1.25 grams per liter at S.T.P. (standard temperature and pressure, $0°C$ and $760 \, mm$ of mercury). Determine the density of nitrogen at $42°C$ and $730 \, mm$ (of mercury).

Solution:

$$\frac{p_1}{\rho_1 T_1} = \frac{p_2}{\rho_2 T_2}, \qquad \frac{760 \, mm}{1.25 \, g/l \times 273°K} = \frac{730 \, mm}{\rho_2 \times (42+273)°K}, \qquad \rho_2 = 1.04 \, g/l$$

9. Determine the volume occupied by $4.0 \, g$ of oxygen at S.T.P. ($0°C$ and $1 \, atm$). The molecular weight of oxygen is 32.

Solution:

Volume of $4.0 \, g \, O_2$ at S.T.P. = number of moles in $4.0 \, g \, O_2 \times$ volume of 1 mole at S.T.P.

$$= \frac{4.0 \, g}{32 \, g/mole} \times 22.4 \, l/mole = 2.8 \, l \, O_2 \text{ at S.T.P.}$$

10. A tank of volume 590 liters contains oxygen at S.T.P. ($0°C$ and $1 \, atm$). Calculate the mass of oxygen in the tank. Molecular weight of oxygen is 32.

Solution:

Mass of $590 \, l \, O_2$ at S.T.P. = number of moles in $590 \, l$ at S.T.P. $\times$ mass of 1 mole

$$= \frac{590 \, l}{22.4 \, l/mole} \times 32 \, g/mole = 843 \, g$$

11. Use the ideal gas equation $pV = nRT$, $R = 0.0821 \, \dfrac{liter \, atm}{°K \, mole}$ to solve each of the following.

(*a*) At $18°C$ and $765 \, mm$ of mercury, 1.29 liters of an ideal gas weighs $2.71 \, g$. Compute the molecular weight of the gas.

(*b*) Compute the volume occupied by $8.00 \, g$ of oxygen at $15°C$ and $750 \, mm$ of mercury. The molecular weight of oxygen is 32.0.

(*c*) Find the density of methane at $20°C$ and $5 \, atm$. Molecular weight of methane is 16.0.

Solution:

(*a*) n (number of moles) = $\dfrac{\text{mass of gas in grams}}{\text{molecular weight of gas}} = \dfrac{m}{M}$. Then from $pV = nRT = \dfrac{m}{M} RT$,

$$M = \frac{mRT}{pV} = \frac{2.71 \, g \times 0.0821 \, l \, atm \, °K^{-1} \, mole^{-1} \times 291°K}{765/760 \, atm \times 1.29 \, l} = 49.8 \, g/mole$$

(*b*) $$V = \frac{mRT}{Mp} = \frac{8 \, g \times 0.0821 \, l \, atm \, °K^{-1} \, mole^{-1} \times 288°K}{32 \, g/mole \times 750/760 \, atm} = 5.99 \, l$$

(*c*) Density ρ in grams/liter = $\dfrac{\text{mass in grams}}{\text{volume in liters}} = \dfrac{m}{V}$. Then from $pV = \dfrac{m}{M} RT$,

$$\rho = \frac{m}{V} = \frac{Mp}{RT} = \frac{16 \, g/mole \times 5 \, atm}{0.0821 \, l \, atm \, °K^{-1} \, mole^{-1} \times 293°K} = 3.33 \, g/l$$

Another Method

Density at standard conditions is $\rho_1 = \dfrac{16.0 \text{ g/mole}}{22.4 \; l/\text{mole}} = \dfrac{16.0}{22.4} \text{ g}/l$.

Now the required density ρ_2 is found by using the formula

$$\frac{p_1}{\rho_1 T_1} = \frac{p_2}{\rho_2 T_2} , \qquad \frac{1 \text{ atm}}{16.0/22.4 \text{ g}/l \;\times\; 273^{\circ}\text{K}} = \frac{5 \text{ atm}}{\rho_2 \;\times\; 293^{\circ}\text{K}} , \qquad \rho_2 = 3.33 \text{ g}/l$$

12. How many molecules are in one milligram of benzene? Molecular weight of benzene is 78.

Solution:

Number of molecules $=$ number of moles in 1 mg $\times$ number of molecules in 1 mole

$\qquad\qquad\qquad\quad = \dfrac{0.001 \text{ g}}{78 \text{ g/mole}} \times 6.02 \times 10^{23} \text{ molecules/mole} = 7.7 \times 10^{18} \text{ molecules}$

13. Mercury diffusion pumps are used in the laboratory to produce a high vacuum. Cold traps are generally placed between the pump and the system to be evacuated. These cause the condensation of mercury vapor and prevent mercury from diffusing back into the system. The maximum pressure of mercury that can exist in the system is the vapor pressure of mercury at the temperature of the cold trap. Calculate the number of mercury vapor molecules per cm^3 in a cold trap maintained at -120°C. The vapor pressure of mercury at this temperature is 10^{-16} mm.

Solution:

Moles in 1 cm^3 $= n = \dfrac{PV}{RT} = \dfrac{\dfrac{10^{-16}}{760} \text{ atm} \times 10^{-3} \, l}{0.0821 \; l \text{ atm} \; ^{\circ}\text{K}^{-1} \text{ mole}^{-1} \times 153^{\circ}\text{K}} = 1 \times 10^{-23} \text{ mole}$

Molecules in 1 cm^3 $= 1 \times 10^{-23} \text{ mole} \times 6 \times 10^{23} \text{ molecules/mole} = 6 \text{ molecules}$

14. In a gaseous mixture at 20°C the partial pressures of the components are as follows: hydrogen 200 mm of mercury, carbon dioxide 150 mm, methane 320 mm, ethylene 105 mm. What is the total pressure of the mixture and the volume percent of hydrogen?

Solution:

Total pressure $=$ sum of partial pressures $= (200 + 150 + 320 + 105) \text{ mm} = 775 \text{ mm}$

Volume fraction of hydrogen $= \dfrac{\text{partial pressure of } H_2}{\text{total pressure of mixture}} = \dfrac{200 \text{ mm}}{775 \text{ mm}} = 0.258 = 25.8\%$

15. In a basal metabolism measurement timed at exactly 6 minutes, a patient exhaled 52.5 liters of air, measured over water at 20°C. The vapor pressure of water at 20°C is 17.5 mm of mercury. The barometric pressure was 750 mm. The exhaled air analyzed 16.75 volume % oxygen. The inhaled air contained 20.32 volume % oxygen. Neglecting any solubility of the gases in water and any difference in the total volume of inhaled and exhaled air, calculate the rate of oxygen consumption by the patient in cm^3 (at 0°C and 760 mm of mercury) per minute.

Solution:

The 52.5 l contains water vapor at a partial pressure of 17.5 mm. The volume V_2 of the exhaled air at 0°C and 760 mm is

$$\frac{p_1 V_1}{T_1} = \frac{p_2 V_2}{T_2} , \qquad \frac{(750 - 17.5) \text{ mm} \times 52.5 \, l}{(20 + 273)^{\circ}\text{K}} = \frac{760 \text{ mm} \times V_2}{273^{\circ}\text{K}} , \qquad V_2 = 47.1 \, l$$

Rate of oxygen consumption $= \dfrac{\text{volume of oxygen } (0^{\circ}\text{C}, 760 \text{ mm}) \text{ consumed}}{\text{time in which this volume was consumed}}$

$\qquad\qquad\qquad\qquad\qquad = \dfrac{(0.2032 - 0.1675) \times 47.1 \, l}{6 \text{ min}} = 0.280 \, l/\text{min} = 280 \text{ cm}^3/\text{min}$

16. What is the kinetic energy of translation of the molecules in 10 grams of ammonia gas at $20°C$? Molecular weight of ammonia is 17.03 grams/mole.

Solution:

$$\text{K.E.} = \frac{1}{2}mv^2 = \frac{3}{2}nRT = \frac{3}{2} \times \frac{10\text{ g}}{17.03\text{ g/mole}} \times 8.31\frac{\text{joules}}{\text{mole}°K} \times 293°K = 2140\text{ joules}$$

17. Calculate the root-mean-square velocity v of a molecule of hydrogen at $20°C$ and 70 cm of mercury pressure. Molecular weight of hydrogen = 2.016 g/mole; 1 atm = 1.013×10^5 nt/m^2.

Solution:

At $0°C$ and 1 atm, 1 mole of hydrogen (0.002016 kg) occupies 22.4 liters (22.4×10^3 cm^3 = 0.0224 m^3) and the density of hydrogen is $\rho_O = 20.16/224$ kg/m^3.

$$\rho = \rho_O \times \frac{T_O}{T} \times \frac{p}{p_O}, \text{ where the subscript } _O \text{ refers to standard conditions } (0°C, 1\text{ atm}).$$

$$v = \sqrt{\frac{3p}{\rho}} = \sqrt{\frac{3p}{\rho_O \times T_O/T \times p/p_O}} = \sqrt{\frac{3p_O}{\rho_O} \times \frac{T}{T_O}} = \sqrt{\frac{3(1.013 \times 10^5\text{ nt/m}^2)}{20.16/224\text{ kg/m}^3} \times \frac{293°K}{273°K}}$$

$$= 1900\text{ m/sec}$$

Notice that changing the pressure does not change the velocity.

SUPPLEMENTARY PROBLEMS

18. (a) Convert $300°K$, $760°K$, $180°K$, to degrees centigrade.   *Ans.* $27°C$, $487°C$, $-93°C$
    (b) Express $0°K$, $273°K$, in degrees fahrenheit.   *Ans.* $-459°F$, $32°F$
    (c) Convert $14°F$ to degrees centigrade and degrees kelvin.   *Ans.* $-10°C$, $263°K$
    (d) Convert $50°F$ and $-200°F$ to degrees rankine.   *Ans.* $510°R$, $260°R$

19. A mass of ammonia gas occupies 40 cubic feet at 758 mm of mercury. Compute its volume at 635 mm of mercury, temperature remaining constant.   *Ans.* 47.8 ft^3

20. A given mass of chlorine occupies 38 cm^3 at $20°C$. Determine its volume at $45°C$, pressure remaining constant.   *Ans.* 41.2 cm^3

21. A quantity of hydrogen is confined in a platinum chamber of constant volume. When the chamber is immersed in a bath of melting ice, the absolute pressure of the gas is 1000 mm of mercury. (a) What is the centigrade temperature when the pressure manometer reads exactly 100 mm of mercury? (b) What pressure will be indicated when the chamber is brought to $100°C$?   *Ans.* $-246°C$, 1366 mm

22. Given 1000 ft^3 of helium at $15°C$ and 763 mm. Determine the volume at $-6°C$ and 420 mm.   *Ans.* 1680 ft^3

23. If a mass of gas occupies 15.7 ft^3 at $60°F$ and 14.7 lb/in^2, determine its volume at $100°F$ and 25 lb/in^2. *Ans.* 9.94 ft^3

24. Calculate the final centigrade temperature required to change 10 liters of helium at $100°K$ and 0.1 atmosphere to 20 liters at 0.2 atmosphere.   *Ans.* $127°C$

25. One mole of a gas occupies 22.4 liters at $0°C$ and 1 atm. (a) What pressure would be required to compress 1 mole of oxygen into a 5-liter container held at $100°C$? (b) What maximum centigrade temperature would be permitted to hold this mass of oxygen in 5 liters if the pressure is not to exceed 3 atmospheres? (c) What capacity would be required to hold the same mass if the conditions of $100°C$ and 3 atm were fixed? *Ans.* 6.12 atm, $-90°C$, 10.2 liters

26. A quantity of gas is contained in the closed limb of a U-tube. The volume of gas at 30°C is 50 cm^3 and the level of mercury in the closed limb is 10 cm below the level in the open limb. The barometer reads 75 cm. Compute the volume of the gas at standard conditions, 0°C and 760 mm of mercury.   *Ans.* 50.4 cm^3

27. A quantity of gas is collected in a graduated tube over mercury. The volume of gas at 20°C is 50 cm^3, and the level of mercury in the tube is 20 cm above the outside mercury level. The barometer reads 75 cm. Determine the volume of the gas at 0°C and 76 cm pressure.   *Ans.* 33.7 cm^3

28. At 0°C and 760 mm of mercury, 28.0 g of nitrogen occupy 22.4 liters. Compute the mass of 10 liters of nitrogen at 25°C and 810 mm.   *Ans.* 12.2 g

29. A certain container holds 2.55 g of neon at 0°C and 1 atmosphere. What mass of neon will it hold at 100°C and 10 atmospheres?   *Ans.* 18.7 g

30. The density of oxygen is 1.43 g/liter at 0°C and 1 atmosphere. Compute the density of oxygen at 17°C and 700 mm of mercury.   *Ans.* 1.24 g/liter

31. At the top of a mountain the thermometer reads 10°C and the barometer reads 70 cm of mercury. At the bottom of the mountain the temperature is 30°C and the pressure is 76 cm of mercury. Compare the density of the air at the top with that at the bottom.   *Ans.* 0.99 (top) to 1.00 (bottom)

32. A tank of volume 5000 cm^3 contains oxygen at standard conditions (0°C, 1 atm). How many grams of oxygen must be pumped into the tank to raise the pressure to 40 atm, there being no change of temperature? Molecular weight of oxygen is 32.   *Ans.* 279 g

33. An automobile tire, assumed to be of constant volume 5 liters, is pumped up from a gauge pressure of 0 to a gauge pressure of 32 lb/in^2, both pressures being measured above atmospheric pressure which is 15 lb/in^2. If the temperature remains constant at 35°C, what mass of air must flow into the tire? Assume the mean molecular weight of air to be 29.   *Ans.* 12.2 g

34. What mass of hydrogen at standard conditions could be contained in a vessel that holds 4.0 g of oxygen at standard conditions? Molecular weight of hydrogen is 2.0, of oxygen is 32.   *Ans.* 0.25 g

35. What volume will 1.216 g of SO$_2$ gas occupy at 18°C and 755 mm? Molecular weight of SO$_2$ is 64.07.   *Ans.* 456 cm^3

36. Compute the density of H$_2$S gas at 27°C and 2.00 atm. Molecular weight of H$_2$S is 34.08.   *Ans.* 2.77 g/l

37. One of the methods for estimating the temperature of the center of the sun is based on the ideal gas law. If the center is assumed to consist of gases whose average molecular weight is 0.7, and if the density and pressure are 90 g/cm^3 and 1.4×10^{11} atm respectively, calculate the temperature.   *Ans.* 1.3×10^7 $^\circ$K

38. A certain strain of tobacco mosaic virus has a molecular weight of 40×10^6. How many molecules of the virus are present in 1 cm^3 of a solution that contains 0.10 mg of virus per cm^3?   *Ans.* 1.5×10^{12} molecules/cm^3

39. An electronic vacuum tube was sealed off during manufacture at a pressure of 1.2×10^{-5} mm at 27°C. Its volume is 100 cm^3. Compute the number of gas molecules remaining in the tube.   *Ans.* 4×10^{13} molecules

40. A mixture of gases at 760 mm pressure contains 65.0 % nitrogen, 15.0 % oxygen, and 20.0 % carbon dioxide by volume. What is the partial pressure of each gas in mm?   *Ans.* N$_2$, 494 mm

41. Exactly 500 cm^3 of nitrogen is collected over water at 25°C and 755 mm. The gas is saturated with water vapor. Compute the volume of the nitrogen in the dry condition at S.T.P. (0°C, 1 atm). Vapor pressure of water at 25°C is 23.8 mm.   *Ans.* 441 cm^3

42. A 250 cm^3 flask contained krypton at 500 mm. A 450 cm^3 flask contained helium at 950 mm. The contents of the two flasks were mixed by opening a stopcock connecting them. Assuming that all operations were carried out at a uniform constant temperature, calculate the final total pressure and the volume percent of each gas in the resulting mixture. Neglect the volume of the stopcock.   *Ans.* 789 mm, 22.6% Kr

43. The respiration of a suspension of yeast cells was measured by observing the decrease of pressure of the gas above the cell suspension. The apparatus was arranged so that the gas was confined to a constant volume, 16.0 cm^3, and the entire pressure change was caused by the uptake of oxygen by the cells. The pressure was measured in a manometer the fluid of which had a density of 1.034 g/cm^3. The entire apparatus was immersed in a thermostat at 37°C. In a 30-minute observation period the fluid in the open side of the manometer dropped 37 mm. Neglecting the solubility of oxygen in the yeast suspension, compute the rate of oxygen consumption by the cells in cubic millimeters of O$_2$ (at 0°C and 760 mm of mercury) per hour.
Ans. 104 mm^3/hr

44. A mercury barometer has acquired some air in the Torricellian vacuum above the mercury. If the barometer reads 700 mm on a day when true barometric pressure is 760 mm, what will it read on a day when barometric pressure is 750 mm? The vertical distance from the bottom mercury level to the inside top surface of the tube is 78 cm. Temperature is assumed constant, and the tube is of uniform bore.   *Ans.* 694 mm

45. A cylindrical diving bell 12 ft high is lowered until water within the bell rises 8 ft. Determine the distance from the top of the bell to the surface of the water.   *Ans.* 64 ft

46. A smooth horizontal cylinder has a uniform cross section area of 4 cm^2 and a length of 200 cm. It contains 5 grams of oxygen (molecular weight 32) at 20°C. The piston of mass 3 kg is held in place by a spring whose compressed length is 12 cm and whose original uncompressed length is 15 cm. (*a*) Find the tension in the spring. (*b*) If the piston be given a slight displacement and released, what will be the period of its oscillation? Consider that the pressure of the gas remains sensibly constant and the inertia of the gas is negligible.   *Ans.* 190 nt, 0.14 sec

47. Compute the mass and the translational kinetic energy of the helium contained at 1 atm and 30°C in a blimp of volume 100,000 liters. Molecular weight of helium is 4.003 g/mole.   *Ans.* 16.1 kg, 1.52×10^7 joules

48. Compute the root-mean-square velocity of the molecules of methane vapor in the atmosphere of Jupiter, which is at −130°C. Molecular weight of methane is 16.04 g/mole.   *Ans.* 471 m/sec

Chapter 19

Calorimetry, Fusion, Vaporization

HEAT is a form of energy. The three units most commonly used in measuring the quantity of heat are defined as follows:

1 calorie (cal) = quantity of heat required to raise the temperature of 1 gram of water through 1 centigrade degree.

Note: Since the calorie was originally defined as stated above, it has been recognized that the energy requirement for raising the temperature of 1 gram of water by 1 degree depends slightly on the temperature, with a variation of about half a percent over the interval from $0°$ to $100°C$. For work requiring an accuracy no greater than one percent, the above definition is satisfactory. For the most precise work, it has been agreed to define the calorie in terms of electrical units of energy, so that 1 calorie = 4.1840 joules. This is very close to the amount of energy required to raise the temperature of 1 gram of water from $16.5°$ to $17.5°C$.

1 kilocalorie or **kilogram-calorie** (kcal or kg-cal) = 1000 calories.

1 British thermal unit (Btu) = quantity of heat required to raise the temperature of 1 pound of water through 1 fahrenheit degree. 1 Btu = $453.6 \times 5/9$ cal = 252 cal.

SPECIFIC HEAT of a substance (is numerically equal to the number of)
$\qquad$ = calories required to raise temperature of 1 gram of substance $1°C$.
$\qquad$ = Btu required to raise temperature of 1 pound of substance $1°F$.

Specific heat is expressed in calories per gram per degree centigrade ($cal/g°C$), and in Btu per pound per degree fahrenheit ($Btu/lb°F$).

From the definitions of the calorie and the Btu, it follows that the specific heat of water is numerically equal to 1 in any system of units (1 $cal/g°C$ or 1 $Btu/lb°F$), neglecting the variations with temperature. Also, the specific heat of any substance is numerically the same in any system of units. Thus the specific heat of pyrex glass is 0.20 $cal/g°C$ or 0.20 $Btu/lb°F$.

HEAT CAPACITY or water equivalent of a body is the quantity of heat required to raise the temperature of the body by one degree. It is measured in calories per degree centigrade ($cal/°C$), and in Btu per degree fahrenheit ($Btu/°F$).

$$\text{Heat capacity of a body } = \text{ mass of body} \times \text{specific heat}$$

HEAT GAINED OR LOST by a body in which there is no change of state
$$= \text{mass} \times \text{specific heat} \times \text{temperature change}$$

Heat (in calories) $=$ mass (grams) $\times$ sp ht ($cal/g°C$) $\times$ temp. change ($°C$)

Heat (in Btu) $=$ mass (pounds) $\times$ sp ht ($Btu/lb°F$) $\times$ temp. change ($°F$)

HEAT OF FUSION of a solid is the amount of heat required to melt 1 unit mass of the solid without changing its temperature.

Heat of fusion of ice = 80 cal per gram, (at 0°C and 1 atmosphere)

= 144 Btu per pound, (at 32°F and 1 atmosphere)

HEAT OF VAPORIZATION of a liquid is the amount of heat required to vaporize 1 unit mass of the liquid without changing its temperature.

Heat of vaporization of water = 540 cal per gram, (at 100°C and 1 atm)

= 972 Btu per pound, (at 212°F and 1 atm)

HEAT OF SUBLIMATION of a substance is the amount of heat required to convert 1 unit mass of it from the solid to the gaseous state at a given temperature.

ABSOLUTE HUMIDITY is the mass of water vapor present per unit volume of the atmosphere. It is usually expressed in g/m^3, in $grains/ft^3$, or in lb/ft^3.

RELATIVE HUMIDITY $= \dfrac{\text{mass of water vapor per unit volume present in the air}}{\text{mass of vapor per unit volume in saturated air at same temperature}}$

$= \dfrac{\text{pressure of water vapor in the air}}{\text{pressure of water vapor in saturated air at same temperature}}$

(since the pressure exerted by the water vapor is approximately proportional to the mass of water vapor per unit volume).

Dew point is the temperature at which the atmosphere would be saturated with the contained water vapor.

SOLVED PROBLEMS

1. (a) How many calories are required to heat 100 grams of copper from 10°C to 100°C? (b) The same quantity of heat is added to 100 grams of aluminum at 10°C. Which gets hotter, the copper or the aluminum? Specific heat of Cu = 0.093, of Al = 0.217.

Solution:

(a) Heat required = mass × specific heat × temperature change

= 100 g × 0.093 cal/g°C × (100 − 10)°C = 840 cal

(b) Since the specific heat of copper is less than that of aluminum, less heat is required to raise the temperature of a mass of copper by 1° than is required for an equal mass of aluminum. Hence the copper becomes hotter.

2. A steam boiler is made of steel and weighs 900 lb. The boiler contains 400 lb of water. Assuming that 70% of the heat is delivered to boiler and water, how many Btu are required to raise the temperature of the whole from 42°F to 212°F? Specific heat of steel is 0.11.

Solution:

Heat needed = mass × specific heat × temperature change

Heat needed for boiler = 900 lb × 0.11 Btu/lb°F × (212 − 42)°F = 1.7×10^4 Btu

Heat needed for water = 400 lb × 1 Btu/lb°F × (212 − 42)°F = 6.8×10^4 Btu

Total Btu required = $\dfrac{(1.7 + 6.8) \times 10^4 \text{ Btu}}{0.70}$ = 1.21×10^5 Btu

3. Exactly 3 g of carbon was burned to CO_2 in a copper calorimeter. The mass of the calorimeter is 1500 g, and the mass of water in the calorimeter is 2000 g. The initial temperature was 20°C and the final temperature 31°C. Calculate the heat value of carbon in calories per gram. Specific heat of copper is 0.093.

Solution:

$$\text{Heat gained} = \text{mass} \times \text{specific heat} \times \text{temperature change}$$

$$\text{Heat gained by calorimeter} = 1500\,g \times 0.093\,cal/g°C \times (31-20)°C = 1530\,cal$$

$$\text{Heat gained by water} = 2000\,g \times 1\,cal/g°C \times (31-20)°C = 22{,}000\,cal$$

$$\text{Heat value of carbon} = \frac{1530\,cal + 22{,}000\,cal}{3\,g} = 7.8 \times 10^3\,cal/g$$

4. Determine the resulting temperature, t, when 150 g of ice at 0°C are mixed with 300 g of water at 50°C.

Solution:

$$\text{Heat to melt ice} = \text{mass} \times \text{heat of fusion} = 150\,g \times 80\,cal/g = 1.20 \times 10^4\,cal$$

Heat to raise temperature of 150 g of water at 0°C to final temperature
$$= \text{mass} \times \text{specific heat} \times \text{temperature change} = 150 \times 1 \times (t-0)\,cal$$

Heat lost by 300 g water $= \text{mass} \times \text{sp ht} \times \text{temp. change} = 300 \times 1 \times (50-t)\,cal$

$$\text{Heat lost} = \text{heat gained}$$
$$300(50-t) = 1.20 \times 10^4 + 150t \qquad \text{from which} \quad t = 6.7°C$$

5. How much heat is given up when 20 g of steam at 100°C is condensed and cooled to 20°C?

Solution:

Heat given up in condensing 20 g of steam at 100°C to water at 100°C
$$= \text{mass} \times \text{heat of vaporization} = 20\,g \times 540\,cal/g = 1.08 \times 10^4\,cal$$

Heat given up in cooling 20 g of water at 100°C to 20°C
$$= \text{mass} \times \text{sp ht} \times \text{temperature change} = 20 \times 1 \times (100-20) = 0.16 \times 10^4\,cal$$

Total heat given up $= (1.08 + 0.16) \times 10^4\,cal = 1.24 \times 10^4\,cal$

6. (a) Convert the heat of fusion of ice, 80 cal/g, to its equivalent in Btu/lb. (b) How many Btu are absorbed by an electric refrigerator in changing 5.0 lb water at 60°F to ice at 32°F?

Solution:

(a) $80\,\dfrac{cal}{g} = 80\,\dfrac{cal}{g} \times \dfrac{1\,Btu}{252\,cal} \times \dfrac{454\,g}{1\,lb} = 80 \times \dfrac{454\,Btu}{252\,lb} = 144\,Btu/lb$

(b) Heat absorbed in changing water at 60°F to water at 32°F
$$= \text{mass} \times \text{specific heat of water} \times \text{temperature change}$$
$$= 5.0\,lb \times 1\,Btu/lb°F \times (60-32)°F = 140\,Btu$$

Heat absorbed in changing water at 32°F to ice at 32°F
$$= \text{mass} \times \text{heat of fusion} = 5.0\,lb \times 144\,Btu/lb = 720\,Btu$$

Total heat absorbed $= 140\,Btu + 720\,Btu = 860\,Btu$

7. Five hundred grams of water and 100 grams of ice are in temperature equilibrium at 0°C. If 200 grams of steam at 100°C are introduced into the mixture, find the final temperature and composition of the mixture.

Solution:

Heat to melt ice and raise temperature of water to final temperature t
$$= (100 \times 80) + 600(t-0) = (8000 + 600t)\,cal$$

Heat given up by steam in condensing and cooling to final temperature t
$$= (200 \times 540) + 200(100-t) = (128{,}000 - 200t)\,cal$$

Then, heat absorbed by cold body $= \text{heat given up by hot body}$
$$8000 + 600t = 128{,}000 - 200t \qquad \text{from which} \quad t = 150°.$$

This means that there was more steam than necessary to raise the temperature of the ice and water to 100°C. Thus the final temperature of the mixture is 100°C and some steam is not condensed. Let m = mass of steam condensed.

Heat to melt ice and raise temperature of water to 100°C

     = $(100 \times 80) + 600(100 - 0)$ = 68,000 cal

Heat given up by m grams of steam in condensing = $540m$ cal

Then 68,000 = $540m$, from which m = 126 g. Hence the final mixture consists of $(200 - 126)$ = 74 g steam and $(600 + 126)$ = 726 g water, all at 100°C.

8. If the air temperature is 77°F and the dew point is 59°F, what is the relative humidity? Pressure of saturated water vapor at 77°F = 23.8 mm, at 59°F = 12.8 mm of Hg.

Solution:

$$\text{Relative humidity} = \frac{\text{saturated pressure of water vapor in air if at dew point}}{\text{pressure of water vapor in saturated air at } 77°}$$

$$= \frac{12.8 \text{ mm}}{23.8 \text{ mm}} = 0.54 = 54\%$$

9. Outside air at 5°C and 20% relative humidity is introduced into a heating and air conditioning plant where it is heated to 20°C and the relative humidity is increased to a comfortable value of 50%. How many grams of water must be evaporated into a cubic meter of 5-degree air to accomplish this? The saturated vapor density at 5°C is 6.8 g/m³, and at 20°C is 17.3 g/m³. The atmospheric pressure is standard.

Solution:

Density of water vapor in air at 5°C = 0.20×6.8 g/m³ = 1.36 g/m³

Comfortable vapor density at 20°C = 0.50×17.3 g/m³ = 8.65 g/m³

One m³ of air at 5°C expands to 293/278 m³ = 1.054 m³ at 20°C.

Mass of water vapor in 1.054 m³ at 20°C = 1.054 m³ $\times$ 8.65 g/m³ = 9.12 g

Mass of water vapor to be added to each m³ of air at 5°C = $(9.12 - 1.36)$ g = 7.76 g

SUPPLEMENTARY PROBLEMS

10. How many calories are required to heat each of the following from 15°C to 65°C: (a) 1 g water, (b) 5 g pyrex glass, (c) 20 g platinum? Specific heat of pyrex glass = 0.20, of platinum = 0.032. *Ans.* 50 cal, 50 cal, 32 cal

11. How many Btu are removed in cooling each of the following from 212°F to 68°F: (a) 1 lb water, (b) 2 lb leather, (c) 3 lb asbestos? Specific heat of leather = 0.36, of asbestos = 0.20. *Ans.* 144 Btu, 104 Btu, 86 Btu

12. The combustion of 5.00 g of coke raised the temperature of one liter of water from 10°C to 47°C. Calculate the heat value of coke in kcal/g. *Ans.* 7.4 kcal/g

13. Furnace oil has a heat of combustion of 19,000 Btu/lb. Assuming that 70% of the heat is useful, how many pounds of oil are required to heat 1000 lb of water from 50°F to 190°F? *Ans.* 10.5 lb

14. A 50 gallon tank full of water is heated from 40°F to 160°F using coal having a heat of combustion of 14,000 Btu/lb. How many pounds of coal are required if 55% of the heat is useful? One gallon of water weighs 8.34 lb. *Ans.* 6.5 lb

15. A 55 gram copper calorimeter contains 250 grams of water at 18°C. When 75 grams of an alloy at 100°C is dropped into the calorimeter, the resulting temperature is 20.4°C. Determine the specific heat of the alloy. Specific heat of copper is 0.093.   *Ans.* 0.102

16. Determine the resulting temperature when 1 kg of ice at 0°C is mixed with 9 kg of water at 50°C. *Ans.* 37°C

17. How much heat is required to change 10 g of ice at 0°C to steam at 100°C?   *Ans.* 7.2 kcal

18. Ten pounds of steam at 212°F is passed into 500 lb of water at 40°F. What is the resulting temperature? *Ans.* 62.4°F

19. The heat of combustion of ethane gas is 373 kcal per mole. Assuming that 60% of the heat is useful, how many liters of ethane measured at standard temperature and pressure must be burned to supply enough heat to convert 50 kg of water at 10°C to steam at 100°C? One mole of a gas occupies 22.4 liters at 0°C and 1 atm. *Ans.* 3150 liters

20. Calculate the heat of fusion of ice from the following data:

Mass of calorimeter	60 g
Mass of calorimeter plus water	460 g
Mass of calorimeter plus water and ice	618 g
Initial temperature of water	38°C
Temperature of mixture	5°C
Specific heat of calorimeter	0.10

Ans. 79.8 cal/g

21. A calorimeter whose water equivalent is 5 lb, contains 45 lb of water and 10 lb of ice at 32°F. What will be the final temperature if 5 lb of steam at 212°F is admitted to the calorimeter and contents?   *Ans.* 98.5°F

22. Determine the final result when 200 g of water and 20 g of ice at 0°C are in a calorimeter whose water equivalent is 30 g, and into which is passed 100 g of steam at 100°C. *Ans.* 49.4 g of steam condensed, final temperature 100°C.

23. Determine the final result when 400 g of water and 100 g of ice at 0°C are in a calorimeter whose water equivalent is 50 g, and into which is passed 10 g of steam at 100°C. *Ans.* 79.9 g of ice melted, final temperature 0°C

24. On a clear day the hygrometer indicated condensation at 5°C when the air temperature was 20°C. Calculate the relative humidity. Pressure of saturated water vapor at 5°C = 6.5 mm, at 20°C = 17.4 mm.   *Ans.* 37%

25. What is the pressure of water vapor in the air on a warm day when the temperature is 86°F and the relative humidity is 60%? Pressure of saturated water vapor at 86°F is 31.7 mm.   *Ans.* 19.0 mm

26. Air at 30°C and 90% relative humidity is drawn into an air conditioning unit and cooled to 20°C, the relative humidity being reduced to 50%. How many grams of water vapor must be removed by the air conditioner from a cubic meter of 30-degree air? The density of saturated water vapor in air at 30°C is 30.4 g/m^3, and at 20°C is 17.3 g/m^3.   *Ans.* 19.0 g/m^3

27. Exactly 100 cm^3 of oxygen is collected over water at 23°C and 800 mm. Compute the standard volume of the dry oxygen (at 0°C and 760 mm of mercury). The vapor pressure of water at 23°C is 21.1 mm. (Pressure of dry oxygen = total pressure − vapor pressure of water.)   *Ans.* 94.5 cm^3

Chapter 20

Transfer of Heat

HEAT IS TRANSMITTED by conduction, convection, and radiation.

CONDUCTION. Consider that a rectangular slab, of thickness l and opposite faces of area A, has one surface at temperature t' and the other at t''. Then $\dfrac{t' - t''}{l}$ is the temperature drop per unit distance, and is called the **temperature gradient**.

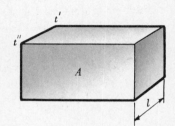

The quantity of heat transmitted per sec (H) from one face to the opposite face is proportional to the area of cross section A and to the temperature gradient. Thus

$$H \;=\; k \times \text{area} \times \text{temperature gradient} \;=\; kA\left(\frac{t' - t''}{l}\right)$$

where k is a proportionality constant which depends only on the nature of the substance, and is called the **coefficient of thermal conductivity** or simply the **thermal conductivity** of the substance.

It follows that k for a given substance is the amount of heat transmitted per unit time per unit area per unit temperature gradient.

When H is expressed in cal/sec, A in cm^2, $(t' - t'')$ in °C, and l in cm, then k is given in cal/sec per °C per cm.

In engineering work, the area is expressed in ft^2, the temperature gradient in °F/inch, and the rate of heat transfer in Btu/hr. Using these units, k for a given substance is the number of Btu transmitted per hr per ft^2 for a temperature gradient of 1°F per inch of thickness.

RADIATION. The ability of a given substance to emit radiation when heated is proportional to its ability to absorb radiation. A **black body** is one which absorbs all the radiant energy falling on it, and emits radiation perfectly freely.

The Stefan-Boltzmann law states that the total radiation at all wavelengths coming from a perfect radiator or black body is proportional to the fourth power of its absolute temperature T. If E is the number of watts radiated per square meter from a black body, then

$$E \;=\; \sigma T^4$$

where the proportionality constant $\sigma = 5.67 \times 10^{-8}$ watt/m^2 per (°K)^4.

SOLVED PROBLEMS

1. An iron plate 2 cm thick has a cross section of 5000 cm^2. One side is at 150°C and the other side is at 140°C. How much heat is transmitted per sec? The thermal conductivity of iron is 0.115 cal/sec per °C per cm.

   Solution:

$$H \;=\; kA\left(\frac{t' - t''}{l}\right) \;=\; 0.115\,\frac{\text{cal}}{\text{sec}\ ^\circ\text{C cm}} \times 5000\ \text{cm}^2 \times \frac{10^\circ\text{C}}{2\,\text{cm}} \;=\; 2880\ \text{cal/sec}$$

2. A plate of nickel 0.4 cm thick has a temperature difference of 32°C between its faces. It transmits 200 kilocalories per hour through an area of 5 cm². Calculate the thermal conductivity of nickel in cgs units.

Solution:

$$k = \frac{H}{A \times (t' - t'')/l} = \frac{200,000/3600 \text{ cal/sec}}{5 \text{ cm}^2 \times (32°C)/(0.4 \text{ cm})} = 0.14 \frac{\text{cal}}{\text{sec } °C \text{ cm}}$$

3. Corkboard transmits 7.0 Btu/day through 1 ft² when the temperature gradient is 1°F/inch. How many Btu are transmitted per day through a corkboard having dimensions 2.5×6 ft and 1.5 in. thick if one face is at 32°F and the other at 65°F?

Solution:

The rate of heat transfer is proportional to the area and to the gradient.

$$H \text{ (Btu/day)} = 7.0 \text{ Btu/day} \times \frac{(2.5 \times 6) \text{ ft}^2}{1 \text{ ft}^2} \times \frac{\frac{(65-32)°F}{1.5 \text{ in.}}}{1°F/\text{in.}} = 2300 \text{ Btu/day}$$

4. A spherical body, diameter 2 cm, is maintained at 600°C. Assuming that it radiates as if it were a black body, at what rate (in watts) is energy radiated from its surface?

Solution:

Surface area A of sphere $= 4\pi(\text{radius})^2 = \pi(\text{diameter})^2 = 4\pi \text{ cm}^2 = 4\pi \times 10^{-4} \text{ m}^2$

Rate $= A\sigma T^4 = (4\pi \times 10^{-4}) \text{ m}^2 \times (5.67 \times 10^{-8}) \frac{\text{watt}}{\text{m}^2 (°K)^4} \times (873°K)^4 = 41.4$ watts

Note. To perform the above multiplication by logarithms: Let x = rate of radiation; then

$\log x = \log 4 + \log 3.14 + \log 10^{-4} + \log 5.67 + \log 10^{-8} + 4(\log 873)$

$\qquad = 0.6021 + 0.4969 - 4 + 0.7536 - 8 + 4(2.9410) = 1.6166$

and $x = $ antilog $1.6166 = 41.4$ watts.

SUPPLEMENTARY PROBLEMS

5. How many grams of water at 100°C could be evaporated per hour per cm² by the heat transmitted through a steel plate 0.2 cm thick, the temperature difference between the plate faces being 100°C? k for the steel is 0.11 cal/(sec °C cm). *Ans.* 367 g

6. What temperature gradient must exist in aluminum in order to transmit 8 cal per sec per cm²? k for aluminum is 0.50 cal/(sec °C cm). *Ans.* 16°C/cm

7. Masonite transmits 0.33 Btu per hour through 1 ft² section when the temperature gradient is 1°F per inch of thickness. How many Btu will be transmitted per day through a board having dimensions 3×6 ft and $\frac{3}{4}$ in. thick, if one face is at 38°F and the opposite face is at 63°F? *Ans.* 4800 Btu/day

8. A small hole (which behaves as a black body), 1 cm² in area, is made in the wall of an electrical furnace heated to 1727°C. How many cal are radiated per sec through this hole? *Ans.* 21.7 cal

Chapter 21

Thermodynamics

MECHANICAL EQUIVALENT OF HEAT, J.

$$J = \frac{\text{work done to produce heat (expressed in mechanical units)}}{\text{heat produced by this work (expressed in heat units)}}$$

The mechanical equivalent of heat is numerically equal to the number of units of mechanical work required to produce unit quantity of heat.

$$J = 4.19 \text{ joules/cal} = 3.09 \text{ ft-lb/cal}$$
$$= 778 \text{ ft-lb/Btu}$$

WORK DONE BY A FLUID in expanding from an initial volume V_1 to a final volume V_2 against a **constant pressure** p is

$$\text{Work} = p(V_2 - V_1)$$

FIRST LAW OF THERMODYNAMICS. When any other kinds of energy are transformed into heat energy, or vice versa, the heat energy is exactly equivalent to the amount of transformed energy.

Consider a system to which is added an amount of heat Q and which at the same time does external work W. Then if Q is greater than W, the difference $(Q - W)$ remains within the system and represents the change in internal energy ΔU of the system. Thus

$$Q - W = \Delta U \qquad \text{or} \qquad Q = \Delta U + W$$

where Q, W and ΔU are expressed in the same units. Q is positive when heat is added to the system, and W is positive when work is done by the system.

SPECIFIC HEATS OF GASES. When a gas is heated at **constant volume** the heat supplied all goes to increase the internal energy of the gas molecules. But when a gas is heated at **constant pressure** the heat supplied not only increases the internal energy of the molecules but also does mechanical work in expanding the gas against the opposing constant pressure. Hence the specific heat of a gas at constant pressure (c_p) is greater than its specific heat at constant volume (c_v). It can be shown that for an ideal gas of molecular weight M,

$$c_p - c_v = R/M$$

where R is the universal gas constant. If c_p and c_v are in cal/g°C, M is expressed in g/mole and $R = 1.99$ cal/mole °C.

The kinetic theory of gases indicates that for monatomic gases (as He, Ne), $c_v = (3/2)R/M$ and $c_p = (5/2)R/M$; and for diatomic gases at ordinary temperatures (as N_2, O_2, CO), $c_v = (5/2)R/M$ and $c_p = (7/2)R/M$.

The ratio c_p/c_v is denoted by γ (gamma). For monatomic gases $\gamma = 5/3 = 1.67$, and for diatomic gases at ordinary temperatures $\gamma = 7/5 = 1.40$.

CONSTANT-PRESSURE (ISOBARIC) PROCESS. When a mass m of gas is heated at constant pressure p,

$$Q = mc_p(T_2 - T_1), \qquad \Delta U = mc_v(T_2 - T_1), \qquad W = Q - \Delta U = m(c_p - c_v)(T_2 - T_1)$$

Also, $W = p(V_2 - V_1)$.

CONSTANT-VOLUME (ISOVOLUMIC) PROCESS. When a mass m of gas is heated at constant volume,

$$W = 0 \qquad \text{and} \qquad Q = \Delta U = mc_v(T_2 - T_1)$$

CONSTANT-TEMPERATURE (ISOTHERMAL) PROCESS. When a mass m of gas expands isothermally against a pressure, the change in internal energy is zero ($\Delta U = 0$) and the heat added equals the external work done by the gas ($Q = W$). Here Boyle's law holds ($p_1 V_1 = p_2 V_2$) and

$$Q = W = p_1 V_1 \log_e \frac{V_2}{V_1} = 2.30\, p_1 V_1 \log_{10} \frac{V_2}{V_1}$$

Note: $\log_e x = (\log_e 10)(\log_{10} x) = 2.30 \log_{10} x$.

AN ADIABATIC PROCESS is one in which heat is not transferred to or from a system during the process. Hence in an adiabatic process

$$Q = 0 = \Delta U + W$$

which indicates that the increase in internal energy of the system equals the external work done on the system, i.e. $\Delta U = -W$. During an adiabatic process,

$$p_1 V_1^{\gamma} = p_2 V_2^{\gamma} \qquad \text{and} \qquad T_1 V_1^{\gamma-1} = T_2 V_2^{\gamma-1} \qquad \text{where } \gamma = c_p/c_v.$$

SECOND LAW OF THERMODYNAMICS. It is impossible for a continuous self-acting machine to transfer heat from a colder to a hotter body. In other words, heat cannot flow of itself from one body to another of higher temperature.

MAXIMUM POSSIBLE EFFICIENCY OF ANY HEAT ENGINE $= \dfrac{T_1 - T_2}{T_1}$

where T_1 = absolute temperature of reservoir which supplies the working substance,

T_2 = absolute temperature of reservoir to which working substance is exhausted.

SOLVED PROBLEMS

1. One pound of fuel, having a heat of combustion of 10,000 Btu/lb, was burned in an engine which raised 6000 lb of water 110 ft. What percentage of the heat was transformed into useful work?

Solution:

$$\text{Efficiency} = \frac{\text{work done by engine}}{\text{work equivalent of heat supplied}} = \frac{6000\,\text{lb} \times 110\,\text{ft}}{10,000\,\text{Btu} \times 778\,\text{ft-lb/Btu}}$$

$$= 0.0848 = 8.48\%$$

2. A crane is operated by a 15 hp gas engine. Taking into account the heat lost by friction in the crane, the efficiency of the engine is 20%. If the combustion value of the gas is 600 Btu per cubic foot, how many cubic feet of gas must be used to lift 3000 lb through a height of 60 ft?

Solution:

$$\text{Total work input} = \frac{\text{useful work}}{\text{efficiency}} = \frac{3000 \text{ lb} \times 60 \text{ ft}}{0.2} = 900,000 \text{ ft-lb}$$

$$\text{Heat equivalent of this work} = \frac{900,000 \text{ ft-lb}}{778 \text{ ft-lb/Btu}} = 1160 \text{ Btu}$$

$$\text{Volume of gas required} = \frac{1160 \text{ Btu}}{600 \text{ Btu/ft}^3} = 1.93 \text{ ft}^3$$

3. A motor supplies 0.4 horsepower to stir 10 gallons of water. Assuming that all the work done goes into heating the water, how long will it take to raise the temperature of the water 12 fahrenheit degrees? One gallon of water weighs 8.34 lb.

Solution:

$$\text{Heat gained by water} = \text{mass} \times \text{specific heat} \times \text{temperature change}$$
$$= (10 \times 8.34) \text{ lb} \times 1 \text{ Btu/lb}^\circ\text{F} \times 12^\circ\text{F} = 1000 \text{ Btu}$$

$$\text{Work (ft-lb) done by motor} = \text{mechanical equivalent (ft-lb) of 1000 Btu}$$
$$(0.4 \times 33,000) \text{ ft-lb/min} \times \text{time} = 1000 \text{ Btu} \times 778 \text{ ft-lb/Btu} \qquad \text{time} = 59 \text{ minutes}$$

4. A copper calorimeter (specific heat 0.093) of mass 108 g contains 800 g of an oil (specific heat 0.520). The liquid is stirred by a rotating paddle which requires a torque of 10 meter-newtons to drive it. The temperature of the liquid is raised 5°C after 141 revolutions. Compute the mechanical equivalent of heat.

Solution:

$$\text{Heat gained} = \text{mass} \times \text{specific heat} \times \text{temperature rise}$$

$$\text{Heat gained by calorimeter} = 108 \text{ g} \times 0.093 \text{ cal/g}^\circ\text{C} \times 5^\circ\text{C} = \quad 50 \text{ cal}$$
$$\text{Heat gained by oil} = 800 \text{ g} \times 0.520 \text{ cal/g}^\circ\text{C} \times 5^\circ\text{C} = \underline{2080 \text{ cal}}$$
$$\text{Total heat gained} = 2130 \text{ cal}$$

$$\text{Work done by paddle} = \text{torque} \times \text{angle in radians}$$
$$= 10 \text{ meter-newtons} \times 2\pi (141) \text{ radians} = 8860 \text{ joules}$$

$$J = \frac{\text{work done to produce heat}}{\text{heat produced by this work}} = \frac{8860 \text{ joules}}{2130 \text{ cal}} = 4.16 \text{ joules/cal}$$

5. In each case find the change in internal energy of the system. (a) A system absorbs 2 Btu of heat and at the same time does 389 ft-lb of external work. (b) A system absorbs 300 cal and at the same time 419 joules of work are done on it. (c) From a gas held at constant volume, 5 Btu of heat is removed.

Solution:

$$\text{Employ the equation} \qquad Q = \Delta U + W$$

where Q, W and ΔU are expressed in the same units. Q is positive when heat is added to the system, negative when removed from the system. W is positive when work is done by the system, negative when done on the system.

(a) $\Delta U = Q - W = 2 \text{ Btu} - 389/778 \text{ Btu} = +1.5 \text{ Btu}$

(b) $\Delta U = Q - W = 300 \text{ cal} - (-419/4.19 \text{ cal}) = +400 \text{ cal}$

(c) Since the volume is unchanged, no work is done during the process.
$$\Delta U = Q - W = -5 \text{ Btu} - 0 = -5 \text{ Btu}$$

6. For each adiabatic process find the change in internal energy. (a) A gas does 5 ft-lb of external work while expanding adiabatically. (b) During an adiabatic compression, 80 joules of work is done on a gas.

Solution:

During an adiabatic process no heat is transferred to or from the system.

(a) $\Delta U = Q - W = 0 - 5$ ft-lb $= -5$ ft-lb

(b) $\Delta U = Q - W = 0 - (-80 \text{ joules}) = +80$ joules

7. One pound of steam at $212°F$ and 14.7 lb/in^2 occupies 26.8 ft^3. (a) What fraction of the observed heat of vaporization of water (970 Btu/lb at $212°F$ and 1 atm) is accounted for by the external work done in expanding water into steam at $212°F$ against atmospheric pressure? The specific volume of water at $212°F$ is 0.0167 ft^3/lb. (b) Determine the increase in internal energy when 1 lb of steam is formed at $212°F$.

Solution:

(a) Work done in expanding 1 lb water into 1 lb steam at constant pressure p

$= p(V_2 - V_1) = (14.7 \times 144) \text{ lb/ft}^2 \times (26.8 - 0.0167) \text{ ft}^3 = 56{,}700$ ft-lb

Heat equivalent of 56,700 ft-lb $= 56{,}700$ ft-lb $\times 1/778$ Btu/ft-lb $= 73$ Btu

Required fraction $= (73 \text{ Btu})/(970 \text{ Btu}) = 0.075 = 7.5\%$

(b) $\Delta U = Q - W = 970$ Btu $- 73$ Btu $= 897$ Btu

8. The temperature of 5 kg of N_2 gas is raised from $10°C$ to $130°C$. (a) If this is accomplished at constant pressure, find the heat Q added, the increase in internal energy ΔU, and the external work W done by the gas. (b) Find the heat required to accomplish this at constant volume. For N_2 gas, $c_v = 0.177$ and $c_p = 0.248$ cal/g$°K$.

Solution:

(a) $Q = mc_p(T_2 - T_1) = 5 \text{ kg} \times 0.248 \text{ kcal/kg}°K \times 120°K = 149$ kcal

$\Delta U = mc_v(T_2 - T_1) = 5 \text{ kg} \times 0.177 \text{ kcal/kg}°K \times 120°K = 106$ kcal

$W = Q - \Delta U = 149 \text{ kcal} - 106 \text{ kcal} = 43$ kcal

(b) At constant volume, $W = 0$ and $Q = \Delta U = mc_v(T_2 - T_1) = 106$ kcal.

9. The specific heat of nitrogen at constant volume is $c_v = 0.177$ cal/g$°C$. Find the specific heat of nitrogen at constant pressure c_p. Molecular weight of $N_2 = 28.0$ g/mole.

Solution:

$$c_p = c_v + \frac{R}{M} = 0.177 \frac{\text{cal}}{\text{g}°C} + \frac{1.99 \text{ cal/mole}°C}{28.0 \text{ g/mole}} = 0.248 \frac{\text{cal}}{\text{g}°C}$$

Or, since N_2 is a diatomic gas,

$$c_p = c_v \times 1.40 = 0.177 \text{ cal/g}°C \times 1.40 = 0.248 \text{ cal/g}°C.$$

10. Compute c_v and c_p for O_2 gas, molecular weight 32.00 g/mole.

Solution:

$$c_v = \frac{5}{2}(\frac{R}{M}) = \frac{5}{2}(\frac{1.99 \text{ cal/mole}°K}{32.0 \text{ g/mole}}) = 0.155 \frac{\text{cal}}{\text{g}°K} \quad \text{and} \quad c_p = \frac{7}{2}(\frac{R}{M}) = 0.218 \frac{\text{cal}}{\text{g}°K}$$

11. How much work is done by a gas in expanding from an initial volume of 3 liters at 20 atm to a final volume of 24 liters, the temperature remaining constant?

Solution:

$$W = p_1 V_1 \log_e \frac{V_2}{V_1} = 2.30(20 \text{ atm})(3l) \log_{10} \frac{24}{3} = 125 \ l\text{-atm}$$

$$= 2.30(20 \times 1.013 \times 10^5 \text{ nt/m}^2)(3 \times 10^{-3} \text{ m}^3)(0.9031) = 1.26 \times 10^4 \text{ joules}$$

12. A volume of 22.4 liters of nitrogen gas at 1 atm and 0°C is adiabatically compressed to 1/10 of its original volume. Find (a) the final pressure, (b) the final temperature, and (c) the external work done on the gas. For N_2 gas, $\gamma = 1.40$, $c_v = 0.178$ cal/g°C, and 1 mole = 28.0 g.

Solution:

(a) $p_1V_1^{\gamma} = p_2V_2^{\gamma}$, $\quad$ (1 atm)$(V_1)^{1.4} = p_2(V_1/10)^{1.4}$, $\quad$ $p_2 = $ (1 atm)$(10^{1.4}) = 25.1$ atm

(b) $T_1V_1^{\gamma-1} = T_2V_2^{\gamma-1}$, $\quad$ (273°K)$(V_1)^{0.4} = T_2(V_1/10)^{0.4}$, $\quad$ $T_2 = $ (273°K)$(10^{0.4}) = 686$°K

$\qquad$ Check: $\dfrac{p_1V_1}{T_1} = \dfrac{p_2V_2}{T_2}$, $\quad$ $\dfrac{1 \text{ atm} \times 22.4\,l}{273°\text{K}} = \dfrac{25.1 \text{ atm} \times 2.24\,l}{686°\text{K}}$, $\quad$ $0.820 = 0.820$

(c) Work done on gas $=$ increase in its internal energy

$\qquad\qquad\qquad\qquad = mc_v(T_2 - T_1)$

$\qquad\qquad\qquad\qquad = $ (28.0 g)(0.178 cal/g°K)(686°K − 273°K) $= 2060$ cal $= 8.63 \times 10^3$ joules

13. Compute the ideal thermal efficiency of a heat engine working between 100°C and 400°C.

Solution:

$\qquad$ Ideal efficiency $= \dfrac{T_1 - T_2}{T_1} = \dfrac{(400+273)°\text{K} - (100+273)°\text{K}}{(400+273)°\text{K}} = 0.446 = 44.6\%$

14. A steam engine operating between a boiler temperature of 410°F and a condenser temperature of 120°F delivers 8 hp. If its efficiency is 30% of that of an ideal heat engine operating between these temperature limits, how many Btu/sec are absorbed by the boiler?

Solution:

$\qquad$ Actual efficiency $= 0.30 \times$ ideal efficiency

$\qquad\qquad\qquad\qquad = 0.30 \times \dfrac{T_1 - T_2}{T_1} = 0.30 \times \dfrac{(410+460)°\text{R} - (120+460)°\text{R}}{(410+460)°\text{R}} = 0.10 = 10\%$

$\qquad$ Power input $= \dfrac{\text{power output}}{\text{efficiency}} = \dfrac{8 \text{ hp}}{0.10} \times \dfrac{550 \text{ ft-lb/sec}}{1 \text{ hp}} \times \dfrac{1 \text{ Btu}}{778 \text{ ft-lb}} = 57$ Btu/sec

SUPPLEMENTARY PROBLEMS

15. Determine the mechanical equivalent of the Btu in terms of the following units of work: foot-pounds, horsepower-hours, kilowatt-hours, joules, liter-atmospheres.
Ans. 778 ft-lb, 3.93×10^{-4} hp-hr, 2.93×10^{-4} kw-hr, 1054 joules, 10.41 l-atm

16. If 10 kg of water falls a distance of 854 meters and all the energy is effective in heating the water, to what temperature will the water be raised if it was at 20°C? *Ans.* 22°C

17. How many Btu per hour are produced in a motor which dissipates 0.25 horsepower as heat, due to friction and electrical resistance? *Ans.* 636 Btu/hr

18. A 100 gram lead bullet, specific heat 0.03, is initially at 20°C. It is fired vertically upward with a speed of 420 meters/sec, and on returning to the starting level strikes a cake of ice at 0°C. How much ice is melted? Assume that all the energy is effective in melting the ice. *Ans.* 27 g ice

19. A boiler and engine deliver 10 horsepower and use 30 lb of coal per hour. If the calorific value of the coal is 15,000 Btu per pound, what percentage of the heat is transformed into work? *Ans.* 5.7%

20. A champion sprinter does mechanical work at the rate of 11 horsepower during a 100 yard dash and is timed 9.3 sec. How much sugar must he eat to provide energy for the dash if the heat of combustion of sugar is 4000 cal/g and the human body is 30% efficient in transforming chemical energy into mechanical energy? *Ans.* 15.2 g

21. An electrical heating coil was placed in a calorimeter containing 380 g of water at 10°C. The coil consumes energy at the rate of 84 watts, and after 10 minutes the temperature of the water rose to 40°C. If the water equivalent of calorimeter and coil is 20 g, what is the mechanical equivalent of heat?   *Ans.* 4.2 joules/cal

22. A 120 lb wheel, of radius of gyration 1 ft, revolves at 480 rpm. Calculate the heat produced when the wheel is brought to rest by friction.   *Ans.* 6.1 Btu

23. An aluminum V-2 rocket fired vertically reaches a maximum altitude of 150 km where it has a temperature of 50°C. If it strikes earth again at a speed of only 600 m/sec, and half of the heat generated by air friction remains in the rocket, what will its temperature be when it strikes earth? Specific heat of Al is 0.22 cal/g°C. *Ans.* 750°C

24. How much external work is done by a gas in expanding from a volume of 3 liters to a volume of 30 liters against a constant pressure of 2 atmospheres?   *Ans.* 5470 joules

25. How much work is done by a gas whose initial volume is 3 liters and whose temperature increases from 27°C to 227°C, pressure remaining constant at 2 atm?   *Ans.* 405 joules

26. Water is boiled at 100°C and 1 atm. Under these conditions 1 g of water occupies 1 cm^3, 1 g of steam occupies 1671 cm^3 and the heat of vaporization is 540 cal/g. Find the external work done when 1 g of steam is formed at 100°C and the increase in internal energy.   *Ans.* 169 joules or 40.4 cal, 500 cal

27. The temperature of 3 kg of krypton (Kr) gas is raised from −20°C to 80°C. (*a*) If this is done at constant pressure, compute the heat added, the increase in internal energy, and the external work done by the gas. (*b*) Find the heat required to do this at constant volume. For the monatomic gas krypton, c_v = 0.0357 and c_p = 0.0595 cal/g°K (computed from the formulas $c_v = (3/2)R/M$ and $c_p = (5/2)R/M$, where M = 83.7 g/mole). *Ans.* (*a*) 17.8, 10.7, 7.1 kcal; (*b*) 10.7 kcal

28. One mole of carbon monoxide (CO) gas is heated from 15°C to 16°C. Determine the increase in its internal energy when heated (*a*) at constant volume, (*b*) at constant pressure. What external work is done by one mole of CO gas while it is being heated from 15°C to 16°C (*c*) at constant volume, (*d*) at constant pressure? For CO, molecular weight = 28.01 g/mole, c_p = 0.248 cal/g°C, and γ = 1.40. *Ans.* (*a*) 4.96 cal, (*b*) 4.96 cal, (*c*) 0, (*d*) 1.99 cal

29. (*a*) Compute c_v of the monatomic gas argon, given c_p = 0.125 cal/g°C and γ = 1.67. (*b*) Compute c_p of the diatomic gas nitric oxide (NO), given c_v = 0.166 cal/g°C and γ = 1.40. *Ans.* (*a*) 0.0749, (*b*) 0.232 cal/g°C

30. Compute c_v and c_p for (*a*) the monatomic gas neon (Ne), (*b*) the diatomic gas hydrogen (H_2). Molecular weight of Ne = 20.18, of H_2 = 2.016 g/mole.   *Ans.* (*a*) 0.148, 0.247; (*b*) 2.47, 3.45 cal/g°K

31. Compute the work done on a gas in compressing it from a volume of 30 liters at 1 atm to a volume of 3 liters, temperature remaining constant.   *Ans.* 6990 joules

32. Five moles of neon gas at 2 atm and 27°C is adiabatically compressed to one-third of its initial volume. Find the final pressure, the final temperature, and the external work done on the gas. For Ne gas, γ = 1.67, c_v = 0.148 cal/g°K, and 1 mole = 20.18 g.   *Ans.* 12.5 atm, 626°K, 2.04×10^4 joules.

33. Determine the theoretical limiting efficiency of a steam engine when steam enters the engine at 400°C and leaves the cylinder at 105°C.   *Ans.* 43.8%

34. What is the ideal thermal efficiency of a heat engine operating between 140°F and 340°F? To what temperature must the upper temperature be raised to give an ideal efficiency of 40%?   *Ans.* 25%, 540°F

Chapter 22

Electrostatics

COULOMB'S LAW. The force F between two point charges q and q' varies directly as the magnitude of each charge and inversely as the square of the distance r between them.

$$F = k \frac{qq'}{r^2}$$

where k is a (dimensional) proportionality constant which depends on the units used for charge, distance and force. F is given in newtons if q and q' are in coulombs, r in meters, and

$$k = 9 \times 10^9 \text{ nt-m}^2/\text{coul}^2$$

If we now define $k = \frac{1}{4\pi\epsilon_O}$,

$$F = \frac{1}{4\pi\epsilon_O} \frac{qq'}{r^2} \qquad \text{where} \quad \epsilon_O = \frac{1}{4\pi k} = 8.85 \times 10^{-12} \text{ coul}^2/\text{nt-m}^2.$$

When the surrounding medium is not a vacuum, forces caused by charges induced in the medium reduce the resultant force between free charges immersed in the medium. The net force is now given by $F = \frac{1}{4\pi\epsilon} \frac{qq'}{r^2}$. For air ϵ is only slightly larger than ϵ_O and for most purposes is taken equal to ϵ_O. For other materials ϵ is given by

$$\epsilon = K\epsilon_O$$

where K is a dimensionless constant called the **dielectric constant** or **specific inductive capacity** of the material between the charges, $\epsilon = K\epsilon_O$ is called the **permittivity** of the material, and ϵ_O the **permittivity of free space**. For a vacuum, $K = 1$ and $\epsilon = \epsilon_O$.

The unit of charge, the coulomb, may be defined as the quantity of charge which, when placed 1 meter from an equal and similar charge in vacuum, repels it with a force of 9×10^9 newtons. Convenient submultiples of the coulomb are

$$1 \mu c = 1 \text{ microcoulomb} = 10^{-6} \text{ coulomb}$$
$$1 \mu\mu c = 1 \text{ micromicrocoulomb} = 10^{-12} \text{ coulomb}$$

The charge carried by an electron $(-e)$ or by a proton $(+e)$ is

$$e = 1.602 \times 10^{-19} \text{ coulomb}$$

The electron mass $= 9.11 \times 10^{-31}$ kg.

The proton mass $= 1836 \times$ electron mass $= 1.67 \times 10^{-27}$ kg.

AN ELECTRIC FIELD exists at any point in space where an electric charge, if placed at that point, would experience an electrical force. The electric intensity (or electric field intensity) at a point is numerically equal to the force exerted on a unit positive charge placed at that point. Unit field intensity is the field which exerts a force of 1 newton on 1 coulomb of charge.

Electric intensity E is a vector quantity. For example, if a positive charge of 1 coulomb is acted upon by a force of 90 newtons directed due west when placed at a certain point in an electric field, the electric intensity at that point is 90 newtons/coulomb directed due west.

$$E \text{ (nt/coul)} \;=\; \frac{F \text{ (nt)}}{q \text{ (coul)}}$$

It follows that the force in newtons acting on a charge q coulombs placed at a point where the electric intensity is E nt/coul is

$$F \text{ (nt)} \;=\; E \text{ (nt/coul)} \;\times\; q \text{ (coul)}$$

ELECTRIC INTENSITY DUE TO A CHARGE. Consider that a charge q', located at point P, is distant r from a point charge q. Then by Coulomb's law the force on q' is $F = k\,(qq'/r^2)$, and thus the electric intensity E at P is

$$E \;=\; \frac{F}{q'} \;=\; k\,\frac{q}{r^2}$$

The electric intensity at a point due to several charges is the vector sum of the intensities due to the individual charges.

POTENTIAL. The potential at a point is the work required to bring unit positive charge from infinity to that point against the electrical forces of the field. Difference of potential between two points is measured by the work required to carry unit positive charge from one point to the other point.

Potential (and potential difference) is a scalar quantity having dimensions of work/charge. It is expressed in volts, and 1 volt = 1 joule/coulomb.

The potential V at a point (in volts) due to a charge q coulombs at a distance r meters is

$$V \;=\; k\,\frac{q}{r}$$

The work W done in transferring a charge q coulombs from one point to another having a difference of potential V is

$$W \text{ (joules)} \;=\; q \text{ (coulombs)} \;\times\; V \text{ (volts)}$$

If the field is uniform (as between two parallel plates), $W = qV = Fr$, where F is the force on the charge q and r the distance between the points. Then $V/r = F/q$ or $V/r = E$, i.e. in a uniform field the electric intensity E in nt/coul equals the **potential gradient** V/r in volts/meter.
(Note. Since 1 volt $= 1\,\dfrac{\text{joule}}{\text{coul}}$, $\;1\,\dfrac{\text{volt}}{\text{m}} = 1\,\dfrac{\text{joule}}{\text{coul m}} = 1\,\dfrac{\text{nt}}{\text{coul}}$.)

A CAPACITOR or **condenser** consists of two conductors separated by an insulator or dielectric.

$$\textbf{Capacitance } C \text{ of a capacitor} \;=\; \frac{\text{charge } q \text{ on either conductor}}{\text{potential difference } V \text{ between conductors}}$$
$$C \text{ (farads)} \;=\; \frac{q \text{ (coulombs)}}{V \text{ (volts)}}$$

A capacitor has capacitance 1 farad (1 f) if it requires 1 coulomb of charge per volt of potential difference between its conductors. Convenient submultiples of the farad are

$$1\,\mu\text{f} \;=\; 1 \text{ microfarad} \;=\; 10^{-6}\,\text{f}$$
$$1\,\mu\mu\text{f} \;=\; 1 \text{ micromicrofarad} \;=\; 10^{-12}\,\text{f}$$

Note. 10^{-12} farad is also called a **picofarad** (pf).

PARALLEL PLATE CAPACITOR. The capacitance of a parallel plate capacitor with two large plates, the area of one side of one plate which is opposed by the other plate being A square meters and the distance between them d meters, is

$$C = K\epsilon_o \frac{A}{d}$$

where K (dimensionless) is called the **dielectric constant** or **specific inductive capacity** of the non-conducting material (the dielectric) between the plates, and $\epsilon_o = 8.85 \times 10^{-12}$ coul²/nt-m². For a vacuum, $K = 1$.

CAPACITORS IN PARALLEL AND SERIES.

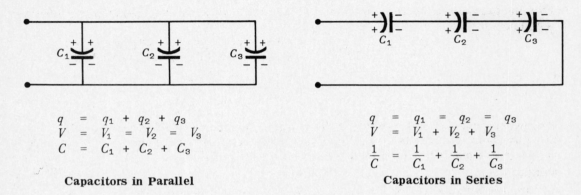

$$q = q_1 + q_2 + q_3$$
$$V = V_1 = V_2 = V_3$$
$$C = C_1 + C_2 + C_3$$

Capacitors in Parallel

$$q = q_1 = q_2 = q_3$$
$$V = V_1 + V_2 + V_3$$
$$\frac{1}{C} = \frac{1}{C_1} + \frac{1}{C_2} + \frac{1}{C_3}$$

Capacitors in Series

The resultant capacitance C of any number of capacitors connected in parallel is the sum of their individual capacitances. The reciprocal of the resultant capacitance C of any number of capacitors connected in series is the sum of the reciprocals of the individual capacitances.

ENERGY STORED IN A CAPACITOR. In a capacitor the potential difference is proportional to the charge ($V = q/C$). While a capacitor is being charged the charge builds up from an initial value zero to a final value q. Hence the potential difference builds up from zero to a final value V, the average value during the process being $\frac{1}{2}V$. Now the work W required to transfer a total charge q through an average potential difference $\frac{1}{2}V$ is $W = q(\frac{1}{2}V)$. Thus the electrical energy W stored in a charged capacitor is

$$W = \tfrac{1}{2}qV = \tfrac{1}{2}CV^2 = \tfrac{1}{2}q^2/C \qquad \text{using } q = CV$$

W is in joules if q is in coulombs, V in volts, and C in farads.

SOLVED PROBLEMS

1. A helium nucleus has charge $+2e$ and a neon nucleus $+10e$, where $e = 1.60 \times 10^{-19}$ coul. With what force do they repel each other when separated by 3 millimicrons?

   Solution:

$$F = k \frac{qq'}{r^2} = 9 \times 10^9 \frac{\text{nt-m}^2}{\text{c}^2} \times \frac{(2 \times 1.60 \times 10^{-19}\text{ c})(10 \times 1.60 \times 10^{-19}\text{ c})}{(3 \times 10^{-9}\text{ m})^2} = 5.12 \times 10^{-10}\text{ nt}$$

2. The normal hydrogen atom consists of a proton nucleus and an orbital electron, each carrying the fundamental charge of magnitude $e = 1.60 \times 10^{-19}$ coul. Assuming that the electron orbit is circular and the separation between the particles is 5.3×10^{-11} meter, find (a) the force of electrical attraction between the particles, (b) the electron's orbital speed. The electron has mass $m = 9.11 \times 10^{-31}$ kg.

Solution:

(a) $F = k \dfrac{qq'}{r^2} = 9 \times 10^9 \dfrac{\text{nt-m}^2}{\text{c}^2} \times \dfrac{(1.60 \times 10^{-19} \text{ c})^2}{(5.3 \times 10^{-11} \text{ m})^2} = 8.2 \times 10^{-8}$ nt

(b) F is the centripetal force that keeps the electron in its circular path. Then

$$F = \frac{mv^2}{r} \quad \text{and} \quad v = \sqrt{\frac{Fr}{m}} = \sqrt{\frac{(8.2 \times 10^{-8} \text{ nt})(5.3 \times 10^{-11} \text{ m})}{9.11 \times 10^{-31} \text{ kg}}} = 2.2 \times 10^6 \text{ m/sec.}$$

3. Find the ratio of the electrical force F_e and the gravitational force F_g between two electrons.

Solution:

$$\frac{F_e}{F_g} = \frac{k(q^2/r^2)}{G(m^2/r^2)} = \frac{kq^2}{Gm^2} = \frac{(9 \times 10^9 \text{ nt-m}^2/\text{coul}^2)(1.60 \times 10^{-19} \text{ coul})^2}{(6.67 \times 10^{-11} \text{ nt-m}^2/\text{kg}^2)(9.11 \times 10^{-31} \text{ kg})^2}$$

$$= 4.16 \times 10^{42}, \quad \text{i.e.} \quad F_e = 4.16 \times 10^{42} F_g$$

4. Two equally charged balls, each of mass 0.1 gram, are suspended from the same point by threads 13 cm long. The balls come to rest 10 cm apart due to repulsion. Determine the charge q on each ball.

Solution:

The two balls are at P and P_1, 10 cm apart. The ball at P is in equilibrium under the action of the three forces: (1) the tension T in the thread; (2) the weight of the ball, $w = mg = 10^{-4} \text{ kg} \times 9.8 \text{ m/sec}^2 = 9.8 \times 10^{-4}$ nt; (3) the horizontal force F of repulsion of the charges. The tension T is equal and opposite to the resultant R of mg and F.

$$AB = \sqrt{(13 \text{ cm})^2 - (5 \text{ cm})^2} = 12 \text{ cm}$$

Triangle PCD is similar to triangle APB; then

$$\frac{F}{mg} = \frac{PB}{AB}, \qquad \frac{F}{9.8 \times 10^{-4} \text{ nt}} = \frac{5 \text{ cm}}{12 \text{ cm}}, \qquad F = 4.1 \times 10^{-4} \text{ nt}$$

$$F = k \frac{qq}{r^2}, \qquad 4.1 \times 10^{-4} \text{ nt} = 9 \times 10^9 \frac{\text{nt-m}^2}{\text{coul}^2} \frac{qq}{(10^{-1} \text{ m})^2},$$

$$q = 2.1 \times 10^{-8} \text{ coul}$$

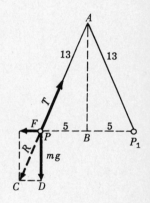

5. Three point charges of +2, +3 and +4 microcoulombs are at the vertices of the equilateral triangle ABP having sides of 10 cm. What is the resultant force R acting on the $+4\mu c$ charge?

Solution:

Force due to $+2 \ \mu c = 9 \times 10^9 \dfrac{(2 \times 10^{-6})(4 \times 10^{-6})}{(0.10)^2} = 7.2$ nt repulsion (P to D)

Force due to $+3 \ \mu c = 9 \times 10^9 \dfrac{(3 \times 10^{-6})(4 \times 10^{-6})}{(0.10)^2} = 10.8$ nt repulsion (P to S)

$\angle APB = \angle SPD = 60°$, $\angle PDC = 180° - 60° = 120°$. In triangle PCD, by the cosine law,

$$R^2 = (7.2)^2 + (10.8)^2 - 2(7.2)(10.8) \cos 120°$$

and $R = 15.7$ nt directed from P to C.

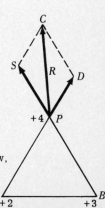

6. Compute (*a*) the electric intensity E in air at a distance 30 cm from a charge $q_1 = 5 \times 10^{-9}$ coulomb, (*b*) the force F on a charge $q_2 = 4 \times 10^{-10}$ coulomb placed 30 cm from q_1.

Solution:

(*a*) $E = k\dfrac{q_1}{r^2} = 9 \times 10^9 \dfrac{\text{nt-m}^2}{\text{coul}^2} \times \dfrac{5 \times 10^{-9}\,\text{coul}}{(3 \times 10^{-1}\,\text{m})^2} = 5 \times 10^2\,\text{nt/coul}$

(*b*) $F = Eq_2 = (5 \times 10^2\,\text{nt/coul})(4 \times 10^{-10}\,\text{coul}) = 2 \times 10^{-7}\,\text{nt}$

7. (*a*) Compute the electric intensity in air midway between two point charges of $+20 \times 10^{-8}$ and -5×10^{-8} coulomb separated by a distance of 10 cm. What is the force on a $+4 \times 10^{-8}$ coul point charge placed midway between the charges? (*b*) If instead of the -5×10^{-8} coul charge we have a $+5 \times 10^{-8}$ coul charge, compute the electric intensity and the force on the $+4 \times 10^{-8}$ coul charge.

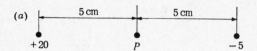 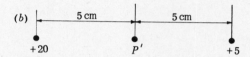

Solution:

(*a*) A positive charge at P would be repelled (toward the right) by the $+20 \times 10^{-8}$ coul charge and attracted (toward the right) by the -5×10^{-8} coul charge. The resultant electric intensity E at P is the vector sum of the intensities due to the individual charges.

$E = k\dfrac{q_1}{r^2} + k\dfrac{q_2}{r^2} = \dfrac{k}{r^2}(q_1 + q_2) = \dfrac{9 \times 10^9}{(.05)^2}(20 + 5)10^{-8} = 9 \times 10^5\,\text{nt/coul}$ toward right

$F = Eq = (9 \times 10^5\,\text{nt/coul})(4 \times 10^{-8}\,\text{coul}) = 3.6 \times 10^{-2}\,\text{nt}$ toward right

(*b*) A positive charge at P' would be repelled (toward the right) by the $+20 \times 10^{-8}$ coul charge and repelled (toward the left) by the $+5 \times 10^{-8}$ coul charge. Hence the resultant intensity E at P' is

$E = k\dfrac{q_1}{r^2} - k\dfrac{q_2}{r^2} = \dfrac{k}{r^2}(q_1 - q_2) = \dfrac{9 \times 10^9}{(.05)^2}(20 - 5)10^{-8} = 54 \times 10^4\,\text{nt/coul}$ toward right

$F = Eq = (54 \times 10^4\,\text{nt/coul})(4 \times 10^{-8}\,\text{coul}) = 2.2 \times 10^{-2}\,\text{nt}$ toward right

8. An electron of mass m kg and charge e coul is projected with initial velocity v m/sec along the axis and midway between two parallel horizontal plates each of length l meters. The electric intensity between the plates is E nt/coul directed downward. A fluorescent screen is placed at a horizontal distance d meters from the plates. Derive formulas for (*a*) the vertical displacement y of an electron just as it leaves the deflecting plates, (*b*) the angle θ the motion of the electron makes with the axis after leaving the plates, (*c*) the vertical distance Y from the axis to the point at which the electron strikes the screen.

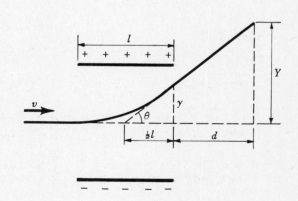

Solution:

(*a*) Upward electrical force on electron = mass × upward acceleration of electron

$$Ee = ma_y, \quad \text{or} \quad a_y = Ee/m$$

Time for electron to pass between plates, $t = l/v$.

Upward displacement when it leaves plates, $y = \frac{1}{2}a_y t^2 = \frac{1}{2}\left(\dfrac{Ee}{m}\right)\left(\dfrac{l}{v}\right)^2$.

(*b*) $\tan\theta = \dfrac{y}{\frac{1}{2}l} = \dfrac{Eel}{mv^2}$ (*c*) $Y = (\frac{1}{2}l + d)\tan\theta = (\frac{1}{2}l + d)\dfrac{Eel}{mv^2}$

9. A tin nucleus has charge $+50e$. Find the potential V at a distance 10^{-12} meter from the nucleus and the potential energy W of a proton at this position. The proton has charge $+e = 1.60 \times 10^{-19}$ coul.

Solution:

$$V = k\frac{q}{r} = 9 \times 10^9 \frac{\text{nt-m}^2}{\text{coul}^2} \times \frac{50(1.60 \times 10^{-19}) \text{ coul}}{10^{-12} \text{ m}} = 7.2 \times 10^4 \frac{\text{joules}}{\text{coul}} \text{ or volts}$$

$$W = q_p V = (1.60 \times 10^{-19} \text{ coul})(7.2 \times 10^4 \text{ joules/coul}) = 1.2 \times 10^{-14} \text{ joule}$$

10. How much work W is required to carry a charge of 5×10^{-8} coul from a point in air 50 cm from a charge of 2×10^{-6} coul to a point 10 cm from it?

Solution:

$$W = \text{charge} \times \text{potential difference between the two points}$$

$$= qV = (5 \times 10^{-8}) \text{coul} \times (9 \times 10^9)(\frac{2 \times 10^{-6}}{0.1} - \frac{2 \times 10^{-6}}{0.5}) \text{ volts} = 7.2 \times 10^{-3} \text{ joule}$$

11. At one corner of a 3×4 cm rectangle is placed a charge of -20 $\mu\mu c$, and at the two adjacent corners are charges of $+10$ $\mu\mu c$. Calculate the potential at the fourth corner P.

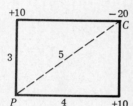

Solution:

The potential at a point depends on its distance from the charges, and not on their directions. $PC = \sqrt{3^2 + 4^2} = 5$ cm.

$$V_P = k\Sigma\frac{q}{r} = 9 \times 10^9 \times (\frac{10 \times 10^{-12}}{.04} + \frac{10 \times 10^{-12}}{.03} - \frac{20 \times 10^{-12}}{.05}) = 1.65 \text{ volts}$$

12. Point charges of $+200$ $\mu\mu c$ and -100 $\mu\mu c$ are fixed at points A and B respectively which are 100 cm apart in air. (a) Calculate the work required to transfer a charge of 5×10^{-4} coul from point C 80 cm from A to point D 20 cm from A, both points being between A and B. (b) Which point is at the higher potential?

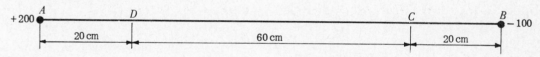

Solution:

(a) Potential at $C = 9 \times 10^9 \frac{\text{nt-m}^2}{\text{coul}^2} \times (\frac{200 \times 10^{-12}}{0.80} - \frac{100 \times 10^{-12}}{0.20}) \frac{\text{coul}}{\text{m}} = -2.25 \text{ volts}$

Potential at $D = 9 \times 10^9 \frac{\text{nt-m}^2}{\text{coul}^2} \times (\frac{200 \times 10^{-12}}{0.20} - \frac{100 \times 10^{-12}}{0.80}) \frac{\text{coul}}{\text{m}} = +7.88 \text{ volts}$

Potential difference V between D and $C = 7.88 - (-2.25) = 10.13$ volts

Work required $= qV = (5 \times 10^{-4} \text{ coul})(10.13 \text{ volts}) = 5.06 \times 10^{-3} \text{ joule}$

(b) D is at the higher potential. Hence the charge of 5×10^{-4} coul has acquired 5.06×10^{-3} joule of additional potential energy in being transferred from C to D.

13. The two horizontal parallel plates of a vacuum tube are 2 cm apart and connected across 120 volts. Find (a) the electric intensity E (assumed uniform) in the space between the plates, (b) the constant force F acting on an electron in the space between the plates, (c) the energy W gained by an electron in traveling 2 cm from cathode to anode, (d) the ratio of the electrical force to the gravitational force on an electron in the field between the plates.

Solution:

(a) $E = \frac{F}{q} = \frac{V}{r} = \frac{120 \text{ v}}{.02 \text{ m}} = 6 \times 10^3 \text{ volts/meter} = 6 \times 10^3 \text{ newtons/coulomb}$

(b) $F = Eq = (6 \times 10^3 \text{ nt/coul})(1.60 \times 10^{-19} \text{ coul}) = 9.6 \times 10^{-16} \text{ nt}$

(c) $W = Fr = (9.6 \times 10^{-16} \text{ nt})(.02 \text{ m}) = 1.92 \times 10^{-17} \text{ nt-m or joule}$

$\quad = qV = (1.60 \times 10^{-19} \text{ coul})(120 \text{ v}) = 1.92 \times 10^{-17} \text{ joule}$

(d) $\dfrac{\text{Electrical force}}{\text{Gravitational force}} = \dfrac{Eq}{mg} = \dfrac{9.6 \times 10^{-16} \text{ nt}}{(9.1 \times 10^{-31} \text{ kg})(9.8 \text{ m/sec}^2)} = 1.08 \times 10^{14}$

The gravitational force is entirely negligible compared with the electrical force.

14. A charged particle remains stationary in an upwardly directed field between two horizontal parallel charged plates separated by 2 cm. Compute the potential difference V between the plates if the particle has mass 4×10^{-13} kg and charge 2.4×10^{-18} coul.

Solution:

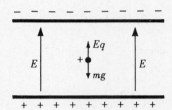

$$\text{Downward weight of particle} = \text{upward electrical force}$$
$$mg = Eq = (V/r)q$$

Then $V = \dfrac{mgr}{q} = \dfrac{(4 \times 10^{-13} \text{ kg})(9.8 \text{ m/sec}^2)(2 \times 10^{-2} \text{ m})}{2.4 \times 10^{-18} \text{ coul}}$

$\quad = 3.3 \times 10^4 \dfrac{\text{kg-m}^2/\text{sec}^2}{\text{coul}} = 3.3 \times 10^4 \dfrac{\text{joules}}{\text{coul}}$ or volts.

15. If electrons are caused to fall through a potential difference of 1500 volts, determine their final speed if they were initially at rest. An electron has mass 9.11×10^{-31} kg and charge -1.60×10^{-19} coul.

Solution:

$$\text{K.E. gained by an electron} = \text{work done by field on an electron}$$
$$\tfrac{1}{2}mv^2 = q(V_2 - V_1)$$

Solving, $v = \sqrt{\dfrac{2q(V_2 - V_1)}{m}} = \sqrt{\dfrac{2(1.60 \times 10^{-19} \text{ coul})(1500 \text{ v})}{9.11 \times 10^{-31} \text{ kg}}} = 2.3 \times 10^7 \text{ m/sec}$

16. A capacitor with air between its plates has a capacitance of 8 microfarads (8 μf). Determine the capacitance when glass is substituted for air. K for glass is 6.

Solution:

Capacitance varies directly with the dielectric constant K. K for air is 1.
Capacitance with glass between plates $= 6 \times 8 \ \mu\text{f} = 48 \ \mu\text{f}$.

17. The capacitance of a capacitor is 300 micromicrofarads ($= 300 \ \mu\mu\text{f} = 300 \times 10^{-12}$ farad). The potential difference between the plates is 1000 volts. Find the charge q on each plate.

Solution: $\quad q = CV = (3 \times 10^{-10} \text{ farad})(10^3 \text{ volts}) = 3 \times 10^{-7} \text{ coulomb}$

18. A given conductor has a potential of 200 volts when charged with 6×10^{-9} coulomb. What is the capacitance of the capacitor formed by the conductor and its surroundings?

Solution:

Capacitance $C = \dfrac{\text{charge } q}{\text{potential } V} = \dfrac{6 \times 10^{-9} \text{ coulomb}}{200 \text{ volts}} = 3 \times 10^{-11} \text{ farad}$

19. A 1.2 microfarad television set capacitor is subjected to a 3000 volt potential difference across its terminals. Compute the energy stored in the capacitor.

Solution: $\quad W = \tfrac{1}{2}CV^2 = \tfrac{1}{2}(1.2 \times 10^{-6} \text{ farad})(3 \times 10^3 \text{ volts})^2 = 5.4 \text{ joules}$

20. Two capacitors, of capacitances $C_1 = 3 \ \mu\mu\text{f}$ and $C_2 = 6 \ \mu\mu\text{f}$, are connected in series and the resulting combination is connected across 1000 volts. Compute (a) the equivalent capacitance C of the combination, (b) the total charge on the combination and the charge taken by each capacitor, (c) the potential difference across each capacitor, (d) the energy W stored in the capacitors.

Solution:

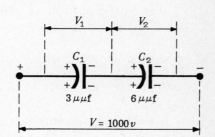

(a) $\dfrac{1}{C} = \dfrac{1}{C_1} + \dfrac{1}{C_2} = \dfrac{1}{3 \ \mu\mu\text{f}} + \dfrac{1}{6 \ \mu\mu\text{f}} = \dfrac{1}{2 \ \mu\mu\text{f}}, \quad C = 2 \ \mu\mu\text{f}$

(b) $q = CV = (2 \times 10^{-12} \ \text{f})(10^3 \ \text{v}) = 2 \times 10^{-9} \ \text{coul}$
The charge on each is also 2×10^{-9} coul.

(c) $V_1 \ (\text{across } C_1) = \dfrac{q}{C_1} = \dfrac{2 \times 10^{-9} \ \text{c}}{3 \times 10^{-12} \ \text{f}} = 667 \ \text{volts}$

$V_2 \ (\text{across } C_2) = \dfrac{q}{C_2} = \dfrac{2 \times 10^{-9} \ \text{c}}{6 \times 10^{-12} \ \text{f}} = 333 \ \text{volts}$

(d) $W = \tfrac{1}{2}qV = \tfrac{1}{2}(2 \times 10^{-9} \ \text{c})(10^3 \ \text{v}) = 10^{-6} \ \text{joule}$

21. Two capacitors, of capacitances $C_1 = 200 \ \mu\mu\text{f}$ and $C_2 = 600 \ \mu\mu\text{f}$, are connected in parallel and then charged to a potential of 120 volts. Determine the charge on each and the equivalent capacitance C of the combination.

Solution:

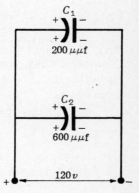

For capacitors connected in parallel, the voltage across each capacitor equals the voltage across the combination.

$q_1 = C_1 V = (200 \times 10^{-12} \ \text{f})(120 \ \text{v}) = 2.4 \times 10^{-8} \ \text{coul}$
$q_2 = C_2 V = (600 \times 10^{-12} \ \text{f})(120 \ \text{v}) = 7.2 \times 10^{-8} \ \text{coul}$
Total charge on combination $= q_1 + q_2 = 9.6 \times 10^{-8}$ coul.

Equivalent capacitance $C = C_1 + C_2 = 800 \ \mu\mu\text{f} = 8 \times 10^{-10} \ \text{f}$.

22. A capacitor consists of two parallel plates separated by a layer of air 0.4 cm thick, the area of each plate being 202 cm^2. (a) Compute its capacitance C. (b) If the capacitor is connected across a 500 volt source, find the charge q on each plate, the energy W stored in the capacitor, and the electric intensity in the air between the plates. (c) If a sheet of mica, 0.4 cm thick and dielectric constant 6, is inserted between the plates, find the additional charge the capacitor will take up and the total energy stored in the capacitor.

Solution:

(a) $C = K\epsilon_0 \dfrac{A}{d} = (1)(8.85 \times 10^{-12} \ \dfrac{\text{coul}^2}{\text{nt-m}^2})(\dfrac{202 \times 10^{-4} \ \text{m}^2}{4 \times 10^{-3} \ \text{m}}) = 44.7 \times 10^{-12} \ \text{f} = 44.7 \ \mu\mu\text{f}$

(b) $q = CV = (44.7 \times 10^{-12} \ \text{f})(500 \ \text{v}) = 2.24 \times 10^{-8} \ \text{coul}$

$W = \tfrac{1}{2}qV = \tfrac{1}{2}(2.24 \times 10^{-8} \ \text{coul})(500 \ \text{v}) = 5.6 \times 10^{-6} \ \text{joule}$

$E = \dfrac{V}{d} = \dfrac{500 \ \text{v}}{4 \times 10^{-3} \ \text{m}} = 1.25 \times 10^5 \ \text{volts/meter} \quad \text{or} \quad 1.25 \times 10^5 \ \text{newtons/coulomb}$

(c) Since V is still the same and C is $K = 6$ times as large, the total charge will be 6 times the initial charge. Hence the additional charge will be 5 times the initial charge, or

$$5 \times 2.24 \times 10^{-8} \ \text{coul} = 11.2 \times 10^{-8} \ \text{coul}$$

The total energy will be 6 times the initial energy, or 3.36×10^{-5} joule.

SUPPLEMENTARY PROBLEMS

23. How many electrons are contained in 1 coulomb of charge? What is the mass and weight of the electrons in 1 coulomb of charge?   *Ans.* 6.2×10^{18} electrons, 5.7×10^{-12} kg, 5.6×10^{-11} nt

24. If two equal charges, each of 1 coulomb, were separated in air by a distance of 1 km, what would be the force between them?   *Ans.* 9000 nt repulsion

25. Determine the force between two free electrons spaced 1 angstrom (10^{-10} m) apart.
  Ans. 2.3×10^{-8} nt repulsion

26. What is the force of repulsion between two argon nuclei when separated by 1 millimicron (10^{-9} m)? The charge on an argon nucleus is $+18e$.   *Ans.* 7.5×10^{-8} nt

27. Two equally charged pith balls are 3 cm apart in air and repel each other with a force of 4×10^{-5} nt. Compute the charge on each ball.   *Ans.* 2×10^{-9} coul

28. Two small equal pith balls are 3 cm apart in air and carry charges of $+3 \times 10^{-9}$ and -12×10^{-9} coul respectively. Compute the force of attraction. If the balls are touched and then separated by a distance of 3 cm, what will be the force between them?
  Ans. 3.6×10^{-4} nt attraction, 2.0×10^{-4} nt repulsion

29. Charges of +2, +3 and −8 microcoulombs are placed in air at the vertices of an equilateral triangle of side 10 cm. Calculate the magnitude of the force acting on the $-8 \ \mu c$ due to the other two charges.
  Ans. 31.4 nt

30. Determine the electric intensity and potential in air at a distance of 3 cm from a charge of 5×10^{-8} coul.
  Ans. 5×10^{5} newtons/coulomb, 1.5×10^{4} volts

31. Compute the electric intensity and potential at a distance of 1 millimicron from a helium nucleus of charge $+2e$. What is the potential energy of a proton at this position?
  Ans. 2.88×10^{9} nt/coul, 2.88 volts, 4.61×10^{-19} joule

32. Determine the acceleration of a proton in an electric field of intensity 500 nt/coul. How many times is this acceleration greater than that due to gravity? The proton mass is 1.67×10^{-27} kg.
  Ans. 4.8×10^{10} m/sec^2, 4.9×10^{9}

33. An electron of mass m kg and charge e coul is projected with horizontal speed v m/sec into an electric field of intensity E nt/coul directed downward. Find: (a) the horizontal and vertical components of its acceleration, a_x and a_y; (b) its horizontal and vertical displacements, x and y, after t sec; (c) the equation of its trajectory.

  Ans. (a) $a_x = 0$, $a_y = \dfrac{Ee}{m}$ (b) $x = vt$, $y = \tfrac{1}{2} a_y t^2 = \tfrac{1}{2}(\dfrac{Ee}{m})t^2$ (c) $y = \tfrac{1}{2}(\dfrac{Ee}{m})(\dfrac{x}{v})^2 = \tfrac{1}{2}(\dfrac{Ee}{mv^2})x^2$, a parabola

34. Determine the electric intensity and potential midway between two charges separated by 6 meters when the charges are (a) $+10^{-8}$ and -10^{-8} coul, (b) $+10^{-8}$ and $+10^{-8}$ coul, (c) $+10^{-8}$ and -10^{-9} coul. (d) Find the force on a charge of -10^{-6} coul placed midway between the charges in (a).
  Ans. (a) 20 nt/coul, 0 v; (b) 0 nt/coul, 60 v; (c) 11 nt/coul, 27 v;
        (d) 2×10^{-5} nt directed toward the $+10^{-8}$ coul

35. What work is required to bring a charge of 2×10^{-7} coul from a point in vacuum 30 cm from a charge of 3×10^{-6} coul to a point 12 cm from it?   *Ans.* 2.7×10^{-2} joule

36. Determine the work done when an electron moves through a potential difference of 6 volts.
  Ans. 9.6×10^{-19} joule

37. Two point charges of $+2 \ \mu c$ and $-3 \ \mu c$ are fixed at points A and B respectively which are 1 meter apart in air. Calculate the position on the straight line passing through A and B of (a) the point of zero electric intensity, (b) the point of zero potential.
  Ans. (a) 4.45 m beyond A and 5.45 m from B.
        (b) 40 cm from A and 60 cm from B; also 2 m beyond A and 3 m from B.

38. In the preceding problem, calculate the work required to transfer a charge of $-5\ \mu c$ from a point 10 cm from A to a point 10 cm from B, both points being between A and B. Which point is at the higher potential?
Ans. 2.0 joules. The point 10 cm from A is at the higher potential, and the $-5\ \mu c$ acquires 2.0 joules of additional potential energy when transferred to a point 10 cm from B.

39. A vacuum tube has two parallel plates, 4 cm apart, at a potential difference of 300 volts. Determine (a) the electric intensity in the space between the plates, (b) the force acting on an electron in the field between the plates, (c) the energy gained by an electron in moving 4 cm from cathode to anode and the speed with which it strikes the anode assuming it is released at the cathode with zero initial speed.
Ans. (a) 7.5×10^3 nt/coul; (b) 1.2×10^{-15} nt; (c) 4.8×10^{-17} joule, 1.03×10^7 m/sec

40. A potential difference of 2.4×10^4 volts maintains a downward directed electric field between two horizontal parallel plates separated by 1.8 cm. Find the charge on an oil droplet of mass 2.2×10^{-10} g which remains stationary in the field between the plates.   *Ans.* 1.6×10^{-18} coul

41. Determine the kinetic energy and speed of a proton after being accelerated through a potential difference of one million volts. A proton has mass 1.67×10^{-27} kg and charge $+1.60 \times 10^{-19}$ coul.
Ans. 1.6×10^{-13} joule, 1.4×10^7 m/sec

42. A heated filament emits electrons which are accelerated to the anode by a potential difference of 500 volts maintained between filament and anode. Find the kinetic energy and speed of an electron as it strikes the anode.   *Ans.* 8.0×10^{-17} joule, 1.3×10^7 m/sec

43. What distance must an electron move in a field of uniform potential gradient 200 volts/cm in order to gain kinetic energy 3.2×10^{-18} joule?   *Ans.* 10^{-3} m

44. A capacitor with air between its plates has capacitance 3 microfarads. What is the capacitance when wax of dielectric constant 2.8 is between the plates?   *Ans.* $8.4\ \mu f$

45. Determine the charge on each plate of a .05 μf capacitor when the potential difference between the plates is 200 volts.   *Ans.* 10 microcoulombs

46. A capacitor is charged with 9.6×10^{-9} coul and has 120 volts potential difference between its terminals. Compute its capacitance and the energy stored in it.   *Ans.* 80 $\mu\mu f$, 5.76×10^{-7} joule

47. Compute the energy stored in a 60 $\mu\mu f$ capacitor (a) when charged to a potential difference of 2000 volts, (b) when the charge on each plate is 3×10^{-8} coul.
Ans. (a) 1.2×10^{-4} joule, (b) 7.5×10^{-8} joule

48. Three capacitors, each of capacitance 120 $\mu\mu f$, are charged each to 500 volts and then connected in series. Determine (a) the capacitance of the system, (b) the potential difference between the end plates, (c) the charge on each capacitor, and (d) the energy stored in the system.
Ans. (a) 40 $\mu\mu f$, (b) 1500 volts, (c) 6×10^{-8} coul, (d) 4.5×10^{-5} joule

49. Two capacitances of 0.3 and 0.5 microfarads are connected in parallel and then charged with 200 microcoulombs. Determine (a) the capacitance and potential of the system and (b) the charge on each capacitor.
Ans. (a) 0.8 μf, 250 volts; (b) 75 μc, 125 μc

50. A 2 μf capacitor is charged to 50 volts and then connected in parallel with a 4 μf capacitor charged to 100 volts. Determine (a) the charge and potential difference of the system, (b) the charge on each capacitor of the system, (c) the energy stored in the system, (d) the total energy stored in the original two capacitors before the parallel connection is made.
Ans. (a) 500 μc, 83.3 volts; (b) 167 μc, 333 μc; (c) 2.08×10^{-2} joule; (d) 2.25×10^{-2} joule

51. (a) Calculate the capacitance of a capacitor consisting of two parallel plates separated by a layer of paraffin wax 0.5 cm thick, the area of each plate being 80 cm^2. The dielectric constant for the wax is 2. (b) If the capacitor is connected to a 100 volt source, calculate the charge on the capacitor and the energy stored in the capacitor.
Ans. (a) 28 $\mu\mu f$, (b) 2800 $\mu\mu c$ or 2.8×10^{-9} coul, 1.4×10^{-7} joule

Chapter 23

Ohm's Law

A CURRENT I of electricity exists in a conductor whenever electric charge q is being transferred from one point to another in that conductor. If charge is transferred at the uniform rate of 1 coulomb per second, then the constant current existing in the conductor is 1 ampere.

$$I \text{ (current)} = \frac{q \text{ (charge transferred)}}{t \text{ (time taken to transfer this charge)}}$$

$$I \text{ (amperes)} = \frac{q \text{ (coulombs)}}{t \text{ (seconds)}}$$

THE POTENTIAL DIFFERENCE V between two points in a conductor is measured by the work W required to transfer unit charge from one point to the other. The **volt** is the potential difference (abbreviated p.d.) between two points in a conductor when 1 joule of work is required to transfer 1 coulomb of charge from one point to the other.

$$V \text{ (potential difference)} = \frac{W \text{ (work to transfer charge)}}{q \text{ (charge transferred)}}$$

$$V \text{ (volts)} = \frac{W \text{ (joules)}}{q \text{ (coulombs)}}$$

If two points of an external circuit have a potential difference V, then a charge q in passing between the two circuit points does an amount of work $W = qV$ as it moves from the higher to the lower potential point.

ELECTROMOTIVE FORCE, ε. An agent such as a battery or generator has an electromotive force (emf) if it does work **on the charge** moving through it, the charge receiving electrical energy as it moves from the lower to the higher potential side. Emf is measured by the p.d. (potential difference) between the terminals when the battery or generator is not delivering current. The units of emf are the same as the units of p.d., since both are measured by work per unit charge. The mks unit of emf is the volt (1 joule per coulomb).

THE RESISTANCE R of a conductor is the property which depends on its dimensions, material and temperature and which determines the current produced in it by a given potential difference. The **ohm** is the resistance of a conductor in which there is a current of 1 ampere when the potential difference between its ends is 1 volt.

$$R \text{ (resistance)} = \frac{V \text{ (potential difference)}}{I \text{ (current)}}$$

$$R \text{ (ohms)} = \frac{V \text{ (volts)}}{I \text{ (amperes)}}$$

OHM'S LAW. The value of the steady electrical current I in a metallic conductor at a constant temperature is equal to the potential difference V between the ends of the conductor divided by the resistance R of the conductor.

$$I \text{ (current)} = \frac{V \text{ (potential difference)}}{R \text{ (resistance)}}$$

$$I \text{ (amperes)} = \frac{V \text{ (volts)}}{R \text{ (ohms)}}$$

Ohm's law may be applied to any part of a circuit or to the entire circuit. Thus the potential difference, or voltage drop, across any part of a conductor is equal to the current I in the conductor multiplied by the resistance R of that part, or $V = IR$.

As applied to the entire circuit (containing a source of emf), Ohm's law states that

$$\text{total current } I \text{ in circuit} = \frac{\text{total emf } \mathcal{E} \text{ in circuit}}{\text{total resistance } R \text{ of circuit}} \quad \text{or} \quad I = \frac{\mathcal{E}}{R}.$$

MEASUREMENT OF RESISTANCE BY AMMETER AND VOLTMETER. The **current** is measured by inserting in series a (**low resistance**) ammeter into the circuit. The **potential difference** is measured by connecting the terminals of a (**high resistance**) voltmeter across the resistance being measured, i.e. in parallel. The **resistance** is computed by dividing the voltmeter reading by the ammeter reading according to Ohm's law, $R = V/I$. (If an *exact* value of the resistance is required, the resistances of the voltmeter and ammeter must be considered parts of the circuit.)

THE TERMINAL VOLTAGE of a battery or generator when it delivers a current I is equal to the total electromotive force (emf or $\mathcal{E}$) minus the potential drop (or voltage drop) in its internal resistance r.

 (1) **When delivering current**, (on discharge):
  Terminal voltage = emf – voltage drop in internal resistance = $\mathcal{E} - Ir$

 (2) **When receiving current**, (on charge):
  Terminal voltage = emf + voltage drop in internal resistance = $\mathcal{E} + Ir$

 (3) **When no current exists**:
  Terminal voltage = emf of battery or generator

SOLVED PROBLEMS

1. A steady current of 5 amp is maintained in a metallic conductor. What charge q in coulombs is transferred through it in 1 minute?

Solution:

$$q = It = 5 \text{ amp} \times 60 \text{ sec} = 300 \text{ coul}$$

2. The electron of a hydrogen atom moves in a circular orbit of radius 5.3×10^{-11} meter with a speed of 2.2×10^6 m/sec. Determine its frequency f and the current I in the orbit.

Solution:

$$f = \frac{v}{2\pi r} = \frac{2.2 \times 10^6 \text{ m/sec}}{2\pi(5.3 \times 10^{-11})\text{m/rev}} = 6.6 \times 10^{15} \text{ rev/sec}$$

The charge passes every point of the orbit 6.6×10^{15} times each second.

$$I = \frac{q}{t} = \frac{q}{1/f} = qf = (1.60 \times 10^{-19} \text{ coul})(6.6 \times 10^{15}/\text{sec}) = 1.06 \times 10^{-3} \text{ amp}$$

3. A current of 20 amp exists in a copper wire of cross section 0.05 cm^2. Calculate the average drift speed of the active electrons in the wire, assuming each atom of the metal contributes one electron to the conduction process. Copper has density 8.92 g/cm^3 and atomic weight 63.5.

Solution:

Mass of 1 cm length of wire = volume $\times$ density = $.05$ cm$^3 \times 8.92$ g/cm^3 = 0.446 g

A mass of 63.5 g Cu contains 6.02×10^{23} atoms and 6.02×10^{23} free electrons.

Free electrons/cm of wire = $\dfrac{0.446 \text{ g/cm}}{63.5 \text{ g}} \times 6.02 \times 10^{23}$ electrons = 4.23×10^{21} elec/cm

20 amp = 20 coul/sec = $20(6.24 \times 10^{18}$ elec)/sec = 1.25×10^{20} electrons/sec passing through a given section of the wire.

Drift speed of active electrons = $\dfrac{1.25 \times 10^{20} \text{ elec/sec}}{4.23 \times 10^{21} \text{ elec/cm}}$ = 2.96×10^{-2} cm/sec

4. What current is in an electric iron having a hot resistance of 22 ohms when connected across a 110 volt line?

Solution:

$$I = \frac{V}{R} = \frac{110 \text{ volts}}{22 \text{ ohms}} = 5 \text{ amperes}$$

5. An electric heater uses 5 amperes when 110 volts are applied to its terminals. Determine its resistance.

Solution:

$$R = \frac{V}{I} = \frac{110 \text{ volts}}{5 \text{ amp}} = 22 \text{ ohms}$$

6. What is the potential drop across an electric hotplate which draws 5 amperes from the line when its hot resistance is 24 ohms?

Solution:

$$V = IR = 5 \text{ amp} \times 24 \text{ ohms} = 120 \text{ volts}$$

7. A dry cell has an emf of 1.52 volts. Determine its internal resistance r if the short-circuit current is 25 amperes.

Solution:

$$r = \frac{\mathcal{E}}{I} = \frac{1.52 \text{ volts}}{25 \text{ amp}} = .061 \text{ ohm}$$

8. The ammeter-voltmeter method is used to measure an unknown resistance R. An ammeter (A) connected in series with the resistance reads 0.3 amp. A voltmeter (V) placed across the ends of the resistance reads 1.5 volts. Compute the value of the resistance R. Neglect instrument losses.

Solution:

$$R = \frac{V}{I} = \frac{1.5 \text{ volts}}{0.3 \text{ amp}} = 5 \text{ ohms}$$

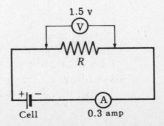

9. A battery of emf 10 volts and internal resistance $r = 1$ ohm is connected to a resistance $R = 4$ ohms. Determine (a) the current in the circuit, (b) the potential drop in the internal resistance and also across the 4 ohm resistance, (c) the terminal voltage of the battery, (d) the reading of a voltmeter connected across the battery terminals in open circuit.

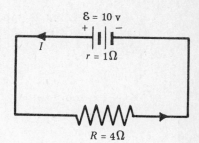

Solution:

(a) $I = \dfrac{\mathcal{E}}{r + R} = \dfrac{10 \text{ volts}}{(1 + 4) \text{ ohms}} = 2$ amp

(b) $V_1 = Ir = 2$ amp $\times$ 1 ohm $= 2$ volts
$V_4 = IR = 2$ amp $\times$ 4 ohms $= 8$ volts

(c) Terminal voltage $= \mathcal{E} - Ir = 10$ volts $- (2 \times 1)$ volts $= 8$ volts
The terminal voltage evidently equals the potential drop in the external circuit.

(d) Assuming the resistance of the voltmeter to be high enough so that it draws negligible current, the voltmeter reading in open circuit gives the emf, 10 volts.

10. A D.C. generator produces an emf of 120 volts on open circuit. With a load of 20 amp the terminal voltage drops to 115 volts. (a) What is the internal resistance r of the generator? (b) What will be the terminal voltage at a load of 40 amp?

Solution:

(a) Emf $-$ terminal voltage $= Ir$ (voltage drop in internal resistance)
120 volts $-$ 115 volts $= 20$ amp $\times r$ $r = 0.25$ ohm

(b) Terminal voltage $=$ emf $- Ir = 120$ volts $- 40$ amp $\times 0.25$ ohm $= 110$ volts

11. A storage battery of emf 20 volts and internal resistance $r = 0.1$ ohm is to be charged from 110 volt mains as shown in the adjoining figure. What resistance R must be placed in series with the battery to limit the charging rate to 15 amp?

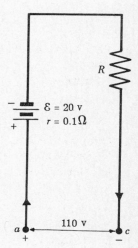

Solution:

Total potential drop in circuit clockwise from a to c $=$ 110 volts
Ir drop $+$ potential drop due to opposing emf $+ IR$ drop $=$ 110 volts
$(15 \times 0.1) + 20 + 15R = 110$
$R = 5.9$ ohms

12. A storage battery has emf 15 volts and internal resistance .05 ohm. Calculate its terminal voltage (a) when it is delivering 10 amp, (b) when it is being charged with 10 amp.

Solution:

(a) Terminal voltage $=$ emf $- Ir$ drop in battery
$= 15$ volts $- (10 \times .05)$ volts $= 14.5$ volts

(b) Terminal voltage $= Ir$ drop $+$ potential drop due to its opposing emf
$= (10 \times .05)$ volts $+ 15$ volts $= 15.5$ volts

13. Two batteries, of emfs 25 and 10 volts and internal resistances 0.4 and 0.1 ohms respectively, are in series with a 2.5 ohm resistor, as shown in Fig. (a) below.
(a) Calculate the current I in the circuit.
(b) Arbitrarily choose the potential at point a as 0 volts and then find the relative potentials (relative to $V_a = 0$ volts) at points b and c.

(c) Determine the potential difference between points a and b, b and c, c and a.
Solution:

(a) Since $\mathcal{E}_1 > \mathcal{E}_2$, the positive direction of the current is clockwise.

$$I = \frac{\Sigma \mathcal{E}}{\Sigma R} = \frac{(25 - 10)\ \text{volts}}{(0.4 + 0.1 + 2.5)\ \text{ohms}} = 5\ \text{amp}$$

(b) $V_a = 0$ volts, arbitrarily chosen.

$V_b = V_a + \mathcal{E}_1 - Ir_1 = 0 + 25 - 5(0.4) = 23$ volts
$V_c = V_b - \mathcal{E}_2 - Ir_2 = 23 - 10 - 5(0.1) = 12.5$ volts

(c) $V_{ab} = V_a - V_b = 0 - 23 = -23$ volts. The negative sign indicates that the potential at b is 23 volts higher than at a. A voltmeter connected across points a and b reads 23 volts.

$V_{bc} = V_b - V_c = 23 - 12.5 = 10.5$ volts, point b being at the higher potential.
$V_{ca} = V_c - V_a = 12.5 - 0 = 12.5$ volts, point c being at the higher potential.

Check: Around the closed circuit, $V_{ab} + V_{bc} + V_{ca} = -23 + 10.5 + 12.5 = 0$ volts.

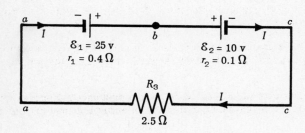

Fig.(a) Problem 13

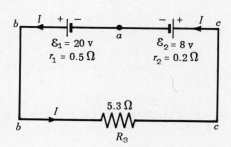

Fig.(b) Problem 14

14. Two batteries, of emfs 20 and 8 volts and internal resistances 0.5 and 0.2 ohms respectively, are in series with a 5.3 ohm resistor as shown in Fig.(b) above.
   (a) Calculate the current I in the circuit.
   (b) Arbitrarily choose the potential at point a as 0 volts and then find the relative potentials (relative to $V_a = 0$ volts) at points b and c.
   (c) Determine the potential differences V_{ab}, V_{bc}, V_{ca}.
Solution:

(a) Since $\mathcal{E}_1 > \mathcal{E}_2$, the positive direction of the current is counterclockwise.

$$I = \frac{\Sigma \mathcal{E}}{\Sigma R} = \frac{(20 - 8)\ \text{volts}}{(0.2 + 0.5 + 5.3)\ \text{ohms}} = 2\ \text{amp}$$

(b) $V_b = V_a + \mathcal{E}_1 - Ir_1 = 0 + 20 - 2(0.5) = 19$ volts
   $V_c = V_b - IR_3 = 19 - 2(5.3) = 8.4$ volts

(c) $V_{ab} = V_a - V_b = -19$ volts, $\quad V_{bc} = V_b - V_c = 10.6$ volts, $\quad V_{ca} = V_c - V_a = 8.4$ volts
   Check: Around the closed circuit, $V_{ab} + V_{bc} + V_{ca} = -19 + 10.6 + 8.4 = 0$ volts.

15. In the figure the circuit is grounded at point a, i.e. the potential at point a is assumed zero ($V_a = 0$). Determine the potentials at points b and c relative to ground.
Solution:

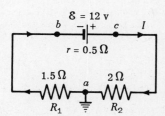

$$I = \frac{\mathcal{E}}{R} = \frac{12\ \text{volts}}{(0.5 + 1.5 + 2)\ \text{ohms}} = 3\ \text{amp}$$

$V_b = V_a - IR_1 = 0 - 3(1.5) = -4.5$ volts, i.e. 4.5 volts below ground.
$V_c = V_b + \mathcal{E} - Ir = -4.5 + 12 - 3(0.5) = +6$ volts, i.e. 6 volts above ground.

Note. $V_{bc} = V_b - V_c = -4.5 - 6 = -10.5$ volts,
   $V_{cb} = V_c - V_b = 6 - (-4.5) = +10.5$ volts.

SUPPLEMENTARY PROBLEMS

16. How many electrons per second pass through a section of wire carrying a current of 1 ampere?
Ans. 6.24×10^{18} electrons/sec

17. Compute the time required to pass 36,000 coulombs through an electroplating bath using a current of 5 amperes.
Ans. 2 hr

18. What is the current through an electric toaster of 8 ohms resistance when it is connected to a 120 volt source?
Ans. 15 amp

19. A lamp draws 1.6 amp when connected to a 120 volt source. What is the hot resistance of the lamp?
Ans. 75 ohms

20. What potential difference is required to pass 3 amp through 28 ohms?   *Ans.* 84 volts

21. Determine the potential difference between the ends of a wire of resistance 5 ohms if 720 coulombs pass through it per minute.   *Ans.* 60 volts

22. A copper busbar carrying 1200 amp has a potential drop of 1.2 millivolts along 24 inches of its length. What is the resistance per foot of the bar?   *Ans.* 5×10^{-7} ohms/ft

23. An ammeter is connected in series with an unknown resistance, and a voltmeter is connected across the terminals of the resistance. If the ammeter reads 1.2 amp and the voltmeter reads 18 volts, compute the value of the resistance.   *Ans.* 15 ohms

24. An electric utility company runs two 100 ft copper wires from the street mains up to a customer's premises. If the wire resistance is 0.100 ohm per 1000 ft, calculate the line voltage drop for an estimated load current of 120 amp D.C.   *Ans.* 2.4 volts

25. When testing the insulation resistance between a motor winding and motor frame, the value obtained is one megohm (10^6 ohms). How much current passes through the insulation of the motor if the test voltage is 1000 volts?   *Ans.* 1 milliamp

26. Compute the internal resistance of an electric generator which has an emf of 120 volts, and a terminal voltage of 110 volts when supplying 20 amp.   *Ans.* 0.5 ohm

27. A dry cell delivering 2 amp has terminal voltage 1.41 volts. What is the internal resistance of the cell if its open circuit voltage is 1.59 volts?   *Ans.* .09 ohm

28. A cell has emf 1.54 volts. When it is in series with a 1 ohm resistance, the reading of a voltmeter connected across the cell terminals is 1.40 volts. Determine its internal resistance.   *Ans.* 0.10 ohm

29. A 5 ohm coil is in series with a lamp and connected to a 100 volt source. Compute the resistance of the lamp if the current in the circuit is 4 amp.   *Ans.* 20 ohms

30. Two resistances, of 12 and 2.4 ohms, are connected in series and then connected to the terminals of an electric generator. The generator produces an emf of 75 volts and has internal resistance 0.6 ohm. Determine (a) the current in the circuit, (b) the potential drop in the 2.4 ohm resistance and in the 12 ohm resistance, (c) the terminal voltage of the generator when the current exists, (d) the reading of the voltmeter connected across the generator terminals in open circuit.
Ans. (a) 5 amp; (b) 12 volts, 60 volts; (c) 72 volts; (d) 75 volts

31. The internal resistance of a 6.4 volt storage battery is .0048 ohm. What is the theoretical maximum current on short circuit? (In practice the leads and connections have some resistance and this value would not be attained.)   *Ans.* 1.3×10^3 amp

32. Calculate the open circuit generator voltage required to supply an electric oven rated at 25 amp if the combined resistance of the heating units is 8.0 ohms, the resistance of the connecting cables is 0.30 ohm, and the internal resistance of the generator is 0.10 ohm.   *Ans.* 210 volts

33. A battery has emf 13.2 volts and internal resistance .024 ohm. If the load current is 20.0 amp, find the terminal voltage.   *Ans.* 12.7 volts

34. What is the maximum allowable discharge current of a 55 cell storage battery having emf 121 volts and total internal resistance 0.100 ohm if the terminal voltage must not fall below 110 volts?   *Ans.* 110 amp

35. A storage battery has emf 25 volts and internal resistance 0.20 ohm. Compute its terminal voltage (a) when it is delivering 8 amp, (b) when it is being charged with 8 amp.

Ans. (a) 23.4 volts, (b) 26.6 volts

36. A battery charger supplies a D.C. current of 10 amp to charge a storage battery which has an open circuit voltage of 5.6 volts. If the voltmeter connected across the charger reads 6.8 volts, what is the internal resistance of the battery at this time?   *Ans.* 0.12 ohm

37. Three series connected cells, each of emf 1.5 volts and internal resistance 2 ohms, are connected in series with a storage battery of unknown emf and internal resistance. The total resistance of the connecting wires is 0.4 ohm. The observed current is 1.25 amp. When the storage battery terminals are reversed, the observed current is 0.18 amp in the opposite direction. Calculate (a) the emf and internal resistance of the storage battery and (b) the reading of a high resistance voltmeter connected across the storage battery for each connection.

   Ans. (a) Solve two simultaneous equations to obtain $\mathcal{E}$ = 6.01 volts, r = 2.01 ohms.
   (b) 3.50 volts, 5.65 volts

38. Referring to Fig. (a) and (b) below, for each circuit determine the current and the potential differences V_{ab}, V_{bc}, V_{ca}.

   Ans. Fig. (a): I = 4 amp, V_{ab} = −17 v, V_{bc} = +10.8 v, V_{ca} = +6.2 v
   Fig. (b): I = 2 amp, V_{ab} = +13.4 v, V_{bc} = −25 v, V_{ca} = +11.6 v

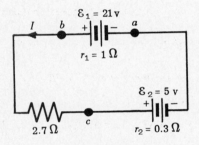

Fig. (a) Problem 38

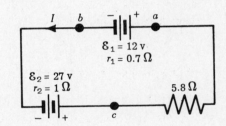

Fig. (b) Problem 38

39. Referring to Fig. (c) below, find the current in the circuit and the terminal voltage of each battery.
   Ans. 4 amp, V_1 = 16 v, V_2 = 12 v, V_3 = 24 v

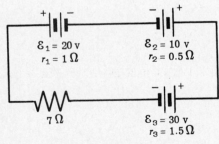

Fig. (c) Problem 39

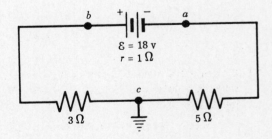

Fig. (d) Problem 40

40. In Fig. (d) above the circuit is grounded at c, i.e. the potential at point c is assumed zero (V_c = 0). Determine the potentials at points a and b relative to ground, and the potential differences V_{ab}, V_{bc}, V_{ca}.

   Ans. V_a = −10 v, V_b = 6 v, V_{ab} = −16 v, V_{bc} = 6 v, V_{ca} = 10 v

Chapter 24

Electrical Energy, Heat, Power

ELECTRICAL ENERGY, HEAT, POWER. The work W in joules done in transferring in a circuit a charge of q coulombs between two terminals having a potential difference V volts is

$$W = qV = (It)V = IVt$$

Since $V = IR$, $IVt = I(IR)t = I^2Rt$. Thus the electrical energy in joules converted into heat in a conductor of resistance R ohms carrying a current I amperes is

$$W = I^2Rt$$

which is called Joule's law of heating. Since 1 joule = 0.239 calorie, the heat H in calories developed in the conductor is

$$H = 0.239\,I^2Rt$$

Since average power $P = W/t = IVt/t = IV$, using Ohm's law ($V = IR$, $I = V/R$) we obtain

$$P = IV = I^2R = V^2/R$$

where P is in joules/sec or watts, I in amperes, V in volts, R in ohms.

> 1 watt = 1 joule/sec = 0.239 cal/sec = 0.738 ft-lb/sec
> 1 kilowatt (kw) = 1000 watts = 1.341 hp = 56.9 Btu/min
> 1 horsepower (hp) = 0.746 kw = 3.30×10^4 ft-lb/min = 42.4 Btu/min

SOLVED PROBLEMS

1. Compute the work and the average power required to transfer 96,000 coulombs of charge in one hour through a potential difference of 50 volts.

   Solution:

   Work $W = qV = 96{,}000$ coul $\times 50$ volts $= 4.8 \times 10^6$ joules

   Power $P = W/t = (4.8 \times 10^6)/(3.6 \times 10^3)$ joules/sec $= 1.33 \times 10^3$ watts $= 1.33$ kw

2. An electric motor takes 5 amp from a 110 volt line. Determine the power input and the energy, in joules and in kw-hr, supplied to the motor in 2 hr.

   Solution:

   Power $P = IV = 5$ amp $\times 110$ volts $= 550$ watts $= 0.55$ kw

   Energy $W = Pt = (IV)t = 550$ watts $\times 2(3600)$ sec $= 3.96 \times 10^6$ joules
   $= 0.55$ kw $\times 2$ hr $= 1.1$ kw-hr

3. An electric iron of resistance 20 ohms takes a current of 5 amp. Calculate the heat, in joules and in calories, developed in 30 seconds.

Solution:

Heat in joules $= I^2Rt = (5\,\text{amp})^2 \times 20\,\text{ohms} \times 30\,\text{sec} = 15 \times 10^3$ joules

Heat in calories $= 0.239\,(I^2Rt) = (0.239\,\text{cal/joule})(15 \times 10^3\,\text{joules}) = 3.6 \times 10^3$ cal

4. An electric heater of resistance 8 ohms draws 15 amp from the service mains. At what rate is heat developed, in watts and in cal/sec? What is the cost of operating the heater for 4 hr at 5¢/kw-hr?

Solution:

Heat rate in watts $= I^2R = (15\,\text{amp})^2 \times 8\,\text{ohms} = 1800\,\text{watts} = 1.8$ kw

Heat rate in cal/sec $= 0.239\,I^2R = 0.239\,(\text{cal/sec})/\text{watt} \times 1800\,\text{watts} = 430$ cal/sec

Cost $= 1.8\,\text{kw} \times 4\,\text{hr} \times 5¢/\text{kw-hr} = 36¢$

5. A coil develops 800 cal/sec when 20 volts are supplied across its ends. Compute its resistance.

Solution:

Heat rate in cal/sec $= 0.239\,I^2R = 0.239\,V^2/R$, $800 = 0.239\,(20)^2/R$, $R = 0.12$ ohm

6. A line having a total resistance of 0.2 ohm delivers 10 kw at 250 volts to a small factory. What is the efficiency of the transmission?

Solution:

Power lost in line $= I^2R = \left(\dfrac{IV}{V}\right)^2 R = \left(\dfrac{10,000\,\text{watts}}{250\,\text{volts}}\right)^2 \times 0.2\,\text{ohm} = 320$ watts

Efficiency $= \dfrac{\text{power delivered by line}}{\text{power supplied to line}} = \dfrac{10\,\text{kw}}{(10 + 0.32)\,\text{kw}} = 0.97 = 97\%$

7. A hoist motor supplied by 240 volts requires 12 amp to lift a ton weight at the rate of 25 ft/minute. Determine the power input to the motor, the power output in horsepower, and the overall efficiency of the system.

Solution:

Power input $= IV = 12\,\text{amp} \times 240\,\text{volts} = 2880\,\text{watts} = 2.88$ kw

$= 2.88\,\text{kw} \times 1.34\,\text{hp/kw} = 3.86$ hp

Power output $= Fv = 2000\,\text{lb} \times 25\,\text{ft/min} \times \dfrac{1\,\text{hp}}{33,000\,\text{ft-lb/min}} = 1.52$ hp

Overall efficiency $= \dfrac{1.52\,\text{hp output}}{3.86\,\text{hp input}} = 0.394 = 39.4\%$

8. What is the cost of electrically heating 50 liters of water from 40°C to 100°C at 4¢/kw-hr?

Solution:

Heat gained by water $=$ mass $\times$ specific heat $\times$ temperature rise

$= (50 \times 10^3)\text{g} \times 1\,\text{cal/g}°\text{C} \times (100 - 40)°\text{C} = 3 \times 10^6$ cal

Cost $= 3 \times 10^6\,\text{cal} \times \dfrac{4.2\,\text{joules}}{1\,\text{cal}} \times \dfrac{1\,\text{kw-hr}}{3.6 \times 10^6\,\text{joules}} \times \dfrac{4¢}{1\,\text{kw-hr}} = 14¢$

SUPPLEMENTARY PROBLEMS

9. A spark of man-made 10 million volt lightning had an energy output of 1.25×10^5 watt-sec. How many coulombs of charge flowed?   *Ans.* .0125 coul

10. A current of 1.5 amp exists in a conductor whose terminals are connected across a potential difference of 100 volts. Compute the total charge transferred in one minute, the work done in transferring this charge, and the power expended in heating the conductor assuming all the electrical energy is converted into heat. *Ans.* 90 coul, 9000 joules, 150 watts

11. An electric motor takes 15 amp at 110 volts. Determine the power input and the cost of operating the motor for 8 hr at 5¢/kw-hr.   *Ans.* 1.65 kw, 66¢

12. A current of 10 amp exists in a line of 0.15 ohm resistance. Compute the rate of production of heat in watts. *Ans.* 15 watts

13. An electric broiler develops 400 cal/sec when the current through it is 8 amp. Determine the resistance of the broiler.   *Ans.* 26 ohms

14. A lamp, designed to be used on a 120 volt line, is rated 75 watts. Compute the hot resistance of the lamp and the current it takes when connected to a 120 volt source.   *Ans.* 192 ohms, 5/8 amp

15. A 25-watt 120-volt bulb has a cold resistance of 45 ohms and a hot resistance of 575 ohms. When the voltage is switched on, what is the instantaneous current? What is the current under normal operation? *Ans.* 2.67 amp, 0.209 amp

16. At a rated current of 400 amp a defective switch blade becomes overheated due to faulty surface contact. A millivoltmeter connected from the jaw to the switch blade shows a 100 millivolt drop. What is the power loss due to the contact resistance?   *Ans.* 40 watts

17. A 10 ohm electric heater operates on a 110 volt line. Compute the rate at which heat is developed, in watts and in cal/sec.   *Ans.* 1210 watts, 290 cal/sec

18. An electric motor, which has 95% efficiency, uses 20 amp at 110 volts. What is the horsepower output of the motor? How many watts are lost in heat? How many calories of heat are developed per sec? If the motor operates for 3 hr, what energy, in joules and in kw-hr, is consumed?
Ans. 2.8 hp, 110 watts, 26.4 cal/sec, 23.8×10^6 joules, 6.6 kw-hr

19. An electric crane uses 8 amp at 150 volts to raise 1000 lb at the rate of 22 ft/min. Determine the efficiency of the system.   *Ans.* 41.4%

20. What should be the resistance of a heating coil which will be used to raise the temperature of 500 g of water from 28°C to the boiling point in 2 minutes, assuming that 25% of the heat is lost? The heater operates on a 110 volt line.   *Ans.* 7.23 ohms

21. Compute the cost per hr at 4¢/kw-hr of electrically heating a room which requires 1 kg per hr of anthracite coal having a heat of combustion of 8 kcal/g.   *Ans.* 37¢/hr

22. Power is transmitted at 80,000 volts between two stations. If the line voltage can be doubled without change in cable size, how much additional power can be transmitted for the same current and what effect does the power increase have on the line heating loss?
Ans. Additional power = 3 × original power; line heating loss remains the same.

23. A power generating station delivers 10 kw at 250 volts into a D.C. distribution feeder of two wires, each 500 ft in length. If the feeder resistance is 0.259 ohm per 1000 ft, compute (a) the power loss in the feeder, (b) the efficiency of the feeder, (c) the voltage at the far end.   *Ans.* 414 watts, 95.9%, 240 volts

24. A storage battery, of emf 6.4 volts and internal resistance .08 ohm, is being charged by a current of 15 amp. Calculate (a) the power loss in internal heating of the battery, (b) the rate at which energy is stored in the battery, (c) its terminal voltage.   *Ans.* (a) 18 watts, (b) 96 watts, (c) 7.6 volts

25. A tank containing 200 liters of water was used as a constant temperature bath. How long would it take to heat the bath from 20°C to 25°C with a 250 watt immersion heater? Neglect the heat capacity of the tank frame and any heat losses to the air.   *Ans.* 4.6 hr

Chapter 25

Resistance and Circuits

RESISTIVITY. The resistance R of a conductor of length l m and cross section area A m² is

$$R = \rho \frac{l}{A} \quad \text{in ohms}$$

where ρ is a constant called **resistivity** or **specific resistance** and depends on the material of which the conductor is made. It is expressed in ohm-meters.

TEMPERATURE AND RESISTANCE.

$$R_t = R_O(1 + \alpha t) \quad \text{in ohms}$$

where R_t = resistance at t°C, R_O = resistance at 0°C,
α = temperature coefficient of resistance of the material of the conductor.

SUPERCONDUCTIVITY. The resistivity of all metals approaches zero as the temperature approaches absolute zero. For some substances (e.g. Pb, Hg, Sn, CbN) the resistivity drops sharply completely to zero at some *transition temperature* above absolute zero (for tin, at 7.2°K). A current once started in a superconductor will flow indefinitely, as there is no I^2R loss. Superconductivity can be destroyed by placing the sample in a sufficiently large magnetic field.

IN A SERIES CIRCUIT:

   Resistance. $R = R_1 + R_2 + R_3 + \cdots$

where R = equivalent resistance of a series combination of conductors having resistances R_1, R_2, R_3, $\cdots$.

   Potential Difference. The total potential difference across several resistors connected in series is equal to the sum of the potential differences across the separate resistors.

   Current in every part of the series circuit is the same.

IN A PARALLEL CIRCUIT:

   Resistance. $\dfrac{1}{R} = \dfrac{1}{R_1} + \dfrac{1}{R_2} + \dfrac{1}{R_3} + \cdots$

where R = equivalent resistance of parallel combination of conductors having resistances R_1, R_2, R_3, $\cdots$. R is always less than the smallest of the individual resistances. Connecting additional resistors in parallel decreases the joint resistance of the combination.

   Potential Difference across several resistors in parallel is the same as that across each of the resistors. The potential difference is the same across all branches.

   Current. The sum of the currents in the branches is equal to the value of the line current. Current values in the different branches vary inversely as the resistances of the different branches.

KIRCHHOFF'S LAWS are employed in the solution of complex circuits.

(1) The sum of the currents directed toward any point in a circuit equals the sum of the currents directed away from that point. If the currents toward a point are considered positive and those away from the same point negative, then this law states that the algebraic sum of all the currents meeting at a common point is zero.

(2) The sum of the rises of potential around any closed circuit equals the sum of the drops of potential in that circuit. In other words, the algebraic sum of the potential differences around a closed circuit is zero.

SOLVED PROBLEMS

1. Compute the resistance of a hardened copper rod 2 meters long and 8 mm in diameter if the resistivity of the material is 1.756×10^{-8} ohm-meter.

   Solution:

   $$R = \rho \frac{l}{A} = 1.756 \times 10^{-8} \text{ ohm-m} \times \frac{2\,\text{m}}{\frac{1}{4}\pi(8 \times 10^{-3}\,\text{m})^2} = 6.99 \times 10^{-4} \text{ ohm}$$

2. The resistance of a coil of insulated copper wire is 3.35 ohms at 0°C. Determine its resistance at 50°C. Temperature coefficient of resistance of the copper wire is 0.00426/°C.

   Solution:

   $$R_t = R_0(1 + \alpha t) = 3.35 \text{ ohms} \times (1 + .00426/°C \times 50°C) = 4.06 \text{ ohms}$$

3. The resistance of a platinum thermometer is 6.00 ohms at 30°C. Determine its resistance at 100°C. Temperature coefficient of resistance of platinum is 0.00392/°C.

   Solution:

   To find R_0 at 0°C: $\quad R_t = R_0(1 + \alpha t), \quad 6.00 = R_0(1 + .00392 \times 30), \quad R_0 = 5.37 \text{ ohms}$

   $$R_{100} = R_0(1 + \alpha t) = 5.37 \text{ ohms} \times (1 + .00392/°C \times 100°C) = 7.48 \text{ ohms}$$

   Note that it is incorrect to use R_0 for initial resistance and t for the temperature change; doing so would lead to an incorrect answer of 7.65 ohms:

   $$R_t = 6.00 \text{ ohms} \times (1 + .00392/°C \times 70°C) = 7.65 \text{ ohms (incorrect)}$$

4. One mil = .001 in. The area of a circle 1 mil in diameter is called a **circular mil**. In the adjoining figure the area of the square is 1 square mil (10^{-6} in²) and the area of the inscribed circle is $\frac{1}{4}\pi$ square mil = 1 circular mil. When the cross section area of a conductor is given in circular mils, the resistivity ρ is expressed in ohm-circular mils per ft and is numerically equal to the resistance in ohms of a circular wire of diameter 1 mil and 1 ft long.

   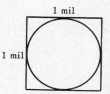

   Number 24 copper wire (American Wire Gage) has diameter .0201 inch. Compute the circular mil area of the wire and the resistance R of 100 ft of the wire at 20°C if the resistivity of the copper at 20°C is 10.37 ohm-circular mils per ft.

   Solution:

   $$\text{Circular mil area} = (\text{diameter in mils})^2 = (20.1 \text{ mils})^2 = 404 \text{ circular mils}$$

   $$R = \rho \frac{l}{A} = 10.37 \frac{\text{ohm-circular mils}}{\text{ft}} \times \frac{100\,\text{ft}}{404 \text{ circular mils}} = 2.57 \text{ ohms}$$

5. Three resistors R_1, R_2 and R_3 are (a) in series and (b) in parallel, as shown in Fig. (a) and (b) respectively. Derive a formula for the equivalent resistance R of each network.

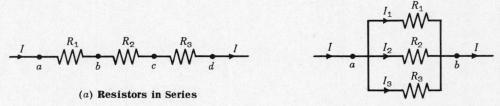

(a) **Resistors in Series**

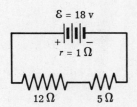

(b) **Resistors in Parallel**

Solution:

(a) For the series network, $V_{ad} = V_{ab} + V_{bc} + V_{cd} = IR_1 + IR_2 + IR_3$

since the current I is the same in each resistor. Dividing by I,

$$V_{ad}/I = R_1 + R_2 + R_3 \quad \text{or} \quad R = R_1 + R_2 + R_3$$

since V_{ad}/I is by definition the equivalent resistance R of the network.

(b) The p.d. across each resistor is the same, i.e. $V_{ab} = I_1 R_1 = I_2 R_2 = I_3 R_3$. Then

$$I_1 = V_{ab}/R_1, \quad I_2 = V_{ab}/R_2, \quad I_3 = V_{ab}/R_3$$

Since the line current I is the sum of the branch currents,

$$I = I_1 + I_2 + I_3 = \frac{V_{ab}}{R_1} + \frac{V_{ab}}{R_2} + \frac{V_{ab}}{R_3}$$

Dividing by V_{ab},

$$\frac{I}{V_{ab}} = \frac{1}{R_1} + \frac{1}{R_2} + \frac{1}{R_3} \quad \text{or} \quad \frac{1}{R} = \frac{1}{R_1} + \frac{1}{R_2} + \frac{1}{R_3}$$

since V_{ab}/I is by definition the equivalent resistance R of the network.

6. Two resistances of 12 and 5 ohms are joined in series and connected to an 18 volt battery of internal resistance $r = 1$ ohm. Compute (a) the current in the circuit, (b) the potential difference across the 12 and 5 ohm resistances, (c) the potential difference across the battery terminals when it is delivering current.

Solution:

(a) $I = \dfrac{\text{emf}}{R} = \dfrac{18 \text{ volts}}{(12 + 5 + 1) \text{ ohms}} = 1 \text{ amp}$

(b) P.d. across 12 ohms $= IR_{12} = 1 \times 12 = 12 \text{ volts}$
P.d. across 5 ohms $= IR_5 = 1 \times 5 = 5 \text{ volts}$

(c) P.d. across terminals $= \text{emf} - Ir = 18 \text{ volts} - (1 \text{ amp} \times 1 \text{ ohm}) = 17 \text{ volts}$

Check: Terminal voltage $=$ potential drop in external circuit $= 12 + 5 = 17 \text{ volts}$.

7. An electrical instrument has 30 ohms resistance and operates best with 50 milliamperes (.050 amp). A dry cell of emf 1.60 volts and internal resistance .06 ohm is available. What resistance R must be connected in series with the instrument and cell in order to limit the current to 50 milliamperes? What is the potential difference across the instrument?

Solution:

$$I = \frac{\text{emf}}{\text{total resistance}}, \quad .05 = \frac{1.6}{.06 + 30 + R}, \quad R = 1.94 \text{ ohms}$$

P.d. across instrument $= IR_{\text{instrument}} = .05 \text{ amp} \times 30 \text{ ohms} = 1.5 \text{ volts}$

8. Compute the joint resistance R of (a) a 0.6 ohm resistor and a 0.2 ohm resistor connected in parallel, (b) three 45 ohm D.C. solenoids connected in parallel.

Solution:

(a) $\dfrac{1}{R} = \dfrac{1}{R_1} + \dfrac{1}{R_2} = \dfrac{1}{0.6} + \dfrac{1}{0.2} = \dfrac{4}{0.6}$ and $R = \dfrac{0.6}{4} = 0.15$ ohm

(b) $\dfrac{1}{R} = \dfrac{1}{R_1} + \dfrac{1}{R_2} + \dfrac{1}{R_3} = \dfrac{1}{45} + \dfrac{1}{45} + \dfrac{1}{45} = \dfrac{3}{45}$ and $R = \dfrac{45}{3} = 15$ ohms

9. What resistance must be placed in parallel with 12 ohms to reduce the combined resistance to 4 ohms?

Solution:

$$\dfrac{1}{R} = \dfrac{1}{R_1} + \dfrac{1}{R_2}, \qquad \dfrac{1}{4} = \dfrac{1}{12} + \dfrac{1}{R_2}, \qquad \dfrac{1}{R_2} = \dfrac{1}{4} - \dfrac{1}{12} = \dfrac{2}{12}, \qquad R_2 = 6 \text{ ohms}$$

10. How many 40 ohm resistors are required to carry 15 amp on a 120 volt line?

Solution:

The resistance of the circuit is to be $R = V/I = 120/15 = 8$ ohms.

The resistors must be in parallel, since the resistance of the circuit is to be decreased. Let x = number of parallel resistors required.

$$\dfrac{1}{R} = \dfrac{1}{R_1} + \dfrac{1}{R_2} + \cdots, \qquad \dfrac{1}{8} = \dfrac{1}{40} + \dfrac{1}{40} + \cdots = \dfrac{x}{40}, \qquad x = \dfrac{40}{8} = 5 \text{ resistors}$$

11. For each of the circuits shown in Fig. (a), (b) and (c), determine the current I through the battery.

Solution:

(a) The 3 and 7 ohms are in parallel; their joint resistance R_1 is found from

$$\dfrac{1}{R_1} = \dfrac{1}{3} + \dfrac{1}{7} = \dfrac{10}{21}, \qquad R_1 = 2.1 \text{ ohms}$$

Then the equivalent resistance of the entire circuit is $R = 2.1 + 5 + 0.4 = 7.5$ ohms, and the battery current is

$$I = \mathcal{E}/R = 30/7.5 = 4 \text{ amp}$$

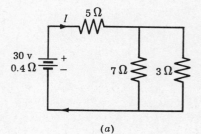

(a)

(b) The 7, 1 and 10 ohms are in series; their joint resistance is 18 ohms. Then 18 ohms is in parallel with 6 ohms; their combined resistance R_1 is given by

$$\dfrac{1}{R_1} = \dfrac{1}{18} + \dfrac{1}{6}, \qquad R_1 = 4.5 \text{ ohms}$$

Hence the equivalent resistance of the entire circuit is $R = 4.5 + 2 + 8 + 0.3 = 14.8$ ohms, and the battery current is

$$I = \mathcal{E}/R = 20/14.8 = 1.35 \text{ amp}$$

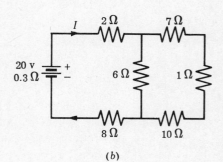

(b)

(c) The 5 and 19 ohms are in series; their joint resistance is 24 ohms. Then 24 ohms is in parallel with 8 ohms; their joint resistance R_1 is given by

$$\dfrac{1}{R_1} = \dfrac{1}{24} + \dfrac{1}{8}, \qquad R_1 = 6 \text{ ohms}$$

Now $R_1 = 6$ ohms is in series with 15 ohms; their joint resistance = $6 + 15 = 21$ ohms. Thus 21 ohms are in parallel with 9 ohms; their combined resistance is found from

$$\dfrac{1}{R_2} = \dfrac{1}{21} + \dfrac{1}{9}, \qquad R_2 = 6.3 \text{ ohms}$$

Hence the equivalent resistance R of the entire circuit is $R = 6.3 + 2 + 0.2 = 8.5$ ohms, and the battery current is

$$I = \mathcal{E}/R = 17/8.5 = 2 \text{ amp}$$

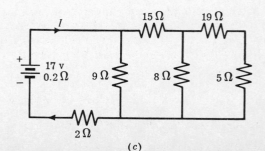

(c)

12. Three coils of 2, 5 and 8 ohms resistance are connected in parallel, with 40 volts across the combination, as shown in Fig. (*a*) below. Determine the current in each coil and the total current to the system.

Solution:

$$I_2 = \frac{40 \text{ volts}}{2 \text{ ohms}} = 20 \text{ amp}, \qquad I_5 = \frac{40 \text{ volts}}{5 \text{ ohms}} = 8 \text{ amp}, \qquad I_8 = \frac{40 \text{ volts}}{8 \text{ ohms}} = 5 \text{ amp}$$

Total current $I = I_2 + I_5 + I_8 = (20 + 8 + 5) \text{ amp} = 33 \text{ amp}$

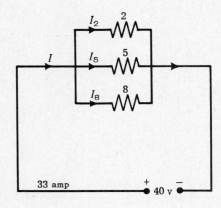

Fig.(*a*) Problem 12

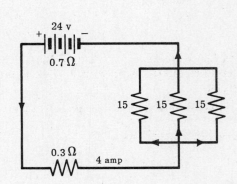

Fig.(*b*) Problem 13

13. A battery of emf 24 volts and internal resistance 0.7 ohm is connected to three 15 ohm coils arranged in parallel, and a 0.3 ohm resistor is connected in series as shown in Fig. (*b*) above. Determine (*a*) the current in the circuit, (*b*) the current in each parallel branch, (*c*) the potential difference across the parallel group and across the 0.3 ohm resistance, (*d*) the terminal voltage of the battery while it delivers current.

Solution:

(*a*) Parallel group resistance R_1: $\quad \dfrac{1}{R_1} = \dfrac{1}{15} + \dfrac{1}{15} + \dfrac{1}{15} = \dfrac{3}{15} \quad$ and $\quad R_1 = 5 \text{ ohms}$

$$I = \frac{\text{emf}}{\text{total } R} = \frac{24 \text{ volts}}{(5 + 0.7 + 0.3) \text{ ohms}} = 4 \text{ amp}$$

(*b*) Since the three parallel resistances are equal, the current is the same in each and is 1/3 of the total current, or $1/3 \times 4$ amp = 1.33 amp.

(*c*) P.d. across parallel group $= IR_1 = 4 \text{ amp} \times 5 \text{ ohms} = 20 \text{ volts}$
P.d. across 0.3 ohm $\qquad = IR_2 = 4 \text{ amp} \times 0.3 \text{ ohm} = 1.2 \text{ volts}$

(*d*) Terminal voltage $=$ potential drop in external circuit $= 20 + 1.2 = 21.2 \text{ volts}$
$\qquad\qquad\qquad\quad = \text{emf} - Ir = 24 \text{ volts} - 4 \text{ amp} \times 0.7 \text{ ohm} = 21.2 \text{ volts}$

14. Each of five cells has emf 2 volts and internal resistance 0.6 ohm. What current will they supply to an external resistance of 17 ohms when they are connected (*a*) in series, (*b*) in parallel?

Solution:

(*a*) $\quad I = \dfrac{\text{total emf}}{\text{total resistance}} = \dfrac{5 \times 2 \text{ volts}}{(5 \times 0.6 + 17) \text{ ohms}} = 0.5 \text{ amp}$

(*b*) $\quad I = \dfrac{\text{total emf}}{\text{total resistance}} = \dfrac{2 \text{ volts}}{(0.6/5 + 17) \text{ ohms}} = 0.117 \text{ amp}$

15. Two groups of cells, each group containing 4 cells in series, are connected in parallel. Each cell has emf 1.50 volts and internal resistance r of .075 ohm. The external resistance of the circuit is 2.35 ohms. Determine the current I in the 2.35 ohm resistance.

Solution:

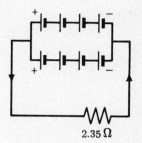

Emf of system of cells $=$ emf of each group of 4 cells
$$= 4 \times 1.5 \text{ volts} = 6 \text{ volts}$$

Resistance of cells $= \dfrac{r \times \text{cells in one group}}{\text{no. of parallel groups}} = \dfrac{.075 \text{ ohm} \times 4}{2}$
$$= 0.15 \text{ ohm}$$

$I = \dfrac{\text{total emf}}{\text{total resistance}} = \dfrac{6 \text{ volts}}{(2.35 + 0.15) \text{ ohms}} = 2.4 \text{ amp}$

2.35 Ω

16. A current I divides between two parallel branches having resistances R_1 and R_2 respectively. Develop formulas for the currents I_1 and I_2 in the parallel branches.

Solution:

The potential drop in each branch is the same, i.e. $I_1 R_1 = I_2 R_2$; also, $I = I_1 + I_2$.

$$I_1 R_1 = I_2 R_2, \qquad I_1 = \frac{R_2}{R_1} I_2 = \frac{R_2}{R_1}(I - I_1), \qquad I_1 R_1 = I R_2 - I_1 R_2,$$

$$I_1(R_1 + R_2) = I R_2, \qquad \text{and} \qquad I_1 = \frac{R_2}{R_1 + R_2} I.$$

Similarly, $\quad I_2 = \dfrac{R_1}{R_1 + R_2} I.$

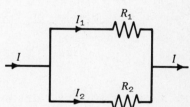

Another method.

P.d. $= IR = I_1 R_1 = I_2 R_2 \quad$ and $\quad IR = I \dfrac{1}{1/R_1 + 1/R_2} = I \dfrac{R_1 R_2}{R_1 + R_2}.$

Then $\quad I_1 = \dfrac{IR}{R_1} = I \dfrac{R_2}{R_1 + R_2} \quad$ and $\quad I_2 = \dfrac{IR}{R_2} = I \dfrac{R_1}{R_1 + R_2}.$

17. A galvanometer having a total resistance $R_1 = 7$ ohms is shunted by a wire of resistance $R_2 = 3$ ohms. What part of the total current I will pass through the instrument and what part through the shunt?

Solution:

Let $I_1 =$ current in galvanometer, $I_2 =$ current in shunt.

$$I_1 = \frac{R_2}{R_1 + R_2} I = \frac{3}{7 + 3} I = 0.3 I$$

$$I_2 = \frac{R_1}{R_1 + R_2} I = \frac{7}{7 + 3} I = 0.7 I$$

18. It is desired that 0.2 of the total current I should pass through an ammeter of resistance .06 ohm. Determine the shunt resistance R_{sh} required.

Solution:

Since the ammeter and shunt are in parallel, the IR drop in each is the same.

$$I_{am} R_{am} = I_{sh} R_{sh}, \qquad (0.2 I)(.06) = (0.8 I) R_{sh}, \qquad R_{sh} = .015 \text{ ohm}$$

19. A coil of unknown resistance X is being measured by means of a Wheatstone bridge. Resistances

L, M and N shown in the adjoining figure are respectively 3, 2 and 10 ohms. The galvanometer G reads zero. Find X.

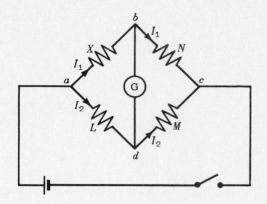

Solution:

When the galvanometer reads zero, the difference in potential $V_{ab} = V_{ad}$ and $V_{bc} = V_{dc}$. Then $I_1X = I_2L$ and $I_1N = I_2M$. Dividing the first equation by the second,

$$\frac{I_1X}{I_1N} = \frac{I_2L}{I_2M}, \quad \frac{X}{N} = \frac{L}{M}, \quad \frac{X}{10 \text{ ohms}} = \frac{3}{2}, \quad X = 15 \text{ ohms}.$$

20. A slidewire bridge is employed to measure an unknown resistance X. AB is a uniform resistance wire; $L = AD = 40$ cm of wire; $M = DB = 60$ cm of wire. Resistance $N = 3$ ohms. The galvanometer reads zero. Find X.

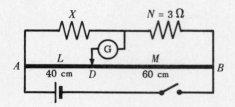

Solution:

The slidewire bridge is a modification of the Wheatstone bridge where a slidewire takes the place of two of the resistances. Since the wire is uniform, the resistance is proportional to the length.

$$\frac{X}{N} = \frac{L}{M}, \quad \frac{X}{3 \text{ ohms}} = \frac{40 \text{ cm}}{60 \text{ cm}}, \quad X = 2 \text{ ohms}$$

21. The values in ohms of the resistances in the circuit shown in Fig. (a) below are as marked. The ammeter reading is 7 amp. Calculate the reading of a very high resistance voltmeter placed between the points P and Q. Which terminal of the voltmeter is positive?

Solution:

Total resistance R: $\quad \dfrac{1}{R} = \dfrac{1}{10+5} + \dfrac{1}{2+18}, \quad R = \dfrac{60}{7}$ ohms

P.d. across each branch, $V = IR = 7(60/7) = 60$ volts. Referring to Fig. (b) below, if we assign +60 volts as the potential of X then the potential of W is zero.

Current in top branch, $I_t = 60/15 = 4$ amp; in bottom branch, $I_b = 60/20 = 3$ amp.

P.d. across 10 ohms $= I_tR_{10} = 4(10) = 40$ volts. Thus Y is at potential +20 volts.
P.d. across 2 ohms $= I_bR_2 = 3(2) = 6$ volts. Thus Z is at potential +54 volts.

The potential of Z is 34 volts higher than the potential of Y. Hence the potential of Q is 34 volts higher than that of P. The voltmeter reads 34 volts and the Q terminal is positive.

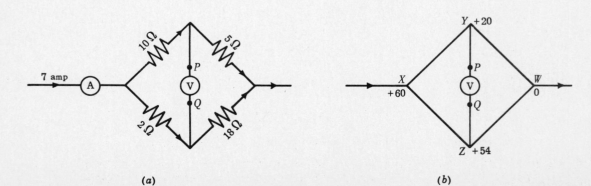

(a)   (b)

22. The current I in a slidewire potentiometer is adjusted with a rheostat so that the galvanometer reads zero when a 1.018 volt standard cell, connected to the slider, intercepts 30 cm of the calibrated resistance wire. An unknown dry cell substituted for the standard cell produces a null balance at 45 cm. What is the dry cell emf?

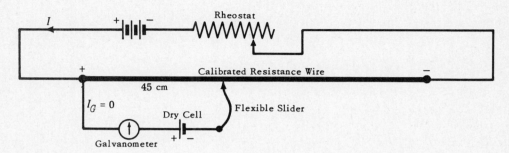

Solution:

The p.d. across 30 cm of resistance wire equals the emf of the standard cell, since no current passes through the cell. Hence 30 cm of wire represent 1.018 volts.

$$\frac{\text{Emf of standard cell}}{\text{Emf of dry cell }(\mathcal{E}_d)} = \frac{30\,\text{cm}}{45\,\text{cm}}, \qquad \frac{1.018\,\text{volts}}{\mathcal{E}_d} = \frac{30\,\text{cm}}{45\,\text{cm}}, \qquad \mathcal{E}_d = 1.527\,\text{volts}$$

23. A 27 volt battery of internal resistance 1 ohm supplies current to the resistances as shown in Diagram I below. (*a*) Determine the currents I_1, I_2, I_3 in the three branches ab, cd, gh respectively. (*b*) Determine the current in and the potential difference across each of the resistances of branch cd.

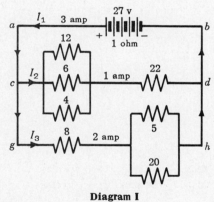

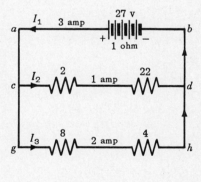

Diagram I   **Diagram II**

Solution:

(*a*) Parallel resistance of 12, 6, 4 ohm group is 2 ohms; of 5, 20 ohm group is 4 ohms. Note that Diagram I simplifies to Diagram II.

$$\text{Parallel resistance of } cd \text{ and } gh: \quad \frac{1}{R} = \frac{1}{2+22} + \frac{1}{8+4} = \frac{3}{24} \quad \text{and} \quad R = 8 \text{ ohms}$$

$$\text{Current supplied by battery,} \quad I_1 = \frac{\text{emf}}{\text{total } R} = \frac{27 \text{ volts}}{(8+1) \text{ ohms}} = 3 \text{ amp}$$

Terminal voltage of battery = 27 volts − 3 amp × 1 ohm = 24 volts. Hence the potential difference across branches cd and gh is 24 volts.

$$\text{Current in } cd, \quad I_2 = \frac{\text{p.d. across } cd}{\text{resistance of } cd} = \frac{24 \text{ volts}}{24 \text{ ohms}} = 1 \text{ amp}$$

$$\text{Current in } gh, \quad I_3 = \text{total current} - \text{current in } cd = 3 \text{ amp} - 1 \text{ amp} = 2 \text{ amp}$$

$$\text{Check:} \quad \text{P.d. across branch } ab = \text{p.d. across branch } cd = \text{p.d. across branch } gh$$
$$24 \text{ volts} = 1 \text{ amp} \times (2+22) \text{ ohms} = 2 \text{ amp} \times (8+4) \text{ ohms}$$

(b) In branch cd, current in 22 ohm resistance is 1 amp.

P.d. across 22 ohm resistance = IR = 1 amp × 22 ohms = 22 volts, leaving (24 − 22) = 2 volts across the 12, 6, 4 ohm parallel group.

Current in 12 ohm of parallel group = V/R = 2/12 = 1/6 amp. Similarly, the currents in the 6 and 4 ohm resistances are 1/3 and 1/2 amp respectively.

24. In the preceding problem, employ Kirchhoff's laws to determine the currents in branches ab, cd and gh.

Solution:

Let I_1, I_2, I_3 be the currents in branches ab, cd, gh respectively. Refer to Diagram II.

By Kirchhoff's First Law. The sum of the currents toward any point in a circuit equals the sum of the currents directed away from that point. At junction c,

$$(1) \quad I_1 = I_2 + I_3$$

By Kirchhoff's Second Law. The algebraic sum of the potential differences around a closed circuit is zero.

Around circuit $bacdb$: $27 − 1I_1 − 2I_2 − 22I_2 = 0$ or   (2) $27 − I_1 − 24I_2 = 0$
Around circuit $cdhgc$: $−2I_2 − 22I_2 + 4I_3 + 8I_3 = 0$ or   (3) $I_3 = 2I_2$

Put $I_3 = 2I_2$ into (1): $I_1 = I_2 + 2I_2 = 3I_2$.
Put $I_1 = 3I_2$ into (2): $27 − 3I_2 − 24I_2 = 0$ or $I_2 = 1$ amp.
Then $I_1 = 3I_2 = 3$ amp, and $I_3 = 2I_2 = 2$ amp.

25. In the circuit shown, determine (a) the current in the 4 ohm resistance and (b) the potential difference across ab, fc, and ed.

Solution:

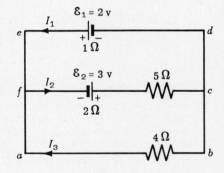

(a) The direction of the current in the 4 ohm resistance is unknown, since $\mathcal{E}_1$ tends to send current from a to b, while $\mathcal{E}_2$ tends to send current from b to a. Hence arbitrarily assume the direction of the current as indicated.

By Kirchhoff's First Law: (1) $I_2 = I_1 + I_3$ at junction f

By Kirchhoff's Second Law:

Around the $fcbaf$ circuit,   (2) $3 − 2I_2 − 5I_2 − 4I_3 = 0$
Around the $fcdef$ circuit,   (3) $3 − 2I_2 − 5I_2 + 2 − 1I_1 = 0$

Simplifying and solving simultaneously equations (1), (2) and (3), we obtain $I_1 = 0.872$ amp, $I_2 = 0.590$ amp, $I_3 = −0.282$ amp.

The current in the 4 ohm resistance is 0.282 amp, from a to b; the minus sign shows that it is opposite to the assumed direction.

(b) The potential differences across ab, fc, and ed must be equal. This serves as a check on the solution of the problem.

P.d. across ab = 0.282 amp × 4 ohms   = 1.13 volts
P.d. across fc = −3 volts + 0.590 amp × (2+5) ohms   = 1.13 volts
P.d. across ed = 2 volts − 0.872 amp × 1 ohm   = 1.13 volts

26. Determine the currents I_1, I_2, and I_3 in the branches of the network shown in the figure below. Arbitrarily assume current directions as indicated.

Solution:

By Kirchhoff's First Law: (1) $I_1 + I_2 + I_3 = 0$ at junction d

By Kirchhoff's Second Law:

Around circuit $abdca$: (2) $15 - 1I_1 - 9.5I_1 + 10 + 0.5I_2 = 0$

> Note. In branch dc we moved (from d to c) opposite to the assumed direction of I_2; hence there is a rise of 10 volts due to the emf of the battery and a rise of $0.5I_2$ volts due to the internal resistance.

Around circuit $cdfec$: (3) $-10 - 0.5I_2 + 1.4I_3 - 3 + 0.1I_3 = 0$

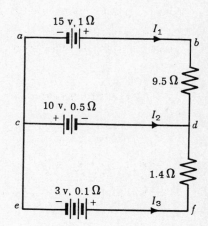

> Note. (A) Here in branch cd we moved (from c to d) in the assumed direction of I_2; hence there is a drop of 10 volts due to the emf and a drop of $0.5I_2$ volts due to the internal resistance.
>
> (B) In dfe we moved (from d to f to e) opposite to the assumed direction of I_3. Hence there is a rise of $1.4I_3$ volts, a rise of $0.1I_3$ volts, and a drop of 3 volts due to the emf.

Simplifying and solving simultaneously equations (1), (2) and (3), we obtain $I_1 = 2$ amp, $I_2 = -8$ amp, $I_3 = 6$ amp. The minus sign indicates that the direction of I_2 is from d to c, i.e. opposite to the assumed direction.

SUPPLEMENTARY PROBLEMS

27. Compute the resistance of 500 ft of german silver wire having a cross section of 0.3 mm². The resistivity of german silver is 33×10^{-6} ohm-cm.   *Ans.* 168 ohms

28. The same power is to be sent over two lines from a power station to a distant point. One current is transmitted at 1000 volts and the other at 20,000 volts. Determine the ratio of the areas of cross sections of the two lines, if the heat loss is to be the same in each one.   *Ans.* 400 : 1

29. A length of wire has resistance 12.64 ohms at 30°C and 11.22 ohms at 0°C. Compute (a) the temperature coefficient of resistance, (b) its resistance if heated to 300°C.
Ans. 4.22×10^{-3} per °C, 25.42 ohms

30. Number 6 copper wire has diameter 0.162 inch. Calculate the circular mil area of the wire and the resistance of 1000 ft of the wire at 20°C if the resistivity of the copper at that temperature is 10.37 ohm-circular mils per ft.   *Ans.* 26,240 CM, 0.395 ohm

31. An electric soldering iron takes 2.9 amp at rated voltage of 120. When in use for long periods of time the copper tip becomes damaged from overheating. An automatic device is arranged to place 50% additional resistance in series with the iron when not in active use so that the iron retains some heat. What is the total resistance for the idle condition and how much current is drawn from the line?   *Ans.* 62.1 ohms, 1.93 amp

32. Compute the joint resistance of 4 and 8 ohms (a) in series, (b) in parallel.   *Ans.* 12, 2.67 ohms

33. Compute the joint resistance (a) of 3, 6 and 9 ohms in parallel, (b) of 3, 4, 7, 10 and 12 ohms in parallel, (c) of three 33 ohm heating elements in parallel, (d) of twenty 100 ohm lamps in parallel.
Ans. (a) 1.64 ohms, (b) 1.10 ohms, (c) 11 ohms, (d) 5 ohms

34. Show that if two resistors R_1 and R_2 are in parallel, with current I_1 in R_1 and I_2 in R_2, then $I_1/I_2 = R_2/R_1$.

35. What resistance must be placed in parallel with 20 ohms to reduce the combined resistance to 15 ohms?
Ans. 60 ohms

36. How many 160 ohm resistors (in parallel) are required to carry 5 amperes on a 100 volt line?   *Ans.* 8

37. Three resistors, of 8, 12 and 24 ohms, are in parallel, and a current of 20 amp is drawn by the combination. Determine the potential difference across the combination and the current in each resistance.
Ans. 80 volts; 10, 6.7, 3.3 amp

38. Two resistors, of 4 and 12 ohms, are connected in parallel across a 22 volt battery having internal resistance 1 ohm. Compute (a) the battery current, (b) the current in the 4 ohm resistor, (c) the terminal voltage of the battery, (d) the current in the 12 ohm resistor.
Ans. (a) 5.5 amp, (b) 4.12 amp, (c) 16.5 volts, (d) 1.38 amp

39. Three resistors, of 40, 60 and 120 ohms, are connected in parallel, and this parallel group is connected in series with 15 and 25 ohms. The whole system is then connected to a 120 volt source. Determine (a) the current in the 25 ohms, (b) the potential drop in the parallel group, (c) the potential drop in the 25 ohms, (d) the current in the 60 ohms, (e) the current in the 40 ohms.
Ans. 2 amp, 40 v, 50 v, 0.67 amp, 1 amp

40. What shunt resistance should be connected in parallel with an ammeter having a resistance of .04 ohm so that 25% of the total current would pass through the ammeter?   *Ans.* .0133 ohm

41. A 36 ohm galvanometer is shunted by a resistance of 4 ohms. What part of the total current will pass through the instrument?   *Ans.* 0.1

42. A relay of resistance 6 ohms operates with a minimum current of .03 amp. It is required that the relay operate when the current in the line attains 0.24 amp. What resistance should be used to shunt the relay?
Ans. 0.857 ohm

43. Show that if two resistances are connected in parallel the rates of heat production in each vary inversely as their resistances.

44. Ten cells, each of emf 1.60 volts and internal resistance .08 ohm, are connected in (a) parallel, (b) series. The external resistance is 2 ohms. For each case, calculate the total resistance of the circuit, the emf and terminal voltage of the battery, and the current in the external circuit.
Ans. (a) 2.008 ohms, 1.60 v, 1.594 v, 0.797 amp; (b) 2.8 ohms, 16.0 v, 11.4 v, 5.71 amp

45. Four groups of cells, each having 5 cells in series, are connected in parallel. Each cell has emf 1.8 volts and internal resistance 0.8 ohm. The external resistance of the circuit is 2 ohms. Calculate the emf of the system of cells, the resistance of the system of cells, the current in the 2 ohm resistance, and the current in each cell.   *Ans.* 9 v, 1 ohm, 3 amp, 0.75 amp

46. Two dry cells, each of emf 1.2 volts and internal resistance 0.4 ohm, are to be connected so as to supply maximum current to an external circuit. How should the cells be arranged if the external resistance is (a) 0.3 ohm, (b) 2.0 ohms?   *Ans.* (a) parallel, (b) series

47. In a slidewire bridge the balance is obtained at a point 25 cm from one end of a wire 100 cm long. The resistance to be tested is connected to that end, and a standard resistance of 3.6 ohms is connected to the other end of the wire. Compute the value of the unknown resistance.   *Ans.* 1.2 ohms

48. The emf of a dry cell is measured by means of a 100 cm slidewire potentiometer. A standard cell of emf 1.0184 volts gives a zero galvanometer reading when 18 cm are intercepted by the potentiometer slider. The dry cell intercepts 24 cm for a zero balance. What is the emf of the dry cell?   *Ans.* 1.36 v

49. In the adjoining figure, find the current in each resistance and the potential difference across each resistance.
Ans. Current in 20 ohm = 3 amp,
                    75 ohm = 2.4 amp,
                    300 ohm = 0.6 amp.
       Potential difference across 20 ohm = 60 v,
                        across 75 ohm = 180 v,
                        across 300 ohm = 180 v.

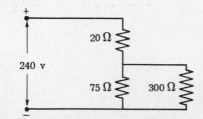

50. In Fig. (a) below, calculate (a) the equivalent resistance of the entire circuit, (b) the total current, (c) the potential difference across points ab, cd and de, (d) the current in each resistance.

    Ans. (a) 15 ohms; (b) 20 amp; (c) V_{ab} = 80 v, V_{cd} = 120 v, V_{de} = 100 v

        (d) I_4 = 20 amp, I_{10} = 12 amp, I_{15} = 8 amp, I_9 = 11.1 amp

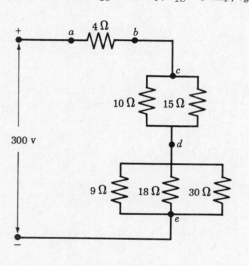

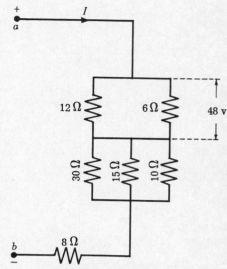

      Fig.(a) Problem 50   **Fig.(b) Problem 51**

51. In the series-parallel circuit shown in Fig. (b) above, the potential difference across the 6 ohm resistance is 48 volts. Determine (a) the total current I, (b) the potential difference across the 8 ohm series resistance, (c) the potential difference across the 10 ohm resistance, (d) the potential difference across the entire circuit ab.   *Ans.* (a) 12 amp, (b) 96 v, (c) 60 v, (d) 204 v

52. In the circuit shown in the adjoining figure, 23.9 calories of heat are produced each second in the 4 ohm resistance. Compute the readings of

  (a) the high resistance voltmeter V_1,

  (b) the high resistance voltmeter V_2,

  (c) the ammeter A.

  Ans. (a) 8 v, (b) 58 v, (c) 5.8 amp

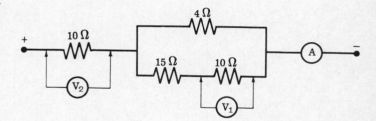

53. In the circuit shown below, the ammeter A registers 2 amp.

  (a) Assuming XY to be a resistance, calculate its value.

  (b) Assuming XY to be a battery of 2 ohms internal resistance which is being charged, calculate its emf.

  (c) Under the conditions of part (b), what is the potential difference between the terminals of XY? Which terminal, X or Y, is at the higher potential?

  Ans. (a) 5 ohms, (b) 6 v, (c) 10 v, Y is higher

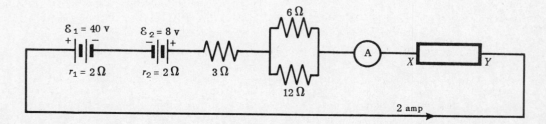

54. For the circuit shown in the adjoining figure, determine (a) the current in each resistance, (b) the *IR* drop across each resistance, (c) the power dissipated by each resistance, (d) the total power dissipated as heat, (e) the total power supplied to the circuit by the battery.

Ans. (a), (b), (c)

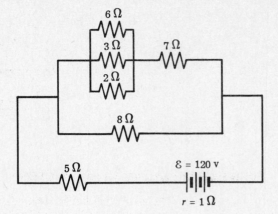

R (ohms)	1	2	3	5	6	7	8
I (amp)	12	3	2	12	1	6	6
IR (v)	12	6	6	60	6	42	48
P (w)	144	18	12	720	6	252	288

(d) 1440 watts, (e) 1440 watts

55. Refer to Fig. (a) below. Two batteries are connected in parallel, with like terminals connected together, and a 0.96 ohm resistance is connected across the combination. One battery has emf 6 volts and internal resistance 0.3 ohm; the other battery has emf 5 volts and internal resistance 0.2 ohm. Use Kirchhoff's laws to determine the current in the 0.96 ohm resistance and the terminal voltage of each battery.

Ans. 5 amp, 4.8 v

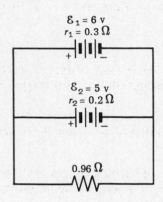

Fig.(a) Problem 55

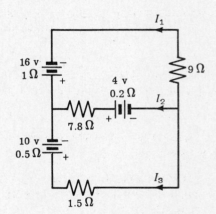

Fig.(b) Problem 56

56. For the network shown in Fig. (b) above, determine (a) the three currents I_1, I_2 and I_3 with their proper signs and (b) the terminal voltages of the three batteries.

Ans. (a) $I_1 = 2$, $I_2 = 1$, $I_3 = -3$ amp; (b) $V_{16} = 14$, $V_4 = 3.8$, $V_{10} = 8.5$ volts

Chapter 26

Electrolysis

FARADAY'S LAWS OF ELECTROLYSIS.

(1) The mass of a substance liberated or deposited at an electrode is proportional to the quantity of electricity (i.e. to the number of coulombs) that has passed through the electrolyte.

(2) The masses of different substances liberated or deposited by the same quantity of electricity are proportional to their equivalent weights.

The **equivalent weight** of an element is its atomic weight divided by its valence. Thus the equivalent weight of copper is $\frac{1}{2}$ an atomic weight for the electrolysis of solutions containing Cu^{++}, because the reaction at the cathode is

$$Cu^{++} + 2e \longrightarrow Cu$$

If a solution of Cu^+ were electrolyzed, the equivalent weight of copper would be the same as the atomic weight because only 1 electron would be involved in the electrode reaction

$$Cu^+ + 1e \longrightarrow Cu$$

When the equivalent weight of a substance is expressed in grams, it is called the **gram-equivalent weight**.

One **faraday**, or 96,500 coulombs, is the quantity of electricity that will deposit 1 gram-equivalent weight of any substance. Thus the mass m in grams of any substance liberated in electrolysis is

$$m = \text{gram-equivalent weight} \times \text{number of faradays transferred.}$$

ELECTROCHEMICAL EQUIVALENT of a substance is the number of grams of that substance liberated by 1 coulomb. Thus the mass m in grams of a substance liberated in electrolysis is

$$m = \text{electrochemical equivalent} \times \text{number of coulombs transferred.}$$

SOLVED PROBLEMS

1. The charge on the electron is 1.602×10^{-19} coulomb. How many electronic charges are contained in one faraday?

Solution:

$$\text{Electrons/faraday} = \frac{9.65 \times 10^4 \text{ coulombs}}{1 \text{ faraday}} \times \frac{1 \text{ electron}}{1.602 \times 10^{-19} \text{ coulomb}}$$

$$= 6.02 \times 10^{23} \text{ electrons/faraday} \quad \text{(Avogadro's Number)}$$

2. A charge of 0.2 faraday is passed through an electrolytic cell containing ferric iron (Fe^{+++}). Assuming that the only cathode reaction is $Fe^{+++} + 3e \longrightarrow Fe$, what mass of iron will be deposited?

Solution:

Equivalent weight of iron = atomic weight/valence = 55.85/3 = 18.62.

Since 1 faraday deposits 1 gram-equivalent weight or 18.62 g of iron, 0.2 faraday will deposit 0.2 (18.62 g) = 3.72 g of iron.

3. How many grams each of tin and zinc would be deposited by the same number of coulombs that deposits 2 grams of silver? Equivalent weight of silver (Ag^+) = 107.88, of tin (Sn^{++}) = 59.35, of zinc (Zn^{++}) = 32.69.

Solution:

Masses of different substances deposited by the same charge are proportional to their equivalent weights.

Then $\dfrac{m_{Sn}}{2\,g} = \dfrac{59.35}{107.88}$ and $\dfrac{m_{Zn}}{2\,g} = \dfrac{32.69}{107.88}$, from which $m_{Sn} = 1.10\,g$, $m_{Zn} = 0.61\,g$.

4. A steady current of 5 amperes maintained for 30 minutes deposits 3.048 grams of zinc at the cathode. Determine the equivalent weight of zinc.

Solution:

One faraday, or 96,500 coul, deposits 1 gram-equivalent weight of a substance.

Since (5 amp × 1800 sec) = 9000 coul deposit 3.048 g Zn, 96,500 coul would deposit (96,500/9000)(3.048 g) = 32.7 g Zn. The equivalent weight of Zn is 32.7.

5. A current of 15 amp is employed to plate nickel in a nickel sulfate bath. Both Ni and H_2 are formed at the cathode. The current efficiency with respect to the formation of Ni is 60%. (*a*) How many grams of nickel are plated on the cathode per hour? (*b*) What is the thickness of the plating if the cathode consists of a sheet of metal 4 cm square which is coated on both faces? Nickel has specific gravity 8.9, atomic weight 58.71, and valence 2. (*c*) What volume of H_2 (S.T.P.) is formed per hour?

Solution:

(*a*) Equivalent weight of Ni = atomic weight/valence = 58.71/2 = 29.4.
   Charge used to form Ni = 0.60 (15 amp × 3600 sec) = 3.24×10^4 coul.

9.65×10^4 coul deposits 1 gram-equivalent weight of an element, or 29.4 g Ni; then

3.24×10^4 coul deposits $29.4\,g \times \dfrac{3.24 \times 10^4 \text{ coul}}{9.65 \times 10^4 \text{ coul}} = 9.9\,g$ Ni.

(*b*) Volume of 9.9 g Ni = mass/density = $(9.9\,g)/(8.9\ g/cm^3)$ = 1.11 cm^3.

Thickness of plating = $\dfrac{\text{volume of plating}}{\text{area of plating}} = \dfrac{1.11\ cm^3}{2\,(4\ cm \times 4\ cm)}$ = .035 cm.

(*c*) Charge used to form H_2 = 0.40 (5.4×10^4 coul) = 2.16×10^4 coul.

Since 9.65×10^4 coul releases 1 g-eq wt of H_2 = $\frac{1}{2}$(22.4 liters) = 11.2 l H_2 (S.T.P.),

2.16×10^4 coul will release $\dfrac{2.16 \times 10^4}{9.65 \times 10^4} \times 11.2\ l$ = 2.5 l H_2.

6. (*a*) Compute the electrochemical equivalent of gold. Gold has atomic weight 197.0 and valence 3. (*b*) What constant current is required to deposit on the cathode 5 g of gold per hour?

Solution:

(*a*) Electrochemical equiv. = $\dfrac{\text{gram-equivalent wt}}{96,500 \text{ coul}} = \dfrac{197.0/3\,g}{96,500 \text{ coul}} = 6.81 \times 10^{-4}$ g/coul

(*b*) Mass deposited = electrochemical equivalent × number of coulombs transferred
   5 g = $(6.81 \times 10^{-4}$ g/coul$)(I \times 3600$ sec), from which I = 2.04 amp

SUPPLEMENTARY PROBLEMS

7. What current is required to pass one faraday per hour through an electroplating bath? How many grams of aluminum and of cadmium will be liberated by one faraday? Equivalent weight of aluminum = 8.99, of cadmium = 56.2. *Ans.* 26.8 amp, 8.99 g Al, 56.2 g Cd

8. How many grams of aluminum are deposited electrolytically in 30 minutes by a current of 40 amp? Equivalent weight of Al is 8.99. *Ans.* 6.71 g

9. A certain current liberates 0.504 g of hydrogen in 2 hr. How many grams of oxygen and of copper (from Cu^{++} solution) can be liberated by the same current maintained for the same time? Equivalent weight of hydrogen = 1.008, of oxygen = 8.00, of copper = 31.8. *Ans.* 4.00 g oxygen, 15.9 g copper

10. A given current releases 2 g of oxygen in 12 minutes. How long will it take the same current to deposit 18 g of copper from a copper sulfate solution? Equivalent weight of oxygen = 8.00, of copper = 31.8. *Ans.* 27.2 minutes

11. An electrolytic cell contains a solution of $CuSO_4$ and an anode of impure copper. How many pounds of copper will be refined (deposited on the cathode) by 150 amp maintained for 12 hr? Equivalent weight of copper is 31.8. *Ans.* 4.7 lb

12. How many hours will it take to produce 100 lb of electrolytic chlorine from NaCl in a cell carrying 1000 amp? The anode efficiency for the chlorine reaction is 85%. Equivalent weight of chlorine is 35.46. *Ans.* 40.3 hr

13. Compute the time required for a current of 3 amp to decompose electrolytically 18 g of water. Equivalent weight of hydrogen = 1.0, of oxygen = 8.0. *Ans.* 18 hr

14. Compute the electrochemical equivalent of magnesium. Magnesium has atomic weight 24.32 and valence 2. *Ans.* 1.26×10^{-4} g/coul

15. The cathode plate of a copper voltameter gains 1.53 g of copper in 30 minutes. Determine the average current. Electrochemical equivalent of copper is 3.294×10^{-4} g/coul. *Ans.* 2.58 amp

Chapter 27

Magnetic Fields of Currents

MAGNETIC FORCES are due to the motion of electric charges, i.e. to electric currents. A magnetic force exists between two charges if and only if both charges are moving relative to an observer. Examples of moving charges are: electric currents in wires, a beam of electrons in a cathode ray tube, and electrons rotating about the atomic nuclei and about their own axes.

A MAGNETIC FIELD is the region surrounding a moving charge. A magnetic field exists at any point where a moving charge experiences a force exclusive of any electrostatic force.

DIRECTION OF MAGNETIC FIELD OF A CURRENT may be determined by a right-hand rule. Point the thumb of the right hand in the direction of the current; then the curled fingers will point in the direction of the field. Thus the magnetic field of a current is clockwise as viewed by an observer looking along the direction of the current. Refer to the figure below.

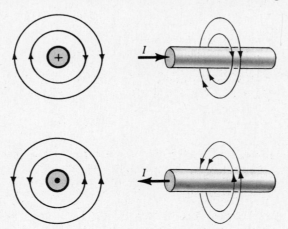

MAGNETIC INDUCTION B, also called **flux density**, is a vector which specifies the magnitude and direction of the magnetic field at a point.

A magnetic field may be represented by lines of induction such that the number of lines piercing perpendicularly a unit area is equal to the magnetic induction in that region. The direction of the lines of induction at any point is that of the magnetic induction vector.

The **magnetic flux** Φ through a surface is the total number of lines of induction extending through it. In a region where the magnetic induction B is uniform and normal to a given area A,

$$\Phi = BA$$

If θ is the angle between the magnetic induction vector B and the normal to the reference area A,

$$\Phi = BA \cos \theta$$

In the mks system, B is expressed in webers/m^2 and Φ in webers.

MAGNETIC FIELD OF A CURRENT. Consider that a current I exists in a wire element of length Δl. The magnetic induction ΔB at point P due to the current element is

$$(1) \qquad \Delta B \ = \ K \frac{I \, \Delta l \, \sin \theta}{r^2}$$

where r is the distance from Δl to P, θ is the angle between r and the current in the element Δl, and K is a proportionality constant depending upon the units used and the medium between Δl and P. The direction of ΔB is perpendicular to the plane determined by Δl and r.

The total magnetic induction B at point P due to a current I in a wire of length l is the vector sum of the contributions of all the elements Δl. Thus

$$(2) \qquad B \ = \ K \, \Sigma \, \frac{I \, \Delta l \, \sin \theta}{r^2}$$

Using mks units, in free space (vacuum) $K = 10^{-7}$ weber per ampere-meter. For nearly all practical purposes K has the same value for air and for non-ferromagnetic materials.

MAGNETIC FIELD OF A FLAT CIRCULAR COIL. To find the magnetic induction at the center of a circular loop of wire of radius r carrying a constant current I, use equation (2). Here $\Sigma \, \Delta l = $ circumference of circle $= 2 \pi r$ and $\sin \theta = \sin 90° = 1$ for any element Δl. Thus $B = K \Sigma \frac{I \, \Delta l \, \sin \theta}{r^2} = K \frac{I(2 \pi r)(1)}{r^2} = K \frac{2 \pi I}{r}$. It follows that for a closely-wound flat circular coil of N turns, the magnetic induction at the center is

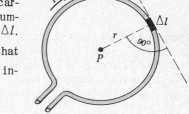

$$B \ = \ K \frac{2 \pi N I}{r}$$

In free space $K = 10^{-7}$ weber per ampere-meter.

MAGNETIC FIELD OF A LONG STRAIGHT WIRE. The magnetic induction B at a perpendicular distance r from the axis of a long straight conductor carrying a current I is

$$B \ = \ K \frac{2I}{r}$$

MAGNETIC FIELD OF A SOLENOID AND TOROID. Consider a long solenoid having N turns of wire and length l, and carrying a current I. The magnetic induction B at any point in the interior is

$$B \ = \ K \frac{4 \pi N I}{l}$$

If the solenoid is wound in the form of a toroid (ring), the same equation applies if $l = $ mean circumference of toroid. The magnetic field is entirely within the toroid.

FORCE ON CONDUCTOR IN MAGNETIC FIELD. AMPERE'S LAW. The force ΔF on a conductor element Δl carrying a current I in a region of magnetic induction B is

$$\Delta F \ = \ B I \Delta l \, \sin \theta$$

where θ is the angle between Δl and the magnetic flux. For a straight conductor of length l in a uniform field, the force on the conductor is

$$F \ = \ B I l \, \sin \theta$$

If the current is perpendicular to the field, $\sin \theta = \sin 90° = 1$ and the force is maximum; if it is parallel to the field, $\sin \theta = 0$ and the force is zero.

The force is perpendicular both to the current and the field, and the conductor tends to move from a region of strong field into a region of weak field.

Using mks units, F is in newtons when B is in webers/m², I in amperes and l in meters. Solving for $B = F/(Il \sin \theta)$, we see that B can also be expressed in newtons per ampere-meter, or 1 weber/m² = 1 nt/amp-m.

FORCE BETWEEN TWO PARALLEL CONDUCTORS. Consider that two wires, carrying currents I_1 and I_2 respectively, are parallel over a length l and separated by a distance r. The magnetic induction at a distance r from the wire carrying current I_1 is $B = 2KI_1/r$, and the force on the other wire carrying current I_2 in this field is $F = BI_2l = (2KI_1/r)I_2l$. Hence the force between the parallel wires is

$$F = 2K \frac{I_1 I_2 l}{r}$$

where F is in newtons, I in amperes, l and r in meters, and $K = 10^{-7}$ nt/amp^2 or weber/amp-m in free space. The force is attractive if I_1 and I_2 are in the same direction; the force is repulsive if I_1 and I_2 are in opposite directions.

The force per unit length is $F/l = 2KI_1I_2/r$. Thus the ampere may be defined as that current which, if existing in each of two infinitely long parallel wires separated by a distance of 1 meter in free space, causes the force on each wire to be 2×10^{-7} newton per meter of length.

TORQUE ON COIL IN MAGNETIC FIELD. The torque L on a coil of N turns carrying current I in a field of magnetic induction B is

$$L = BINA \cos \theta$$

where A is the area of the coil and θ is the angle the plane of the coil makes with the field. When the plane of the coil is parallel to the field, $\cos \theta = \cos 0 = 1$ and the torque is a maximum. When the plane of the coil is normal to the field, the torque is zero.

The torque is given in meter-newtons when B is in nt/amp-m (webers/m^2), I in amp, and A in m^2.

FORCE ON A MOVING CHARGE IN A MAGNETIC FIELD. Consider that a charge q moves with velocity v in a field of magnetic induction B and covers a distance l in time t. Then $l = vt$ and the moving charge represents a current $I = q/t$. Substituting $Il = (q/t)(vt) = qv$ in $F = BIl \sin \theta$, the force on the charge is

$$F = Bqv \sin \theta$$

where θ is the angle between vectors B and v. Consistent mks units are F in newtons, B in webers/m^2, q in coulombs, v in m/sec. The direction of F is perpendicular to the vectors B and v.

PATH OF CHARGED PARTICLE IN MAGNETIC FIELD. When a particle of mass m, charge q and initial velocity v moves normal to a field of magnetic induction B, the force acting on it is $F = Bqv$ directed perpendicular both to B and v. Since F is constant in magnitude and directed always at right angles to v, the particle has uniform circular motion with radius r and centripetal acceleration $a = v^2/r$. Now combining $F = ma = mv^2/r$ and $F = Bqv$, we have $mv^2/r = Bqv$ from which

$$r = \frac{mv}{Bq}$$

A **cyclotron** is used to accelerate massive particles (e.g. protons, deuterons, alpha particles) by applying a small voltage many times in succession as the particles spiral outward in a magnetic field. This is possible because the angular velocity $\omega = v/r = Bq/m$ of a particle is independent of its speed and of the radius of its path, as long as v is small compared with the speed of light.

A **mass spectrograph** is used to determine the masses of positively charged ions, and to measure the relative abundance of isotopes. Positive ions having the same charge q and velocity v enter a uniform magnetic field B perpendicular to the vector v and thus are caused to move in a circular path of radius $r = mv/Bq$. Since v/Bq is the same for all ions, the mass m of the ion is proportional to r.

RATIO OF ELECTRONIC CHARGE TO MASS. Consider that an electron stream with velocity v passes through two mutually perpendicular electric and magnetic fields, that the electric field deflects each electron upward and the magnetic field deflects each electron downward, and that when both fields act simultaneously the resultant deflection is zero. The electrostatic force on each electron of mass m and charge e in an electric field E is $F = eE$, and the magnetic force $F = Bev$. Since the forces balance, $eE = Bev$ and

$$v = \frac{E}{B}$$

If the electric field is cut off and the magnetic field maintained, each electron will move in the magnetic field in a circular path of radius $r = mv/Be$. Substituting $v = E/B$ and solving for e/m,

$$\frac{e}{m} = \frac{E}{B^2 r}$$

The ratio $e/m = 1.759 \times 10^{11}$ coul/kg. Since $e = 1.602 \times 10^{-19}$ coul, the rest mass of the electron is $m = 1.602 \times 10^{-19}/(1.759 \times 10^{11}) = 9.107 \times 10^{-31}$ kg.

THE ELECTRON-VOLT (ev) is the energy acquired by a body whose charge equals that of the electron, when the body falls through a potential difference of one volt.

$$1 \text{ electron-volt} = (1.602 \times 10^{-19} \text{ coul})(1 \text{ volt}) = 1.602 \times 10^{-19} \text{ joule}$$

SOLVED PROBLEMS

1. Compute the magnetic induction (or flux density) in air at a point 5 cm from a long straight wire carrying a current of 15 amperes.
   Solution:

   $$B = K\frac{2I}{r} = 10^{-7}\frac{\text{weber}}{\text{amp-m}} \times \frac{30 \text{ amp}}{5 \times 10^{-2} \text{ m}} = 6 \times 10^{-5} \text{ weber/m}^2$$

2. A circular coil of 40 turns of wire and negligible section has diameter 32 cm. What current must exist in the coil to produce a flux density of 3×10^{-4} weber/m^2 at its center?
   Solution:

   $$B = K\frac{2\pi NI}{r}, \qquad 3 \times 10^{-4}\frac{\text{weber}}{\text{m}^2} = 10^{-7}\frac{\text{weber}}{\text{amp-m}} \times \frac{2\pi(40)I}{0.16 \text{ m}}, \qquad I = 1.9 \text{ amp}$$

3. Compute the flux density at the center of the air core of a long solenoid having 9 turns of wire per cm of length and carrying a current of 6 amperes.
   Solution:

   $$B = K\frac{4\pi NI}{l} = 4\pi K\frac{N}{l}I = 4\pi \times 10^{-7}\frac{\text{weber}}{\text{amp-m}} \times \frac{9 \text{ turns}}{10^{-2} \text{ m}} \times 6 \text{ amp} = 6.8 \times 10^{-3} \text{ weber/m}^2$$

4. A charge of 4×10^{-6} coul moves at 15 revolutions per second in a circle of radius 20 cm. What is the magnetic induction at the center of the circle?
   Solution:

   Current in circle, $I = q/t = (4 \times 10^{-6} \text{ coul})/(1/15 \text{ sec}) = 6 \times 10^{-5}$ amp

   $$B = K\frac{2\pi NI}{r} = 10^{-7}\frac{\text{weber}}{\text{amp-m}} \times \frac{2\pi(1)(6 \times 10^{-5} \text{ amp})}{0.2 \text{ m}} = 1.88 \times 10^{-10}\frac{\text{weber}}{\text{m}^2}$$

5. A circular coil of 30 turns and radius 24 cm is mounted with its plane vertical and in the magnetic meridian at a place where the horizontal component of the earth's magnetic induction is $B_e = 2.5 \times 10^{-5}$ weber/m^2. Determine the current in the coil if a small magnetic needle at the center is deflected 52°.

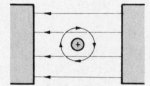

Solution:

At the center of the coil, the current I causes a magnetic induction $B_C = 10^{-7}(2\pi NI/r)$ which is perpendicular to the plane of the coil and to the earth's field. The compass needle points in the direction of the resultant of B_e and B_C.

$$\tan 52° = \frac{B_C}{B_e} = \frac{10^{-7}(2\pi NI/r)}{B_e}$$

$$I = \frac{r}{2\pi \times 10^{-7}N} B_e \tan 52° = \frac{0.24 \text{ m}}{2\pi \times 10^{-7} \text{ weber/amp-m} \times 30} \times 2.5 \times 10^{-5} \frac{\text{weber}}{\text{m}^2} \times 1.28 = 0.41 \text{ amp}$$

6. Determine the magnitude and direction of the force on a horizontal conductor 5 cm long and carrying 30 amp of current from south to north, if placed in air in a horizontal magnetic field of flux density 0.8 weber/m^2 directed from east to west.

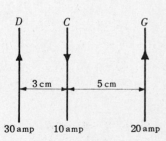

Solution:

$$F = BIl \sin \theta = 0.8 \text{ weber/m}^2 \times 30 \text{ amp} \times .05 \text{ m} \times 1 = 1.2 \text{ nt}$$

The direction of the force is found by drawing the field which surrounds the conductor due to the current in it. This field and the applied field build up below the wire, and tend to cancel above the wire. The strong resultant field is then below the wire, and the force on the wire is upward, into the region of weak field.

7. Two long parallel wires, C and D, are 10 cm apart in air and carry currents of 6 and 4 amp respectively. Compute the force of attraction on each meter length of wire if the currents are (*a*) in the same direction, (*b*) in opposite directions.

Solution:

(*a*) Flux density at D due to current in C is $B_D = K \dfrac{2I_C}{r}$.

$$F = B_D I_D l = (K \frac{2I_C}{r})I_D l = 2K \frac{I_C I_D l}{r}$$

$$= 2 \times 10^{-7} \frac{\text{weber}}{\text{amp-m}} \times \frac{(6 \text{ amp})(4 \text{ amp})(1 \text{ m})}{0.1 \text{ m}} = 4.8 \times 10^{-5} \text{ nt attraction}$$

(*b*) 4.8×10^{-5} nt repulsion

8. Two fixed parallel wires of great length, D and G, are hung vertically 8 cm apart. In D there is a current of 30 amp and in G 20 amp, both currents being in an upward direction. A third vertical wire C of great length carries a downward current of 10 amp and is suspended so as to hang at a distance 3 cm from D and 5 cm from G. Determine the force acting on each 25 cm length of C.

Solution:

Resultant flux density at C due to currents in D and G is

$$B_C = 2K \frac{I_D}{r_D} - 2K \frac{I_G}{r_G} = 2K(\frac{I_D}{r_D} - \frac{I_G}{r_G}) = 2 \times 10^{-7}(\frac{30}{.03} - \frac{20}{.05}) = 1.2 \times 10^{-4} \frac{\text{weber}}{\text{m}^2}.$$

$$F = B_C I_C l = 1.2 \times 10^{-4} \text{ weber/m}^2 \times 10 \text{ amp} \times 0.25 \text{ m} = 3 \times 10^{-4} \text{ nt toward } G.$$

9. Calculate the torque required to hold a vertical rectangular coil of height 12 cm and width 10 cm and having 40 turns of wire, when the coil is suspended in a uniform magnetic field of flux density 0.25 weber/m^2 and carries a current of 2 amp. The plane of the coil is parallel to the direction of the field.

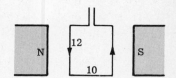

Solution:

The length of wire on each side of the coil that is perpendicular to the field = 40 (0.12 m) = 4.8 m. The force on each side of the coil (i.e. on right and on left side) is

$$F = BIl = 0.25 \text{ weber/m}^2 \times 2 \text{ amp} \times 4.8 \text{ m} = 2.4 \text{ nt}$$

A force of 2.4 nt tends to push the left side of the coil toward the reader (forward, out of the page). Also, a force of 2.4 nt tends to push the right side of the coil away from the reader (backward, into the page). These two equal forces, acting in opposite directions not in the same straight line, produce a couple.

Torque of couple = one of equal forces × perpendicular distance between them
$$= 2.4 \text{ nt} \times 0.1 \text{ m} = 0.24 \text{ m-nt}$$

Otherwise: Torque = $BINA$ = 0.25 weber/m^2 × 2 amp × 40 × .012 m^2 = 0.24 m-nt

10. A thin coil, of 10 turns of wire and diameter 2 cm, is mounted in the interior of a solenoid having 200 turns of wire and 25 cm long. If a current of 0.5 amp exists in the coil and 2.4 amp in the solenoid, compute the torque L required to hold the coil with its axis perpendicular to that of the solenoid.

Solution:

Let the subscripts s and c refer to the solenoid and coil respectively. The flux density in the interior of the solenoid is $B = 4\pi K N_s I_s / l$.

$$L = BINA = (4\pi K \frac{N_s I_s}{l})(I_c)(N_c)(\pi r^2) = 4\pi^2 K \frac{N_s N_c I_s I_c r^2}{l}$$

$$= 4\pi^2 \times 10^{-7} \frac{\text{weber}}{\text{amp-m}} \times \frac{200(10)(2.4 \text{ amp})(0.5 \text{ amp})(10^{-4} \text{ m}^2)}{0.25 \text{ m}} = 3.79 \times 10^{-6} \text{ m-nt}$$

11. Determine the magnetic induction at a point P along the axis of a closely-wound circular coil of N turns and distant y from the plane of the coil.

Solution:

The flux density at P due to the current element Δl is $\Delta B = K \frac{I \Delta l}{z^2}$ since z is perpendicular to Δl. Since ΔB is normal to z,

$$\Delta B_{\text{axis}} = \Delta B \sin \alpha = K \frac{I \Delta l}{z^2} \times \frac{r}{z}$$

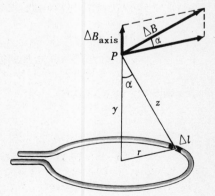

Since $\Sigma \Delta l = 2\pi r$, the total magnetic induction at P due to a current I in a circular coil of N turns is

$$B_{\text{axis}} = K \frac{I(2\pi r N)}{z^2} \times \frac{r}{z} = K \frac{2\pi N I r^2}{z^3}$$

considering that for the entire coil the vector sum of the components of B normal to the axis is zero.

12. A proton enters a magnetic field of flux density 1.5 weber/m^2 with a velocity of 2×10^7 m/sec at an angle of 30° with the field. Compute the force on the proton.

Solution:

$$F = Bqv \sin \theta = (1.5 \text{ weber/m}^2)(1.6 \times 10^{-19} \text{ coul})(2 \times 10^7 \text{ m/sec})(0.5) = 2.4 \times 10^{-12} \text{ nt}$$

Note. 1 (weber/m^2)(coul)(m/sec) = 1 (nt/amp-m)(amp-sec)(m/sec) = 1 nt

13. Charged particles with varying velocities enter a region having an electric field E and a magnetic field $B = 0.4$ weber/m^2, the vectors v, B and E being perpendicular to each other. Determine the electric field required to permit the undeflected passage of only particles with velocity 2×10^5 m/sec.

Solution:

For undeflected passage, the electrostatic force $F = qE$ on a particle having charge q balances the magnetic force $F = Bqv$ on the particle. Then $qE = Bqv$ and

$$E = Bv = (0.4 \text{ weber/m}^2)(2 \times 10^5 \text{ m/sec}) = 8 \times 10^4 \text{ nt/coul or volts/m.}$$

Note. 1 (weber/m^2)(m/sec) = 1 (nt/amp-m)(m/sec) = 1 nt/amp-sec = 1 nt/coul

14. A cathode ray beam is bent in a circle of radius 2 cm by a field of magnetic induction 4.5×10^{-3} weber/m^2. Calculate the velocity of the electrons.

Solution:

The force on an electron of mass m and charge e moving with velocity v normal to a field of magnetic induction B is $F = Bev$ directed perpendicular to both B and v. Since F is constant in magnitude and directed always perpendicular to v, the electron has uniform circular motion with centripetal acceleration v^2/r. Then $F = Bev = mv^2/r$ and

$$v = \frac{Ber}{m} = \frac{(4.5 \times 10^{-3} \text{ weber/m}^2)(1.60 \times 10^{-19} \text{ coul})(2 \times 10^{-2} \text{ m})}{9.11 \times 10^{-31} \text{ kg}} = 1.58 \times 10^7 \text{ m/sec.}$$

Note. $1 \dfrac{(\text{weber/m}^2)(\text{coul})(\text{m})}{\text{kg}} = 1 \dfrac{(\text{nt/amp-m})(\text{amp-sec})(\text{m})}{\text{kg}} = 1 \dfrac{\text{nt sec}}{\text{kg}}$

$$= 1 \frac{(\text{kg m/sec}^2)(\text{sec})}{\text{kg}} = 1 \frac{\text{m}}{\text{sec}}$$

15. Alpha particles are accelerated through a potential difference of 1000 volts and then enter a magnetic field of flux density 0.2 weber/m^2 perpendicular to their direction of motion. Calculate the radius of their path. An alpha particle has mass 6.68×10^{-27} kg and charge $+2e$.

Solution:

Since kinetic energy $= \frac{1}{2}mv^2 = qV$, $v = \sqrt{2qV/m}$. Then

$$r = \frac{mv}{Bq} = \frac{m}{Bq}\sqrt{\frac{2qV}{m}} = \frac{1}{B}\sqrt{\frac{2mV}{q}}$$

$$= \frac{1}{0.2 \text{ weber/m}^2}\sqrt{\frac{2(6.68 \times 10^{-27} \text{ kg})(10^3 \text{ volts})}{2 \times 1.60 \times 10^{-19} \text{ coul}}} = 3.23 \times 10^{-2} \text{ m}$$

16. A cyclotron in which the flux density is 1.4 weber/m^2 is employed to accelerate protons. How rapidly should the electric field between the dees be reversed? The proton has mass 1.67×10^{-27} kg and charge $+e$.

Solution:

The electric field should be reversed in the time required for the protons to move through a semicircle or π radians. From $r = mv/Bq$, the constant angular velocity of the protons in radians/sec is $v/r = Bq/m$. Hence the required number of times per sec is

$$\frac{v/r}{\pi} = \frac{Bq}{\pi m} = \frac{(1.4 \text{ webers/m}^2)(1.60 \times 10^{-19} \text{ coul})}{3.14(1.67 \times 10^{-27} \text{ kg})} = 4.27 \times 10^7 \text{ per sec}$$

SUPPLEMENTARY PROBLEMS

17. Compute the flux density (or magnetic induction) in air at a point 6 cm from a long straight wire carrying a current of 9 amp. *Ans.* 3×10^{-5} weber/m^2

18. A closely-wound flat circular coil of 25 turns of wire has diameter 10 cm and carries a current of 4 amp. Determine the flux density in air (a) at its center, (b) at a point along the axis of the coil and distant 12 cm from the plane of the coil. *Ans.* (a) 1.26×10^{-3} weber/m^2, (b) 7.15×10^{-5} weber/m^2

19. A solenoid 50 cm long and 2 cm in diameter is wound with 4000 turns of wire. Compute the magnetic induction at the center of the air core when a current of 0.25 amp exists in the winding.   *Ans*. 2.51×10^{-3} weber/m^2

20. A ring solenoid is wound uniformly with 750 turns of copper wire and the mean diameter of its air core is 10 cm. What current in the winding will produce a flux density of 1.8×10^{-3} weber/m^2 in its interior?   *Ans*. 0.6 amp

21. The electron of a hydrogen atom moves in a circular orbit of radius 5.3×10^{-11} m with a speed of 2.2×10^6 m/sec. Determine the magnetic induction at the center of the orbit.   *Ans*. 12.5 weber/m^2

22. A circular coil of 20 turns of wire and radius 10 cm is mounted with its plane vertical and in the magnetic meridian at a place where the horizontal component of the earth's magnetic induction is 2×10^{-5} weber/m^2. What is the current in the coil if a small compass needle at the center of the coil is deflected 45°?   *Ans*. 0.16 amp

23. A wire 15 cm long is at right angles to a uniform field of magnetic induction 0.4 weber/m^2. (a) What is the force on the wire when it carries a current of 6 amp? (b) What is the force if the wire makes an angle of 30° with the field?   *Ans*. 0.36 nt, 0.18 nt

24. What is the direction of the force, due to the earth's magnetic field, on a wire carrying current vertically downward?   *Ans*. Horizontally toward east

25. Two long parallel wires are 4 cm apart and carry currents of 2 and 6 amp respectively in the same direction. Compute the force between the wires per meter of wire length.   *Ans*. 6×10^{-5} nt/m attraction

26. Two long and fixed parallel wires, A and B, are 10 cm apart in air and carry currents of 40 amp and 20 amp respectively in opposite directions. Determine the resultant flux density (a) on a line midway between the wires and parallel to them, (b) on a line 8 cm from wire A and 18 cm from wire B. (c) What is the force per meter on a long third wire, midway between A and B and in their plane, when it carries a current of 5 amp in the same direction as the current in A?
Ans. (a) 2.4×10^{-4} weber/m^2, (b) 7.8×10^{-5} weber/m^2, (c) 1.2×10^{-3} nt/m toward A

27. A rectangular coil of 25 turns is suspended in a field of magnetic induction 0.2 weber/m^2. The plane of the coil is parallel with the direction of the field. The dimensions of the coil are 15 cm perpendicular to the field and 12 cm parallel to the field. What is the current in the coil if there is a torque of 5.4 m-nt acting on it?   *Ans*. 60 amp

28. An ion carrying a charge of $+2e$ enters a magnetic field of flux density 1.2 weber/m^2 with a velocity of 2.5×10^5 m/sec perpendicular to the field. Determine the force on the ion.   *Ans*. 9.6×10^{-14} nt

29. A charged particle with velocity v enters a region having an electric field E and a magnetic field B, the vectors v, B and E being perpendicular to each other. If the particle continues to move in a straight line, make a sketch showing the relative directions of v, B and E and determine their mathematical relation.
Ans. $E = Bv$

30. Calculate the velocity of neon ions which pass undeflected through a region having an electric field $E = 7.7 \times 10^3$ volts/m and a magnetic field $B = 0.14$ weber/m^2, the vectors v, E and B being mutually perpendicular.
Ans. 5.5×10^4 m/sec

31. What might be the mass of a positive ion which is moving at 10^7 m/sec and is bent into a circle of radius 1.55 m by a magnetic field of 0.134 weber/m^2? There are several possible answers.
Ans. If the ion has a single charge, $m = 3.32 \times 10^{-27}$ kg; if the ion has a double charge, $m = 6.64 \times 10^{-27}$ kg; etc.

32. An electron moving with kinetic energy 6×10^{-16} joule enters a field of magnetic induction 4×10^{-3} weber/m^2 at right angles to its motion. Calculate the radius of its path.   *Ans*. 5.17 cm

33. Alpha particles, of mass 6.68×10^{-27} kg and charge $+2e$, are accelerated in a cyclotron in which the uniform flux density is 1.25 weber/m^2. How rapidly should the electric field between the dees be reversed? What is the velocity and kinetic energy of an alpha particle when it moves with radius 25 cm?
Ans. 1.91×10^7 per sec, 1.50×10^7 m/sec, 7.52×10^{-13} joule or 4.69×10^6 ev

34. A beam of electrons passes undeflected through two mutually perpendicular electric and magnetic fields. Now if the electric field is cut off and the same magnetic field maintained, the electrons move in the magnetic field in a circular path of radius 1.14 cm. Determine the ratio of the electronic charge to mass if the electric field has potential gradient 8×10^3 volts/m and the magnetic field has flux density 2×10^{-3} weber/m^2.
Ans. $e/m = 1.75 \times 10^{11}$ coul/kg

Chapter 28

Magnets and Magnetic Circuits

PERMEABILITY. The magnetic induction B inside a ring solenoid or toroid **in vacuum** was given as $B = K \frac{4\pi NI}{l} = \frac{4\pi}{10^7} \frac{NI}{l}$. Now if the toroid core is magnetic material instead of vacuum, B is increased greatly. Thus B in the toroid depends on NI/l and also on properties of the material in the toroid.

Let μ_r be the ratio of the magnetic induction in the toroid with a core of magnetic material to the magnetic induction with a vacuum core. Then the magnetic induction in the material is $B = \mu_r \frac{4\pi}{10^7} \frac{NI}{l} = \mu \frac{NI}{l}$, where μ_r is called the **relative permeability** of the material and $\mu = \mu_r \frac{4\pi}{10^7}$ is called the **permeability** of the material.

Since μ_r for a vacuum or free space is exactly 1, the permeability of a vacuum, denoted by μ_0, is

$$\mu_0 = \frac{4\pi}{10^7} \frac{\text{weber}}{\text{ampere-meter}}$$

and for any substance the relative permeability is

$$\mu_r \text{ (relative permeability)} = \frac{\mu \text{ (permeability of substance)}}{\mu_0 \text{ (permeability of free space)}}$$

The mks unit of permeability is the weber per ampere-meter. The relative permeability of a substance is a dimensionless number.

MAGNETIC FIELD INTENSITY, H, within any medium is defined as the ratio

$$H = \frac{B}{\mu}$$

where B is the magnetic induction and μ the permeability of the medium. Thus for a toroid of mean circumference l and wound with N turns carrying a current I, the field intensity is

$$H = \frac{B}{\mu} = \frac{\mu NI/l}{\mu} = \frac{NI}{l}$$

The mks unit of field intensity is the ampere-turn per meter.

MAGNETIC MOMENT OF A COIL. The torque L on a coil of N turns carrying a current I in a field of magnetic induction B was shown to be $L = BINA$, where the plane of the coil is parallel to the field. We define the magnetic moment M of the coil by the equation

$$M = \frac{L}{B} = \frac{BINA}{B} = INA$$

where the units of M are amp-m^2.

MAGNETIC POLES. Although magnetic poles do not actually exist, the concept is often useful in simplifying calculations involving magnets.

A bar magnet of length l placed with its axis normal to a field B has a torque L acting on it which tends to rotate the axis to a position parallel to B, and its magnetic moment $M = L/B$. We now define the **pole strength** p of each end face of the magnet as

$$p = \frac{M}{l}$$

where p is in amp-m, since M is in amp-m^2. The force exerted on each pole is

$$F \text{ (nt)} = B \text{ (nt/amp-m)} \times p \text{ (amp-m)}$$

the force on a north pole being in the same direction as B and the force on a south pole being directed opposite to B.

FORCE BETWEEN TWO MAGNETIC POLES. If two point poles of strength p and p' are separated in free space by a distance r, the force between them is

$$F = K\frac{pp'}{r^2}$$

where $K = \mu_o/4\pi = 10^{-7}$ nt/amp^2 (weber/amp-m), using mks units.

MAGNETIC FIELD OF A POLE. The force exerted by a pole p on another pole p' at a distance r from it in free space is $F = Kpp'/r^2$. Also, the magnetic induction at p' is $B = F/p'$. Then $B = (Kpp'/r^2)/p'$ or

$$B = K\frac{p}{r^2}$$

where B is the magnetic induction at a distance r from a pole of strength p.

THE MAGNETIC CIRCUIT. The magnetic flux Φ inside a closed ring solenoid of uniform cross section area A and mean circumference l is

$$\Phi = BA = \mu HA = \mu\frac{NI}{l}A$$

where μ is the permeability of the core material. Rearranging this expression gives the law of the magnetic circuit:

$$\Phi = \frac{NI}{l/\mu A} \qquad \text{or} \qquad \text{flux} = \frac{\text{magnetomotive force (mmf)}}{\text{reluctance } (\mathfrak{R})}$$

Magnetomotive force (NI) causes the establishment of flux in the circuit. Flux is analogous to current in the electric circuit, magnetomotive force (mmf) to emf, and reluctance to resistance. Flux is given in webers, magnetomotive force in ampere-turns, and reluctance ($l/\mu A = NI/\Phi$) in ampere-turns per weber.

SOLVED PROBLEMS

1. A solenoid is 40 cm long, has section area 8 cm^2, and is wound with 300 turns of wire which carry a current of 1.2 amp. The relative permeability of its iron core is assumed to be 600. Compute the field intensity (or magnetizing force) H, the magnetic induction (or flux density) B, and the flux Φ in the iron core.

    Solution: $H = NI/l = (300 \text{ turns})(1.2 \text{ amp})/(0.4 \text{ m}) = 900 \text{ amp-turns/m}$

    $$B = \mu H = \mu_r \mu_O H = 600 \times \frac{4\pi}{10^7} \frac{\text{weber}}{\text{amp-m}} \times 900 \frac{\text{amp-turns}}{\text{m}} = 0.678 \frac{\text{weber}}{\text{m}^2}$$

    $$\Phi = \mu H A = BA = (0.678 \text{ weber/m}^2)(8 \times 10^{-4} \text{ m}^2) = 5.42 \times 10^{-4} \text{ weber}$$

2. For a field intensity (or magnetizing force) $H = 200$ amp-turns/m, the flux density in an iron core of a solenoid is $B = 0.14$ weber/m^2. Determine the permeability μ and the relative permeability μ_r of the iron.

    Solution: $\mu = \dfrac{B}{H} = \dfrac{0.14 \text{ weber/m}^2}{200 \text{ amp-turns/m}} = 7 \times 10^{-4} \dfrac{\text{weber}}{\text{amp-m}}$, $\mu_r = \dfrac{\mu}{\mu_O} = \dfrac{7 \times 10^{-4} \text{ weber/amp-m}}{4\pi \times 10^{-7} \text{ weber/amp-m}} = 557$

3. A ring solenoid has a section area of 6 cm^2 and the magnetic induction in its air core is 10^{-3} weber/m^2. What is the magnetic induction B and flux Φ in the solenoid if an iron core of assumed relative permeability 500 replaces the air core?

    Solution: $B = 500 \times 10^{-3} \dfrac{\text{weber}}{\text{m}^2} = 0.5 \dfrac{\text{weber}}{\text{m}^2}$, $\Phi = BA = 0.5 \dfrac{\text{weber}}{\text{m}^2} \times 6 \times 10^{-4} \text{ m}^2 = 3 \times 10^{-4} \text{ weber}$

4. A bar magnet has poles of 48 amp-m which are 25 cm apart. What is the magnetic moment M of the magnet? What torque L is required to hold this magnet at an angle of 30° with a uniform magnetic field of flux density 0.15 nt/amp-m? If this magnet is pivoted at the center, what force acting perpendicular to the magnet and 6 cm from the pivot is required?

    Solution:

    $M = pl = 48 \text{ amp-m} \times 0.25 \text{ m} = 12 \text{ amp-m}^2$

    $L = BM \sin\theta = 0.15 \text{ nt/amp-m} \times 12 \text{ amp-m}^2 \times 0.5 = 0.9 \text{ m-nt}$

    $F = \text{torque/distance} = (0.9 \text{ m-nt})/(.06 \text{ m}) = 15 \text{ nt}$

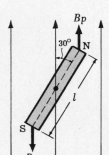

5. A bar magnet 15 cm long has pole strengths of 6 amp-m. Determine the force on a unit north pole in air at a point P 10 cm from each pole.

    Solution:

    Force on a unit north pole at P due to N pole alone

    $$= K\frac{pp'}{r^2} = 10^{-7} \frac{\text{nt}}{\text{amp}^2} \times \frac{(6 \times 1)(\text{amp-m})^2}{(0.1 \text{ m})^2} = 6 \times 10^{-5} \text{ nt repulsion.}$$

    This repulsion is in the direction PA. The force due to the S pole alone is also 6×10^{-5} nt, but in the direction PC.

    Lay off equal distances PA and PC to represent the two forces on the pole at P and complete the parallelogram. Diagonal PD represents the resultant force and is computed to be 9×10^{-5} nt directed horizontally from P to D.

6. A bar magnet 25 cm long has pole strengths of 12 amp-m. Compute the magnetic induction in air at a point in line with the axis of the magnet and 5 cm away from its north pole. What is the force on a north pole of strength 8 amp-m placed at that point?

    Solution:

    Since $B = Kp/r^2$, the flux density at P due to the N pole is $Kp/(.05 \text{ m})^2$ directed to the right and the

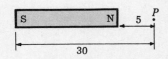

flux density at P due to the S pole is $Kp/(0.30 \text{ m})^2$ directed to the left. The resultant flux density at P is

$$B = Kp\left[\frac{1}{(.05 \text{ m})^2} - \frac{1}{(.30 \text{ m})^2}\right] = 10^{-7}\frac{\text{nt}}{\text{amp}^2} \times 12 \text{ amp-m} \times \frac{389}{\text{m}^2} = 4.67 \times 10^{-4}\frac{\text{nt}}{\text{amp-m}} \text{ toward right.}$$

$$F = Bp = 4.67 \times 10^{-4} \text{ nt/amp-m} \times 8 \text{ amp-m} = 3.74 \times 10^{-3} \text{ nt toward right.}$$

7. A circular coil of 8 turns and radius 5 cm carries a current of 3 amp. Compute the force on a pole of 60 amp-m placed at the center of the coil.
Solution:

$$F = Bp = (K\frac{2\pi NI}{r})p = 10^{-7}\frac{2\pi \times 8 \times 3}{.05}\frac{\text{nt}}{\text{amp-m}} \times 60 \text{ amp-m} = 1.81 \times 10^{-2} \text{ nt}$$

8. (a) How much work is done in carrying a magnet pole of 50 amp-m in any circular path around a long straight wire carrying a current of 3 amp? (b) How much work is done in carrying the 50 amp-m pole a distance of 4 cm along the axis and near the center of a long solenoid having 12 turns of wire per cm and carrying a current of 3 amp?
Solution:

(a) $W = F \times 2\pi r = Bp \times 2\pi r = (2KI/r)p \times 2\pi r = 4\pi KIp$
    $= 4\pi \times 10^{-7} \text{ nt/amp}^2 \times 3 \text{ amp} \times 50 \text{ amp-m} = 1.88 \times 10^{-4} \text{ joule}$

(b) $W = Fd = Bpd = 4\pi K(N/l)Ipd$
    $= 4\pi \times 10^{-7} \text{ nt/amp}^2 \times 1200 \text{ turns/m} \times 3 \text{ amp} \times 50 \text{ amp-m} \times .04 \text{ m} = 9.02 \times 10^{-3} \text{ joule}$

> **Another Method.** The work done in carrying the pole around a wire in a circular path (or any path) is $4\pi KIp$ joules, as shown in (a). Since the field outside the solenoid can be neglected, all the work is done along the path inside the solenoid. Hence the work required to carry the pole a distance of 4 cm, i.e. through 48 turns, inside the solenoid is
>
> $$W = 48(4\pi KIp) = 48(1.88 \times 10^{-4} \text{ joule}) = 9.02 \times 10^{-3} \text{ joule}$$

9. An iron ring has a section area of 4 cm^2 and a mean diameter of 20 cm. It is wound uniformly with 500 turns of wire and a current of 1 amp exists in the winding. The relative permeability of the iron is 1200. Compute the flux density and the flux in the iron.
Solution:

$$B = \mu H = 1200\mu_0\frac{NI}{l} = 1200 \times \frac{4\pi}{10^7}\frac{\text{weber}}{\text{amp-m}} \times \frac{500 \times 1}{0.2\pi}\frac{\text{amp-turns}}{\text{m}} = 1.2\frac{\text{webers}}{\text{m}^2}$$

$$\Phi = BA = (1.2 \text{ webers/m}^2)(4 \times 10^{-4} \text{ m}^2) = 4.8 \times 10^{-4} \text{ weber}$$

$$\text{Or,} \quad \Phi = \frac{\text{mmf}}{\Re} = \frac{NI}{\dfrac{l}{\mu A}} = \frac{500 \times 1 \text{ amp-turns}}{\dfrac{0.2\pi \text{ m}}{(1200 \times 4\pi \times 10^{-7} \text{ weber/amp-m})(4 \times 10^{-4} \text{ m}^2)}} = 4.8 \times 10^{-4} \text{ weber}$$

10. An electromagnet having a total flux of 1.2×10^{-3} weber is wound with a coil of 600 turns carrying a current of .08 amp. Compute the reluctance $\Re$ of the magnetic circuit.
Solution:
$$\Re = \frac{\text{mmf}}{\text{flux}} = \frac{NI}{\Phi} = \frac{600 \times .08 \text{ amp-turns}}{1.2 \times 10^{-3} \text{ weber}} = 4 \times 10^4\frac{\text{amp-turns}}{\text{weber}}$$

11. The air gap of a magnetic circuit has a cross section of 24 cm^2 and a length of 0.8 cm. The remainder of the magnetic circuit consists of 100 cm of iron of cross section 20 cm^2 and relative permeability 600. How many ampere-turns (NI) are required to produce a flux of 1.2×10^{-4} weber in the air gap?

Solution: The total flux is the same throughout the magnetic circuit.

$$\Re_{\text{gap}} = \frac{l}{\mu A} = \frac{8 \times 10^{-3}}{(4\pi \times 10^{-7})(24 \times 10^{-4})} = \frac{10^8}{12\pi}, \quad \Re_{\text{iron}} = \frac{1}{(600 \times 4\pi \times 10^{-7})(20 \times 10^{-4})} = \frac{10^8}{48\pi}$$

$$NI = \text{mmf} = \Phi\Re = 1.2 \times 10^{-4} \text{ weber} \times (\frac{10^8}{12\pi} + \frac{10^8}{48\pi})\frac{\text{amp-turns}}{\text{weber}} = 398 \text{ amp-turns}$$

SUPPLEMENTARY PROBLEMS

12. A flux of 9×10^{-4} weber is produced in the iron core of a solenoid. When the iron core is removed, a flux (in air) of 5×10^{-7} weber is produced in the same solenoid by the same current. What is the relative permeability of the iron?   *Ans.* 1800

13. The flux density in an iron core of a ring solenoid is 0.54 weber/m^2 when the field intensity (or magnetizing force) is 360 amp-turns/m. What is the permeability and the relative permeability of the iron? *Ans.* 1.5×10^{-3} weber/amp-m, 1.19×10^{3}

14. A solenoid has section area 15 cm^2 and 700 turns per meter which carry a current of 0.5 amp. Compute the field intensity H, flux density B and flux Φ in its core if it has (a) an air core, (b) an iron core of relative permeability 1000.   *Ans.* (a) 350 amp-turns/m, 4.4×10^{-4} weber/m^2, 6.6×10^{-7} weber
(b) 350 amp-turns/m, 4.4×10^{-1} weber/m^2, 6.6×10^{-4} weber

15. A circular coil of diameter 7 cm has 24 turns of wire which carry a current of 0.75 amp. Compute the magnetic moment of the coil.   *Ans.* 6.9×10^{-2} amp-m^2

16. What is the magnetic moment of a bar magnet having poles of 7 amp-m and 12 cm apart?   *Ans.* 0.84 amp-m^2

17. When a magnet of magnetic moment 1.5 amp-m^2 is placed at right angles to a magnetic field of flux density 0.16 weber/m^2, the force exerted on one of the poles is 0.8 nt. What is the length of the magnet?   *Ans.* 0.3 m

18. Calculate the torque required to hold a magnet, of magnetic moment 3.6 amp-m^2, at an angle of 60° with a field of magnetic induction 0.25 weber/m^2. If the magnet is pivoted at the center, what force acting perpendicular to the magnet and 12 cm from the pivot is required?   *Ans.* 0.78 m-nt, 6.5 nt

19. A bar magnet 30 cm long has poles of 16 amp-m. When it is placed in a uniform magnetic field at an angle of 30° with the direction of the field, the turning couple acting on the magnet is .048 m-nt. Determine the flux density.   *Ans.* .02 weber/m^2

20. A circular coil of radius 10 cm has 25 turns of wire which carry a current of 2 amp. Determine the force acting on a pole of 5 amp-m placed at the center of the coil.   *Ans.* 1.57×10^{-3} nt

21. Two unlike magnet poles attract each other with a force of .03 nt at a distance of 4 cm in air. If one pole is 50 amp-m, what is the other pole strength?   *Ans.* 9.6 amp-m

22. A magnet pole experiences a force of 0.8 nt in a uniform field of flux density .05 weber/m^2. Determine the strength of the pole.   *Ans.* 16 amp-m

23. A south pole of a very long bar magnet has a strength of 36 amp-m. Compute the flux density in air at a point 3 cm from this pole.   *Ans.* 4×10^{-3} weber/m^2

24. A bar magnet 16 cm long has pole strengths of 40 amp-m. Determine the force on a south pole of 5 amp-m placed in air at a point in line with the axis of the magnet and 4 cm away from its north pole.
Ans. 1.2×10^{-2} nt toward magnet

25. A bar magnet NS is 10 cm long and has poles of 20 amp-m. Calculate the flux density at a point P in air where angle $NPS = 90°$ and $NP = SP$.   *Ans.* 5.7×10^{-4} weber/m^2

26. A bar magnet 15 cm long has poles of 24 amp-m. Calculate the magnetic induction in air at a point 9 cm from the S pole and 12 cm from the N pole.   *Ans.* 3.40×10^{-4} weber/m^2

27. How many ampere-turns are required to produce a flux of 2×10^{-4} weber in an iron ring of mean circumference 100 cm and cross section 5 cm^2? The relative permeability of the iron is 500.   *Ans.* 637 amp-turns

28. An iron ring, of section area 4 cm^2 and mean diameter 10 cm, is wound with 5 turns of wire per cm. The permeability of the iron is 2000. Compute (a) the reluctance of the core, (b) the magnetomotive force produced by a current of 0.5 amp in the winding, and (c) the flux in the core when the winding carries 0.5 amp.
Ans. 3.12×10^{5} amp-turns/weber, 78.5 amp-turns, 2.52×10^{-4} weber

29. An iron ring, of section area 8 cm^2 and mean diameter 15 cm, is wound with 400 turns of wire. The ring has an air gap 0.2 cm long and the relative permeability of the iron is 500. What current in the winding will produce a flux of 1×10^{-4} weber?   *Ans.* 0.73 amp

Chapter 29

Galvanometers, Ammeters, Voltmeters

A GALVANOMETER is an instrument which detects and measures very small electric currents. D'Arsonval galvanometers, used for D.C. measurements, have a permanent magnet between whose poles is suspended a moving coil by means of a fine wire or ribbon.

When no current is in the coil, the plane of the coil is parallel to the magnetic field. A current set up in the coil causes it to rotate until the torque due to the interaction of the field of the magnet and the current in the coil is balanced by the restoring torque exerted on the coil by the twisted suspension. The torque on the coil, and hence the angular deflection of the coil, is proportional to the current.

AMMETERS. If a low resistance shunt is connected in parallel with a galvanometer, the instrument may be used to measure larger currents and is called an ammeter. The shunt will bypass a large part of the current but will allow a definite part to pass through the coil, so that with proper calibration an exact reading of the total current can be obtained.

The ammeter is connected in series with a circuit and hence it must have low resistance. To increase the range of an ammeter, a suitable low resistance is connected in parallel with the ammeter.

VOLTMETERS. If a high resistance is connected in series with a galvanometer, the instrument may be used to measure the potential difference between two points of a circuit and is called a voltmeter. The current in the coil will be proportional to the potential difference between the two points.

The voltmeter is connected in parallel across the points whose potential difference is desired and hence it must have high resistance. To extend the range of a voltmeter, a suitable high resistance is connected in series with the voltmeter.

SOLVED PROBLEMS

1. A galvanometer has resistance 50 ohms and requires .01 amp for full scale deflection. (*a*) What shunt (i.e. parallel) resistance R_{sh} will convert the galvanometer into an ammeter reading 10 amp full scale? (*b*) What series resistance R_{se} will convert the instrument into a voltmeter reading 100 volts full scale?

Solution:

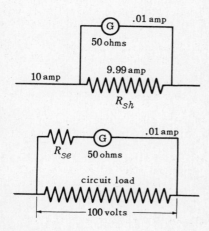

(*a*) When the line current is 10 amp, the galvanometer current must be .01 amp and the shunt current (10 − .01) = 9.99 amp. Since the galvanometer and shunt are in parallel, the potential difference V across each is the same; then

$$V_g = V_{sh}, \qquad I_g R_g = I_{sh} R_{sh}, \qquad .01 \times 50 = 9.99 \times R_{sh}, \qquad \text{and}$$
$$R_{sh} = .050 \text{ ohm}$$

(*b*) When a potential difference $V = 100$ volts is impressed across the combined (galvanometer + series) resistance, a current $I = .01$ amp must pass through the galvanometer and series resistance; then

$$V = I(R_g + R_{se}), \qquad 100\text{v} = (.01\text{ amp})(50\text{ ohms} + R_{se}), \qquad \text{and} \qquad R_{se} = 9950 \text{ ohms.}$$

2. An ammeter has resistance .006 ohm and reads 1 amp per scale division. What shunt resistance will cause it to read 5 amp per scale division?

Solution:

When the line current is 5 amp, the ammeter current must be 1 amp and the shunt current $(5-1) = 4$ amp. Since the ammeter and shunt are in parallel, the potential difference V across each is the same; then

$$V_a = V_{sh}, \qquad I_a R_a = I_{sh} R_{sh}, \qquad 1 \times .006 = 4 \times R_{sh}, \qquad \text{and} \qquad R_{sh} = .0015 \text{ ohm}.$$

3. A voltmeter has resistance 4000 ohms and reads 1 volt per scale division. What resistance, connected in series with the voltmeter, will cause the instrument to read 10 volts per scale division?

Solution:

When 1 volt is impressed across the voltmeter, the voltmeter current is $I = 1/4000$ amp. It is required that when a potential difference $V = 10$ volts is impressed across the combined voltmeter and series resistance, a current $I = 1/4000$ amp should exists in the voltmeter and series resistance.

$$V = I(R_v + R_{se}), \qquad 10 \text{ v} = (1/4000 \text{ amp})(4000 \text{ ohms} + R_{se}), \qquad R_{se} = 36,000 \text{ ohms}.$$

4. A 250 ohm circuit is connected across 100 volt mains as shown. The voltmeter has resistance 1000 ohms and the ammeter has negligible resistance. (*a*) What power is dissipated in the 250 ohm circuit? (*b*) What is the apparent power obtained by multiplying the ammeter and voltmeter readings?

Solution:

The voltmeter reads 100 volts, since the IR drop in the ammeter is negligible.

(*a*) Current in 250 ohm circuit = $V_C/R_C = 100/250 = 0.4$ amp

Power in 250 ohm circuit = $V_C I_C = 100 \times 0.4 = 40$ watts

(*b*) Current in voltmeter = $V_v/R_v = 100/1000 = 0.1$ amp

Total current read by ammeter = $0.4 + 0.1 = 0.5$ amp

Apparent power = voltmeter reading $\times$ ammeter reading

$\qquad\qquad\qquad = 100 \text{ v} \times 0.5 \text{ amp} = 50$ watts

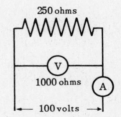

SUPPLEMENTARY PROBLEMS

5. An ammeter has resistance 2 ohms and the shunt has resistance .001 ohm. Determine the instrument current when the line current is 50 amp.   *Ans.* .025 amp

6. A galvanometer has resistance 28 ohms and requires 1 milliampere for full scale deflection. What is the resistance required, and how connected, to convert the galvanometer (*a*) into an ammeter reading 0.25 amp full scale, (*b*) into a voltmeter reading 0.2 volt full scale?   *Ans.* (*a*) 0.112 ohm in parallel, (*b*) 172 ohms in series

7. A galvanometer has resistance 600 ohms and requires 100 microamperes for full scale deflection. It is to be converted for use either as (*a*) a 0-100 milliammeter or (*b*) a 0-100 millivoltmeter. In each case, what size shunt or multiplier is required?   *Ans.* (*a*) 0.601 ohm in parallel, (*b*) 400 ohms in series

8. An ammeter has resistance .009 ohm and reads 1 amp per scale division. What shunt resistance will make it read 10 amp per scale division?   *Ans.* .001 ohm

9. A voltmeter has resistance 2000 ohms and reads 1 volt per scale division. What resistance must be inserted in series with the voltmeter to make it read 4 volts per scale division?   *Ans.* 6000 ohms

10. A voltmeter has resistance 15,000 ohms and has a full scale of 15 volts. How can the range be extended to read 150 volts full scale?   *Ans.* 135,000 ohms in series

11. A voltmeter of resistance 26,000 ohms is employed to measure a large unknown resistance. When the instrument is connected across D.C. mains it reads 140 volts. When it is connected in series with the unknown resistance across the same mains, the voltmeter reads 40 volts. What is the value of the unknown resistance?   *Ans.* 65,000 ohms

12. An ammeter of negligible resistance is connected in series with a parallel combination consisting of a 2000 ohm voltmeter and an unknown resistance. If the voltmeter reads 120 volts and the ammeter reads 0.60 amp, determine the unknown resistance.   *Ans.* 222 ohms

Chapter 30

Electromagnetic Induction

ELECTROMAGNETIC INDUCTION. An emf is induced in a circuit whenever there is a change in the magnetic flux linked with the circuit.

DIRECTION OF INDUCED EMF. LENZ'S LAW. The induced current flows in such a direction as to oppose, by its electromagnetic action, the motion or cause by which it is produced. Thus if the induced current in a coil is caused by an increase in flux through the coil, the induced current is in such a direction as to set up magnetic lines that are in opposite direction to the lines of the original field. If a moving wire cuts magnetic flux, the induced current is in such a direction as to set up a magnetic field that opposes the motion.

FARADAY'S LAW OF ELECTROMAGNETIC INDUCTION. The magnitude of the emf induced in a coil is proportional to the time rate of change of flux ($\Delta\Phi/\Delta t$) linked with the coil and to the number of turns (N) in the coil. When the flux through a coil changes, an emf is induced in each turn; and since the turns are in series, the total emf induced in the coil is the sum of the emf's of the turns. The average emf is

$$\mathcal{E} = -N\frac{\Delta\Phi}{\Delta t}$$

where the minus sign indicates that the induced emf opposes the cause which produces it (Lenz's law). The emf $\mathcal{E}$ is in volts if $\Delta\Phi/\Delta t$ is in webers/sec.

We may also think of the emf as being caused by a conductor cutting lines of magnetic flux. Thus if a circuit has N conductors in series and if each conductor cuts flux at the rate of 1 weber/sec, the average emf induced in the circuit is N volts.

EMF INDUCED IN MOVING CONDUCTOR. The emf induced in a straight conductor of length l moving with velocity v perpendicular to a field of magnetic induction B is

$$\mathcal{E} = Blv$$

where B, l and v are mutually perpendicular. The emf $\mathcal{E}$ is in volts when B is in webers/m², l in meters, and v in m/sec.

SOLVED PROBLEMS

1. A copper bar 30 cm long is perpendicular to a field of flux density 0.8 weber/m² and moves at right angles to the field with a speed of 50 cm/sec. Determine the emf induced in the bar.
   Solution:
$$\mathcal{E} = Blv = 0.8 \text{ weber/m}^2 \times 0.3 \text{ m} \times 0.5 \text{ m/sec} = 0.12 \text{ volt}$$

2. A coil of 50 turns is pulled in .02 sec from between the poles of a magnet where its area includes 31×10^{-5} weber to a place where its area includes 1×10^{-5} weber. Determine the average emf induced in the coil.

Solution:

Neglecting the sign of the emf, $\quad \mathcal{E} \;=\; N \dfrac{\Delta \Phi}{\Delta t} \;=\; 50 \times \dfrac{(31-1) \times 10^{-5} \text{ weber}}{2 \times 10^{-2} \text{ sec}} \;=\; 0.75 \text{ volt}$

3. A coil of wire, of 20 turns and area 400 cm², is rotating uniformly at 10 rps about an axis in the plane of the coil and perpendicular to a uniform field of flux density 0.3 weber/m². What is the average emf induced in the coil?

Solution:

Consider that the plane of the coil is perpendicular to the field at a given instant. When the coil rotates through 90° its plane passes from a position (perpendicular to the field) where a maximum number of flux lines thread its area to a position (parallel to the field) where zero lines thread its area. Thus as the coil rotates through 360°, or 1 revolution, each turn of wire cuts 4 times the maximum number of flux lines threading its area. Then, neglecting the sign of the emf,

$$\mathcal{E} \;=\; N \dfrac{\Delta \Phi}{\Delta t} \;=\; 20 \times \dfrac{4\,(0.3 \text{ weber/m}^2 \times .04 \text{ m}^2)}{0.1 \text{ sec}} \;=\; 9.6 \text{ volts}$$

4. A copper disc of 10 cm radius is rotating at 20 rps about its axis and with its plane perpendicular to a uniform field of flux density 0.6 weber/m². What is the potential difference between the circumference and the center?

Solution:

In 1/20 sec each radial strip (from axis to circumference) cuts once all the flux lines threading the disk.

Flux threading disk, $\Phi \;=\; BA \;=\; 0.6 \text{ weber/m}^2 \times \pi (0.1 \text{ m})^2 \;=\; 6\pi \times 10^{-3} \text{ weber}$.

$\mathcal{E} \;=\; \text{flux cut per sec} \;=\; 20\,(6\pi \times 10^{-3}) \text{ weber/sec} \;=\; 0.38 \text{ volt}$.

5. A 5 ohm coil, of 100 turns and diameter 6 cm, is placed between the poles of an electromagnet and perpendicular to the flux. When the coil is suddenly removed from the field of the electromagnet, a charge of 10^{-4} coulomb is sent through a 595 ohm galvanometer connected to the coil. Compute the flux density B between the poles of the electromagnet.

Solution:

Let Φ = change of flux when coil is removed from field. Then $\mathcal{E} \;=\; N(\Phi/t) \;=\; IR$ and

$$B \;=\; \dfrac{\Phi}{A} \;=\; \dfrac{(It)R}{NA} \;=\; \dfrac{(10^{-4} \text{ coul}) \times (595+5) \text{ ohms}}{100 \times \pi(.03 \text{ m})^2} \;=\; 0.212 \text{ weber/m}^2$$

6. How much charge q will flow through a 200 ohm ballistic galvanometer connected to a 400 ohm circular coil of 1000 turns wound on a wooden stick 2 cm in diameter, if a magnetic field intensity of 9000 ampere-turns/meter parallel to the length of the stick is decreased suddenly to zero?

Solution:

As in the preceding problem, $IR \;=\; N \dfrac{\Phi}{t} \;=\; N \dfrac{BA}{t} \;=\; N \dfrac{\mu H A}{t}$. Then

$$q \;=\; It \;=\; \dfrac{N}{R} \mu H A \;=\; \dfrac{1000 \text{ turns}}{(200+400) \text{ ohms}} \times \dfrac{4\pi}{10^7} \dfrac{\text{weber}}{\text{amp-m}} \times 9000 \dfrac{\text{amp-turns}}{\text{m}} \times \pi(.01 \text{ m})^2$$

$$=\; 5.9 \times 10^{-6} \dfrac{\text{weber}}{\text{ohm}} \text{ or coul}$$

since $\quad 1 \dfrac{\text{weber}}{\text{ohm}} \;=\; 1 \dfrac{\text{volt-sec}}{\text{volt/amp}} \;=\; 1 \text{ amp-sec} \;=\; 1 \text{ coul}$.

7. A solenoid of 1200 evenly spaced turns is wound on an iron core 80 cm long and 3 cm in diameter. The relative permeability of the iron is assumed to have the constant value 50. A secondary coil of 10,000 turns is wound around the central portion of the solenoid. If a current of 2 amp through the primary coil is reduced to zero in .01 sec, what average emf is induced in the secondary coil?

Solution:

The flux through the secondary equals that through the primary, since at the center the flux lines are confined to the interior of the solenoid.

Let N_1 and N_2 be the number of turns in the primary and secondary, respectively.

$$\text{Initial } \Phi = BA = (\mu \frac{N_1 I}{l})A = 50(\frac{4\pi}{10^7}) \frac{\text{weber}}{\text{amp-m}} \times \frac{1200 \times 2}{0.8} \frac{\text{amp-turns}}{\text{m}} \times \frac{\pi}{4}(.03\,\text{m})^2$$
$$= 1.33 \times 10^{-4} \text{ weber}$$

$$\text{Emf induced in secondary} = N_2 \frac{\text{change of flux}}{\text{time taken}} = 10^4 \frac{1.33 \times 10^{-4} \text{ weber}}{10^{-2} \text{ sec}} = 133 \text{ volts}$$

SUPPLEMENTARY PROBLEMS

8. A train is moving directly south with uniform speed of 10 m/sec. If the vertical component of the earth's magnetic induction is 5.4×10^{-5} weber/m^2, compute the emf induced in a car axle 1.2 m long. *Ans.* 6.5×10^{-4} volt

9. A coil 20 cm square has 50 turns of wire. The coil rotates at 360 rpm about an axis in the plane of the coil and perpendicular to a uniform field of flux density .04 weber/m^2. (*a*) Compute the maximum flux passing through the coil and the average emf induced in the coil. (*b*) Consider that the coil is stationary and its plane is perpendicular to the field. If the field is cut off in .04 sec, find the average emf induced in the coil during this period. (*c*) Now consider that the same coil is stationary and makes an angle of 60° with the direction of the field of flux density .04 weber/m^2. If the field becomes zero in .04 sec, find the average emf induced during this period. *Ans.* (*a*) 1.6×10^{-3} weber, 1.92 v; (*b*) 2.00 v; (*c*) 1.73 v

10. A rectangular wooden frame of area 0.1 m^2 carries a coil of 200 turns around its edge, and is set up with its plane vertical and at right angles to the horizontal component of the earth's magnetic induction at a place where the horizontal component is 1.8×10^{-5} weber/m^2. The frame is suddenly rotated about a vertical axis through 180°. If the resistance of the circuit is 36 ohms, what charge will flow in it? *Ans.* 2×10^{-5} coul

11. Given an air-core solenoid of length 1 meter and diameter 2 cm, whose primary coil has 2000 evenly spaced turns. How many turns must a secondary coil have in order that an emf of 2 volts be induced when the primary current changes from 0 to 10 amp in .01 sec? *Ans.* 2530 turns

12. A coil of 200 turns and resistance 60 ohms is wound on an iron core of 30 cm^2 section area and constant relative permeability 160, and the terminals of the coil are connected to a capacitor of capacitance 50 microfarads. If an external magnetic field intensity of 3200 ampere-turns/meter is applied, parallel to the length of the iron core, what potential difference will be acquired by the condenser? *Ans.* 129 volts

Chapter 31

Self-Inductance and Mutual Inductance

SELF-INDUCTANCE. When the current in a circuit is changing, the magnetic flux linking the same circuit changes. This change in flux causes an emf to be induced in the circuit. The induced emf ε is proportional to the time rate of change of current, $\Delta I/\Delta t$, if the permeability is constant.

$$\varepsilon = -L\frac{\Delta I}{\Delta t}$$

where L is a constant called the **self-inductance** of the circuit. The negative sign indicates that the self-induced emf (it is a back emf) opposes the change of current which produces it.

When ε is in volts and $\Delta I/\Delta t$ in amp/sec, L is in **henrys**. The self-inductance of a circuit is 1 henry if an emf of 1 volt is induced in it when the current changes at the rate of 1 amp/sec.

MUTUAL INDUCTANCE. When a current in a (primary) circuit is changing, an emf is induced in a neighboring (secondary) circuit which is interlinked by any part of the primary flux. The induced secondary emf ε_2 is proportional to the time rate of change of the primary current, $\Delta I_1/\Delta t$.

$$\varepsilon_2 = M\frac{\Delta I_1}{\Delta t}$$

where M is a constant called the **mutual inductance** of the system. If ε is in volts and $\Delta I/\Delta t$ in amp/sec, M is in henrys.

ENERGY OF A MAGNETIC FIELD of a circuit is

$$W \text{ (joules)} = \tfrac{1}{2}LI^2$$

where L = self-inductance of circuit in henrys, I = current in amperes.

SELF-INDUCTANCE OF A SOLENOID. The emf induced in a coil of N turns when the time rate of change of flux is $\Delta\Phi/\Delta t$ is $\varepsilon = -N(\Delta\Phi/\Delta t)$. Equating this with $\varepsilon = -L(\Delta I/\Delta t)$ gives $L = N(\Delta\Phi/\Delta I)$. If the flux changes uniformly with the current (assuming constant permeability) and if the flux value is Φ when the current value is I, then

$$L = \frac{N\Phi}{I}$$

which indicates that a circuit has self-inductance of 1 henry if it produces 1 flux linkage ($N\Phi$) per ampere of current in that circuit.

Consider that a solenoid has a core of permeability μ, length l and section area A. Then $\Phi = BA$, where $B = \mu NI/l$, and

$$L = \frac{N\Phi}{I} = \frac{N}{I}BA = \frac{N}{I}(\mu\frac{NI}{l})A = \frac{N^2\mu A}{l}$$

SOLVED PROBLEMS

1. A direct current of 2 amp in a coil of 400 turns causes a flux of 10^{-4} weber to link the turns of the coil. Compute (a) the average counter emf induced in the coil if the current is interrupted in .08 sec, (b) the inductance of the coil, and (c) the energy stored in the magnetic field.

Solution:

(a) $\mathcal{E} = N\dfrac{\Delta\Phi}{\Delta t} = 400\dfrac{(10^{-4}-0)\text{ weber}}{.08\text{ sec}} = 0.5$ volt (neglecting the sign of the emf)

(b) $\mathcal{E} = L\dfrac{\Delta I}{\Delta t}$, $\quad$ 0.5 volt $= L\dfrac{(2-0)\text{ amp}}{.08\text{ sec}}$, $\quad$ and $\quad L = .02$ henry

or $\quad L = \dfrac{N\Phi}{I} = \dfrac{400\times10^{-4}\text{ weber}}{2\text{ amp}} = .02$ henry $= 20$ millihenrys

(c) $W = \frac{1}{2}LI^2 = \frac{1}{2}(.02\text{ henry})(2\text{ amp})^2 = .04$ joule

2. Coils A and B are placed near each other and have 200 and 800 turns respectively. A direct current of 2 amp in coil A produces a flux of 2.5×10^{-4} weber in A and 1.8×10^{-4} weber in B. Determine (a) the self-inductance of A, (b) the mutual inductance of A and B, (c) the average emf induced in B when the current in A is interrupted in 0.3 sec.

Solution:

(a) $L_A = \dfrac{N_A\Phi_A}{I_A} = \dfrac{200(2.5\times10^{-4}\text{ weber})}{2\text{ amp}} = .025$ henry

(b) $M = \dfrac{N_B\Phi_B}{I_A} = \dfrac{800(1.8\times10^{-4}\text{ weber})}{2\text{ amp}} = .072$ henry

(c) $\mathcal{E}_B = M\dfrac{\Delta I_A}{\Delta t} = .072$ henry $\times \dfrac{(2-0)\text{ amp}}{0.3\text{ sec}} = 0.48$ volt

or $\quad \mathcal{E}_B = N_B\dfrac{\Delta\Phi_B}{\Delta t} = 800\dfrac{1.8\times10^{-4}\text{ weber}}{0.3\text{ sec}} = 0.48$ volt

3. A coil of resistance 15 ohms and inductance 0.6 henry is connected to a 120 volt D.C. line. At what rate will the current in the coil rise (a) at the instant the coil is connected to the line? (b) at the instant the current reaches 80% of its maximum (Ohm's law) value?

Solution:

Impressed voltage − back emf of self-induction = potential drop in resistance

$$V - L\dfrac{dI}{dt} = IR$$

(a) At the starting instant, $I = 0$ and hence $IR = 0$. Then

$$V = L\dfrac{dI}{dt} \quad\text{and}\quad \dfrac{dI}{dt} = \dfrac{V}{L} = \dfrac{120\text{ volts}}{0.6\text{ henry}} = 200\text{ amp/sec}$$

(b) Maximum value of current (when back emf of self-induction is zero, i.e. when dI/dt approaches zero) $= \dfrac{V}{R} = \dfrac{120\text{ volts}}{R}$. Then

$$V - L\dfrac{dI}{dt} = IR, \quad 120 - 0.6\dfrac{dI}{dt} = (0.8\times\dfrac{120}{R})R \quad\text{and}\quad \dfrac{dI}{dt} = 40\text{ amp/sec}$$

4. A wooden ring, of section area 10 cm² and mean circumference 40 cm, is wound with 300 turns of wire. Compute the inductance of the ring solenoid.

Solution:

$$L = \mu A\dfrac{N^2}{l} = \dfrac{4\pi}{10^7}\dfrac{\text{weber}}{\text{amp-m}} \times 10^{-3}\text{ m}^2 \times \dfrac{(300)^2}{0.4\text{ m}} = 2.8\times10^{-4}\text{ henry}$$

Note. $1\dfrac{\text{weber}}{\text{amp-m}}\times\text{m}^2\times\dfrac{1}{\text{m}} = 1\dfrac{\text{weber}}{\text{amp}} = 1\dfrac{\text{volt-sec}}{\text{amp}} = 1\dfrac{\text{volt}}{\text{amp/sec}} = 1$ henry

SUPPLEMENTARY PROBLEMS

5. An emf of 8 volts is induced in a given coil when the current in it changes at the rate of 32 amp/sec. Compute the inductance of the coil.   *Ans.* 0.25 henry

6. A direct current of 2.5 amp creates a flux of 1.4×10^{-4} weber in a coil of 500 turns. What is the inductance of the coil?   *Ans.* 28 millihenrys

7. The mutual inductance between the primary and secondary of a transformer is 0.3 henry. Compute the induced emf in the secondary when the primary current changes at the rate of 4 amp/sec.   *Ans.* 1.2 volts

8. A coil of inductance 0.2 henry is connected to a 90 volt D.C. supply line. At what rate will the current in the coil grow (*a*) at the instant the coil is connected to the line? (*b*) at the instant the current reaches two-thirds of its maximum value?   *Ans.* 450 amp/sec, 150 amp/sec

9. Two neighboring coils, A and B, have 300 and 600 turns respectively. A current of 1.5 amp in A causes 1.2×10^{-4} weber to pass through A and 0.9×10^{-4} weber through B. Determine (*a*) the self-inductance of A, (*b*) the mutual inductance of A and B, and (*c*) the average induced emf in B when the current in A is interrupted in 0.2 sec.   *Ans.* 24 millihenrys, 36 millihenrys, 0.27 volt

10. A coil of inductance 0.48 henry carries a current of 5 amperes. Compute the energy of its magnetic field.   *Ans.* 6 joules

11. The iron core of a solenoid has a length of 40 cm, a cross section of 5.0 cm^2, and is wound with 10 turns of wire per cm of length. Compute the inductance of the solenoid, assuming the relative permeability of the iron to be constant at 500.   *Ans.* 126 millihenrys

12. Show that (*a*) 1 nt/amp^2 = 1 weber/amp-m = 1 henry/m,   (*b*) 1 coul^2/nt-m^2 = 1 farad/m.
(1 weber = 1 volt-sec, 1 henry = 1 volt/(amp/sec), 1 farad = 1 coul/volt.)

13. The speed of light in free space is given by $c = 1/\sqrt{\epsilon_0 \mu_0}$. Find c, given the permittivity of free space $\epsilon_0 = \dfrac{1}{36\pi \times 10^9} \dfrac{\text{coul}^2}{\text{nt-m}^2}$ and the permeability of free space $\mu_0 = \dfrac{4\pi}{10^7} \dfrac{\text{weber}}{\text{amp-m}}$.

Ans. 3×10^8 m/sec

Chapter 32

Electric Generators and Motors

ELECTRIC GENERATORS are machines that convert mechanical energy into electrical energy. They consist fundamentally of a magnetic field produced by electromagnets or by permanent magnets, and of an armature having an iron core and carrying conductors on its surface. When the armature is revolved the conductors cut the magnetic flux and an alternating emf is induced in each conductor. If a direct current is desired, a commutator is used.

In most types of direct current generators the field is stationary and the armature rotates, while in alternating current generators the armature usually is stationary and the field rotates. In either case, the emf is generated by the *relative* motion of the armature conductors and the magnetic field.

ELECTRIC MOTORS convert electrical energy into mechanical energy.

The armature of a motor is closely similar to that of a generator. When a motor is running, the armature conductors cut magnetic flux; hence they develop an induced emf, called the **back emf** or **counter emf**, which opposes the impressed voltage.

The armature of a shunt motor is connected directly across the supply line. Since the back emf of the armature opposes the line voltage, the net potential difference which causes current through the armature is

$$\text{Net p.d. across armature} = \text{line voltage} - \text{back emf}$$

and

$$\text{Armature current} = \frac{\text{line voltage} - \text{back emf}}{\text{armature resistance}}$$

The mechanical power P developed within the armature of a motor is

$$P \text{ (watts)} = \text{armature current (amperes)} \times \text{back emf (volts)}$$

The useful mechanical power delivered to the pulley is slightly less, due to friction, windage and iron losses.

SOLVED PROBLEMS

ELECTRIC GENERATORS

1. A 2 pole generator has a drum armature with a cylindrical core 20 cm long and 10 cm in diameter, and 200 armature conductors arranged in 2 parallel paths. The flux density in the air gap is 0.5 weber/m². If the armature is driven at 30 rps, what is the average emf generated?

Solution:

Flux in air gap, $\Phi = BA = (0.5 \text{ weber/m}^2)(0.2 \times 0.1 \text{ m}^2) = .01$ weber.

Each conductor cuts .01 weber twice per revolution. Then in 1 sec or 30 revolutions, each conductor cuts $2(30)(.01) = 0.6$ weber. As there are 200 conductors in 2 parallel paths, the number of conductors in series in each path is $200/2 = 100$. (The emf's in series are additive.)

Average emf = flux cut per sec by 100 conductors in series
= 100×0.60 weber/sec = 60 volts

193

2. A 6 pole generator with fixed field excitation develops an emf of 100 volts when operating at 1500 rpm. At what speed must it rotate to develop 120 volts?

Solution: The flux cut per sec, and hence the emf, varies directly as the speed.

Speed = $120/100 \times 1500$ rpm = 1800 rpm.

3. A shunt generator has armature resistance .08 ohm and develops a total induced emf of 120 volts when driven at its rated speed. What is the terminal voltage V if the armature current is 50 amp?

Solution: V = emf − IR drop in armature = 120 volts − $(50 \times .08)$ volts = 116 volts

4. A shunt generator has armature resistance .06 ohm and shunt-field resistance 100 ohms. What power is developed in the armature when it delivers 40 kilowatts at 250 volts to an external circuit?

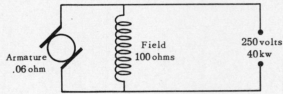

Solution:

Current in external circuit, $I_x = \dfrac{\text{watts } (IV)}{\text{volts } (V)}$

$= \dfrac{40{,}000 \text{ watts}}{250 \text{ volts}} = 160$ amp

Field current, $I_f = V_f/R_f = (250 \text{ volts})/(100 \text{ ohms}) = 2.5$ amp

Armature current, $I_a = I_x + I_f = 162.5$ amp

Total induced emf, $\mathcal{E} = 250$ volts + $I_a R_a$ drop in armature

$= 250$ volts + $(162 \times .06)$ volts = 260 volts

Power developed by armature = $I_a \mathcal{E}$ = 162.5 amp $\times$ 260 volts = 42.2 kw

Another Method.

Power loss in armature = $I_a^2 R_a$ = $(162.5 \text{ amp})^2 \times .06$ ohm = 1.6 kw

Power loss in field = $I_f^2 R_f$ = $(2.5 \text{ amp})^2 \times 100$ ohms = 0.6 kw

Power developed = power delivered + power loss in armature + power loss in field

$= 40$ kw + 1.6 kw + 0.6 kw = 42.2 kw

5. At what speed must an 8 pole A.C. generator rotate to produce an emf having a frequency of 60 cycles per sec?

Solution:

For each pair of poles there is produced one cycle (360 electrical degrees) per revolution. Hence 8 poles give 4 cycles per revolution.

Required angular speed = $\dfrac{60 \text{ cycles/sec}}{4 \text{ cycles/rev}}$ = 15 rev/sec = 900 rpm

ELECTRIC MOTORS

6. The armature of a 4 pole shunt motor carries 320 surface conductors, arranged in four parallel paths, which cut a flux of .025 weber per pole. (*a*) Determine the back emf developed by the armature when rotating at 900 rpm. (*b*) What is the impressed voltage V if the armature resistance R_a is 0.1 ohm and the armature current I_a is 40 amp?

Solution:

(*a*) Each conductor cuts .025 weber 4 times per revolution. Then in 1 sec or 15 revolutions, each conductor cuts $4(15)(.025) = 1.5$ weber. Since the 320 conductors are in 4 parallel paths, there are $320/4 = 80$ conductors is series in each path.

Back emf, $\mathcal{E}_b$ = flux cut per sec by 80 conductors in series
$= 80 \times 1.5$ weber/sec = 120 volts

(*b*) Impressed voltage, V = $\mathcal{E}_b + I_a R_a$ = 120 volts + (40×0.1) volts = 124 volts

7. A shunt motor has armature resistance .05 ohm and is connected to 120 volt mains. (*a*) What is the armature current at the starting instant, i.e. before the armature develops any back emf? (*b*) What starting rheostat resistance *R*, in series with the armature, will limit the starting current to 60 amp? (*c*) With no starting resistance, what back emf is generated when the armature current

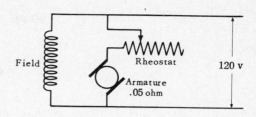

is 20 amp? (*d*) If this machine were running as a generator, what would be the total induced emf developed by the armature when the armature is delivering 20 amp at 120 volts to the shunt field and external circuit?

Solution:

(*a*) Armature current $= \dfrac{\text{impressed voltage}}{\text{armature resistance}} = \dfrac{120 \text{ volts}}{.05 \text{ ohm}} = 2400 \text{ amp}$

(*b*) Armature current $= \dfrac{\text{impressed voltage}}{.05 \text{ ohm} + R}$, $\quad 60 \text{ amp} = \dfrac{120 \text{ volts}}{.05 \text{ ohm} + R}$, $\quad R = 1.95 \text{ ohms}$

(*c*) Back emf $=$ impressed voltage $-$ voltage drop in armature resistance
$\qquad\qquad = 120 \text{ volts} - (20 \times .05) \text{ volts} = 119 \text{ volts}$

(*d*) Induced emf $=$ terminal voltage $+$ voltage drop in armature resistance
$\qquad\qquad = 120 \text{ volts} + (20 \times .05) \text{ volts} = 121 \text{ volts}$

8. A shunt motor has armature resistance 0.25 ohm and field resistance 150 ohms. It is connected across 120 volt mains and is generating a back emf of 115 volts. Compute: (*a*) the armature current I_a, the field current I_f, and the total current I_t taken by the motor; (*b*) the total power taken by the motor; (*c*) the power lost in heat in the armature and field circuits; (*d*) the electrical efficiency of this machine (when only heat losses in the armature and field are considered).

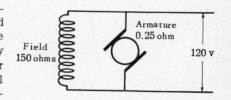

Solution:

(*a*) $I_a = \dfrac{\text{impressed voltage} - \text{back emf}}{\text{armature resistance}} = \dfrac{(120 - 115) \text{ volts}}{0.25 \text{ ohm}} = 20 \text{ amp}$

$\quad I_f = \dfrac{\text{impressed voltage}}{\text{field resistance}} = \dfrac{120 \text{ volts}}{150 \text{ ohms}} = 0.80 \text{ amp.} \qquad I_t = I_a + I_f = 20.80 \text{ amp.}$

(*b*) Power input $= 120 \text{ volts} \times 20.80 \text{ amp} = 2496 \text{ watts}$

(*c*) $I_a^2 R_a$ loss in armature $= (20 \text{ amp})^2 \times 0.25 \text{ ohm} = 100 \text{ watts}$

$\quad I_f^2 R_f$ loss in field $\quad\;\; = (0.80 \text{ amp})^2 \times 150 \text{ ohms} = 96 \text{ watts}$

(*d*) Power output $=$ power input $-$ power losses $= 2496 - (100 + 96) = 2300 \text{ watts}$
$\qquad\qquad\quad\; =$ armature current $\times$ back emf $= 20 \text{ amp} \times 115 \text{ volts} = 2300 \text{ watts}$

$\quad$ Efficiency $= \dfrac{\text{power output}}{\text{power input}} = \dfrac{2300 \text{ watts}}{2496 \text{ watts}} = 0.921 = 92.1\%$

9. A motor has back emf 110 volts and armature current 90 amp when running at 1500 rpm. Determine the power and the torque developed within the armature.

Solution: Power $=$ armature current $\times$ back emf $= 90 \text{ amp} \times 110 \text{ volts} = 9900 \text{ watts}$

$\qquad\qquad$ Torque $= \dfrac{\text{power}}{\text{angular speed}} = \dfrac{9900 \text{ watts}}{(2\pi \times 25) \text{ rad/sec}} = 63.0 \text{ nt-m} = 46.5 \text{ lb-ft}$

10. A motor armature develops a torque of 100 lb-ft when it draws 40 amp from the line. Determine the torque developed if the armature current is increased to 70 amp and the magnetic field strength is reduced to 80% of its initial value.

Solution: The torque developed by the armature of a given motor is proportional to the armature current and to the field strength.

$\qquad$ Hence, torque $= 100 \text{ lb-ft} \times 70/40 \times 0.80 = 140 \text{ lb-ft}$.

SUPPLEMENTARY PROBLEMS

ELECTRIC GENERATORS

11. Determine the separate effects on the induced emf of a generator if (a) the flux per pole is doubled, (b) the speed of the armature is doubled.   *Ans.* doubled, doubled

12. The armature of a 2 pole shunt generator has 400 conductors arranged in 2 parallel paths and cutting 6×10^{-3} weber per pole at 1800 rpm. Compute the average emf generated.   *Ans.* 72 v

13. A 4 pole D.C. generator has 240 armature conductors arranged in 4 parallel paths and cutting 2×10^{-2} weber per pole at 1500 rpm. What is the average emf generated?   *Ans.* 120 v

14. The emf induced in the armature of a shunt generator is 596 volts. The armature resistance is 0.1 ohm. (a) Compute the terminal voltage when the armature current is 460 amp. (b) The field resistance is 110 ohms. Determine the field current, and the current and power delivered to the external circuit.
Ans. (a) 550 v, (b) 5 amp, 455 amp, 250 kw

15. A dynamo delivers 30 amp at 120 volts to an external circuit when operating at 1200 rpm. What torque is required to drive the generator at this speed if the total power losses are 400 watts?
Ans. 31.8 m-nt or 23.5 lb-ft

16. A 75-kw 230-volt shunt generator has a generated emf of 243.5 volts. If the field current is 12.5 amp at rated output, what is the armature resistance?   *Ans.* .04 ohm

17. How many cycles per sec are generated by a 12 pole alternator when driven at 250 rpm?   *Ans.* 25 cycles/sec

ELECTRIC MOTORS

18. A bipolar shunt generator has an armature with 500 surface conductors, arranged in two parallel paths, which cut a flux of 8×10^{-3} weber per pole. Compute the back emf it develops when run as a motor at 1500 rpm.
Ans. 100 v

19. The active length of each armature conductor of a motor is 30 cm and the flux density directly under the poles is 1 weber/m². A current of 15 amp is in each conductor. Determine the force acting on each conductor when directly under the poles.   *Ans.* 4.5 nt

20. A shunt motor with armature resistance .08 ohm is connected to 120 volt mains. With 50 amp in the armature, compute the back emf and the mechanical power developed within the armature.   *Ans.* 116 v, 5.8 kw

21. A shunt motor is connected to a 110 volt line. When the armature generates a back emf of 104 volts the armature current is 15 amp. Compute the armature resistance.   *Ans.* 0.4 ohm

22. A shunt dynamo has an armature resistance of 0.12 ohm. (a) If it is connected across 220 volt mains and is running as a motor, what is the induced (back) emf when the armature current is 50 amp? (b) If this machine is running as a generator, what is the induced emf when the armature is delivering 50 amp at 220 volts to the shunt field and external circuit?   *Ans.* 214 v, 226 v

23. A shunt motor has a speed of 900 rpm when connected to 120 volt mains and delivering 12 horsepower. The total losses are 1048 watts. Compute the power input, the line current and the motor torque.
Ans. 10 kw, 83.3 amp, 70 lb-ft

24. A shunt motor has armature resistance 0.20 ohm and field resistance 150 ohms, and draws 30 amp when connected to a 120 volt supply line. Determine the field current, the armature current, the back emf, the mechanical power developed within the armature, and the electrical efficiency of the machine.
Ans. 0.80 amp, 29.2 amp, 114.2 v, 3.33 kw, 92.5%

25. A shunt motor develops 80 m-nt torque when the flux density in the air gap is 1 weber/m² and the armature current is 15 amp. What is the torque when the flux density is 1.3 weber/m² and the armature current is 18 amp?   *Ans.* 125 m-nt

26. A shunt motor has a field of resistance 200 ohms, an armature of resistance 0.5 ohm, and is connected to 120 volt mains. The motor draws a current of 4.6 amp when running at full speed. What current will be drawn by the motor if the speed is reduced to 90% of full speed by application of a load?   *Ans.* 28.2 amp

Chapter 33

Alternating Currents

PERIOD AND FREQUENCY. The **period** of an alternating emf or current is the time required for the emf or current to go through one complete cycle of change.

$$1 \text{ cycle } = 360 \text{ electrical degrees } = 2\pi \text{ electrical radians}$$

The **frequency** of an alternating emf or current is the number of cycles made per sec. If an alternator has 2 poles, the emf and current generated will pass through 1 cycle once per revolution of the armature or field. A 4 pole alternator will give 2 cycles per revolution. In general,

$$\text{Frequency (cycles/sec)} = \text{number of pairs of poles} \times \text{speed in rps.}$$

INSTANTANEOUS VALUES of an alternating emf and current are (assuming the wave form to be a sine curve):

$$\mathcal{E}_{\text{instantaneous}} = \mathcal{E}_{\text{maximum}} \sin \omega t = \mathcal{E}_{\text{maximum}} \sin 2\pi f t$$

$$I_{\text{instantaneous}} = I_{\text{maximum}} \sin \omega t = I_{\text{maximum}} \sin 2\pi f t$$

where f = frequency, in cycles/sec
$\omega = 2\pi f$ = angular velocity, in electrical radians per sec
t = time in seconds after the sine function passes its zero value in an increasing direction.

EFFECTIVE OR ROOT-MEAN-SQUARE (RMS) VALUES. An alternating current is said to have a rms or effective value of 1 amp if it develops heat in a resistance at the same rate as a direct steady current of 1 amp.

$$\mathcal{E}_{\text{rms}} = \frac{\mathcal{E}_{\text{max}}}{\sqrt{2}} = 0.707\,\mathcal{E}_{\text{max}} \qquad I_{\text{rms}} = \frac{I_{\text{max}}}{\sqrt{2}} = 0.707\,I_{\text{max}}$$

A.C. voltmeters and ammeters are calibrated to read effective values.

PHASE. In an alternating current circuit containing only resistance (without inductance or capacitance), the voltage and current attain their maximum values at the same instant and their zero values at the same instant; and the voltage and current are said to be **in phase**.

In a circuit containing only resistance and inductance, the inductance causes the current to **lag** behind the voltage – the current is **out of phase** with the voltage. In a circuit containing only resistance and capacitance, the current **leads** the voltage or the voltage lags behind the current. The angle of lag or lead is called the **phase angle**, and depends on the amounts of inductance, capacitance, and resistance in the circuit.

INDUCTIVE REACTANCE X_L in ohms: $\qquad X_L = 2\pi f L$
where f = frequency in cycles per second, L = inductance in henrys.

CAPACITIVE REACTANCE X_C in ohms: $\qquad X_C = \dfrac{1}{2\pi f C} \qquad$ where C = capacitance in farads.

IMPEDANCE Z of a circuit containing inductance and capacitance in series with resistance R:

$$Z = \sqrt{R^2 + (X_L - X_C)^2} = \sqrt{R^2 + (2\pi f L - \frac{1}{2\pi f C})^2}$$

The terms X_L, X_C, Z and R are all in ohms. Ohm's law for this circuit is

$$I \text{ (in rms amperes)} = \frac{V \text{ (in rms volts)}}{Z \text{ (in ohms)}}$$

RESONANCE occurs when $X_L = X_C$, i.e. when $2\pi f L = 1/2\pi f C$. It follows that the resonance frequency or natural frequency of a circuit containing inductance and capacitance in series is

$$f = \frac{1}{2\pi \sqrt{LC}}$$

POWER used in A.C. circuit $= VI \times$ power factor $= VI \cos \phi = VI \frac{R}{Z}$

where V and I are rms (effective) values, and ϕ is the phase angle between the voltage and current.

A TRANSFORMER is a device to raise or lower voltage in an alternating current circuit. It consists of a primary and a secondary coil wound on a common iron core. An alternating current in one coil creates a continuously changing magnetic flux through the core, and this change of flux induces an alternating emf in the other coil. The efficiency of a transformer is usually very high. Then, neglecting losses,

$$\text{Power in primary} = \text{power in secondary}$$
$$\mathcal{E}_1 I_1 = \mathcal{E}_2 I_2$$

The voltage ratio is the same as the ratio of the number of turns; the current ratio is the inverse ratio of the number of turns.

$$\frac{\mathcal{E}_1}{\mathcal{E}_2} = \frac{N_1}{N_2} \quad \text{and} \quad \frac{I_1}{I_2} = \frac{N_2}{N_1}$$

SOLVED PROBLEMS

1. An 8 pole alternator operates at 900 rpm and develops an emf represented by a sine curve having a maximum value of 300 volts. Compute (a) the frequency of the emf, (b) the instantaneous value of the emf 1/720 sec after passing its zero value, (c) the rms or effective value of the emf.

Solution:

(a) Frequency = pairs of poles × rps = 4 cycles/rev × 15 rev/sec = 60 cycles/sec

(b) In 1/720 sec the sine curve makes 1/720 sec × 60 cycles/sec = 1/12 cycle. Since 1 cycle = 360 electrical degrees, 1/12 cycle = 30°.

$$\mathcal{E}_{\text{instantaneous}} = \mathcal{E}_{\text{maximum}} \sin 30° = 300 \text{ volts} \times 0.500 = 150 \text{ volts}$$

(c) $\mathcal{E}_{\text{rms}} = 0.707 \mathcal{E}_{\text{maximum}} = 0.707 \times 300 \text{ volts} = 212 \text{ volts}$

2. A coil having inductance 0.14 henry and resistance 12 ohms is connected across a 110-volt 25-cycle line. Compute (a) the current in the coil, (b) the phase angle between the current and supply voltage, (c) the power factor, (d) the power absorbed by the coil.

Solution:

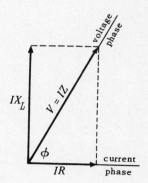

(a) $X_L = 2\pi f L = 2\pi(25)(0.14) = 22.0$ ohms

$Z = \sqrt{R^2 + X_L^2} = \sqrt{(12)^2 + (22)^2} = 25.1$ ohms

$I = \dfrac{V}{Z} = \dfrac{110 \text{ volts}}{25.1 \text{ ohms}} = 4.38$ amp

(b) $\tan\phi = \dfrac{X_L}{R} = \dfrac{22 \text{ ohms}}{12 \text{ ohms}} = 1.83, \quad \phi = 61°\,20'$

The voltage leads the current by 61° 20'.

(c) Power factor $= \cos\phi = \cos 61°\,20' = 0.479$

(d) Power $= VI\cos\phi = 110 \text{ volts} \times 4.38 \text{ amp} \times 0.479 = 231$ watts

3. A capacitor is in series with a resistance of 30 ohms and connected to a 220 volt A.C. line. The reactance of the capacitor is 40 ohms. Determine (a) the current in the circuit, (b) the phase angle between the current and supply voltage, (c) the power factor.

Solution:

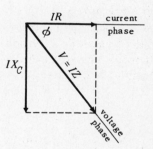

(a) $Z = \sqrt{R^2 + X_C^2} = \sqrt{(30)^2 + (40)^2} = 50$ ohms

$I = \dfrac{V}{Z} = \dfrac{220 \text{ volts}}{50 \text{ ohms}} = 4.4$ amp

(b) $\tan\phi = \dfrac{X_C}{R} = \dfrac{-40 \text{ ohms}}{30 \text{ ohms}} = -1.33, \quad \phi = -53°$

The minus sign indicates that the voltage **lags** the current by 53°.

(c) $\cos\phi = \cos -53° = \cos 53° = 0.60$

4. A potential difference of 110 volts, 60 cycles is impressed on a series circuit consisting of a non-inductive resistance of 100 ohms, a coil of 0.10 henry inductance and negligible resistance, and a capacitor of capacitance 20 microfarads. Compute (a) the current in the circuit and (b) the phase angle between the current and supply voltage.

Solution:

The potential difference across the resistance (IR) is in phase with the current. The potential difference across the inductance (IX_L) leads the current by 90°, while that across the capacitance (IX_C) lags the current by 90°. The effective p.d. applied to the circuit is the vector sum of these potential differences.

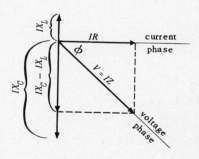

(a) $X_L = 2\pi f L = 2\pi \times 60 \times 0.10 = 38$ ohms

$X_C = \dfrac{1}{2\pi f C} = \dfrac{1}{2\pi \times 60 \times (20 \times 10^{-6})} = 133$ ohms

$Z = \sqrt{R^2 + (X_L - X_C)^2} = \sqrt{(100)^2 + (38 - 133)^2}$
$= 138$ ohms

$I = \dfrac{V}{Z} = \dfrac{110 \text{ volts}}{138 \text{ ohms}} = 0.797$ amp

(b) $\tan\phi = \dfrac{X_L - X_C}{R} = \dfrac{38 - 133}{100} = -0.950$ and $\phi = -43°\,30'$, voltage lagging

5. A series circuit connected across a 200-volt 60-cycle line consists of a capacitor of capacitive reactance 30 ohms, a noninductive resistor of 44 ohms, and a coil of inductive reactance 90 ohms and resistance 36 ohms. Determine (a) the current in the circuit, (b) the potential difference across each unit, (c) the power factor of the circuit, (d) the power absorbed by the circuit.

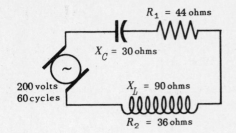

Solution:

(a) $Z = \sqrt{(R_1 + R_2)^2 + (X_L - X_C)^2} = \sqrt{(44 + 36)^2 + (90 - 30)^2}$
$= 100$ ohms

$I = \dfrac{V}{Z} = \dfrac{200 \text{ volts}}{100 \text{ ohms}} = 2 \text{ amp}$

(b) Potential drop across capacitor $= IX_C = 2 \text{ amp} \times 30 \text{ ohms} = 60 \text{ volts}$

Potential drop across resistor $= IR_1 = 2 \text{ amp} \times 44 \text{ ohms} = 88 \text{ volts}$

Impedance of coil $= \sqrt{R_2^2 + X_L^2} = \sqrt{(36)^2 + (90)^2} = 97 \text{ ohms}$

Potential drop across coil $= 2 \text{ amp} \times 97 \text{ ohms} = 194 \text{ volts}$

(c) Power factor of circuit $= \cos\phi = R/Z = 80/100 = 0.80$

(d) Power used $= VI \cos\phi = 200 \text{ volts} \times 2 \text{ amp} \times 0.80 = 320 \text{ watts}$
$= I^2R = (2 \text{ amp})^2 \times (44 + 36) \text{ ohms} = 320 \text{ watts}$

6. Calculate the resonant frequency of a circuit of negligible resistance containing an inductance of 40 millihenrys and a capacitance of 600 micromicrofarads.

Solution:

$$f = \frac{1}{2\pi\sqrt{LC}} = \frac{1}{2\pi\sqrt{40 \times 10^{-3} \text{ henry} \times 600 \times 10^{-12} \text{ farad}}} = 32.5 \text{ kilocycles/sec}$$

7. A step-up transformer is used on a 120 volt line to furnish 1800 volts. The primary has 100 turns. How many turns are in the secondary?

Solution:

$$\frac{\mathcal{E}_1}{\mathcal{E}_2} = \frac{N_1}{N_2} \quad \text{or} \quad \frac{120 \text{ volts}}{1800 \text{ volts}} = \frac{100 \text{ turns}}{N_2}, \quad \text{from which} \quad N_2 = 1500 \text{ turns}$$

8. A transformer used on a 120 volt line delivers 2 amperes at 900 volts. What current is drawn from the line? Assume 100% efficiency.

Solution:

Power in primary $=$ power in secondary

$I_1 \times 120 \text{ volts} = 2 \text{ amp} \times 900 \text{ volts} \qquad I_1 = 15 \text{ amp}$

9. A step-down transformer operates on a 2500 volt line and supplies a load of 80 amperes. The ratio of the primary winding to the secondary winding is 20:1. Assuming 100% efficiency, determine the secondary voltage $\mathcal{E}_2$, the primary current I_1, and the power output P_2.

Solution:

$$\mathcal{E}_2 = (1/20)\mathcal{E}_1 = 125 \text{ volts}, \quad I_1 = (1/20)I_2 = 4 \text{ amp}, \quad P_2 = \mathcal{E}_2 I_2 = 10 \text{ kw}$$

SUPPLEMENTARY PROBLEMS

10. An alternating current in a 10 ohm resistance produces heat at the rate of 360 watts. Determine the effective values of the current and voltage.   *Ans.* 6 amp, 60 volts

11. Determine the number of revolutions per minute that a 6-pole alternator must make to produce a frequency of 60 cycles/sec.   *Ans.* 1200 rpm

12. A voltmeter reads 220 volts when connected across the terminals of an alternator. Determine the maximum value of the emf.   *Ans.* 311 volts

13. A coil has resistance 20 ohms and inductance 0.35 henry. Compute its reactance and its impedance to an alternating current of 25 cycles/sec.   *Ans.* 55.0 ohms, 58.5 ohms

14. A current of 30 milliamperes is taken by a 4 microfarad capacitor connected across an alternating current line having a frequency of 500 cycles/sec. Compute the reactance of the capacitor and the voltage across the capacitor.   *Ans.* 80 ohms, 2.4 volts

15. A coil has inductance 0.10 henry and resistance 12 ohms. It is connected to a 110-volt 60-cycle line. Determine (*a*) the reactance of the coil, (*b*) the impedance of the coil, (*c*) the current through the coil, (*d*) the phase angle between current and supply voltage, (*e*) the power factor of the circuit, (*f*) the reading of a wattmeter connected in the circuit.

   Ans. (*a*) 37.7 ohms   (*c*) 2.78 amperes   (*e*) 0.303
          (*b*) 39.6 ohms   (*d*) voltage leads by $72°20'$ (*f*) 92.6 watts

16. A 10 microfarad capacitor is in series with a 40 ohm resistance and connected to a 110-volt 60-cycle line. Calculate (*a*) the capacitive reactance, (*b*) the impedance of the circuit, (*c*) the current in the circuit, (*d*) the phase angle between the current and supply voltage, (*e*) the power factor of the circuit.

   Ans. (*a*) 266 ohms   (*c*) 0.409 amp   (*e*) 0.149
          (*b*) 269 ohms   (*d*) voltage lags by $81°\,25'$

17. A circuit having a resistance, an inductance and a capacitance in series is connected to a 110 volt alternating current line. The resistance = 9.0 ohms, the inductive reactance = 28 ohms, and the capacitive reactance = 16 ohms. Compute (*a*) the impedance of the circuit, (*b*) the current, (*c*) the phase angle between this current and the supply voltage, (*d*) the power factor of the circuit.

   Ans. (*a*) 15.0 ohms, (*b*) 7.33 amp, (*c*) voltage leads by $53°8'$, (*d*) 0.60

18. An experimenter has a coil of inductance 3 millihenrys and wishes to construct a circuit whose resonant frequency is 1000 kilocycles. What should be the value of the capacitor used?   *Ans.* 8.44 micromicrofarads

19. A circuit has a resistor of resistance 11 ohms, a coil of inductive reactance 120 ohms and a capacitor of capacitive reactance 120 ohms connected in series to a 110-volt 60-cycle line. What is the potential difference across each circuit element?

   Ans. 110, 1200, 1200 volts. Note that in a series resonant circuit high voltages, far in excess of supply voltage, can be built up.

20. A step-down transformer is used on a 2200 volt line to deliver 110 volts. How many turns are in the primary winding if the secondary has 25 turns?   *Ans.* 500

21. A step-down transformer is used on a 1650 volt line to deliver 45 amp at 110 volts. What current is drawn from the line? Assume 100% efficiency.   *Ans.* 3 amp

22. A step-up transformer operates on a 110 volt line and supplies a load of 2 amp. The ratio of the primary and secondary winding is 1:25. Determine the secondary voltage, the primary current, and the power output. Assume 100% efficiency.   *Ans.* 2750 volts, 50 amp, 5.5 kw

Chapter 34

Wave Motion and Sound

LONGITUDINAL AND TRANSVERSE WAVES. In wave motion in a material medium, particles of the medium vibrate about their positions of equilibrium. The wave energy is carried forward, but not the medium.

Most forms of wave motion can be classified into two types: transverse and longitudinal. A transverse wave is one in which vibrations of particles of the medium are perpendicular to the direction of motion of the wave energy. A longitudinal, or compressional, wave is one in which the vibration of the medium is (forward and backward) parallel to the direction of propagation of the wave.

PERIOD, FREQUENCY, WAVELENGTH, SPEED. The **period** of a vibrating particle is the time required for one vibration. The **frequency** is the number of vibrations made per second (frequency = 1/period). The **wavelength** is the shortest distance between two vibrating particles which are in phase. The **amplitude** is the maximum displacement of the vibrating particle from its undisturbed position.

$$\text{Speed of a wave} \quad = \quad \text{frequency} \times \text{wavelength}$$
$$v \quad = \quad f\lambda$$

SPEED OF A LONGITUDINAL WAVE depends on the elasticity and density of the medium.

$$\text{In liquids:} \quad v \quad = \quad \sqrt{\frac{B}{\rho}} \quad = \quad \sqrt{\frac{\text{bulk modulus}}{\text{density of liquid}}}$$

$$\text{In solids:} \quad v \quad = \quad \sqrt{\frac{Y}{\rho}} \quad = \quad \sqrt{\frac{\text{Young's modulus}}{\text{density of solid}}}$$

$$\text{In gases:} \quad v \quad = \quad \sqrt{\frac{\gamma p}{\rho}} \quad = \quad \sqrt{\frac{\gamma \times \text{pressure of gas}}{\text{density of gas}}}$$

where $\gamma = \dfrac{\text{specific heat of gas at constant pressure}}{\text{specific heat of gas at constant volume}}$. For monatomic gases $\gamma = 1.67$, and for air and most diatomic gases $\gamma = 1.40$, approximately.

SPEED OF A TRANSVERSE WAVE in a streched string or wire is

$$v \quad = \quad \sqrt{\frac{F}{\mu}} \quad = \quad \sqrt{\frac{\text{tension in string}}{\text{mass per unit length}}}$$

SOUND is longitudinal wave motion that can be perceived by the auditory nerve. It consists of a series of condensations and rarefactions, and can be transmitted by any type of elastic matter but not by vacuum.

SPEED OF SOUND IN AIR at $0°C$ is 331 meters/sec or 1087 ft/sec, and increases approximately 0.6 meter/sec or 2 ft/sec for each degree centigrade rise. The speed is independent of changes in barometric pressure, frequency, and wavelength.

The effect of temperature on the speed of sound in a gas is expressed more accurately by the equation

$$\frac{v_1}{v_2} = \sqrt{\frac{T_1}{T_2}}$$

where v_1 and v_2 are the speeds at the **absolute** temperatures T_1 and T_2 respectively.

BEATS. The pulsations of maximum and minimum disturbance produced by the superposition of two sound waves of slightly different frequencies are called beats. The number of beats per second is equal to the difference between the frequencies of the two sound waves which are combined.

MUSICAL INTERVALS. When two notes have frequencies which are in the ratio of 2:1, the two notes are said to differ by an **octave**. If the frequency ratio is 3:2, the interval is called a **fifth**. Other harmonious musical intervals occur when the frequencies are in other simple ratios of integers, such as 5:3, 5:4, etc. It is impossible to tune an instrument so that **all** intervals are in simple ratios. The compromise which is generally used is called **equal temperament**.

HARMONICS. The term **harmonics** refers to a series of frequencies which have whole number ratios. If f is the lowest frequency of the series, called the first harmonic, then the other harmonics have frequencies $2f$, $3f$, $4f$, $5f$, etc.

OVERTONES. The lowest frequency which a vibrating string, air column, or other vibrating body emits is called the **fundamental** frequency. The next higher frequency the vibrating body can emit is the first overtone, the next higher frequency is the second overtone, etc. The overtones may or may not be harmonics of the fundamental. For example, the overtones of a bell are not harmonics at all, since their frequencies are not integral multiples of the fundamental frequency.

STATIONARY OR STANDING WAVES. A standing wave may be set up in a vibrating body such as an air column, string, or rod. Two waves of equal frequencies and amplitudes traveling in opposite directions in a medium produce a standing wave.

A **displacement node** is a point on a standing wave where the displacement of the particle is zero at all times. A **displacement antinode** is a point on the standing wave where the amplitude of vibration is greatest. The distance between two adjacent nodes or between two adjacent antinodes is a half-wavelength.

VIBRATING STRINGS. A stretched string produces its fundamental tone, or first harmonic, when it vibrates as a whole with an antinode at its center and a node at each end. Since the distance between two adjacent nodes is half a wavelength, the wavelength λ of its fundamental mode of vibration is twice its length, or $2l$.

The frequency f of its fundamental mode of vibration is

$$f_{\text{fundamental}} = \frac{v}{\lambda} = \frac{\sqrt{F/\mu}}{2l} = \frac{1}{2l}\sqrt{\frac{F}{\mu}}$$

Overtones are produced when the string vibrates in segments. The first overtone (second harmonic), second overtone (third harmonic), etc., are produced when the string vibrates respectively in 2 segments, 3 segments, etc. If f is the frequency of the fundamental tone, the frequencies of the first and second overtones are respectively $2f$ and $3f$.

VIBRATING AIR COLUMNS. An open end of a tube is an antinode, and a closed end a node.

Closed tube.

The wavelength of the fundamental tone, or first harmonic, produced by a tube closed at one end is 4 times the length of the tube. If f is the frequency of the fundamental, the frequencies of the overtones, or upper harmonics, are $3f$, $5f$, $7f$, $9f$, etc. – only odd harmonics are possible. In this case the second overtone is the fifth harmonic.

Open tube.

The wavelength of the fundamental tone produced by a tube open at both ends is 2 times the length of the tube. If f is the frequency of the fundamental, the frequencies of the overtones are $2f$, $3f$, $4f$, $5f$, etc. – all harmonics are possible.

RESONANCE. Acoustic resonance exists when a body is caused to vibrate by sound waves having the same frequency as its natural frequency of vibration. In this case, the free vibrations re-enforce the forced ones and a large amplitude of vibration is developed.

DOPPLER EFFECT. When a source of sound waves and an observer are approaching each other, the observed pitch of the sound is increased; while if they are receding from each other, the observed pitch is lowered. The observed pitch of a sound depends essentially on the number of waves reaching the ear per second.

Let f = true frequency of sounding body, f' = observed frequency, V = speed of sound, and v = speed of moving body. Then

(a) When the **source moves**, $\qquad f' = \dfrac{fV}{V \mp v}$

where the negative and positive signs refer respectively to the approach and recession of the sounding body.

(b) When the **observer moves**, $\qquad f' = \dfrac{f(V \pm v)}{V}$

where the positive and negative signs refer respectively to the approach and recession of the observer.

INTENSITY AND LOUDNESS. The **intensity** of a sound wave is the amount of wave energy transmitted per unit time (i.e. the power transmitted) per unit area perpendicular to the direction of propagation. The intensity I of a sound of frequency f vibrations per sec and amplitude r meters is

$$I \,(\text{watts/m}^2) \;=\; 2\pi^2 f^2 r^2 v\rho$$

where v = speed of sound in m/sec and ρ = density of undisturbed medium in kg/m^3.

Loudness is a subjective physiological sensation which increases with the intensity of the sound, but no simple relation exists between loudness and intensity. The sensation of loudness is only roughly proportional to the common logarithm (to the base 10) of the intensity of the sound.

The **bel** and the **decibel** (0.1 bel) are units of **intensity level** (and very roughly of loudness level). The intensity level, expressed in decibels, of a sound of intensity I_1 with reference to a sound of intensity I_2 is

$$\text{Intensity level of } I_1 \text{ in decibels} \;=\; 10 \log \frac{I_1}{I_2}$$

The smallest difference in loudness that the ear can distinguish is approximately 1 decibel (1db).

SOLVED PROBLEMS

1. A longitudinal wave of frequency 100 vibrations per sec has a wavelength of 11 ft. Find the speed of propagation.
   Solution:
   $$v = f\lambda = 100/\text{sec} \times 11\,\text{ft} = 1100\,\text{ft/sec}$$

2. What is the pitch or frequency of the tone made by a siren having a disk with 15 holes and making 20 revolutions per sec?
   Solution:
   $$\text{Pitch or frequency} = 15\,\text{vibrations/rev} \times 20\,\text{rev/sec} = 300\,\text{vibrations/sec}$$

3. The speed of sound in water is 1450 m/sec. Compute the bulk modulus B of water.
   Solution:
   $$v = \sqrt{B/\rho}, \qquad B = \rho v^2 = (10^3\,\text{kg/m}^3)(1450\,\text{m/sec})^2 = 2.1 \times 10^9\,\text{nt/m}^2$$

4. Calculate the speed of sound in air at $0°C$ and a pressure of 760 mm of mercury (1 atm). Density of air at standard conditions = 1.293 g/liter, density of mercury = 13.6 g/cm^3, $\gamma = 1.40$.
   Solution:
   $$v = \sqrt{\frac{\gamma p\ (\text{nt/m}^2)}{\rho\ (\text{kg/m}^3)}} = \sqrt{\frac{1.40 \times 0.76\,\text{m} \times (13.6 \times 10^3)\,\text{kg/m}^3 \times 9.8\,\text{m/sec}^2}{1.293\,\text{kg/m}^3}} = 331\,\text{m/sec}$$

5. Compute the speed of sound in helium gas at $800°C$ and 2.3 atmospheres pressure. Molecular weight of helium is 4.00, and $\gamma = 1.66$.
   Solution:
   One mole of an ideal gas occupies 22.4 liters = $22.4 \times 10^{-3}\,\text{m}^3$ at $273°K$ and 1 atm.
   $$v = \sqrt{\frac{\gamma p}{\rho}} = \sqrt{\frac{1.66 \times 2.3 \times 0.76\,\text{m} \times (13.6 \times 10^3)\,\text{kg/m}^3 \times 9.8\,\text{m/sec}^2}{\dfrac{4.00 \times 10^{-3}\,\text{kg}}{22.4 \times 10^{-3}\,\text{m}^3} \times \dfrac{273°K}{(273 + 800)°K} \times \dfrac{2.3\,\text{atm}}{1\,\text{atm}}}} = 1.92 \times 10^3\,\text{m/sec}$$

   Note that the pressure 2.3 atm cancels out of the above equation.

   Another Method.

   From the ideal gas equation $pV = nRT = (m/M)RT$, where m is the mass of gas and M the molecular weight, we have $p(V/m) = RT/M$ or $p/\rho = RT/M$. Then
   $$v = \sqrt{\gamma \frac{p}{\rho}} = \sqrt{\gamma \frac{RT}{M}} = \sqrt{1.66 \times \frac{8.31\,\text{joules/(}°K\,\text{mole)} \times 1073°K}{4.00 \times 10^{-3}\,\text{kg/mole}}} = 1.92 \times 10^3\,\text{m/sec}$$

   Note that for a given gas γ, R and M are constants and v varies as the square root of the absolute temperature, i.e. $v_1/v_2 = \sqrt{T_1/T_2}$.

6. A tuning fork makes 284 vib/sec in air. Compute the wavelength of the tone emitted at $25°C$.
   Solution:
   The speed of sound in dry air at $0°C$ is 331 m/sec or 1087 ft/sec, and increases approximately by 0.6 m/sec or 2 ft/sec per centigrade degree rise.

   Speed v at $25°C$ = 331 m/sec + 0.6 (25) m/sec = 346 m/sec.

   Or, $v = v_0\sqrt{T/T_0} = 331\,\text{m/sec} \times \sqrt{(273 + 25)/273} = 346\,\text{m/sec}$.

   Wavelength $\lambda = v/f = (346\,\text{m/sec})/(284/\text{sec}) = 1.22\,\text{m}$.

7. A metal string of mass 0.50 g and length 50 cm is under a tension of 88.2 nt. (*a*) Compute the speed of a transverse wave in the string. (*b*) Determine the frequencies of its fundamental tone, first overtone, and second overtone.

   Solution:

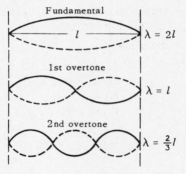

   (*a*) $v = \sqrt{\dfrac{F}{\mu}} = \sqrt{\dfrac{88.2 \text{ nt}}{(5 \times 10^{-4} \text{ kg})/(5 \times 10^{-1} \text{ m})}} = 297$ m/sec

   (*b*) The wavelength of the fundamental tone is twice the length of the string. The frequencies of the first and second overtones are respectively twice and thrice the frequency of the fundamental.

   $f_{\text{fund}} = \dfrac{v}{\lambda_{\text{fund}}} = \dfrac{297 \text{ m/sec}}{2 \times 0.50 \text{ m}} = 297/\text{sec}$

   $f_{\text{1st overtone}} = 2 \times 297/\text{sec} = 594/\text{sec}$

   $f_{\text{2nd overtone}} = 3 \times 297/\text{sec} = 891/\text{sec}$

8. Determine the fundamental frequency of vibration of a rope 20 ft long weighing 4 lb and stretched with a tension of 40 lb.

   Solution: $v = \sqrt{\dfrac{F}{\mu}} = \sqrt{\dfrac{40 \text{ lb}}{(4/32 \text{ slug})/(20 \text{ ft})}} = 80$ ft/sec, $\quad f_{\text{fund}} = \dfrac{v}{\lambda_{\text{fund}}} = \dfrac{80 \text{ ft/sec}}{2 \times 20 \text{ ft}} = 2/\text{sec}$

9. A string of length 80 cm and mass 0.2 g is attached to one end of a tuning fork which makes 250 vibrations/sec. What tension applied to the string will cause it to vibrate in 4 segments?

   Solution:

   Length of each segment = $\tfrac{1}{4} \times 80$ cm = 20 cm = $\tfrac{1}{2}\lambda$
   Wavelength λ of stationary waves = 40 cm
   $v = f\lambda = 250/\text{sec} \times 0.40 \text{ m} = 100$ m/sec

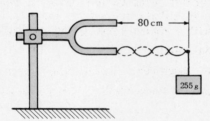

   $v = \sqrt{F/\mu}, \quad F = \mu v^2 = \dfrac{2 \times 10^{-4} \text{ kg}}{8 \times 10^{-1} \text{ m}}(100 \text{ m/sec})^2$

   $\quad\quad = 2.5 \text{ nt} = $ weight of 255 g.

10. A rod 200 cm long is clamped 50 cm from one end and set into longitudinal vibration. The lowest frequency produced by the rod is 3000 vibrations per sec. What is the speed of sound in the rod?

    Solution:

    There must be a node at the clamped point, and there must be an antinode at each free end. The mode of vibration with fewest nodes which satisfies these conditions is shown in the diagram.

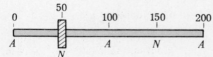

    Wavelength λ = 2 × distance between nodes = 2 × 100 cm = 200 cm
    $v = f\lambda = 3000/\text{sec} \times 2.00 \text{ m} = 6000$ m/sec

11. A Kundt's tube is employed to measure the speed of sound in a steel rod. The rod, clamped at its center, is stroked to vibrate longitudinally and emits its fundamental tone. The length of the rod is 90 cm and the distance between the nodes (powder heaps) of the standing waves in the air column of the tube is 6 cm. The speed of sound in air at room temperature is 340 m/sec. What is the speed of sound in the steel rod?

    Solution:

    The rod vibrates with a node at its clamped center and antinodes at both free ends.

    Wavelength of the sound in rod = 2 × length of rod = 2 × 90 cm = 180 cm.

    Wavelength of the sound in air = 2 × distance between nodes = 12 cm.

    Since frequency of waves in rod = frequency of waves in air, we have

    $f = \dfrac{v_{\text{rod}}}{\lambda_{\text{rod}}} = \dfrac{v_{\text{air}}}{\lambda_{\text{air}}} \quad$ and $\quad v_{\text{rod}} = v_{\text{air}}\dfrac{\lambda_{\text{rod}}}{\lambda_{\text{air}}} = 340 \text{ m/sec} \times \dfrac{180 \text{ cm}}{12 \text{ cm}} = 5100$ m/sec.

12. A 680 g brass rod is 100 cm long and 1 cm in diameter, and a 990 g steel rod is 165 cm long and 1 cm in diameter. Each rod is clamped at its midpoint and stroked longitudinally so as to emit its fundamental tone. The brass rod is in tune with a 50 cm length of a certain sonometer wire while the steel rod is in tune with a 52 cm length of the same sonometer wire. If Young's modulus of the steel is 30×10^6 lb/in^2, compute Young's modulus of the brass.

Solution:

Let f_b, f_s = frequency of sound emitted by brass and steel rod, respectively
L_b, L_s = length of brass and steel rod, respectively
l_b, l_s = respective lengths of sonometer wire
Y_b, Y_s = Young's modulus for the brass and steel, respectively. Then

$$(1) \quad f_b = \frac{1}{2L_b}\sqrt{\frac{Y_b}{\rho_b}} = \frac{1}{2l_b}\sqrt{\frac{F}{\mu}} \qquad \text{and} \qquad (2) \quad f_s = \frac{1}{2L_s}\sqrt{\frac{Y_s}{\rho_s}} = \frac{1}{2l_s}\sqrt{\frac{F}{\mu}}$$

where $\rho_b = \dfrac{\text{mass}}{\text{volume}} = \dfrac{m_b}{\pi r^2 L_b}$ and $\rho_s = \dfrac{m_s}{\pi r^2 L_s}$.

Dividing (1) by (2) and solving for Y_b,

$$Y_b = Y_s \times \left(\frac{l_s}{l_b}\right)^2 \times \frac{L_b}{L_s} \times \frac{m_b}{m_s} = 30 \times 10^6 \text{ lb/in}^2 \times \left(\frac{52}{50}\right)^2 \times \frac{100}{165} \times \frac{680}{990} = 13.5 \times 10^6 \text{ lb/in}^2$$

13. (a) How many beats per sec are heard when two tuning forks, of frequencies 200 and 205 per sec respectively, are sounded together? (b) What is the frequency of a fork which makes 4 beats/sec with a standard fork of 300 vibrations/sec?

Solution:

(a) Beats/sec = difference between frequencies = (205 − 200)/sec = 5/sec.

(b) The frequency is 4 more or less than that of the standard fork, i.e. 304 or 296/sec.

14. Determine the shortest length of closed pipe and of open pipe that will resonate in air at $0°$C with a fork of frequency 160/sec.

Solution:

Wavelength of the sound, $\lambda = v/f = (1087 \text{ ft/sec})/(160/\text{sec}) = 6.8$ ft

Shortest resonant length of closed pipe = $\frac{1}{4}\lambda = \frac{1}{4}(6.8 \text{ ft}) = 1.7$ ft
Shortest resonant length of open pipe = $\frac{1}{2}\lambda = \frac{1}{2}(6.8 \text{ ft}) = 3.4$ ft

15. Determine the pitch or frequency of the fundamental, and also of the first two overtones, of (a) a closed pipe, (b) an open pipe. Each pipe is 67 cm long. Air temperature is $20°$C.

Solution:

(a) Speed of sound at $20°$C = 331 m/sec + 0.6(20) m/sec = 343 m/sec
   Wavelength of fundamental = 4 × length of closed pipe = 4 × 67 cm = 2.68 m
   Frequency of fundamental = v/λ = (343 m/sec)/(2.68 m) = 128/sec

   There is also resonance when the frequency is any odd multiple of that of the fundamental. Hence there will be resonance at 3 × 128 = 384/sec and at 5 × 128 = 640/sec.

(b) Wavelength of fundamental = 2 × length of open pipe = 2 × 67 cm = 1.34 m
   Frequency of fundamental = v/λ = (343 m/sec)/(1.34 m) = 256/sec

   There is also resonance when the frequency is any integral multiple of that of the fundamental. Hence there will be resonance at 2 × 256 = 512/sec and at 3 × 256 = 768/sec.

16. A uniform siren disc has diameter 50 cm, mass 2 kg, and 40 small evenly spaced holes. A jet of air is blown through the holes into a closed pipe 30 cm long. If the disc is set into motion by a 1/20 hp motor which is 60% efficient at all speeds, how long after closing the switch will the pipe be heard to resonate (a) in its fundamental, (b) in its first overtone? The room temperature is 25°C.

Solution:

(a) Fundamental frequency of closed pipe $= \dfrac{\text{speed of sound}}{4 \times \text{pipe length}} = \dfrac{(331+15)\,\text{m/sec}}{4 \times 0.30\,\text{m}} = 288\ \text{vib/sec}$

Angular speed of disc, $\omega = 2\pi/40\ \text{rad/vib} \times 288\ \text{vib/sec} = 45.2\ \text{rad/sec}$

K.E. of disc $= \frac{1}{2}I\omega^2 = \frac{1}{2}[\frac{1}{2}(2\ \text{kg})(0.25\ \text{m})^2](45.2\ \text{rad/sec})^2 = 63.8\ \text{joules}$

Time to reach frequency of fundamental $= \dfrac{63.8\ \text{joules}}{0.05\ \text{hp} \times 746\ (\text{joules/sec})/\text{hp} \times 0.60} = 2.85\ \text{sec}$

(b) Time to reach $3 \times$ fundamental frequency $= 3^2 \times 2.85\ \text{sec} = 25.6\ \text{sec}$

17. A tuning fork of frequency 400 per sec is moved away from an observer and towards a flat wall with a speed of 6 ft/sec. What is the apparent frequency (a) of the unreflected sound waves coming directly to the observer, and (b) of the sound waves coming to the observer after reflection? (c) How many beats per sec are heard? Assume the speed of sound in air to be 1100 ft/sec.

Solution:

(a) The fork is receding from observer. $f' = \dfrac{fV}{V+v} = \dfrac{400 \times 1100}{1100+6} = 398/\text{sec}$

(b) The fork is approaching the wall. $f' = \dfrac{fV}{V-v} = \dfrac{400 \times 1100}{1100-6} = 402/\text{sec}$

(c) Beats/sec $=$ difference between frequencies $= (402-398)/\text{sec} = 4/\text{sec}$

18. An automobile moving at 30 m/sec is approaching a factory whistle having a frequency of 500/sec. If the speed of sound in air is 340 m/sec, what is the apparent pitch of the whistle as heard by the driver?

Solution:

$$f' = \dfrac{f(V+v)}{V} = \dfrac{500/\text{sec} \times (340+30)\,\text{m/sec}}{340\ \text{m/sec}} = 544/\text{sec}$$

19. Compute the intensity of a sound wave in air at standard conditions (0°C, 1 atm) if its frequency is 800/sec and its amplitude 0.001 cm. Standard density of air $= 0.001293\ \text{g/cm}^3$.

Solution:

$$I\ (\text{watts/m}^2) = 2\pi^2 f^2 r^2 v\rho = 2(3.14)^2(800/\text{sec})^2(10^{-5}\ \text{m})^2(331\ \text{m/sec})(1.293\ \text{kg/m}^3)$$
$$= 54 \times 10^{-2}\ \text{watts/m}^2 = 54\ \text{microwatts/cm}^2$$

20. Two sound waves have intensities of 10 and 500 microwatts/cm^2 respectively. How many decibels is the "louder" sound above the other?

Solution:

Decibels $= 10 \log (I_1/I_2) = 10 \log (500/10) = 10 \log 50 = 10(1.7) = 17\ \text{decibels}$

21. Find the ratio of the intensities of two sounds if one is 8 decibels "louder" than the other.

Solution:

Decibels $= 10 \log (I_1/I_2)$, $8 = 10 \log (I_1/I_2)$, $I_1/I_2 = \text{antilog } 0.8 = 6.3$

SUPPLEMENTARY PROBLEMS

22. The average person can hear sounds ranging in frequency from about 20 to 20,000 vibrations per sec. Determine the wavelength in each case, taking the speed of sound to be 340 m/sec. *Ans.* 17 m, 1.7 cm

23. (*a*) Diagram two Simple Harmonic Curves whose wavelengths are 3:1 and amplitudes 2:1, starting in the same phase, and show the resultant curve. (*b*) Repeat starting the two in opposite phases.

24. (*a*) Diagram two Simple Harmonic Curves whose wavelengths are 2:1 and amplitudes 3:1, starting in the same phase, and show the resultant curve. (*b*) Repeat starting the two in opposite phases.

25. An increase in pressure of 1 atmosphere causes a certain volume of water to decrease in volume by 5×10^{-5} of its original volume. Calculate the wavelength in water of sound of frequency 200/sec. *Ans.* 7.1 m

26. The speed of sound in air at $0°C$ is 331 m/sec. Compute the speed at $24°C$ (*a*) by using the approximate correction of 60 cm/sec per degree C, (*b*) by using the exact formula. *Ans.* 345 m/sec

27. Determine the pitch and wavelength of the tone produced by a siren having a disk with 40 holes and making 1200 rpm. The air temperature is $15°C$. *Ans.* 800/sec, 42.5 cm

28. In an experiment to determine the speed of sound, two stations A and B were chosen distant 5 km from each other. Two observers, each equipped with gun and stopwatch, were employed. The observer at A heard the report of B's gun 15.5 sec after seeing its flash. Later, A fired his gun and the observer at B heard the report 14.5 sec after seeing the flash. Determine the speed of sound and the component of the speed of the wind along the line joining A to B. *Ans.* 334 m/sec, 11.1 m/sec

29. A shell fired at a target half a mile distant was heard to strike it 5 sec after leaving the gun. Compute the average speed of the bullet, the air temperature being $20°C$. *Ans.* 994 ft/sec

30. Given that the speed of sound in air at standard conditions is 331 m/sec, determine the speed of sound in hydrogen at $0°C$ and 1 atmosphere. The specific gravity of hydrogen relative to air is 0.069. For each gas, $\gamma = 1.40$. *Ans.* 1260 m/sec

31. Determine the speed of sound in carbon dioxide at a pressure of 0.5 atm and a temperature of $400°C$. Molecular weight of CO_2 = 44; ratio of specific heats = 1.30. *Ans.* 407 m/sec

32. Compute the molecular weight of a gas for which γ is known to be 1.40 and in which the speed of sound at $0°C$ is 1260 m/sec. *Ans.* 2; gas is hydrogen

33. Young's modulus of copper is 11×10^{10} nt/m^2, and the density of copper is 8.8 g/cm^3. What is the speed of sound in copper? *Ans.* 3540 m/sec

34. A flexible cable, 100 ft long and weighing 16 lb, is stretched between two poles with a force of 450 lb. If the cable is struck at one end, how long will it take the transverse wave to travel to the other end and return? *Ans.* 2/3 sec

35. A wire under tension vibrates with a fundamental frequency of 256 per sec. What would be the fundamental frequency if the wire were half as long, twice as thick, and under one-fourth the tension? *Ans.* 128/sec

36. Steel and silver wires of the same diameter and length are stretched with equal tensions. The specific gravities are 7.8 and 10.6 respectively. What is the fundamental frequency of the silver wire, that of the steel being 200/sec? *Ans.* 172/sec

37. A string has mass 3 grams and length 60 cm. What must be the tension so that when vibrating transversely its first overtone has frequency 200/sec? *Ans.* 72 nt

38. (*a*) At what point should a stretched string be plucked to make its fundamental tone (first harmonic) most prominent? At what point should it be plucked and at what point touched (*b*) to make its first overtone (second harmonic) most prominent? (*c*) to make its second overtone (third harmonic) most prominent? *Ans.* (*a*) center
    (*b*) plucked at $\frac{1}{4}$ of its length from one end, then touched at center
    (*c*) plucked at 1/6 of its length from one end, then touched at 1/3 of its length from one end.

39. What must be the length of an iron rod so as to emit its fundamental tone (320/sec), if it is clamped at its center and the speed of sound in the iron is 5000 m/sec? *Ans.* 7.81 m

40. A bar, 1 cm^2 $\times$ 200 cm and mass 2 kg, is clamped at its center. When vibrating longitudinally it emits its fundamental tone in unison with a tuning fork making 1000 vibrations/sec. How much will the bar be elongated if, when clamped at one end, a stretching force of 980 nt is applied at the other end? *Ans.* 0.01225 cm

41. A rod 120 cm long is clamped at the center and is stroked in such a way as to give its first overtone. Make a drawing showing the location of the nodes and antinodes, and determine at what other points the rod might be clamped and still emit the same tone.   *Ans.* 20 cm from either end

42. A metal bar, 6 meters long, clamped at its center and vibrating longitudinally in such a manner that it gives its first overtone, vibrates in unison with a tuning fork marked 1200 vibrations/sec. Compute the speed of sound in the metal.   *Ans.* 4800 m/sec

43. A metal rod 5 ft long, clamped at its middle and vibrating longitudinally, emits its fundamental tone. When vibrating with a tuning fork making 1004 vibrations per sec, 4 beats/sec are produced, and 2 beats/sec with a tuning fork making 998 vibrations per sec. If the specific gravity of the rod is 8, determine the modulus of elasticity (Young's modulus).   *Ans.* 11×10^6 lb/in^2

44. In Kundt's tube experiment the metal rod, 120 cm long, is clamped at its center and emitting its fundamental tone. The distance between the first and seventh nodes of the standing waves in the air column of the tube is 60 cm. The speed of sound in air at the room temperature is 345 m/sec. Compute the speed of sound in the rod.   *Ans.* 4140 m/sec

45. A Kundt's tube is filled with air at 15°C and the distance between the dust heaps is 10.0 cm. It is then filled with hydrogen at 15°C and the dust heaps are 38.5 cm apart. (*a*) Determine the speed of sound in hydrogen if the speed of sound in air is 340 m/sec, both gases being at 15°C. (*b*) How many vibrations per sec are produced in the rod?   *Ans.* 1310 m/sec, 1700/sec

46. Determine the length of the shortest air column in a cylindrical jar that will strongly reenforce the sound of a tuning fork having a vibration rate of 512/sec, the temperature being 15°C.   *Ans.* 16.6 cm

47. The lowest note on a pipe organ is C_O (16.35 vibrations/sec). Find the length of an open organ pipe that gives this note at 22°C.   *Ans.* 34.6 ft

48. A closed pipe resonates to a tuning fork having a frequency of 300/sec when the shortest length of the air column is 28 cm and the next length is 84 cm. What is the speed of sound in air at the room temperature?   *Ans.* 336 m/sec

49. A closed organ pipe is 2 ft long. What are the frequencies of the first three overtones, the temperature being 18°C?   *Ans.* 421, 702, 983 per sec

50. An open pipe and a closed pipe are each 45 in. long. Compute the wavelength of the fourth overtone of each.   *Ans.* 18 in., 20 in.

51. The shortest air column in a tube 10 cm in diameter closed at one end which will resonate to a given tuning fork is found to be 30 cm long when the temperature is 20°C. If the correction for the end effect (to be added to the tube length) is 0.285 times the diameter, what is the frequency of the fork?   *Ans.* 261/sec

52. Five beats per second are heard when a banjo string and an organ pipe are sounded together. Decreasing the tension in the string tends to remove the beats. The pipe is 60 cm long, closed at one end, and emits its first overtone. The string is 20 cm long, has mass 2 grams, and is vibrating so as to give its fundamental tone. Taking the speed of sound in air to be 332 m/sec, find the tension in the string.   *Ans.* 282 nt

53. A locomotive speeding at 60 mi/hr blows a whistle, the frequency of which is 2000/sec. If the speed of sound in air is 1100 ft/sec, compute the observed pitch of the whistle before reaching the observer and after passing the observer.   *Ans.* 2170/sec, 1850/sec

54. The fog horns of two ships have identical frequencies of 200/sec and are sounded simultaneously. The velocity of sound in air is 332 m/sec. Assume that ship A is stationary and ship B is moving along the line joining the two ships. The captain on A hears a note of 204/sec coming from ship B. State whether B is approaching or receding from A, and calculate the speed of ship B relative to A.
Ans. B approaches A at 6.51 m/sec

55. With what speed is a man moving away from a sounding body if the observed pitch of the sound is lowered by 10%, the speed of sound being 1100 ft/sec?   *Ans.* 110 ft/sec

56. Calculate the intensity of a sound wave in air at 0°C and 1 atm if its amplitude is 0.002 mm and its wavelength is 66.2 cm. Standard density of air (0°C, 1 atm) is 0.001293 g/cm^3.   *Ans.* 0.844 microwatt/cm^2

57. What sound intensity is 3 decibels "louder" than a sound of intensity 10 microwatts/cm^2?
Ans. 20 microwatts/cm^2

Chapter 35

Illumination and Photometry

LUMINOUS INTENSITY I **AND LUMINOUS FLUX** F.

The luminous intensity of a point source is expressed in **candles**.

The amount of flux radiating out from a uniform point source of 1 candle through 1 unit solid angle (1 steradian) is 1 **lumen**. Thus 1 lumen is the amount of luminous flux radiating from a 1 candle source normally upon a spherical surface of area 1 ft^2 at a distance of 1 ft from the source, or upon a surface of 1 m^2 at a distance of 1 m.

Since there are 4π unit solid angles (4π steradians) about a point source, the total luminous flux F emitted by a source of luminous intensity I is

$$F \text{ (lumens)} = 4\pi \text{ (lumens/candles)} \times I \text{ (candles)}$$

where F is in lumens if I is in candles. Note that a 1 candle source radiates 1 lumen per steradian, or 1 candle = 1 lumen/steradian. A 1 candle source radiates a total of 4π lumens.

THE ILLUMINANCE E, or illumination, of a surface is the luminous flux incident per unit area of the surface.

$$E \text{ (lumens/m}^2\text{)} = \frac{F \text{ (lumens)}}{A \text{ (m}^2\text{)}}$$

Units of illuminance are the lumen/m^2 and the lumen/ft^2, also called the foot-candle.

Consider that a point source of luminous intensity I candles is at the center of a sphere of radius r meters. Then $4\pi I$ lumens are incident perpendicularly on a spherical surface of area $4\pi r^2$ m^2 at a distance r m from the source, and the illuminance E of the surface, expressed in lumens/m^2, is

$$E = \frac{F}{A} = \frac{4\pi I}{4\pi r^2} = \frac{I}{r^2}$$

It follows that if a point source of luminous intensity I is distant r from a surface of area A and if the luminous flux makes an angle i with the normal to the surface, then the illuminance of the surface is

$$E = \frac{I}{r^2} \cos i$$

PRINCIPLE OF PHOTOMETRY. The luminous intensities of two sources (I_1 and I_2) producing equal illuminance E on a screen are directly proportional to the squares of their distances (r_1 and r_2) from the screen. Thus

$$\text{since } E = \frac{I_1}{r_1^2} = \frac{I_2}{r_2^2}, \quad \text{then } \frac{I_1}{I_2} = \frac{r_1^2}{r_2^2}.$$

SOLVED PROBLEMS

1. A 60 watt tungsten incandescent lamp has a luminous intensity of 66.5 candles. Determine the total luminous flux F radiated by the lamp and the luminous "efficiency" of the lamp.

Solution:

$$F = 4\pi I = 4\pi \text{ lumens/candle} \times 66.5 \text{ candles} = 836 \text{ lumens}$$

Luminous efficiency $= (836 \text{ lumens})/(60 \text{ watts}) = 13.9 \text{ lumens/watt}$

2. Compute the illumination E of a small surface distant 120 cm from a lamp of luminous intensity 72 candles (a) if the surface is normal to the luminous flux, (b) if the normal to the surface makes an angle of 30° with the light rays.

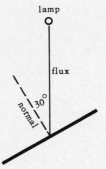

Solution:

(a) $E = \dfrac{I}{r^2} = \dfrac{72 \text{ candles}}{(1.2 \text{ m})^2} = 50 \text{ lumens/m}^2$

(b) $E = \dfrac{I}{r^2} \cos 30° = \dfrac{72 \text{ candles}}{(1.2 \text{ m})^2} \times 0.866 = 43.3 \text{ lumens/m}^2$

3. A photoelectric cell measures the illumination received from the sun as 10^5 lumens/m². If the distance between earth and sun is 1.5×10^{11} m, compute the luminous intensity of the sun.

Solution:

$$I = Er^2 = (10^5 \text{ lumens/m}^2)(1.5 \times 10^{11} \text{ m})^2 = 2.25 \times 10^{27} \text{ candles}$$

4. An unknown lamp placed 90 cm from a photometer screen gives the same illumination as a standard 32 candle lamp at a distance of 60 cm from the screen. Compute the luminous intensity I_1 of the lamp under test.

Solution:

$$\frac{I_1}{I_2} = \frac{r_1^2}{r_2^2}, \qquad \frac{I_1}{32 \text{ candles}} = \frac{(90 \text{ cm})^2}{(60 \text{ cm})^2}, \qquad \text{and } I_1 = 72 \text{ candles}$$

5. Two lamps of 20 and 40 candles respectively are 10 ft apart. At what two points on the straight line passing through the lamps will the illumination produced by each be equal?

Solution:

Let x = distance of 20 candle lamp from point of equal illumination; then
$10 - x$ = distance of 40 candle lamp from point of equal illumination.

At the point of equal illumination, $\dfrac{I_1}{I_2} = \dfrac{r_1^2}{r_2^2}$ or $\dfrac{20 \text{ candles}}{40 \text{ candles}} = \dfrac{x^2}{(10-x)^2}$.

Simplifying and solving, $x^2 + 20x - 100 = 0$ and $x = \dfrac{-20 \pm \sqrt{(20)^2 - 4(1)(-100)}}{2(1)}$

$$= 4.14 \text{ and } -24.14.$$

The first solution represents a point P_1 between the lamps and 4.14 ft from the 20 candle lamp. The second solution represents a point P_2 24.14 ft from the 20 candle lamp and 34.14 ft from the 40 candle lamp.

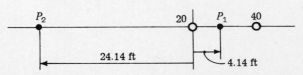

SUPPLEMENTARY PROBLEMS

6. What is the luminous intensity of a 200 watt tungsten lamp whose efficiency is 18 lumens/watt?
   Ans. 287 candles

7. Determine the illuminance at a distance 5 m from a 200 candle source.   *Ans.* 8 lumens/m^2

8. How many lumens pass through a spherical area of 0.3 m^2 having a radius of 4 m, if an 800 candle source is at the center?   *Ans.* 15 lumens

9. At what distance from a screen will a 27 candle lamp provide the same illumination as a 75 candle lamp 15 ft from the screen?   *Ans.* 9 ft

10. Determine the illumination on a surface 7 ft distant from a 125 candle source (*a*) if the surface is normal to the light rays, (*b*) if the normal to the surface makes an angle of 15° with the rays.
    Ans. 2.55 lumens/ft^2, 2.46 lumens/ft^2

11. Compute the illumination at the edge of a circular table of radius 1 m, if a 200 candle source is suspended 3 m above its center.   *Ans.* 19.0 lumens/m^2

12. How much should a 60 watt lamp be lowered to double the illumination on an object which is 6 ft directly under it?   *Ans.* 1.76 ft

13. A 40 watt, 110 volt lamp is rated 11.0 lumens/watt. At what distance from the lamp is the maximum illumination 5 lumens/ft^2 (ft-candles)?   *Ans.* 2.65 ft

14. Two lamps of 5 and 20 candles respectively are 150 cm apart. At what point between them will the illumination produced by each be equal?   *Ans.* 50 cm from 5 candle lamp

15. A frosted light bulb having an effective surface area of 50 cm^2 gives an illuminance of 8 lumens/m^2 at a distance of 5 m. Compute (*a*) the total luminous flux radiating from the lamp and (*b*) the luminance of the light bulb in candles/m^2.   *Ans.* 800π lumens, 4×10^4 candles/m^2

16. An air-cooled searchlight bulb has an efficiency of 25 lumens/watt. The searchlight is powered by a generator of efficiency 80% to which power is supplied by a belt passing around a pulley of diameter 16 cm. If the difference in tension of the two portions of the belt is 98 nt, calculate the angular speed of the generator required to give 4 lumens/ft^2 of illumination on the ground. The reflector system of the searchlight concentrates all the light into a circle on the ground 50 ft in diameter.   *Ans.* 478 rpm

Chapter 36

Reflection of Light

LAWS OF REFLECTION. The angle of incidence is the angle between the incident ray and the normal to the reflecting surface at the point of incidence. The angle of reflection is the angle between the reflected ray and the normal to the surface.

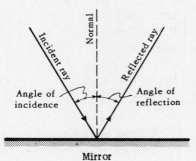

In regular reflection: (*1*) The incident ray, reflected ray and normal to the reflecting surface lie in the same plane. (2) The angle of incidence equals the angle of reflection.

PLANE MIRRORS form images that are erect, virtual, of the same size as the object, and as far behind the reflecting surface as the object is in front of it.

SPHERICAL MIRRORS. The **principal focus** of a spherical mirror is the point F where rays parallel to and very close to the principal axis XX of the mirror are focused. This focus is real for a concave mirror and virtual for a convex mirror. It is located on the principal axis XX and halfway between the center of curvature C and the mirror.

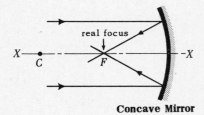
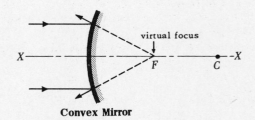

Concave Mirror **Convex Mirror**

Concave mirrors form real and inverted images of objects located outside of the principal focus. If the object is between the principal focus and the mirror, the image is virtual, erect and enlarged.

Convex mirrors produce only virtual, erect and smaller images.

MIRROR EQUATION for both concave and convex spherical mirrors:

$$\frac{1}{p} + \frac{1}{q} = \frac{2}{r} = \frac{1}{f}$$

where p = object distance from mirror, q = image distance from mirror,
    r = radius of curvature of mirror, f = focal length of mirror = $\frac{1}{2}r$.

p is positive when the object is in front of the mirror.
q is positive when the image is real, i.e. in front of the mirror.
q is negative when the image is virtual, i.e. behind the mirror.
r and f are positive for a concave mirror and negative for a convex mirror.

SIZE OF IMAGE formed by a concave or convex spherical mirror:

$$\text{Linear magnification} = \frac{\text{size of image}}{\text{size of object}} = \frac{\text{image distance from mirror}}{\text{object distance from mirror}} = \frac{q}{p}$$

SOLVED PROBLEMS

1. Two plane mirrors make an angle of 30° with each other. Locate graphically four images of a luminous point A placed between the two mirrors.

Solution:

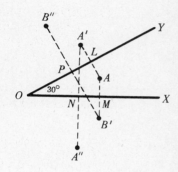

From A draw normals AA' and AB' to the mirrors OY and OX respectively, making $AL = LA'$ and $AM = MB'$. Then A' and B' are images of A.

Next, from A' and B' draw normals to OX and OY respectively, making $A'N = NA''$ and $B'P = PB''$. Then A'' is the image of A' in OX, and B'' is the image of B' in OY.

The four images of A are A', B', A'', B''.

2. A man is 5 ft 4 in. tall and can just see his image in a vertical plane mirror 9 ft away. His eyes are 5 ft from the floor level. Determine the height and position of the mirror.

Solution:

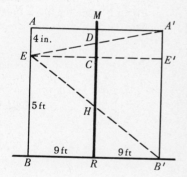

Let AB be the position and height of the man; his eyes are at E.

Then $A'B'$ is the image of AB in the mirror MR, and DH represents the height and position of the shortest mirror necessary for the eye to view the image $A'B'$.

Triangle $A'EB'$ is similar to triangle DEH; then

$$\frac{A'B'}{DH} = \frac{EE'}{EC}, \qquad \frac{16/3 \text{ ft}}{DH} = \frac{18}{9} \quad \text{and} \quad DH = 8/3 \text{ ft.}$$

Triangle $EB'B$ is similar to triangle $HB'R$; then

$$\frac{EB}{HR} = \frac{BB'}{RB'}, \qquad \frac{5 \text{ ft}}{HR} = \frac{18}{9} \quad \text{and} \quad HR = 5/2 \text{ ft.}$$

The shortest mirror DH is 2 ft 8 in. high and 2 ft 6 in. above the floor.

3. A ray of light IO is incident upon a small plane mirror which is attached to a galvanometer coil. The mirror reflects this ray upon a straight scale SC 1 meter distant and parallel to the undeflected mirror MM. When the current through the instrument has a certain value, the mirror turns through an angle of 8° and assumes the position $M'M'$. Across what distance on the scale will the spot of light move?

Solution:

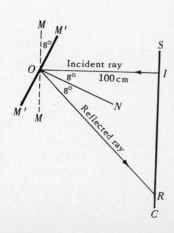

When the mirror turns through 8°, the normal to it also turns through 8° and the incident ray makes an angle of 8° with the normal NO to the deflected mirror $M'M'$. Since the incident ray IO and the reflected ray OR make equal angles with the normal, $\angle IOR$ is twice the angle through which the mirror has turned, or 16°.

$$IR = IO \tan \angle IOR = 100 \text{ cm} \times 0.287 = 28.7 \text{ cm}$$

4. A concave spherical mirror has a radius of curvature 4 ft. A real object OO', 5 in. high, is placed 3 ft in front of the mirror. By construction and computation, determine the position and height of the image II'.

Solution:

     C = center of curvature, 4 ft from mirror. F = principal focus, 2 ft from mirror.

To construct the figure:

     Two of the following 3 convenient rays from O will locate the image.

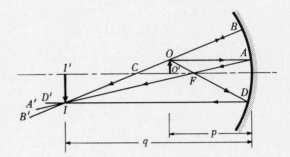

1. Draw the ray OA parallel to the principal axis. This ray, like all parallel rays, is reflected through the principal focus F in the direction AFA'.

2. Draw the ray OB in the same direction as if it passed through the center of curvature C. This ray is normal to the mirror and is reflected back on itself in the direction BCB'.

3. A ray OFD passes through the principal focus F and, like all rays passing through F, is reflected parallel to the principal axis in the direction DD'.

     The intersection I of any two of these reflected rays is the image of O. Thus II' represents the position and size of the image of OO'.

     The image is real, inverted, magnified, and at a greater distance from the mirror than the object.

     Note. If the object were at II', the image would be at OO' (real, inverted, smaller).

By the Mirror Equation. $\dfrac{1}{p} + \dfrac{1}{q} = \dfrac{2}{r}$, $\dfrac{1}{3} + \dfrac{1}{q} = \dfrac{2}{4}$, $q = 6$ ft

     The image is real (since q is positive) and 6 ft from the mirror.

$\dfrac{\text{Size of image}}{\text{Size of object}} = \dfrac{q}{p} = \dfrac{6\,\text{ft}}{3\,\text{ft}} = 2$ Height of image $= 2 \times 5\,\text{in.} = 10\,\text{in.}$

5. An object OO' is 25 cm from a concave spherical mirror of radius 80 cm. Determine the position and relative size of its image II'.

Solution:

To construct the figure. Choose 2 convenient rays coming from O.

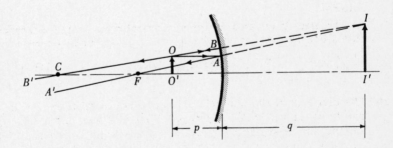

1. A ray OA, parallel to the principal axis, is reflected through the principal focus F, 40 cm from the mirror.

2. A ray OB, in the line of the radius COB, is normal to the mirror and is reflected back on itself through the center of curvature C.

     The reflected rays, AA' and BB', do not meet but appear to originate from a point I behind the mirror. Thus II' represents the relative position and size of the image of OO'. The image is virtual (behind the mirror), erect and magnified.

By the Mirror Equation. $\dfrac{1}{p} + \dfrac{1}{q} = \dfrac{2}{r}$, $\dfrac{1}{25} + \dfrac{1}{q} = \dfrac{2}{80}$, $q = -66.7$ cm

     The image is virtual (since q is negative) and 66.7 cm behind the mirror.

Linear magnification $= \dfrac{\text{size of image}}{\text{size of object}} = \dfrac{q}{p} = \dfrac{66.7\,\text{cm}}{25\,\text{cm}} = 2.67$ times

6. An object 6 cm high is located 30 cm in front of a convex spherical mirror of radius 40 cm. Determine the position and height of its image.

Solution:

To construct the figure. Choose two convenient rays coming from O.

1. A ray OA, parallel to the principal axis, is reflected in the direction AA' as if it passed through the principal focus F.

2. A ray OB, directed toward the center of curvature C, is normal to the mirror and is reflected back on itself.

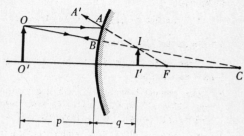

The reflected rays, AA' and BO, never meet but appear to originate from a point I behind the mirror. Then II' represents the size and position of the image of OO'.

All images formed by convex mirrors are virtual, erect, and reduced in size.

By the Mirror Equation. $\quad \dfrac{1}{p} + \dfrac{1}{q} = \dfrac{2}{r}, \qquad \dfrac{1}{30} + \dfrac{1}{q} = -\dfrac{2}{40}, \qquad q = -12 \text{ cm}$

The image is virtual (q is negative) and 12 cm behind the mirror.

$$\frac{\text{Size of image}}{\text{Size of object}} = \frac{q}{p} = \frac{12 \text{ cm}}{30 \text{ cm}} = 0.4 \qquad \text{Height of image} = 0.4 \times 6 \text{ cm} = 2.4 \text{ cm}$$

7. Where should an object be placed with reference to a concave spherical mirror of radius 180 cm in order to form a real image having half its linear dimensions?

Solution:

Size of image $= \frac{1}{2} \times$ size of object; hence $q = p/2$.

$$\frac{1}{p} + \frac{1}{q} = \frac{2}{r}, \qquad \frac{1}{p} + \frac{2}{p} = \frac{2}{180}, \qquad p = 270 \text{ cm from mirror}$$

8. How far must a man stand in front of a concave spherical mirror of radius 120 cm in order to see an erect image of his face four times its natural size?

Solution:

The erect image must be virtual; hence q is negative, and $q = -4p$.

$$\frac{1}{p} + \frac{1}{q} = \frac{2}{r}, \qquad \frac{1}{p} - \frac{1}{4p} = \frac{2}{120}, \qquad p = 45 \text{ cm from mirror}$$

9. What kind of spherical mirror must be used and what must be its radius, in order to give an erect image 1/5 as large as an object placed 15 in. in front of it?

Solution:

An erect image produced by a spherical mirror is virtual; hence $q = -p/5 = -15/5 = -3$ in. As the virtual image is smaller than the object, a convex mirror is required.

$$\frac{1}{p} + \frac{1}{q} = \frac{2}{r}, \qquad \frac{1}{15} - \frac{1}{3} = \frac{2}{r}, \qquad r = -7.5 \text{ in. (convex mirror)}$$

10. The diameter of the sun subtends an angle of approximately 32 minutes (32') at any point on the earth. Determine the position and diameter of the solar image formed by a concave spherical mirror of radius 400 cm.

Solution:

Since the sun is very distant, p is very large and $1/p$ is practically zero.

$$\frac{1}{p} + \frac{1}{q} = \frac{2}{r} \qquad \text{or} \qquad 0 + \frac{1}{q} = \frac{2}{400}$$

Solving, $q = 200$ cm. The image is at the principal focus F, 200 cm from the mirror.

The diameter of the sun and its image II' subtend equal angles at the center of curvature C of the mirror.

$$I'I = 2(I'F) = 2(CF \tan 16') = 2 \times 200 \text{ cm} \times 0.00465 = 1.86 \text{ cm}$$

SUPPLEMENTARY PROBLEMS

11. Two plane mirrors are parallel to each other and spaced 20 cm apart. A luminous point is placed between them and 5 cm from one mirror. Determine the distance from each mirror of the three nearest images in each.
Ans. 5, 35, 45 cm; 15, 25, 55 cm

12. A ray of light makes an angle of 25° with the normal to a plane mirror. If the mirror is turned through 6°, making the angle of incidence 31°, through what angle is the reflected ray rotated?
Ans. 12°

13. Describe the image of a candle flame located 4 in. from a concave spherical mirror of radius 6.4 in.
Ans. real, inverted, 16 in. before mirror, magnified 4 times

14. Describe the image of an object spaced 20 cm from a concave spherical mirror of radius 60 cm.
Ans. virtual, erect, 60 cm behind mirror, magnified 3 times

15. How far should an object be spaced from a concave spherical mirror of radius 36 cm in order to form a real image 1/9 its size?   *Ans.* 180 cm

16. An object 7 cm high is placed 15 cm from a convex spherical mirror of radius 45 cm. Describe its image.
Ans. virtual, erect, 9 cm behind mirror, 4.2 cm high

17. What is the focal length of a convex spherical mirror which produces an image 1/6 the size of an object spaced 1 ft from the mirror?   *Ans.* −2.4 in.

18. It is desired to cast the image of a lamp, magnified 5 times, upon a wall 12 ft distant from the lamp. What kind of spherical mirror is required and what is its position?
Ans. concave, radius 5 ft, 3 ft from lamp

19. Compute the position and diameter of the image of the moon in a polished sphere of diameter 20 cm. The diameter of the moon is 2200 miles and its distance from the earth is 240,000 miles, approximately.
Ans. 5 cm inside sphere, 0.46 mm

Chapter 37

Refraction of Light

REFRACTION. Consider a ray of light passing obliquely from medium A into medium B. If the speed of light is greater in A than in B, the ray is bent toward the normal NN to the surface of separation, as shown in the adjoining figure; if it is less in A than in B, the ray is bent away from the normal.

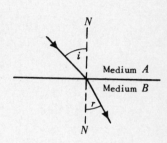

A constant n of the two media is defined by the ratio

$$n = \frac{\text{speed of light in } A}{\text{speed of light in } B} = \frac{\sin i}{\sin r}$$

where i is called the angle of incidence, r the angle of refraction, and n the **index of refraction** of B relative to A. When A is vacuum, n is called simply the (absolute) index of refraction of medium B.

Since the speeds of light in air and in vacuum are practically equal, the refractive index of a substance relative to air is practically equal to that relative to vacuum.

Speed of light in air $= 3.00 \times 10^8$ m/sec $= 1.86 \times 10^5$ mi/sec.

The direction of a light ray can be reversed. Hence, regardless of the direction of the ray, the larger angle is often termed the angle of incidence i and the smaller angle is termed the angle of refraction r, and n is greater than 1.

CRITICAL ANGLE. Suppose that light passes from one medium into another in which its speed is greater, e.g. from water into air. Then the angle between the ray and the normal in air is always greater than the angle between the ray and the normal in water. The angle in water for which the angle in air is $90°$ is the **critical angle** of water. Whenever the critical angle is exceeded, light is totally reflected at the surface of separation (and the angle of incidence MON = angle of reflection $M'ON$).

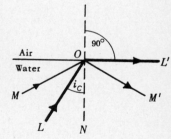

Let n = index of refraction of water. Then at the critical angle i_c,

$$n = \frac{\sin i}{\sin r} = \frac{\sin 90°}{\sin i_c} = \frac{1}{\sin i_c} \quad \text{or} \quad \sin i_c = \frac{1}{n}$$

REFRACTION THROUGH A PRISM. The refractive index n of the material of a triangular prism can be determined from the relation

$$n = \frac{\sin \frac{1}{2}(A + D)}{\sin \frac{1}{2}A}$$

where A = refracting angle of prism,
D = angle of minimum deviation.

SOLVED PROBLEMS

1. The speed of light in water is $\frac{3}{4}$ that in air. What is the effect on the frequency and wavelength of light in passing from air into water? Compute the refractive index of water.

Solution:

Speed of a wave = frequency × wavelength.

The same number of light waves that leave the air per sec pass into the water. Therefore the frequency is the same in both media, and the wavelength in water is $\frac{3}{4}$ that in air.

$$\text{Refractive index of water} = \frac{\text{speed of light in air}}{\text{speed of light in water}} = \frac{1}{\frac{3}{4}} = 1.33$$

2. A ray of light strikes the surface of crown glass at an incident angle of 50°. Determine the directions of the reflected and refracted rays. The refractive index of the crown glass is 1.50.

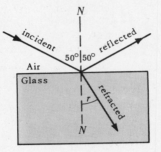

Solution:

The incident and reflected rays make equal angles of 50° with the normal NN. The refracted ray makes an angle r with the normal NN.

$$n = \frac{\sin 50^\circ}{\sin r} \quad \text{or} \quad 1.50 = \frac{0.766}{\sin r}$$

from which $\sin r = 0.511$ and $r = 30.7^\circ$.

3. A microscope is sharply focused on a mark. When a parallel plate of glass 4.8 mm thick is placed over the mark, the microscope has to be raised 1.8 mm to refocus. What is the refractive index of the glass?

Solution:

$$n = \frac{\text{real depth of glass}}{\text{apparent depth of glass}} = \frac{4.8 \text{ mm}}{(4.8 - 1.8) \text{mm}} = 1.6$$

4. The refractive index of diamond is 2.42. What is the critical angle i_C of light passing from diamond into air?

Solution:

$$\sin i_C = \frac{1}{n} = \frac{1}{2.42} = 0.413 \quad \text{and} \quad i_C = 24.4^\circ$$

5. The index of refraction of water (relative to air) is 1.33, and of a specimen of crown glass (relative to air) is 1.54. Calculate the index of refraction of glass relative to water, and the critical angle between glass and water.

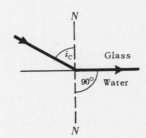

Solution:

Let V_a, V_w and V_g be the speeds of light in air, water and glass respectively. The index of refraction of glass relative to water is

$$n' = \frac{V_w}{V_g} = \frac{V_a/n_w}{V_a/n_g} = \frac{n_g}{n_w} = \frac{1.54}{1.33} = 1.16$$

Glass is a more highly refracting medium than water. Hence there can be no critical angle for light passing from water into glass, since the angle of refraction will always be smaller than the angle of incidence. But there is a critical angle of incidence i_C for light passing from glass into water.

$$\sin i_C = \frac{1}{n'} = \frac{1}{1.16} = 0.862 \quad \text{and} \quad i_C = 59.6^\circ$$

LENSES IN CONTACT. When two thin lenses having focal lengths f_1 and f_2 are in contact, the focal length f of the combination is given by the equation

$$\frac{1}{f} = \frac{1}{f_1} + \frac{1}{f_2}$$

SOLVED PROBLEMS

1. An object OO', 4 cm high, is 20 cm in front of a thin convex lens of focal length +12 cm. Determine the position and height of its image II'.

Solution:

<u>To construct the figure:</u>

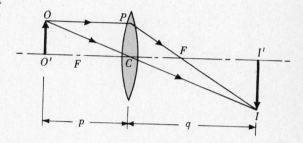

The following 2 convenient rays from O will locate the image.

1. A ray OP, parallel to the principal axis, must after refraction pass through the principal focus F.

2. A ray passing through the optical center C of a thin lens is not appreciably deviated. Hence ray OCI may be drawn as a straight line.

The intersection I of these two rays is the image of O. Thus II' represents the position and size of the image of OO'. The image is real, inverted, enlarged, and at a greater distance from the lens than the object.

(If the object were at II', the image would be at OO' — real, inverted, smaller.)

<u>**By computation:**</u> $\quad \frac{1}{p} + \frac{1}{q} = \frac{1}{f}, \qquad \frac{1}{20} + \frac{1}{q} = \frac{1}{12}, \qquad q = 30 \text{ cm}$

The image is real (since q is positive) and 30 cm behind the lens.

$$\frac{\text{Size of image}}{\text{Size of object}} = \frac{q}{p} = \frac{30 \text{ cm}}{20 \text{ cm}} = 1.5. \qquad \text{Height of image} = 1.5 \times 4 \text{ cm} = 6 \text{ cm}.$$

2. An object OO' is 5 in. in front of a convex lens of focal length +7.5 in. Determine the position and magnification of its image II'.

Solution:

<u>To construct the figure:</u>

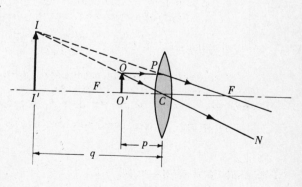

Choose 2 convenient rays from O.

1. A ray OP, parallel to the principal axis, is refracted so as to pass through the principal focus F.

2. A ray OCN, through the optical center of the lens, is drawn as a straight line.

These two rays do not meet but appear to originate from a point I. Thus II' represents the position and size of the image of OO'.

When the object is between F and C, the image is virtual, erect and enlarged.

<u>**By computation:**</u> $\quad \frac{1}{p} + \frac{1}{q} = \frac{1}{f}, \qquad \frac{1}{5} + \frac{1}{q} = \frac{1}{7.5}, \qquad q = -15 \text{ in.}$

Since q is negative, the image is virtual (on the same side of the lens as the object) and 15 in. in front of the lens.

Linear magnification $= \dfrac{\text{size of image}}{\text{size of object}} = \dfrac{q}{p} = \dfrac{15 \text{ in.}}{5 \text{ in.}} = 3 \text{ diameters}$

3. An object OO', 9 cm high, is 27 cm in front of a concave lens of focal length −18 cm. Determine the position and height of its image II'.

Solution:

To construct the figure:

Choose 2 convenient rays from O.

1. A ray OP, parallel to the principal axis, is refracted outward in the direction D as if it passed through the principal focus F.

2. A ray through the optical center of the lens is drawn as a straight line OC.

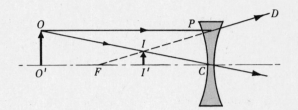

Then II' is the image of OO'. Images formed by concave or divergent lenses are virtual, erect and smaller.

By computation: $\dfrac{1}{p} + \dfrac{1}{q} = \dfrac{1}{f}$, $\dfrac{1}{27} + \dfrac{1}{q} = -\dfrac{1}{18}$, $q = -10.8$ cm

Since q is negative, the image is virtual and 10.8 cm in front of the lens.

Linear magnification $= \dfrac{q}{p} = \dfrac{10.8 \text{ cm}}{27 \text{ cm}} = 0.40$.   Height of image $= 0.40(9 \text{ cm}) = 3.6$ cm.

4. Compute the position and focal length of the converging lens which will project the image of a lamp, magnified 4 diameters, upon a screen spaced 10 ft from the lamp.

Solution:

Given $p + q = 10$ and $q = 4p$. Hence $p + 4p = 10$, $p = 2$; and $q = 8$.

$$\frac{1}{f} = \frac{1}{p} + \frac{1}{q} = \frac{1}{2} + \frac{1}{8} = \frac{5}{8}, \qquad f = \frac{8}{5} = +1.6 \text{ ft}$$

5. In what two positions will a converging lens of focal length +7.5 in. form images of a luminous object on a screen spaced 40 in. from the object?

Solution:

Given $p + q = 40$ and $f = +7.5$.   Thus $\dfrac{1}{p} + \dfrac{1}{40-p} = \dfrac{1}{7.5}$.

Then $p^2 - 40p + 300 = 0$ or $(p - 10)(p - 30) = 0$, from which $p = 10$ and $p = 30$. The two lens positions are 10 in. and 30 in. from the object.

6. A lens has a convex surface of radius 20 cm and a concave surface of 40 cm, and is made of glass of refractive index 1.54. Compute the focal length of the lens, and state whether it is a converging or a diverging lens.

Solution:

$$\frac{1}{f} = (n-1)\left(\frac{1}{r_1} + \frac{1}{r_2}\right) = (1.54 - 1)\left(\frac{1}{20} - \frac{1}{40}\right) = \frac{0.54}{40}, \qquad f = +74.1 \text{ cm}$$

Since f turns out to be positive, the lens is converging.

7. A double convex lens has faces of radii 18 and 20 cm. When an object is 24 cm from the lens, a real image is formed 32 cm from the lens. Determine (a) the focal length of the lens and (b) the refractive index of the lens material.

Solution:

(a) $\dfrac{1}{f} = \dfrac{1}{p} + \dfrac{1}{q} = \dfrac{1}{24} + \dfrac{1}{32} = \dfrac{7}{96}$, $f = \dfrac{96}{7} = +13.7$ cm

(b) $\dfrac{1}{f} = (n-1)\left(\dfrac{1}{r_1} + \dfrac{1}{r_2}\right)$, $\dfrac{1}{13.7} = (n-1)\left(\dfrac{1}{18} + \dfrac{1}{20}\right)$, $n = 1.69$

8. A glass lens has a focal length of +10 cm in air. Compute its focal length in water. Refractive index of the glass = 3/2, of water = 4/3.

Solution:

Relative refractive index n' when light passes from water into glass $= \dfrac{3/2}{4/3} = \dfrac{9}{8}$.

Let f = focal length of lens in air, f' = focal length of lens in water.

In air, (1) $\dfrac{1}{f} = (n-1)(\dfrac{1}{r_1} + \dfrac{1}{r_2})$; in water, (2) $\dfrac{1}{f'} = (n'-1)(\dfrac{1}{r_1} + \dfrac{1}{r_2})$.

Dividing (1) by (2): $\dfrac{f'}{f} = \dfrac{(n-1)}{(n'-1)}$, $\dfrac{f'}{10} = \dfrac{3/2-1}{9/8-1}$, $f' = +40$ cm

9. A double convex lens has faces of radii 20 cm each. The index of refraction of the glass is 1.50. Compute the focal length of this lens in air and when immersed in carbon disulfide, of refractive index 1.63.

Solution:

Since the glass is a less highly refracting medium than the carbon disulfide, the lens becomes a diverging lens when immersed.

(1) In air: $\dfrac{1}{f} = (n-1)(\dfrac{1}{r_1} + \dfrac{1}{r_2}) = (1.50-1)(\dfrac{1}{20} + \dfrac{1}{20})$, $f = +20$ cm (converging lens)

(2) In carbon disulfide: The glass is optically less dense than the liquid, and the index of refraction of glass relative to liquid is $n' = 1.50/1.63 = 0.92$.

$$\dfrac{1}{f} = (0.92-1)(\dfrac{1}{20} + \dfrac{1}{20}), \qquad f = -125 \text{ cm (diverging lens)}$$

10. Two thin lenses, of focal lengths +9 and −6 cm respectively, are placed in contact. Calculate the focal length of the combination.

Solution:

$$\dfrac{1}{f} = \dfrac{1}{f_1} + \dfrac{1}{f_2} = \dfrac{1}{9} - \dfrac{1}{6} = \dfrac{-1}{18}, \qquad f = -18 \text{ cm (diverging)}$$

11. A certain achromatic lens is formed from two thin lenses in contact, having powers of +10 and −6 diopters respectively. Determine the power and focal length of the combination.

Solution:

Power $= +10 - 6 = +4$ diopters. Focal length $= \dfrac{1}{+4}$ meter $= +25$ cm.

12. A lens of focal length f projects upon a screen the image of a luminous object magnified M times. Show that the lens distance from the screen is $f(M+1)$.

Solution:

$$\dfrac{1}{f} = \dfrac{1}{p} + \dfrac{1}{q}, \qquad pq = fq + fp, \qquad \text{and} \qquad q = \dfrac{fq}{p} + \dfrac{fp}{p} = f(\dfrac{q}{p} + \dfrac{p}{p}) = f(M+1)$$

SUPPLEMENTARY PROBLEMS

13. Draw diagrams to locate qualitatively the position, nature and size of image formed by a converging lens of focal length f for the following object distances: (a) infinity, (b) greater than $2f$, (c) equal to $2f$, (d) between $2f$ and f, (e) equal to f, (f) less than f.

14. Determine the nature, position and linear magnification of the image formed by a thin converging lens of focal length +100 cm when the object distance from the lens is (a) 150 cm, (b) 75 cm.
    Ans. (a) Real, inverted, 300 cm beyond lens, 2:1.
         (b) Virtual, erect, 300 cm in front of lens, 4:1.

15. In what two positions of the object will its image be enlarged 8 times by a lens of focal length +4 cm?
    Ans. 4.5 cm from lens, image is real and inverted;
         3.5 cm from lens, image is virtual and erect.

16. What is the nature and focal length of the lens that will form a real image having one-third the dimensions of an object spaced 9 cm from the lens?   Ans. converging, +2.25 cm

17. Describe fully the image of an object 10 in. high and spaced 28 in. from a diverging lens of focal length −7 in.
    Ans. Virtual, erect, smaller, 5.6 in. in front of lens, 2 in. high

18. Compute the focal length of the lens which will give an erect image 10 inches from the lens when the object distance from the lens is (a) 200 in., (b) very great.   Ans. (a) −10.5 in., (b) −10 in.

19. A luminous object and a screen are 12.5 ft apart. What is the position and focal length of the lens which will throw upon the screen an image of the object magnified 24 diameters?
    Ans. 0.50 ft from object, +0.48 ft

20. A plano-concave lens has a spherical surface of radius 12 cm, and its focal length is −22.2 cm. Compute the refractive index of the lens material.   Ans. 1.54

21. A convexo-concave lens has faces of radii 3 and 4 cm respectively, and is made of glass of refractive index 1.6. Determine (a) its focal length and (b) the linear magnification of the image when the object is 28 cm from the lens.   Ans. +20 cm, 2.5:1

22. A double convex glass lens has faces of radii 8 cm each. Compute its focal length in air and when immersed in water. Refractive index of the glass = 1.50, of water = 1.33.   Ans. +8 cm, +32 cm

23. Two thin lenses, of focal lengths +12 and −30 cm respectively, are in contact. Compute the focal length and power of the combination.   Ans. +20 cm, +5 diopters

Chapter 39

Optical Instruments

COMBINATION OF THIN LENSES. When a lens is used in combination with another lens to form an image: (1) compute the position of the image produced by the first lens alone, disregarding the second lens; (2) then consider this image as the object for the second lens and locate its image as produced by the second lens alone. This latter image is the final image required.

If the image formed by the first lens alone is computed to be in back of the second lens, then that image is a virtual object for the second lens and its distance from the second lens is considered negative.

SOLVED PROBLEMS

1. A certain nearsighted person cannot see distinctly objects beyond 80 cm from the eye. What is the power in diopters of the spectacle lenses which will enable him to see distant objects clearly?

   Solution:

   The image must be on the same side of the lens as the distant object (hence the image is virtual and $q = -80$ cm), and nearer to the lens than the object (hence diverging or negative lenses are indicated). As the object is at a great distance, p is very large and $1/p$ is practically zero.

   $$\frac{1}{p} + \frac{1}{q} = \frac{1}{f}, \qquad 0 - \frac{1}{80} = \frac{1}{f}, \qquad f = -80 \text{ cm (diverging)}$$

   $$\text{Power in diopters} = \frac{1}{f \text{ in meters}} = \frac{1}{-0.80 \text{ m}} = -1.25 \text{ diopters}$$

2. A certain farsighted person cannot see clearly objects closer to the eye than 75 cm. Determine the power of the spectacle lenses which will enable him to read type at a distance of 25 cm.

   Solution:

   The image must be on the same side of the lens as the type (hence the image is virtual and $q = -75$ cm), and farther from the lens than the type (hence converging or positive lenses are prescribed).

   $$\frac{1}{f} = \frac{1}{25} - \frac{1}{75}, \quad f = +37.5 \text{ cm.} \qquad \text{Power} = \frac{1}{+0.375 \text{ m}} = +2.67 \text{ diopters.}$$

3. A projection lens of focal length 1 ft throws a picture of a slide 2×3 in. upon a screen 30 ft from the lens. Compute the dimensions of the image.

   Solution:

   Distance p of slide from lens: $\dfrac{1}{p} = \dfrac{1}{f} - \dfrac{1}{q} = \dfrac{1}{1} - \dfrac{1}{30} = \dfrac{29}{30}$

   Linear magnification of image $= \dfrac{q}{p} = \dfrac{30 \text{ ft}}{30/29 \text{ ft}} = 29$

   The length and width of the slide are each magnified 29 times.

   Size of image $= (29 \times 2 \text{ in.})(29 \times 3 \text{ in.}) = 58 \times 87 \text{ in.}$

4. A camera gives a clear image of a distant landscape when the lens is 8 in. from the plate. What adjustment is required to get a good photograph of a map placed 6 ft from the lens?

Solution:

When the camera is focused for distant objects (for parallel rays), the distance between lens and plate is the focal length of the lens, 8 in.

For an object 6 ft distant: $\dfrac{1}{q} = \dfrac{1}{f} - \dfrac{1}{p} = \dfrac{1}{8 \text{ in.}} - \dfrac{1}{72 \text{ in.}}$, $\quad q = 9$ in.

The lens should be moved away from the plate a distance of $(9 - 8)$ in. $= 1$ in.

5. With a given illumination and plate, the correct exposure for a camera lens set at $f/12$ is $1/5$ sec. What is the proper exposure time with the lens working at $f/4$?

Solution:

$f/12$ means that the diameter of the opening, or stop, of the lens is $1/12$ of the focal length; $f/4$ means that it is $1/4$ of the focal length.

The amount of light passing through the opening is proportional to its area, and therefore to the square of its diameter. As the diameter of the stop at $f/4$ is three times that at $f/12$, $3^2 = 9$ times as much light will pass through the lens at $f/4$, and the correct exposure at $f/4 = 1/9 \times$ exposure time at $f/12 = 1/45$ sec.

6. An engraver who has normal eyesight uses a converging lens of focal length 8 cm which he holds very close to his eye. At what distance from the work should the lens be placed, and what is the magnifying power of the lens?

Solution:

When a converging lens is used as a magnifying glass, the object is between the lens and the principal focal plane. The virtual, erect and enlarged image forms at the distance of distinct vision, 25 cm from the eye.

$$\frac{1}{p} + \frac{1}{q} = \frac{1}{f}, \quad \frac{1}{p} + \frac{1}{-25} = \frac{1}{8}, \quad p = \frac{200}{33} = 6.06 \text{ cm}$$

$$\text{Magnifying power} = q/p = 25/6.06 = 4.13 \text{ diameters}$$

Otherwise: By formula, magnifying power $= 25/f_{cm} + 1 = 25/8 + 1 = 4.13$ diameters.

7. In a compound microscope, the objective and eyepiece have focal lengths of $+0.8$ and $+2.5$ cm respectively. The real image $A'B'$ formed by the objective is 16 cm from the objective. Determine the total magnification if the eye is held close to the eyepiece and views the virtual image $A''B''$ at a distance of 25 cm.

Solution:

Let p_O = object distance from objective,
$\quad q_O$ = real-image distance from objective.

$$\frac{1}{p_O} = \frac{1}{f_O} - \frac{1}{q_O} = \frac{1}{0.8} - \frac{1}{16} = \frac{19}{16}, \quad p_O = \frac{16}{19} \text{ cm}$$

Linear magnification by objective

$$= \frac{q_O}{p_O} = \frac{16}{16/19} = 19$$

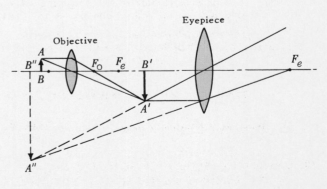

Magnifying power of eyepiece

$$= \frac{25}{f_e} + 1 = \frac{25}{2.5} + 1 = 11 \text{ diameters}$$

Magnifying power of instrument $= 19 \times 11 = 209$ diameters

8. Two positive lenses, having focal lengths of +2 and +5 cm respectively, are 14 cm apart. An object AB is placed 3 cm in front of the +2 lens. Determine the position and magnification of the final image $A''B''$ formed by this combination of lenses.

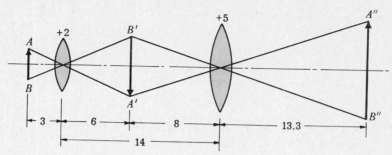

Solution:

To locate image $A'B'$ by +2 lens alone: $\dfrac{1}{q} = \dfrac{1}{f} - \dfrac{1}{p} = \dfrac{1}{2} - \dfrac{1}{3} = \dfrac{1}{6}$, $\quad q = 6$ cm

The image $A'B'$ is real, inverted, and 6 cm beyond the +2 lens.

To locate the final image $A''B''$: The image $A'B'$ is $(14-6)$ cm = 8 cm in front of the +5 lens and is taken as a real object for the +5 lens.

$\dfrac{1}{q'} = \dfrac{1}{5} - \dfrac{1}{8}$, $\quad q' = 13.3$ cm. $\qquad A''B''$ is real, erect, and 13.3 cm from +5 lens.

Total linear magnification $= \dfrac{A''B''}{AB} = \dfrac{A'B'}{AB} \times \dfrac{A''B''}{A'B'} = \dfrac{6}{3} \times \dfrac{13.3}{8} = 3.33$

9. A telephoto lens consists of a converging lens of focal length +6 cm placed 4 cm in front of a diverging lens of focal length −2.5 cm. (*a*) Locate the image of a very distant object. (*b*) Compare the size of the image formed by this lens combination with the size of the image that could be produced by the positive lens alone.

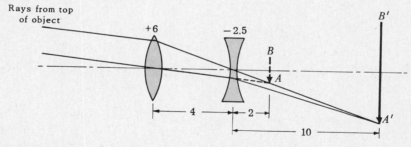

Solution:

(*a*) If the negative lens were not employed, the image AB would be formed at the principal focal plane of the +6 lens, 6 cm distant from the +6 lens. The negative lens decreases the convergence of the rays refracted by the positive lens and causes them to focus at $A'B'$ instead of at AB.

The image AB (that would have been formed by the +6 lens alone) is $(6-4) = 2$ cm beyond the −2.5 lens and is taken as the (virtual) object for the −2.5 lens. Then $p = -2$ cm (negative because AB is virtual).

$$\frac{1}{q} = \frac{1}{f} - \frac{1}{p} = -\frac{1}{2.5} + \frac{1}{2} = \frac{1}{10}, \quad q = +10 \text{ cm}$$

The final image $A'B'$ is real and 10 cm beyond the negative lens.

(*b*) Linear magnification by negative lens $= \dfrac{\text{size } A'B'}{\text{size } AB} = \dfrac{q}{p} = \dfrac{10 \text{ cm}}{2 \text{ cm}} = 5$

10. Compute the magnifying power of a telescope, having objective and eyepiece lenses of focal lengths +60 and +3 cm respectively, when focused for parallel rays.

Solution:

Magnifying power $= \dfrac{\text{focal length of objective}}{\text{focal length of eyepiece}} = \dfrac{60 \text{ cm}}{3 \text{ cm}} = 20$ diameters

SUPPLEMENTARY PROBLEMS

11. A certain farsighted person cannot see clearly objects closer to the eye than 60 cm. Determine the focal length and power of the spectacle lenses which will enable him to read a book at a distance of 25 cm.
   Ans. +42.9 cm, +2.33 diopters

12. A certain nearsighted person cannot see clearly objects beyond 50 cm from the eye. Determine the focal length and power of the glasses which will enable him to see distant objects clearly.
   Ans. −50 cm, −2 diopters

13. A projection lens is employed to produce pictures 7.5 × 10 ft from slides 3 × 4 in. on a screen 75 ft from the lens. Compute its focal length.   *Ans.* 29 in.

14. A camera gives a life-size picture of a flower when the lens is 20 in. from the plate. What is the distance between lens and plate when snapping a flock of birds high overhead?   *Ans.* 10 in.

15. What is the maximum stop rating of a camera lens having a focal length of +10 in. and a diameter of 2 in.? If the correct exposure at $f/6$ is 1/90 sec, what exposure is needed when the diaphragm is changed to $f/9$?
   Ans. $f/5$, 1/40 sec

16. What is the magnifying power of a lens of focal length +2 cm when used as a magnifying glass (or simple microscope)? The lens is held close to the eye, and the virtual image forms at the distance of distinct vision, 25 cm from the eye.   *Ans.* 13.5×

17. When the object distance from a converging lens is 5 in., a real image is formed 20 in. from the lens. What magnification is produced by this lens when it is used as a magnifying glass, the distance of most distinct vision being 10 in.?   *Ans.* 3.5×

18. In a compound microscope, the focal lengths of the objective and eyepiece are +0.5 and +2 cm respectively. The instrument is focused on an object 0.52 cm from the objective lens. Compute the magnifying power of the microscope if the virtual image is viewed by the eye at a distance of 25 cm.   *Ans.* 338×

19. A refracting astronomical telescope has a magnifying power of 150× when adjusted for minimum eyestrain using an eyepiece of focal length +1.2 in. (*a*) Determine the focal length of the objective lens. (*b*) How far apart must the two lenses be in order to project a real image of a distant object on a screen one foot from the eyepiece?   *Ans.* (*a*) +180 in., (*b*) 181.33 in.

20. The large telescope at Mt. Palomar has a concave objective mirror of diameter 200 in. and radius of curvature 150 ft. What is the magnifying power of the instrument when used with an eyepiece of focal length 0.5 in.?   *Ans.* 1800 diameters

21. An astronomical telescope, having an objective lens of focal length +80 cm, is focused on the moon. How much must the eyepiece be drawn out in order to focus on an object 40 meters distant?   *Ans.* 1.63 cm

22. A lens combination consists of two positive lenses, having focal lengths of +4 and +8 cm respectively, which are spaced 16 cm apart. Locate and describe the final image of an object placed 12 cm in front of the +4 lens.   *Ans.* 40 cm beyond +8 lens, real and erect

23. Two lenses, having focal lengths of +6 and −10 cm respectively, are spaced 1.5 cm apart. Locate and describe the image of an object 30 cm in front of the +6 lens.
   Ans. 15 cm beyond negative lens, real and inverted, 5/8 as large as the object

24. A telephoto lens consists of a positive lens of focal length +3.5 cm placed 2 cm in front of a negative lens of focal length −1.8 cm. (*a*) Locate the image of a very distant object. (*b*) Determine the focal length of the single lens which would form as large an image of a distant object as is formed by this lens combination.
   Ans. (*a*) Real image 9 cm in back of negative lens, (*b*) +21 cm

25. An opera glass has an objective of focal length +3.6 in. and a negative eyepiece of focal length −1.2 in. How far apart must the two lenses be in order to view with minimum eyestrain an object 36 ft distant?
   Ans. 2.4 in.

Chapter 40

Dispersion of Light

DISPERSION OF LIGHT. White light is composed of a large number of waves of different frequencies and wavelengths. Each component frequency produces a characteristic color sensation. The wavelengths (in air) comprising the visible spectrum range from about 780 mμ (7800 A) at the red end to about 380 mμ (3800 A) at the violet end.

The refractive index of transparent optical materials increases with decreasing wavelength, being greater for the shorter (violet) waves than for the longer (red) waves. Hence when a beam of white light passes through a refracting medium its component frequencies (colors) become separated, or *dispersed*, and spread out into a colored spectrum.

Chromatic aberration is due to the dispersion of white light in passing through a lens. This lens defect results in a blurred and colored image.

$$1 \text{ micron } (\mu) = 10^{-6} \text{ m}, \qquad 1 \text{ millimicron } (m\mu) = 10^{-9} \text{ m}, \qquad 1 \text{ angstrom } (A) = 10^{-10} \text{ m}.$$

SOLVED PROBLEMS

1. What angular dispersion between the C (red region) and F (blue region) spectral lines is produced by a flint-glass prism whose refracting angle is 12°? The refractive indices of the glass for the C and F lines are 1.644 and 1.664 respectively.

Solution:

Prisms are usually used in a position of minimum deviation, as shown. When the prism angle A is small, the angular deviation D is also small. Since the sines of small angles are very nearly proportional to their angles, when the prism angle is small the equation

$n = \dfrac{\sin \frac{1}{2}(A + D)}{\sin \frac{1}{2} A}$ may be simplified to $n = \dfrac{A + D}{A}$ or $D = A(n - 1)$.

Dispersion between C and F lines = deviation of F line − deviation of C line

$$= D_F - D_C = A(n_F - 1) - A(n_C - 1)$$
$$= A(n_F - n_C) = 12°(1.664 - 1.644) = 0.24°$$

2. It is required to fit a 10° crown-glass prism with a flint-glass prism so as to achromatize the region between the C and F spectral lines. (a) What must be the angle of the flint-glass prism? (b) What is the deviation produced by the prism combination, as computed for the D line? (The D line is located in the yellow region of the spectrum and is taken as the mean ray between the C and F lines.)

Indices of the crown glass for C, D, F lines: $n_C = 1.514$, $n_D = 1.517$, $n_F = 1.523$.
Indices of the flint glass for C, D, F lines: $n'_C = 1.644$, $n'_D = 1.650$, $n'_F = 1.664$.

Solution:

(a) Dispersion by each prism between C and F lines = deviation of F − deviation of C
Dispersion by crown-glass prism $= A(n_F - 1) - A(n_C - 1) = A(n_F - n_C)$
Dispersion by flint-glass prism $= A'(n'_F - 1) - A'(n'_C - 1) = A'(n'_F - n'_C)$

231

Achromatism obtains when the dispersion produced by the crown-glass prism equals (annuls) that produced by the flint-glass prism. Then

$$A(n_F - n_C) = A'(n_F' - n_C')$$
$$10°(1.523 - 1.514) = A'(1.664 - 1.644) \qquad A' = 4.5°$$

(b) Resultant deviation of D line produced by the prism combination

$$= \text{deviation of } D \text{ line by crown-glass prism} - \text{deviation of } D \text{ line by flint}$$
$$= A(n_D - 1) - A'(n_D' - 1) = 10°(1.517 - 1) - 4.5°(1.650 - 1) = 2.24°$$

3. It is desired to fit a $12°$ crown-glass prism with a flint-glass prism so that the combination will produce dispersion, but without deviation of the mean D line. The indices of the crown and flint glass for the D line are respectively 1.520 and 1.650. What should be the angle of the flint-glass prism?

Solution:

Deviation of D line by crown-glass prism $=$ deviation of D line by flint

$$A(n_D - 1) = A'(n_D' - 1)$$
$$12°(1.520 - 1) = A'(1.650 - 1)$$
$$A' = 9.6°$$

4. Compute the dispersive power of a light flint glass in the region between the C and F spectral lines. The D line is taken as the mean ray between lines C and F. Indices of the glass for C, D, F lines: $n_C = 1.571$, $n_D = 1.575$, $n_F = 1.585$.

Solution:

Dispersive power of the flint glass between the Fraunhofer lines C and F

$$= \frac{\text{dispersion by small-angle prism between the } C \text{ and } F \text{ lines}}{\text{deviation of the mean } D \text{ line}}$$

$$= \frac{A(n_F - n_C)}{A(n_D - 1)} = \frac{n_F - n_C}{n_D - 1} = \frac{1.585 - 1.571}{1.575 - 1.000} = 0.0243$$

SUPPLEMENTARY PROBLEMS

5. A beam of white light is incident upon water at an angle of $60°$. The indices of water for the Fraunhofer lines A (red region) and H (violet region) are 1.330 and 1.344 respectively. Calculate the angular separation of the A and H lines in water.   *Ans.* $0.50°$ or $30'$

6. A parallel beam of white light strikes a double convex lens having faces of radii $+32$ and $+48$ cm. The refractive indices of the glass for the A (red region) and H (violet region) spectral lines are respectively 1.578 and 1.614. Determine the distance between the focal points of the red and violet radiations.   *Ans.* 1.95 cm

7. The blue F line of the hydrogen spectrum has a wavelength of 486.1 millimicrons. (a) Express this length in meters, in microns, and in angstroms. (b) What is the frequency of this radiation? The speed of light in air is 3.00×10^8 m/sec.   *Ans.* 4.861×10^{-7} m, 0.4861 micron, 4861 angstroms, 6.17×10^{14} vib/sec

8. A $10°$ prism is made of the heaviest flint glass having refractive indices of 1.879 and 1.919 for the C and F lines respectively. Compute the dispersion (degrees) and the length (cm) of the spectrum between the C and F lines produced by the prism on a screen 3 meters distant and normal to the average direction of the emerging light.   *Ans.* $0.40°$ or $24'$, 2.1 cm

9. An achromatic lens having a focal length of $+20$ cm is to be constructed by combining a crown-glass lens with a flint-glass lens. What must be the focal lengths (f_1 and f_2) of the component lenses if the dispersive powers (δ_1 and δ_2) of the crown and flint glass used are 0.0158 and 0.0324 respectively?
Hint: Achromatism obtains when $\delta_1/f_1 + \delta_2/f_2 = 0$ or $f_2 = -(\delta_2/\delta_1)f_1$.
Ans. $+10.2$ cm (crown), -20.9 cm (flint)

Chapter 41

Interference and Diffraction of Light

INTERFERENCE AND DIFFRACTION. Consider that two trains of waves originate from a point source and have the same wavelength and amplitude. If the waves are superposed, destructive interference (annulment, darkness) occurs at points where they meet in opposite phase, and constructive interference (reenforcement, brightness) occurs where they meet in the same phase.

Diffraction refers to the spreading of light waves around the edges of apertures and opaque obstacles, and to the interference patterns produced by this deviation of light from a rectilinear path.

DIFFRACTION BY A SINGLE SLIT: $\qquad m\lambda = s \sin\theta \qquad$ for normal incidence

where m = order of the diffracted band, λ = wavelength of the light, s = width of the slit, θ = angle between the normal to the slit and the rays which cancel out to give the mth **dark** band.

DIFFRACTION GRATING EQUATION: $\qquad m\lambda = d \sin\theta \qquad$ for normal incidence

where m = order of the diffracted image, λ = wavelength of the light, d = grating space, θ = angle between the diffracted light and the normal to the grating.

DIFFRACTION OF X–RAYS by reflection from a crystal: $\qquad m\lambda = 2d \sin\theta$

where m = order of the diffracted image, λ = wavelength of the radiation, d = distance between atomic or ionic planes in the crystal, θ = angle (between the x-ray beam and the face of the crystal) at which the diffracted beam has maximum intensity, often called the glancing angle.

SOLVED PROBLEMS

1. Monochromatic light from a point source illuminates two parallel and narrow slits, the centers of the slit openings being 0.8 mm apart. An interference pattern forms on a screen placed parallel to the plane of the slits and 50 cm away. The distance between two adjacent dark interference fringes is 0.304 mm. Compute the wavelength λ of the light.

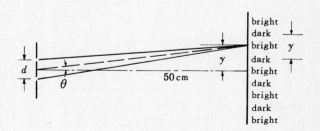

Solution:

Let d = distance between the slits. The distance y between adjacent dark fringes is the same as the distance from the central bright fringe to the first order bright fringe, provided the angles are small, as in this problem, and $\sin\theta$ can be taken equal to $\tan\theta$.

$$m\lambda = d \sin\theta, \qquad 1 \times \lambda = .08 \text{ cm} \times .0304/50, \qquad \lambda = 4.86 \times 10^{-5} \text{ cm} = 486 \text{ m}\mu = 4860 \text{ A}$$

2. A slight movement of one of the two mirrors of a Michelson interferometer causes 150 dark fringes to sweep across the field when blue light of wavelength 4800 angstroms illuminates the instrument. Through what distance was the mirror moved?

Solution:

Consider that the field is initially dark. Now if the mirror is moved $\frac{1}{2}\lambda$ distance, the change of optical path of light reflected by this mirror is $2 \times \frac{1}{2}\lambda = 1\lambda$ and the field again will appear dark. It follows that a displacement of 150 dark fringes is observed when the mirror moves through $150(\frac{1}{2}\lambda) = 150(2400 \text{ A}) = .036 \text{ mm}$.

3. Two plane glass plates touch at one edge and are separated at the opposite edge by a strip of gold leaf. When the air wedge is examined with sodium light of wavelength 5893 angstroms reflected normally from its two surfaces, 12 dark interference fringes are observed. What is the thickness of the gold leaf?

Solution: The difference in thickness of the air film at two adjacent dark fringes is $\frac{1}{2}\lambda$.

Thickness of gold leaf $= 12(\frac{1}{2} \times 5.893 \times 10^{-5} \text{ cm}) = 3.54 \times 10^{-4} \text{ cm}$

4. A convex lens is placed on a plane glass surface and illuminated from above with red light of wavelength 6700 angstroms. The interference pattern, caused by light reflected from the convex and plane surfaces of the air film, consists of a dark spot at the point of contact surrounded by bright and dark rings, the radius r of the 20th dark ring being 1.1 cm. Compute the radius of curvature R of the lens.

Solution:

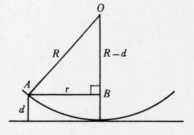

The reflections at the convex and plane surfaces of the air film are of different nature in that reflection at the convex surface takes place at the boundary of a medium (air) of lower refractive index, while reflection at the plane surface occurs at the boundary of a medium (glass) of higher refractive index. In such cases, the act of reflection by itself involves a phase displacement of $\frac{1}{2}\lambda$ between the two reflected rays.

Then the total phase displacement between light reflected at the convex and plane surfaces of the air film is $\frac{1}{2}\lambda$ **plus** the path difference, the latter (for normal incidence) being equal at any point to twice the thickness of the air film. When this total **phase displacement** is $1/2\ \lambda,\ 3/2\ \lambda,\ 5/2\ \lambda$, etc., there is annulment or darkness; when it is $1\lambda,\ 2\lambda,\ 3\lambda$, etc., there is reenforcement or brightness. It follows that darkness occurs at points where the thickness of the **air film** is $0\ \lambda$ (point of contact, phase displacement $= 1/2\ \lambda$), $1/2\ \lambda$ (phase displacement $= \frac{1}{2}\lambda + 2 \times \frac{1}{2}\lambda = 3/2\ \lambda$), 1λ (phase displacement $= \frac{1}{2}\lambda + 2 \times 1\lambda = 5/2\ \lambda$), $3/2\ \lambda,\ 2\lambda$, etc.; and brightness occurs where the thickness of the **air film** is $1/4\ \lambda$ (phase displacement $= 1\lambda$), $3/4\ \lambda,\ 5/4\ \lambda$, etc.

The difference in thickness of the air film at two adjacent dark rings is $\frac{1}{2}\lambda$. Hence its thickness d at the 20th dark ring is $d = 20(\frac{1}{2} \times .000067 \text{ cm}) = .00067 \text{ cm}$.

Let O = center of curvature of the lens. Then in right triangle ABO:

$$R^2 = r^2 + (R-d)^2 = r^2 + R^2 - 2Rd + d^2 \qquad \text{or} \qquad 2Rd = r^2 + d^2$$

As d^2 is negligible compared with r^2, $\quad R = \dfrac{r^2}{2d} = \dfrac{(1.1 \text{ cm})^2}{2(.00067 \text{ cm})} = 903 \text{ cm.}$

5. What is the least thickness of a soap film which will appear black when viewed with sodium light reflected normally? The refractive index of the soap solution is 1.38 for sodium light.

Solution:

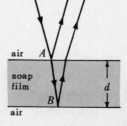

The retardation (phase displacement) of ray b relative to ray a is $\frac{1}{2}\lambda$ due to reflection itself, and $2dn$ due to the path difference (for normal incidence), where d is the film thickness. When this retardation ($\frac{1}{2}\lambda + 2dn$) is $1/2\ \lambda,\ 3/2\ \lambda$, etc., there is annulment and darkness; when it is $1\lambda,\ 2\lambda,\ 3\lambda$, etc., there is reenforcement and brightness. Hence the film of minimum thickness (other than zero thickness) which will appear black in reflected light produces a retardation of $3/2\ \lambda$.

$$3/2\ \lambda = 1/2\ \lambda + 2dn, \qquad d = \frac{\lambda}{2n} = \frac{5893 \times 10^{-8} \text{ cm}}{2 \times 1.38} = 2.14 \times 10^{-5} \text{ cm}$$

6. A single slit of width 0.1 mm is illuminated by parallel light of wavelength 6000 A, and diffraction bands are observed on a screen 40 cm from the slit. How far is the third dark band from the central bright band?

Solution:

For a single slit, the **dark** bands are located by the equation $m\lambda = s \sin\theta$.

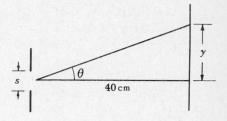

$$\sin\theta = \frac{m\lambda}{s} = \frac{3(6 \times 10^{-7}\text{ m})}{10^{-4}\text{ m}} = .018$$

Since θ is a very small angle, $\tan\theta$ is approximately equal to $\sin\theta$. Hence the required distance y on the screen is

$$y = 40\text{ cm} \times \tan\theta = 40\text{ cm} \times .018 = 0.72\text{ cm}$$

7. Red light falls normally on a diffraction grating ruled 4000 lines/cm, and the second order image is diffracted $34°$ from the normal. Compute the wavelength of the light.

Solution:

$$\lambda = \frac{d\sin\theta}{m} = \frac{1/4000\text{ cm} \times 0.559}{2} = 6.99 \times 10^{-5}\text{ cm} = 699\text{ m}\mu = 6990\text{ A}$$

8. The figure shows a laboratory setup for grating experiments. The diffraction grating has 5000 lines/cm and is 1 meter from the slit which is illuminated with sodium light. On either side of the slit, and parallel to the grating, are two meter sticks. The eye, placed close to the grating, sees virtual images of the slit as if projected along the lengths of the meter stick. Determine the wavelength of the light if each first order image is 31 cm from the slit.

Solution:

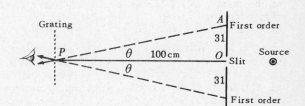

$$\sin\theta = \frac{OA}{PA} = \frac{31}{\sqrt{(100)^2 + (31)^2}}$$
$$= 0.295$$

$$\lambda = \frac{d\sin\theta}{m} = \frac{0.0002\text{ cm} \times 0.295}{1}$$
$$= 59 \times 10^{-6}\text{ cm} = 590\text{ m}\mu = 5900\text{ A}$$

9. Green light of wavelength 5400 angstroms is diffracted by a grating ruled 2000 lines/cm. (*a*) Compute the angular deviation of the 3rd order image. (*b*) Is a 10th order image possible?

Solution:

(*a*) $\sin\theta_3 = \dfrac{m\lambda}{d} = \dfrac{3(5.4 \times 10^{-5}\text{ cm})}{5 \times 10^{-4}\text{ cm}} = 0.324, \qquad \theta = 18.9°$

(*b*) $\sin\theta_{10} = \dfrac{m\lambda}{d} = \dfrac{10(5.4 \times 10^{-5}\text{ cm})}{5 \times 10^{-4}\text{ cm}} = 1.08$ (impossible)

Since the value of $\sin\theta$ cannot exceed 1, a 10th order image is impossible.

10. Show that, in a spectrum of white light obtained with a grating, the red ($\lambda_r = 7000$ angstroms) of the 2nd order overlaps the violet ($\lambda_v = 4000$ angstroms) of the 3rd order.

Solution:

For red of 2nd order: $\qquad \sin\theta_{r_2} = \dfrac{m\lambda_r}{d} = \dfrac{2 \times 0.00007}{d} = \dfrac{0.00014}{d}$

For violet of 3rd order: $\qquad \sin\theta_{v_3} = \dfrac{m\lambda_v}{d} = \dfrac{3 \times 0.00004}{d} = \dfrac{0.00012}{d}$

As $\sin\theta_{r_2} > \sin\theta_{v_3}$, $\theta_{r_2} > \theta_{v_3}$. Thus the angle of diffraction of red in the 2nd order is greater than that of violet in the 3rd order.

11. A parallel beam of x-rays is diffracted by a rock salt crystal, the first order maximum being obtained when the glancing angle of incidence is $6° 50'$. The distance between the ionic planes of the crystal is 2.81×10^{-8} cm. Calculate the wavelength of the radiation.

Solution:

$$\lambda = \frac{2d \sin \theta}{m} = \frac{2 \times 2.81 \times 10^{-8} \text{ cm} \times 0.119}{1} = 0.669 \times 10^{-8} \text{ cm} = 0.669 \text{ A}$$

SUPPLEMENTARY PROBLEMS

12. Red light of wavelength 6438 angstroms, from a point source, passes through two parallel and narrow slits which are 1 mm apart. Determine the distance between the central bright fringe and the third dark interference fringe formed on a screen parallel to the plane of the slits and 1 meter away.   *Ans.* 1.61 mm

13. Two flat glass plates are pressed together at the top edge and separated at the bottom edge by a strip of tinfoil. The air wedge is examined in yellow sodium light (wavelength 5893 angstroms) reflected normally from its two surfaces, and 42 dark interference fringes are observed. Compute the thickness of the tinfoil. *Ans.* 1.24×10^{-3} cm

14. A mixture of yellow light of wavelength 5800 angstroms and blue light of wavelength 4500 angstroms is incident normally on an air film .00029 mm thick. What is the color of the reflected light?   *Ans.* blue

15. A transparent film of glass of refractive index 1.50 is introduced normally in the path of one of the interfering beams of a Michelson interferometer which is illuminated with blue light of wavelength 486 mμ. This causes 500 dark fringes to sweep across the field. Determine the thickness of the film. [Considering that the light passes twice through the glass film, the increased optical path of light reflected by one of the mirrors is $2(n-1)d$, where n = refractive index of the glass, 1 = refractive index of the air it replaces, and d = thickness of the film.]   *Ans.* .0243 cm

16. A single slit of width 0.14 mm is illuminated by monochromatic light and diffraction bands are observed on a screen 200 cm away. If the second dark band is 1.6 cm from the central bright band, what is the wavelength of the light?   *Ans.* 5600 A

17. Green light of wavelength 5000 angstroms is incident normally on a grating, and the second order image is diffracted $32°$ from the normal. How many lines/cm are marked on the grating?   *Ans.* 5300 lines/cm

18. A narrow beam of yellow light of wavelength 6000 angstroms is incident normally on a diffraction grating ruled 2000 lines/cm, and images are formed on a screen parallel to the grating and 1 meter distant. Compute the distance along the screen from the central bright line to the first order lines.   *Ans.* 12.1 cm

19. Blue light of wavelength 4700 angstroms is diffracted by a grating ruled 5000 lines/cm. (*a*) Compute the angular deviation of the 2nd order image. (*b*) What is the highest order image theoretically possible with this wavelength and grating?   *Ans.* $28°$, 4th

20. Determine the ratio of the wavelengths of two spectral lines if the 2nd order image of one line coincides with the 3rd order image of the other line, both lines being examined by means of the same grating. *Ans.* 3:2

21. A spectrum of white light is obtained with a grating ruled 2500 lines/cm. Compute the angular separation between the violet (λ_v = 4000 angstroms) and red (λ_r = 7000 angstroms) in the (*a*) first order, (*b*) second order. (*c*) Does yellow (λ_y = 6000 angstroms) in the third order overlap the violet in the fourth order? *Ans.* $4° 20'$, $8° 57'$, yes

22. A spectrum of the sun's radiation in the infrared region is produced by a grating. What is the wavelength being studied, if the infrared line in the first order occurs at an angle of $25°$ with the normal, and the 4th order image of the hydrogen line of wavelength 6563 angstroms occurs at $30°$?   *Ans.* 22,200 A

23. How far apart are the diffracting planes in a NaCl crystal for which x-rays of wavelength 1.54 A make a glancing angle θ of $15° 54'$ in the first order?   *Ans.* 2.81 A

Chapter 42

Quantum Physics, Relativity, Wave Mechanics

QUANTUM THEORY. Radiant energy of frequency f can be emitted or absorbed only in discrete amounts that are integer multiples of hf, where h is Planck's constant. Each package or quantum of radiant energy is given by

$$W = hf$$

where W is the energy of the quantum in joules, Planck's constant $h = 6.624 \times 10^{-34}$ joule-sec, and f is the frequency of the radiation.

A PHOTON is a quantum of electromagnetic energy. All photons do not have the same energy. Thus blue light comes in larger packages than does red light. The blue light has a shorter wavelength and hence a higher frequency.

Two sources of light of the same frequency (i.e. of the same color) emit identical photons of energy hf. A bright source emits more photons per second than does a weak source of the same color, but the individual photons from the two sources have the same energy.

PHOTOELECTRIC EFFECT. When light is incident on a metallic surface, under certain conditions electrons are ejected. Consider that a photon of energy hf collides with an electron at or near the surface of a metal, that the photon transfers all its energy hf to the electron, and that the minimum energy (work function) required to free the electron from the surface is W_{min}. Then the maximum kinetic energy $\frac{1}{2}mv_{max}^2$ of the ejected electron is given by Einstein's photoelectric equation

$$\tfrac{1}{2}mv_{max}^2 = hf - W_{min}$$

The energy of the ejected electron may be found by determining what potential difference V must be applied to stop its motion; then $\frac{1}{2}mv^2 = Ve$.

For any surface, the light must be of short enough wavelength so that the photon hf has enough energy to eject the electron. At the threshold, the photon's energy just equals the work function. If the frequency is too low, hf is insufficient and not a single photoelectron will be ejected, regardless of the intensity of the source. For ordinary metals the threshold lies in the visible or ultraviolet. X-rays will always eject photoelectrons; far infrared or heat photons will never do so.

BOHR'S THEORY OF THE HYDROGEN ATOM. To account for the line spectrum of the hydrogen atom, Bohr made three assumptions:

 (*1*) The electron can exist in certain orbits without radiating energy, even though radiation would be expected because of the centripetal acceleration.

 (*2*) The allowed orbits are those for which 2π times the angular momentum ($2\pi I\omega$) is an integral multiple of Planck's constant h, i.e.,

$$2\pi I\omega = nh$$

 where I = moment of inertia = mr^2, ω = angular velocity of electron in orbit, n = an integer (1, 2, 3, ...).

 (*3*) If the electron goes from one orbit of energy W_2 to another orbit of lower energy W_1, a photon of energy $hf = W_2 - W_1$ is radiated.

The Bohr theory was later extended and applied to a few more complex atoms.

In wave mechanics the concept of definite electronic orbits about the nucleus has been discarded, but the idea of different energy levels for the atom remains.

RELATIVITY.

1. **The special theory of relativity** is concerned with bodies which are in **uniform** motion relative to each other. Einstein's postulates are:

   (*a*) All motion is relative. It is impossible to determine absolute motion.

   (*b*) The measured speed of light in free space is constant, independent of the motion of the source or the motion of the observer.

2. **Variation of mass** is predicted by the special theory. The mass of a moving body is larger than its mass when at rest.

$$m = \frac{m_O}{\sqrt{1 - v^2/c^2}}$$

where m = mass when moving, m_O = mass when at rest, v = speed of body relative to observer, c = speed of light = 2.998×10^8 m/sec.

   A body cannot travel faster than the speed of light, since its mass would then tend toward infinity and an infinite force would be needed to accelerate it to a higher speed.

3. **Energy and mass are equivalent**. If a body has rest mass m_O, and mass m when moving with speed v, its kinetic energy is

$$W_k = (m - m_O)c^2$$

where $m = m_O/\sqrt{1 - v^2/c^2}$. Thus the kinetic energy of a body equals its change of mass times c^2.

   In general, mass m and energy W are interchangeable according to the equation

$$W = mc^2$$

   Thus 1 kg of mass, if annihilated, would be replaced by $(3 \times 10^8)^2$ joules of energy.

4. **The general theory of relativity** is concerned with bodies which are accelerated relative to each other, and leads to a new concept of gravitation, and to corrections to Newton's Second Law. These effects are observable only in large-scale astronomical phenomena.

WAVE MECHANICS.

1. The equivalence of mass and energy given by $W = mc^2$ indicates that a photon of energy $hf = h(c/\lambda)$ may be considered as a particle of mass m given by $hf = mc^2$ or

$$m = hf/c^2 = h/c\lambda,$$

and the wavelength of the photon, which has the speed of light c, may be expressed in terms of its momentum mc,

$$\lambda = h/mc$$

   The particle nature of radiation was confirmed by Compton's scattering experiment in which x-ray photons are considered as particles having energy hf and momentum h/λ.

2. Similarly, a moving particle, such as an electron, exhibits wave characteristics and the wavelength λ associated with a particle of mass m moving with speed v is

$$\lambda = h/mv$$

   This concept was suggested by de Broglie and confirmed by Davisson and Germer who showed that electrons produce diffraction patterns when projected upon a single-crystal nickel target, and by G.P. Thomson who secured diffraction of electrons by thin films.

   The **electron microscope** has a much higher resolving power than does an ordinary microscope. By applying sufficient potential difference, the electron velocities are made large, and the associated wavelengths are small compared with the wavelengths of visible light. Just as in an ordinary microscope, resolving power varies inversely as the wavelength used.

SOLVED PROBLEMS

1. Compute the energy W of a photon of red light of wavelength 6000 angstroms.
Solution:

$$W = hf = h\frac{c}{\lambda} = 6.62 \times 10^{-34} \text{ joule-sec} \times \frac{3 \times 10^8 \text{ m/sec}}{6000 \times 10^{-10} \text{ m}} = 3.31 \times 10^{-19} \text{ joule}$$

2. What potential difference must be applied to stop the fastest photoelectrons emitted by a nickel surface under the action of ultraviolet light of wavelength 2000 angstroms? The work function of nickel is 5.01 ev.
Solution:

Energy of photon $= hf = h\dfrac{c}{\lambda}$

$$= 6.62 \times 10^{-34} \text{ joule-sec} \times \frac{3 \times 10^8 \text{ m/sec}}{2000 \times 10^{-10} \text{ m}} \times \frac{1 \text{ ev}}{1.60 \times 10^{-19} \text{ joule}} = 6.21 \text{ ev}$$

Energy of emitted electron $= 6.21 \text{ ev} - 5.01 \text{ ev} = 1.20 \text{ ev}.$
Hence a negative retarding potential difference of 1.20 volts is required.

3. Will photoelectrons be emitted by a copper surface, of work function 4.4 ev, when illuminated by visible light?
Solution:

Threshold $\lambda = \dfrac{c}{f} = \dfrac{hc}{hf} = \dfrac{(6.62 \times 10^{-34} \text{ joule-sec})(3 \times 10^8 \text{ m/sec})}{4.4(1.60 \times 10^{-19}) \text{ joule}} = 2.82 \times 10^{-7} \text{ m} = 2820 \text{ A}$

Hence visible light (4000 A to 7600 A) cannot eject photoelectrons from copper.

4. The wavelength of the yellow sodium D_1 line is 5896 angstroms. What is the difference in energy between the two energy levels involved in the emission or absorption of this line?
Solution:

$$\Delta W = hf = h\frac{c}{\lambda} = 6.62 \times 10^{-34} \text{ joule-sec} \times \frac{3 \times 10^{18} \text{ A/sec}}{5896 \text{ A}} = 3.37 \times 10^{-19} \text{ joule}$$

5. Employ Bohr's theory of the hydrogen atom to derive expressions for (a) the radii r of the electronic orbits, (b) the energy W of the electron in an orbit of radius r, (c) the energy radiated by the hydrogen atom when the electron passes from an outer to an inner orbit.
Solution:

(a) Assume the electron of mass m and charge $-e$ coul revolves with speed v m/sec and radius r meters about the nucleus of charge $+e$ coul. The attractive force between them in mks units is $F = ke^2/r^2$ nt, where $k = 9 \times 10^9$ nt-m^2/coul^2, and this equals the centripetal force $F = mv^2/r$ which maintains the electron in its circular path. Since $v = r\omega$, where ω is the angular speed in radians/sec,

$$ke^2/r^2 = mv^2/r = m\omega^2 r \qquad \text{or} \qquad ke^2/r = m\omega^2 r^2 \qquad (1)$$

The total energy W of the revolving electron is, using (1),

$$W = \text{P.E.} + \text{K.E.} = -eV + \tfrac{1}{2}mv^2 = -e(ke/r) + \tfrac{1}{2}m(\omega r)^2 = -k\frac{e^2}{2r} \qquad (2)$$

The negative sign indicates that W is zero when r becomes infinite and that W becomes increasingly negative (smaller) as the electron approaches the nucleus, i.e. the atom radiates (loses) energy as the electron jumps into orbits of smaller r.

Bohr assumed the allowed orbits are those for which the angular momentum of the electron is $I\omega = nh/2\pi$, where n is an integer and h is Planck's constant. Since $I = mr^2$, the allowed orbits are such that $mr^2\omega = nh/2\pi$. Putting $\omega = nh/2\pi mr^2$ in equation (1), $ke^2/r = m(nh/2\pi mr^2)^2 r^2$, from which the allowed radii of the electronic orbits are determined by

$$r = \frac{1}{k}\frac{n^2h^2}{4\pi^2me^2}$$

(b) Substituting in (2),

$$W = -k^2 \frac{2\pi^2 m e^4}{n^2 h^2}$$

which is the energy of the electron rotating in the nth orbit.

(c) When the electron jumps from a higher n_2th orbit to a lower n_1th orbit, the energy of the emitted photon is hf and

$$W_2 - W_1 = hf = \frac{k^2 2\pi^2 m e^4}{h^2}\left(\frac{1}{n_1^2} - \frac{1}{n_2^2}\right).$$

Since $f = \frac{c}{\lambda}$,

$$\frac{1}{\lambda} = \frac{k^2 2\pi^2 m e^4}{h^3 c}\left(\frac{1}{n_1^2} - \frac{1}{n_2^2}\right).$$

6. Compute the mass of an electron traveling at half the speed of light.

   Solution:

$$m = \frac{m_O}{\sqrt{1 - v^2/c^2}} = \frac{m_O}{\sqrt{1 - (\tfrac{1}{2}c)^2/c^2}} = \frac{m_O}{\sqrt{1 - \tfrac{1}{4}}} = \frac{m_O}{\sqrt{3/4}}$$

$$= 1.154\, m_O = 1.154\,(9.11 \times 10^{-31}\text{ kg}) = 1.05 \times 10^{-30}\text{ kg}$$

7. If one gram of matter could be converted entirely into energy, what would be the value of the energy so produced, at 1¢ per kilowatt-hour?

   Solution:

$$W = mc^2 = (10^{-3}\text{ kg})(3 \times 10^8\text{ m/sec})^2 = 9 \times 10^{13}\text{ joules}$$

$$\text{Value of energy} = 9 \times 10^{13}\text{ joules} \times \frac{1\text{ kw-hr}}{3.6 \times 10^6\text{ joules}} \times \frac{\$.01}{1\text{ kw-hr}} = \$250,000$$

8. Compute the mass m and speed v of electrons having kinetic energy 1.5 Mev.

   Solution:

$$W_k = (m - m_O)c^2$$

$$(1.5 \times 10^6\text{ ev})(1.60 \times 10^{-19}\text{ joule/ev}) = (m - 9.11 \times 10^{-31}\text{ kg})(3 \times 10^8\text{ m/sec})^2$$

$$m = 35.8 \times 10^{-31}\text{ kg, nearly four times rest mass}$$

From $m = \dfrac{m_O}{\sqrt{1 - v^2/c^2}}$ obtain $v = c\sqrt{1 - (m_O/m)^2} = 3 \times 10^8\sqrt{1 - (9.11/35.8)^2} = 2.90 \times 10^8\ \dfrac{\text{m}}{\text{sec}}$.

9. Determine the energy required to give an electron a speed 0.9 that of light, starting from rest.

   Solution:

$$W_k = c^2(m - m_O) = c^2\left(\frac{m_O}{\sqrt{1 - v^2/c^2}} - m_O\right) = m_O c^2\left(\frac{1}{\sqrt{1 - v^2/c^2}} - 1\right)$$

$$= (9.11 \times 10^{-31}\text{ kg})(3 \times 10^8\text{ m/sec})^2\left(\frac{1}{\sqrt{1 - (0.9)^2}} - 1\right) = 1.061 \times 10^{-13}\text{ joule} = 6.63 \times 10^5\text{ ev}$$

10. Show that $W_k = (m - m_O)c^2$ reduces to $W_k = \tfrac{1}{2}m_O v^2$ when v is very much smaller than c.

    Solution:

$$W_k = (m - m_O)c^2 = \left(\frac{m_O}{\sqrt{1 - v^2/c^2}} - m_O\right)c^2 = m_O c^2\left[(1 - v^2/c^2)^{-1/2} - 1\right]$$

Let $b = -v^2/c^2$ and expand $(1 + b)^{-1/2}$ by the binomial theorem. Then

$$(1 + b)^{-1/2} = 1 + (-1/2)b + \frac{(-1/2)(-3/2)}{2!}b^2 + \ldots = 1 + \frac{1}{2}\frac{v^2}{c^2} + \frac{3}{8}\frac{v^4}{c^4} + \ldots$$

and

$$W_k = m_O c^2\left[(1 + \frac{1}{2}\frac{v^2}{c^2} + \frac{3}{8}\frac{v^4}{c^4} + \ldots) - 1\right] = \frac{1}{2}m_O v^2 + \frac{3}{8}m_O v^2\frac{v^2}{c^2} + \ldots$$

If v is very much smaller than c, the terms after $\tfrac{1}{2}m_O v^2$ are negligibly small and we may write $W_k = \tfrac{1}{2}m_O v^2$.

11. Compute the wavelength associated with electrons whose speed is .01 the speed of light.

Solution:

$$\lambda = \frac{h}{mv} = \frac{6.62 \times 10^{-34} \text{ joule-sec}}{(9.11 \times 10^{-31} \text{ kg})(10^{-2} \times 3 \times 10^{8} \text{ m/sec})} = 2.42 \times 10^{-10} \text{ m} = 2.42 \text{ A}$$

Since here v is small compared with c, m can be taken equal to m_O.

12. What potential difference is required in an electron microscope to give electrons a wavelength of 0.5 angstrom?

Solution:

$$\text{K.E. of electron} = \tfrac{1}{2} mv^2 = \tfrac{1}{2} m \left(\frac{h}{m\lambda}\right)^2 = \frac{h^2}{2m\lambda^2} \qquad (\text{since } \lambda = \frac{h}{mv})$$

$$= \frac{(6.62 \times 10^{-34} \text{ joule-sec})^2}{2(9.11 \times 10^{-31} \text{ kg})(0.5 \times 10^{-10} \text{ m})^2} \times \frac{1 \text{ ev}}{1.60 \times 10^{-19} \text{ joule}} = 601 \text{ ev}$$

Hence the required potential difference is 601 volts.

SUPPLEMENTARY PROBLEMS

13. Compute the energy of a photon of blue light of wavelength 4500 angstroms, in joules and in electron-volts. *Ans.* 4.41×10^{-19} joule, 2.76 ev

14. Determine the wavelength of a photon of energy 600 ev. *Ans.* 20.7 A

15. What is the work function of sodium metal if the photoelectric threshold wavelength is 6800 A? *Ans.* 1.83 ev

16. Determine the maximum kinetic energy of photoelectrons ejected from a potassium surface by ultraviolet light of wavelength 2000 A. What retarding potential difference is required to stop the emission of electrons? The photoelectric threshold wavelength of potassium is 4400 A. *Ans.* 3.39 ev, 3.39 v

17. With what speed will the fastest photoelectrons be emitted from a surface whose threshold wavelength is 6000 A, when the surface is illuminated with light of wavelength 4000 A? *Ans.* 6.03×10^{5} m/sec

18. Electrons with maximum kinetic energy of 3 ev are ejected from a metal surface by ultraviolet radiation of wavelength 1500 A. Determine the work function of the metal, the threshold wavelength of the metal, and the retarding potential difference required to stop the emission of electrons. *Ans.* 5.28 ev, 2350 A or 235 mμ, 3 v

19. At what speed must a particle move in order to double its rest mass? *Ans.* 2.60×10^{8} m/sec

20. At what potential difference must an x-ray tube be operated in order that the shortest wavelength produced be 0.5 angstrom? *Ans.* 2.48×10^{4} v

21. Compute the rest mass energy of an electron. *Ans.* 0.512 Mev

22. Determine the mass and speed of an electron having kinetic energy 100 Kev (10^5 ev). *Ans.* 1.09×10^{-30} kg, 1.64×10^{8} m/sec

23. (a) For a particle of rest mass m_O and speed v, give formulas for the total energy W_t, the kinetic energy W_k, and the momentum p. (b) Show that $W_t^2 = (W_k + m_O c^2)^2 = p^2 c^2 + m_O^2 c^4$. (c) Show that $v W_t = p c^2$. (d) Show that $p^2 c^2 = 2 m_O c^2 W_k + W_k^2$.

Ans. $W_t = \dfrac{m_O c^2}{\sqrt{1 - v^2/c^2}}$, $\quad W_k = m_O c^2 \left(\dfrac{1}{\sqrt{1 - v^2/c^2}} - 1\right)$, $\quad p = \dfrac{m_O v}{\sqrt{1 - v^2/c^2}}$

24. Compute the wavelength of an electron having speed 10^6 m/sec. *Ans.* 7.27 A

25. What is the wavelength associated with an electron which has been accelerated by a potential difference of 9000 volts? Neglect any change in electron mass. *Ans.* 0.129 A

26. What is the wavelength associated with an electron which has been accelerated by a potential difference of 1.024×10^6 volts? *Ans.* 0.0086 A

Chapter 43

Nuclear Physics

INTRODUCTION. In ordinary chemical reactions, the atoms of the reactant molecules regroup themselves to form the product molecules. In such reactions, the outer electrons of the atoms undergo rearrangements in being transferred wholly or in part from one atom to another. The atomic nuclei, on the other hand, change their relative positions with respect to each other, but are themselves unchanged.

There are reactions in which the nuclei themselves are broken down, and in which the product materials do not contain the same elements as the reactants. The physics of such nuclear reactions is called nuclear physics. Some nuclear processes, such as radioactivity, consist of the spontaneous disintegration of individual nuclei. These reactions occur at rates that are not affected by ordinary laboratory conditions, such as temperature or pressure. Most of the known nuclear reactions, however, result from the interaction of two nuclei or from the impact of a sub-atomic particle upon a nucleus. Processes from this latter class are very sensitive to the experimental control of the energy and relative positions of the reacting particles.

FUNDAMENTAL PARTICLES. For the purposes of this chapter the fundamental particles occurring in nuclear reactions will be limited to the proton, neutron, negative electron, and the positive electron, or positron. The charge of an electron is $-e$, and $+e$ is an equal but opposite charge. The mass units are units on the **physical atomic mass scale**, which will be explained in a later paragraph.

SOME FUNDAMENTAL PARTICLES

PARTICLE	SYMBOL	MASS	CHARGE
Proton	p, $_1H^1$	1.00760	$+e$
Neutron	n, $_0n^1$	1.00898	0
Electron	$_{-1}e^0$, $_{-1}\beta^0$	0.0005488	$-e$
Positron	$_{+1}e^0$, $_{+1}\beta^0$	0.0005488	$+e$

THE NUCLEI OF THE ELEMENTS are believed to consist of protons and neutrons. Since neutrons have no charge, the charge on a nucleus is equal to the number of protons. The number of protons in a nucleus is equal to the atomic number, by definition.

The mass of a nucleus is close to (within a fraction of a percent) the sum of the masses of its constituent protons and neutrons. Since the mass of a proton and the mass of a neutron are each close to 1 on the atomic mass scale, the mass of the nucleus should be close to some integral number on the same scale. An atom consists of its nucleus plus a number of electrons equal to the atomic number. Since the contribution of the electrons to the total mass of the atom, even in an atom containing 100 electrons, is a very small fraction of 1 mass unit, the total mass of an atom should also be a number close to an integral value. The **integral** number which is close to the mass of an atom is called the **mass number** of that atom. The mass number of an atom is the sum of the numbers of protons and neutrons in the nucleus.

ISOTOPES. Atoms are known which have the same atomic number, but different mass numbers. Such atoms are called **isotopes** of each other. Isotopic nuclei have the same number of protons, but different numbers of neutrons.

For example, ordinary oxygen consists of three isotopes, having mass numbers 16, 17, and 18. Each of the isotopes has the atomic number 8. These isotopes are designated by the symbols $_8O^{16}$, $_8O^{17}$, and $_8O^{18}$; or simply by O^{16}, O^{17}, and O^{18} (it being understood that oxygen always has an atomic number 8). The subscript 8 represents the atomic number. The superscript represents the mass number. In each isotope there are 8 protons in the nucleus, but the number of neutrons is 8, 9, or 10, depending on the particular isotope.

PHYSICAL ATOMIC MASS SCALE. The physical atomic mass scale was adopted to provide an absolute standard of comparison of the masses of **specific isotopes**. This scale is based on the arbitrary assignment of an atomic mass of exactly 16 to O^{16}.

Since 6.025×10^{23} atoms of O^{16} have mass 16 g, 1 atom of O^{16} has mass $16/(6.025 \times 10^{23})$ g, and 1 atomic mass unit (amu) is

$$1 \text{ amu } = \frac{1}{16} \times \text{ mass of the } O^{16} \text{ atom}$$

$$= \frac{1}{16} \times \frac{16}{6.025 \times 10^{23}} \text{ g } = 1.66 \times 10^{-27} \text{ kg}$$

BINDING ENERGIES. The mass of an atom, in general, is not equal to the sum of the masses of its component protons, neutrons, and electrons. If we could imagine a reaction in which free protons, neutrons, and electrons combine to form an atom, we would find that the mass of the atom is slightly less than the mass of the component parts and also that a tremendous amount of energy is released when the reaction occurs. The loss in mass is exactly equal to the mass equivalent of the released energy, according to the Einstein equation $W = mc^2$. Then

$$1 \text{ amu } = mc^2 = (1.66 \times 10^{-27} \text{ kg})(3 \times 10^8 \text{ m/sec})^2$$

$$= 1.49 \times 10^{-10} \text{ joule}$$

$$= 931 \text{ Mev} \qquad \text{(since 1 ev} = 1.60 \times 10^{-19} \text{ joule)}$$

The binding energy of an atom is the energy calculated by the equation $W = mc^2$, usually expressed in Mev. The percentage loss of mass is different for each isotope of any element. Some typical atomic masses for some of the lighter isotopes are given in the following table. These masses are for neutral atoms and include the orbital electrons.

ATOMIC MASSES (amu)

$_0n^1$	1.00899	$_3Li^7$	7.01822
$_1H^1$	1.00814	$_4Be^7$	7.01916
$_1H^2$	2.01474	$_4Be^8$	8.00785
$_1H^3$	3.01700	$_4Be^9$	9.01504
$_2He^4$	4.00388	$_6C^{12}$	12.00384
$_2He^6$	6.02079	$_7N^{14}$	14.00755
$_3Li^6$	6.01702	$_8O^{16}$	16.00000

NUCLEAR EQUATIONS. The rules for balancing nuclear equations are different from the rules for balancing ordinary chemical equations.

(1) Each particle is assigned a superscript equal to its mass number and a subscript equal to its atomic number or nuclear charge.

(2) A free proton is the nucleus of the hydrogen atom, and is assigned the notation $_1H^1$.

(3) A free neutron is assigned zero atomic number because it has no charge. The mass number of a neutron is 1. The notation for a neutron is $_0n^1$.

(4) An electron (beta-particle or β-particle) is assigned the mass number zero and the atomic number –1; hence the notation $_{-1}e^0$.

(5) A positron is assigned the mass number zero and atomic number +1; hence the notation $_{+1}e^0$.

(6) An alpha-particle (α-particle) is a helium nucleus, and is therefore represented by the notation $_2He^4$ or $_2\alpha^4$.

(7) Gamma radiation (γ) is a form of light, emitted as photons of energy hf, and has zero mass number and zero charge.

(8) In a balanced equation the sum of the subscripts (atomic numbers) must be the same on the two sides of the equation. The sum of the superscripts (mass numbers) must also be the same on the two sides of the equation. Thus the equation for the primary radioactivity of radium is

$$_{88}Ra^{226} \longrightarrow {}_{86}Rn^{222} + {}_2He^4$$

Many nuclear processes may be indicated by a short-hand notation, in which a light bombarding particle and a light product particle are represented by symbols in parentheses between the symbols for the initial target nucleus and the final product nucleus. The symbols n, p, d, α, e, γ are used to represent neutron, proton, deuteron ($_1H^2$), alpha, electron, and gamma rays respectively. Examples of the corresponding long- and short-hand notation for several reactions follow.

$$_7N^{14} + {}_1H^1 \longrightarrow {}_6C^{11} + {}_2He^4 \qquad N^{14}\,(p,\,\alpha)\,C^{11}$$

$$_{13}Al^{27} + {}_0n^1 \longrightarrow {}_{12}Mg^{27} + {}_1H^1 \qquad Al^{27}\,(n,\,p)\,Mg^{27}$$

$$_{25}Mn^{55} + {}_1H^2 \longrightarrow {}_{26}Fe^{55} + 2\,{}_0n^1 \qquad Mn^{55}\,(d,\,2n)\,Fe^{55}$$

The slow neutron is a very efficient agent in causing transmutations, since it has no positive charge and hence can approach the nucleus without being repelled. A charged particle such as a proton must have a high energy in order to cause a transformation. Because of their small mass, even very high energy electrons are relatively inefficient in causing transmutations.

HALF-LIFE. The stability of a radioactive nucleus toward spontaneous decay is measured by its half-life. The half-life is defined as the time in which half of any large sample of identical nuclei will undergo decomposition. This is a fixed number for each type of nucleus and may be given the symbol T. Thus a collection of radioactive atoms will be reduced to one-fourth ($\frac{1}{2} \times \frac{1}{2}$) its original number in a time equal to $2T$, to one-eighth in $3T$, and so on.

SOLVED PROBLEMS

1. How many protons, neutrons, and electrons are there in each of the following atoms:
(a) He^3, (b) C^{12}, (c) Pb^{206}?

Solution:

(a) The atomic number of He is 2; therefore the nucleus must contain 2 protons. Since the mass number of this isotope is 3, the sum of the protons and neutrons in the nucleus must equal 3; therefore there is 1 neutron. The number of electrons in the atom is the same as the atomic number, 2.

(b) The atomic number of carbon is 6; hence the nucleus must contain 6 protons. The number of neutrons in the nucleus is equal to $(12-6)$, or 6. The number of electrons is the same as the atomic number, 6.

(c) The atomic number of lead is 82; hence there are 82 protons in the nucleus. The number of neutrons is $(206-82)$, or 124. There are 82 electrons.

2. What is the binding energy of C^{12}?

Solution:

One atom of C^{12} consists of 6 protons, 6 electrons, and 6 neutrons. The mass of the uncombined protons and electrons is the same as that of six H^1 atoms. The component particles may thus be considered as 6 H^1 atoms and 6 neutrons. A mass balance may be computed on the physical atomic mass scale.

Mass of 6 H^1 atoms = 6×1.0081	=	6.0486
Mass of 6 neutrons = 6×1.0090	=	6.0540
Total mass of component particles	=	12.1026
Mass of C^{12}	=	12.0038
Loss in mass on formation of C^{12}	=	0.0988
Binding energy = 931×0.0988 Mev	=	92.0 Mev

3. What is the overall energy balance in the $Li^7(p,n)Be^7$ reaction?

Solution:

The change of mass for the reaction must be computed.

Reactants		Products	
$_3Li^7$	7.01822	$_0n^1$	1.00899
$_1H^1$	1.00814	$_4Be^7$	7.01916
	8.02636		8.02815

Increase of mass = $8.02815 - 8.02636 = 0.00179$.

A corresponding amount of energy must be consumed, equal to 931×0.00179 Mev, or 1.67 Mev. This energy is supplied as kinetic energy of the bombarding proton, and is **part** of the acceleration requirement for the proton supplied by a cyclotron or some other accelerating device.

4. Complete the following nuclear equations.

(a) $_7N^{14} + _2He^4 \longrightarrow _8O^{17} + $ ---

(b) $_4Be^9 + _2He^4 \longrightarrow _6C^{12} + $ ---

(c) $_4Be^9 (p, \alpha)$ ---

(d) $_{15}P^{30} \longrightarrow _{14}Si^{30} + $ ---

(e) $_1H^3 \longrightarrow _2He^3 + $ ---

(f) $_{20}Ca^{43} (\alpha, $ ---$) _{21}Sc^{46}$

Solution:

(a) The sum of the subscripts on the left is $(7+2) = 9$. The subscript of the first product on the right is 8. Hence the second product on the right must have a subscript (net charge) of 1.

The sum of the superscripts on the left is $(14+4) = 18$. The superscript of the first product on the right is 17. Hence the second product on the right must have a superscript (mass number) of 1.

The particle with a nuclear charge 1 and a mass number 1 is the proton, $_1H^1$.

(b) The nuclear charge of the second product particle (its subscript) is $(4+2)-6 = 0$. The mass number of the particle (its superscript) is $(9+4)-12 = 1$. Hence the particle must be the neutron, $_0n^1$.

(c) The reactants, $_4Be^9$ and $_1H^1$, have a combined nuclear charge of 5 and mass number of 10. In addition to the α-particle, a product will be formed of charge $5-2 = 3$, and mass $10-4 = 6$. This is $_3Li^6$, since lithium is the element of atomic number 3.

(d) The nuclear charge of the second particle is $15-14 = +1$. The mass number is $30-30 = 0$. Hence the particle must be a positron, $_{+1}e^0$.

(e) The nuclear charge of the second particle is $1-2 = -1$. Its mass number is $3-3 = 0$. Hence the particle must be a β-particle, or negative electron, $_{-1}e^0$.

(f) The reactants, $_{20}Ca^{43}$ and $_2He^4$, have a combined nuclear charge of 22 and mass number 47. The ejected product will have a charge $22-21 = 1$, and mass $47-46 = 1$. This is a proton and should be represented in the parentheses by p.

5. An isotopic species of lithium hydride, Li^6H^2, is a potential nuclear fuel on the basis of the following reaction.

$$_3Li^6 + {}_1H^2 \longrightarrow 2\ {}_2He^4$$

Calculate the expected power production, in kilowatts, associated with the consumption of 1.00 gram of Li^6H^2 per day. Assume 100% efficiency in the process.

Solution:

The change of mass for the reaction is first computed.

$$\begin{array}{rl}
_3Li^6 & 6.01702 \\
_1H^2 & 2.01474 \\
\text{Total mass of reactants} & 8.03176 \\
2\ _2He^4 = 2\times4.00388 & 8.00776 \\
\text{Loss in mass} & 0.02400
\end{array}$$

For each gram of the hydride consumed, the loss in mass is $0.02400/8.03 = 0.00299$ g. The corresponding energy production is

$$\text{Energy } W = mc^2 = (2.99\times10^{-6}\text{ kg})(3\times10^8\text{ m/sec})^2 \times \frac{1\text{ kw-hr}}{3.6\times10^6\text{ joules}} = 7.48\times10^4\text{ kw-hr}$$

$$\text{Power } P = W/t = (7.48\times10^4\text{ kw-hr})/(24\text{ hr}) = 3.12\times10^3\text{ kw}$$

SUPPLEMENTARY PROBLEMS

Atomic Number: Ag, 47; Ar, 18; Be, 4; C, 6; Cd, 48; Co, 27; Ge, 32; I, 53; K, 19; Mg, 12; Mn, 25; N, 7; Na, 11; Sr, 38; Te, 52; U, 92; Xe, 54.

6. Determine the number of (a) nuclear protons, (b) nuclear neutrons, (c) electrons, in each of the following atoms: (1) Ge^{70}, (2) Ge^{72}, (3) Be^9, (4) U^{235}.

Ans. (1): (a) 32, (b) 38, (c) 32   (3): (a) 4, (b) 5, (c) 4
      (2): (a) 32, (b) 40, (c) 32   (4): (a) 92, (b) 143, (c) 92

7. By natural radioactivity, U^{238} emits an α-particle. The heavy residual nucleus is called UX_1. UX_1 in turn emits a β-particle. The heavy residual nucleus from this radioactive process is called UX_2. Determine the atomic numbers and mass numbers of (a) UX_1 and (b) UX_2.   *Ans.* (a) 90, 234; (b) 91, 234

8. By radioactivity, $_{93}Np^{239}$ emits a β-particle. The residual heavy nucleus is also radioactive, and gives rise to U^{235} by the radioactive process. What small particle is emitted simultaneously with the formation of U^{235}?   *Ans.* α-particle

9. Complete the following equations.

(a) $_{11}Na^{23} + _2He^4 \longrightarrow _{12}Mg^{26} + ?$ (c) $Ag^{106} \longrightarrow Cd^{106} + ?$ (e) $_{48}Cd^{105} + _{-1}e^0 \longrightarrow ?$

(b) $_{29}Cu^{64} \longrightarrow _{+1}e^0 + ?$ (d) $_5B^{10} + _2He^4 \longrightarrow _7N^{13} + ?$ (f) $_{92}U^{238} \longrightarrow _{90}Th^{234} + ?$

Ans. (a) $_1H^1$, (b) $_{28}Ni^{64}$, (c) $_{-1}e^0$, (d) $_0n^1$, (e) $_{47}Ag^{105}$, (f) $_2He^4$

10. Complete the notations for the following nuclear processes.

(a) $Mg^{24}(d, \alpha)$?   (c) $Ar^{40}(\alpha, p)$?   (e) $Te^{130}(d, 2n)$?

(b) $Mg^{26}(d, p)$?   (d) $C^{12}(d, n)$?   (f) $Mn^{55}(n, \gamma)$?   (g) $Co^{59}(n, \alpha)$?

Ans. (a) Na^{22}, (b) Mg^{27}, (c) K^{43}, (d) N^{13}, (e) I^{130}, (f) Mn^{56}, (g) Mn^{56}

11. If an atom of U^{235}, after absorption of a slow neutron, undergoes fission to form an atom of Xe^{139} and an atom of Sr^{94}, what other particles are produced, and how many?   *Ans.* 3 neutrons

12. One of the stablest nuclei is Mn^{55}. The atomic mass of the neutral Mn^{55} atom is 54.956 amu. Determine its binding energy.   *Ans.* 481 Mev

13. How much energy is released during each of the following reactions?

(a) $_1H^1 + _3Li^7 \longrightarrow 2 \; _2He^4$ (b) $_1H^3 + _1H^2 \longrightarrow _2He^4 + _0n^1$ *Ans.* (a) 17.3 Mev, (b) 17.6 Mev

14. In the $N^{14}(n, p)C^{14}$ reaction, the proton is ejected with an energy of 0.6 Mev; very slow neutrons may be used. Calculate the mass of the C^{14} atom.   *Ans.* 14.0077 amu

15. The sun's energy is believed to come from several series of nuclear reactions, the overall result of each of which is the transformation of 4 hydrogen atoms into one helium atom. (In the balanced equation two positrons are also formed. These are quickly converted into energy as gamma radiation by annihilation reactions with two electrons. The two electrons that disappear are the excess orbital electrons from the original hydrogen atoms no longer needed to neutralize the charge of the resulting helium nucleus. The annihilation energy is automatically included in the energy release if the masses of only the helium and hydrogen atoms are considered.) How much energy is released in the formation of one helium atom?   *Ans.* 26.7 Mev

16. A gamma-ray photon disappears and an electron-positron pair is formed. What was the energy of the photon if the total kinetic energy of the electron-positron pair is 0.78 Mev?   *Ans.* 1.80 Mev

17. It is proposed to use the nuclear fusion reaction

$$2 \; _1H^2 \longrightarrow _2He^4 + \text{energy}$$

to produce industrial electric power. If the output is to be 50,000 kilowatts and the energy of the above reaction is used with 30% efficiency, how many grams of deuterium fuel will be needed per day?   *Ans.* 25 grams

18. A sample of river water was found to contain 8×10^{-18} tritium atoms, $_1H^3$, per atom of ordinary hydrogen. Tritium decomposes radioactively with a half-life of 12.5 years. What will be the ratio of tritium to normal hydrogen atoms 50 years after the original sample was taken if the sample is stored in a place where additional tritium atoms cannot be formed?   *Ans.* 5×10^{-19}

Appendix A

Significant Figures

INTRODUCTION. The following discussion is intended to give the elementary student some workable rules of procedure, but is not intended to replace the rigorous treatment of a text on the theory of measurements.

The numerical value of every observed measurement is an approximation. No physical measurement, such as mass, length, time, volume, velocity, is ever absolutely correct. The accuracy (reliability) of every measurement is limited by the reliability of the measuring instrument, which is never absolutely reliable.

Consider that the length of an object is recorded as 15.7 cm. By convention, this means that the length was measured to the **nearest** tenth of a centimeter and that its exact value lies between 15.65 and 15.75 cm. If this measurement were exact to the nearest hundredth of a centimeter, it would have been recorded as 15.70 cm. The value 15.7 cm represents **three significant figures** $(1, 5, 7)$, while the value 15.70 represents **four significant figures** $(1, 5, 7, 0)$. A significant figure is one which is known to be reasonably reliable.

Similarly, a recorded mass of 3.4062 g, observed with an analytical balance, means that the mass was determined to the nearest tenth of a milligram and represents five significant figures $(3, 4, 0, 6, 2)$, the last figure (2) being reasonably correct and guaranteeing the certainty of the preceding four figures.

In elementary measurements in physics and chemistry, the last figure is estimated and is also considered as a significant figure.

ZEROS. A recorded mass of 28 g represents two significant figures $(2, 8)$. If the same mass were written as 0.028 kg it would still contain only two significant figures. Zeros appearing as the first figures of a number are not significant, since they merely locate the decimal point. However, the values 0.0280 kg and 0.280 kg represent three significant figures (2, 8, and the last zero); the value 1.028 kg represents four significant figures $(1, 0, 2, 8)$; and the value 1.0280 kg represents five significant figures $(1, 0, 2, 8, 0)$. Similarly, the value 209.00 for the atomic weight of bismuth contains five significant figures.

The statement that a body of ore weighs 9800 lb does not indicate definitely the accuracy of the weighing. The last two zeros may have been used merely to locate the decimal point. If it was weighed to the nearest hundred pounds, the weight contains only two significant figures and may be written exponentially as 9.8×10^3 lb. If weighed to the nearest ten pounds it may be written as 9.80×10^3 lb, which indicates that the value is accurate to three significant figures. Since the zero in this case is not needed to locate the decimal point, it must be a significant figure. If the object was weighed to the nearest pound, the weight could be written as 9.800×10^3 lb (four significant figures). Likewise, the statement that the velocity of light is 186,000 mi/sec is accurate to three significant figures, since this value is accurate only to the nearest thousand miles per second; to avoid confusion, it may be written as 1.86×10^5 mi/sec. (It is customary to place the decimal point after the first significant figure.)

ROUNDING OFF. A number is rounded off to the desired number of significant figures by dropping one or more digits to the right. When the first digit dropped is less than 5, the last digit retained should remain unchanged; when it is more than 5, 1 is added to the last digit retained. When it is exactly 5, 1 is added to the last digit retained if that digit is odd; otherwise it is dropped. Thus successive approximations to 3.14159 are 3.1416, 3.142, 3.14, 3.1, 3. The quantity 51.75 g may be rounded off to 51.8 g, 51.65 g to 51.6 g, 51.85 g to 51.8 g.

ADDITION AND SUBTRACTION. The answer should be rounded off after adding or subtracting, so as to retain digits only as far as the first column containing estimated figures. (Remember that the last significant figure is estimated.)

Examples. Add the following quantities expressed in grams.

(1)	25.340	(2)	58.0	(3)	4.20	(4)	415.5
	5.465		0.0038		1.6523		3.64
	0.322		0.00001		0.015		0.238
	31.127 g (*Ans.*)		58.00381		5.8673		419.378
			= 58.0 g (*Ans.*)		= 5.87 g (*Ans.*)		= 419.4 g (*Ans.*)

MULTIPLICATION AND DIVISION. The answer should be rounded off to contain only as many significant figures as are contained in the least exact factor.

For example, when multiplying 7.485×8.61, or when dividing $0.1342 \div 1.52$, the answer should be given in three significant figures.

Consider the division $\frac{9.84}{9.3} = 1.06$, to three places. By the rule given above, the answer should be 1.1 (two significant figures). However, a difference of 1 in the last place of 9.3 (9.3 ± 0.1) results in an error of about 1%, while a difference of 1 in the last place of 1.1 (1.1 ± 0.1) yields an error of roughly 10%. Thus the answer 1.1 is of much lower percentage accuracy than 9.3. Hence in this case the answer should be 1.06, since a difference of 1 in the last place of the least exact factor used in the calculation (9.3) yields a percentage of error about the same (about 1%) as a difference of 1 in the last place of 1.06 (1.06 ± 0.01). Similarly, $0.92 \times 1.13 = 1.04$.

In nearly all academic and commercial calculations, a precision of only two to four significant figures is required. Therefore the student is advised to use an inexpensive 10-inch slide rule which is accurate to three or four significant figures, or the table of logarithms in the Appendix, which is accurate to four significant figures. The efficient use of a slide rule or log table will save very much time in calculations without sacrificing accuracy.

EXERCISES

1. How many significant figures are given in the following quantities?

(a) 454 g   (e) 0.0353 ft   (i) 1.118×10^{-3} g   *Ans.* (a) 3, (b) 2, (c) 4, (d) 4, (e) 3
(b) 2.2 lb   (f) 1.0080 g   (j) 1030 g/cm^2 (f) 5, (g) 3, (h) 2, (i) 4
(c) 2.205 lb   (g) 14.0 ml   (k) 125,000 lb   (j) 3 or 4
(d) 0.3937 in.   (h) 9.3×10^7 mi   (k) 3, 4, 5, or 6

2. Add: (a) 703   g   (b) 18.425 cm   (c) 0.0035 *l*   (d) 4.0   lb   *Ans.* (a) 711 g
                  7   g   7.21 cm   0.097 *l*   0.632 lb   (b) 30.6 cm
              0.66 g   5.0   cm   0.225 *l*   0.148 lb   (c) 0.326 *l*
                                                                         (d) 4.8 lb

3. Subtract: (a) 7.26 lb   (b) 562.4 ft   (c) 34   kg   *Ans.* (a) 7.1 lb
                   0.2 lb   16.8 ft   0.2 kg   (b) 545.6 ft, (c) 34 kg

4. Multiply: (a) 2.21×0.3 (d) 107.88×0.610 *Ans.* (a) 0.7   (d) 65.8
           (b) 72.4×0.084 (e) 12.4×84 (b) 6.1   (e) 1.04×10^3
           (c) 2.02×4.113 (f) 72.4×8.6 (c) 8.31   (f) 6.2×10^2

5. Divide: (a) $\dfrac{97.52}{2.54}$ (b) $\dfrac{14.28}{0.714}$ (c) $\dfrac{0.032}{0.004}$ (d) $\dfrac{9.8}{9.3}$ *Ans.* (a) 38.4   (c) 8
                                                                         (b) 20.0   (d) 1.05

Trigonometry Needed for College Physics

FUNCTIONS OF AN ACUTE ANGLE. The trigonometric functions most often used are the sine, cosine and tangent. It is convenient to put the definitions of the functions of an acute angle in terms of the sides of a right triangle.

In any right triangle: The **sine** of either acute angle is equal to the length of the side opposite that angle divided by the length of the hypotenuse. The **cosine** of either acute angle is equal to the length of the side adjacent to that angle divided by the length of the hypotenuse. The **tangent** of either acute angle is equal to the length of the side opposite that angle divided by the length of the side adjacent to that angle.

If A, B, and C are the vertices of any right triangle (C is the right angle) and a, b, and c the sides opposite respectively, as shown in the diagram, then

$$\sin A = \frac{\text{side opposite } A}{\text{hypotenuse}} = \frac{a}{c} \qquad \sin B = \frac{\text{side opposite } B}{\text{hypotenuse}} = \frac{b}{c}$$

$$\cos A = \frac{\text{side adjacent } A}{\text{hypotenuse}} = \frac{b}{c} \qquad \cos B = \frac{\text{side adjacent } B}{\text{hypotenuse}} = \frac{a}{c}$$

$$\tan A = \frac{\text{side opposite } A}{\text{side adjacent } A} = \frac{a}{b} \qquad \tan B = \frac{\text{side opposite } B}{\text{side adjacent } B} = \frac{b}{a}$$

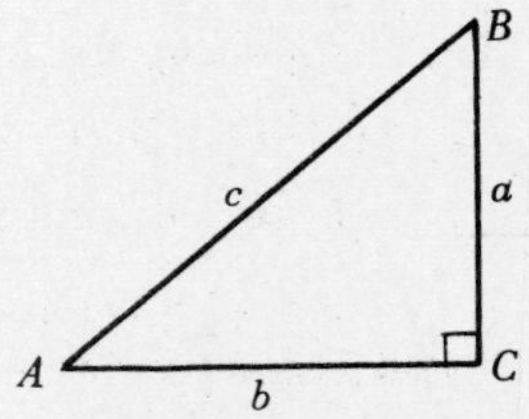

Note that $\sin A = \cos B$; thus the sine of any angle equals the cosine of its complementary angle. For example, $\sin 30° = \cos (90° - 30°) = \cos 60°$, and
$$\cos 50° = \sin (90° - 50°) = \sin 40°.$$

As an angle increases from $0°$ to $90°$, its sine increases from 0 to 1, its tangent increases from 0 to infinity, and its cosine decreases from 1 to 0.

LAW OF SINES AND OF COSINES. These two laws give the relations between the sides and angles of *any* plane triangle. In any plane triangle with angles A, B, and C and sides opposite a, b, and c respectively, the following relations apply:

Law of Sines:
$$\frac{a}{\sin A} = \frac{b}{\sin B} = \frac{c}{\sin C}$$

or
$$\frac{a}{b} = \frac{\sin A}{\sin B}, \quad \frac{b}{c} = \frac{\sin B}{\sin C}, \quad \frac{c}{a} = \frac{\sin C}{\sin A}$$

Law of Cosines:
$$a^2 = b^2 + c^2 - 2bc \cos A$$
$$b^2 = a^2 + c^2 - 2ac \cos B$$
$$c^2 = a^2 + b^2 - 2ab \cos C$$

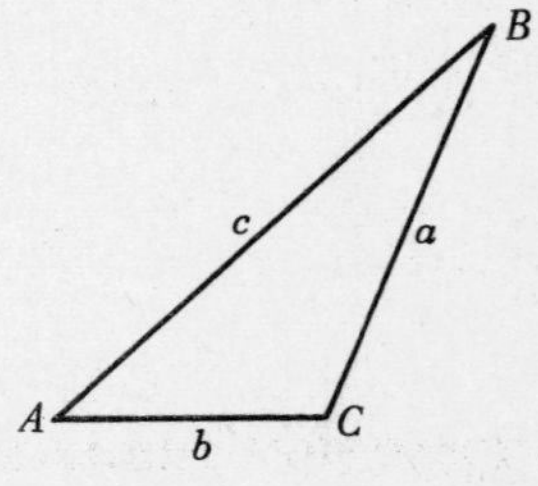

If the angle θ is between $90°$ and $180°$, as in the case of angle C in the above diagram, then
$$\sin \theta = \sin (180° - \theta) \qquad \text{and} \qquad \cos \theta = -\cos (180° - \theta).$$

Thus $\quad \sin 120° = \sin (180° - 120°) = \sin 60° = 0.866$

and $\quad \cos 120° = -\cos (180° - 120°) = -\cos 60° = -0.500.$

SOLVED PROBLEMS

1. In right triangle ABC, given $a = 8$, $b = 6$, $C = 90°$. Find the values of the sine, cosine, and tangent of angle A and of angle B.

Solution:

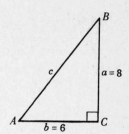

$$c = \sqrt{8^2 + 6^2} = \sqrt{100} = 10$$

$\sin A$	$=$	a/c	$=$	$8/10$	$= 0.80$	$\sin B = b/c = 6/10 = 0.60$
$\cos A$	$=$	b/c	$=$	$6/10$	$= 0.60$	$\cos B = a/c = 8/10 = 0.80$
$\tan A$	$=$	a/b	$=$	$8/6$	$= 1.33$	$\tan B = b/a = 6/8 = 0.75$

2. Given a right triangle with one acute angle = $40°$ and hypotenuse = 400. Find the other sides and angles.

Solution:

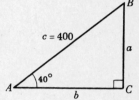

$$\sin 40° = a/400 \qquad \text{and} \qquad \cos 40° = b/400$$

In the table of natural trigonometric functions, we find that $\sin 40° = 0.6428$ and $\cos 40° = 0.7660$.

$$a = 400 \sin 40° = 400(0.6428) = 257$$
$$b = 400 \cos 40° = 400(0.7660) = 306$$
$$B = 90° - 40° = 50°$$

3. Given triangle ABC with $A = 64°$, $B = 71°$, $b = 40$. Find a, c.

Solution:

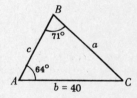

$$C = 180° - (A + B) = 180° - (64° + 71°) = 45°$$

By law of sines, $\dfrac{a}{\sin A} = \dfrac{b}{\sin B}$ and $\dfrac{c}{\sin C} = \dfrac{b}{\sin B}$.

$$a = \frac{b \sin A}{\sin B} = \frac{40 \sin 64°}{\sin 71°} = \frac{40(0.8988)}{0.9455} = 38.0$$

$$c = \frac{b \sin C}{\sin B} = \frac{40 \sin 45°}{\sin 71°} = \frac{40(0.7071)}{0.9455} = 29.9$$

4. (*a*) If $\cos A = 0.438$, find A to the nearest degree. (*b*) If $\sin B = 0.8000$, find B to the nearest tenth of a degree. (*c*) If $\cos C = 0.7120$, find C to the nearest tenth of a degree.

Solution:

(*a*) In the table of natural trigonometric functions, under Cosine, we find that .438 corresponds most nearly to $64°$. Hence $A = 64°$.

(*b*) In the table of natural trigonometric functions, we find that the angle whose sine is 0.8000 lies between $53°$ and $54°$. We interpolate to find the required angle.

$\sin 54° = .8090$		$.8000 = .8000$			
$\sin 53° = .7986$		$\sin 53° = .7986$		Then $B = (53 + \frac{14}{104})° = 53.1°$.
Difference $= .0104$		Diff. $= .0014$			

(*c*)

$\cos 44° = .7193$		$.7120 = .7120$			
$\cos 45° = .7071$		$\cos 45° = .7071$		Then $C = (45 - \frac{49}{122})° = 44.6°$.
Difference $= .0122$		Diff. $= .0049$			

5. Given triangle ABC with $A = 130.8°$, $a = 525$, $c = 421$. Find b, B, C.

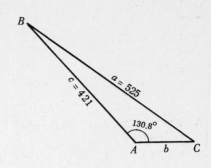

Solution:

$$\sin 130.8° = \sin (180° - 130.8°) = \sin 49.2° = 0.757$$

For C: $\sin C = \dfrac{c \sin A}{a} = \dfrac{421 \sin 130.8°}{525} = \dfrac{421 (0.757)}{525}$

$$= 0.607 \quad \text{from which } C = 37.4°.$$

For B: $B = 180° - (C + A) = 180° - (37.4° + 130.8°) = 11.8°.$

For b: $b = \dfrac{a \sin B}{\sin A} = \dfrac{525 \sin 11.8°}{\sin 130.8°} = \dfrac{525 (0.204)}{0.757} = 142$

6. Given triangle ABC with $a = 14$, $b = 8$, $C = 130°$. Find c, A, B.

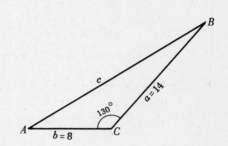

Solution:

$$\cos 130° = -\cos (180° - 130°) = -\cos 50° = -0.643$$

For c: By the law of cosines,

$$c^2 = a^2 + b^2 - 2ab \cos 130°$$
$$= 14^2 + 8^2 - 2(14)(8)(-0.643)$$
$$= 404, \quad \text{and } c = \sqrt{404} = 20.1.$$

For A: By the law of sines, $\sin A = \dfrac{a \sin C}{c} = \dfrac{14 (0.766)}{20.1}$

$$= 0.533, \quad \text{and } A = 32.2°.$$

For B: $B = 180° - (A + C) = 180° - (32.2° + 130°) = 17.8°.$

EXERCISES

7. Solve each right triangle ABC, with $C = 90°$, given:

(a) $A = 23.3°$, $c = 346$ *Ans.* $B = 66.7°$, $a = 137$, $b = 318$

(b) $B = 49.2°$, $b = 222$ $A = 40.8°$, $a = 192$, $c = 293$

(c) $A = 66.6°$, $a = 113$ $B = 23.4°$, $b = 48.9$, $c = 123$

(d) $a = 25.4$, $b = 38.2$ $A = 33.6°$, $B = 56.4°$, $c = 45.9$

(e) $b = 673$, $c = 888$ $A = 40.7°$, $B = 49.3°$, $a = 579$

8. Solve each oblique triangle ABC, given:

(a) $a = 125$, $A = 54.6°$, $B = 65.2°$ *Ans.* $b = 140$, $c = 133$, $C = 60.2°$

(b) $b = 321$, $A = 75.3°$, $C = 38.5°$ $a = 339$, $c = 218$, $B = 66.2°$

(c) $b = 215$, $c = 150$, $B = 42.7°$ $a = 299$, $A = 109.1°$, $C = 28.2°$

(d) $a = 512$, $b = 426$, $A = 48.8°$ $c = 680$, $B = 38.8°$, $C = 92.4°$

(e) $b = 50.4$, $c = 33.3$, $B = 118.5°$ $a = 25.1$, $A = 26.0°$, $C = 35.5°$

(f) $b = 120$, $c = 270$, $A = 118.7°$ $a = 344$, $B = 17.8°$, $C = 43.5°$

(g) $a = 24.5$, $b = 18.6$, $c = 26.4$ $A = 63.2°$, $B = 42.7°$, $C = 74.1°$

(h) $a = 6.34$, $b = 7.30$, $c = 9.98$ $A = 39.3°$, $B = 46.9°$, $C = 93.8°$

Appendix C

Exponents

A. The following is a partial list of powers of 10.

$$10^0 = 1$$
$$10^1 = 10$$
$$10^2 = 10 \times 10 = 100$$
$$10^3 = 10 \times 10 \times 10 = 1000$$
$$10^4 = 10 \times 10 \times 10 \times 10 = 10,000$$
$$10^5 = 10 \times 10 \times 10 \times 10 \times 10 = 100,000$$
$$10^6 = 10 \times 10 \times 10 \times 10 \times 10 \times 10 = 1,000,000$$

$$10^{-1} = \frac{1}{10} = 0.1$$
$$10^{-2} = \frac{1}{10^2} = \frac{1}{100} = 0.01$$
$$10^{-3} = \frac{1}{10^3} = \frac{1}{1000} = 0.001$$
$$10^{-4} = \frac{1}{10^4} = \frac{1}{10,000} = 0.0001$$

In the expression 10^5, the **base** is 10 and the **exponent** is 5.

B. In multiplication, exponents of like bases are added.

(1) $a^3 \times a^5 = a^{3+5} = a^8$

(2) $10^2 \times 10^3 = 10^{2+3} = 10^5$

(3) $10 \times 10 = 10^{1+1} = 10^2$

(4) $10^7 \times 10^{-3} = 10^{7-3} = 10^4$

(5) $(4 \times 10^4)(2 \times 10^{-6}) = 8 \times 10^{4-6} = 8 \times 10^{-2}$

(6) $(2 \times 10^5)(3 \times 10^{-2}) = 6 \times 10^{5-2} = 6 \times 10^3$

C. In division, exponents of like bases are subtracted.

(1) $\dfrac{a^5}{a^3} = a^{5-3} = a^2$

(2) $\dfrac{10^2}{10^5} = 10^{2-5} = 10^{-3}$

(3) $\dfrac{8 \times 10^2}{2 \times 10^{-6}} = \dfrac{8}{2} \times 10^{2+6} = 4 \times 10^8$

(4) $\dfrac{5.6 \times 10^{-2}}{1.6 \times 10^4} = \dfrac{5.6}{1.6} \times 10^{-2-4} = 3.5 \times 10^{-6}$

D. Any number may be expressed as an integral power of 10, or as the product of two numbers one of which is an integral power of 10 (e.g., $300 = 3 \times 10^2$).

(1) $22,400 = 2.24 \times 10^4$

(2) $7,200,000 = 7.2 \times 10^6$

(3) $454 = 4.54 \times 10^2$

(4) $0.454 = 4.54 \times 10^{-1}$

(5) $0.0454 = 4.54 \times 10^{-2}$

(6) $0.00006 = 6 \times 10^{-5}$

(7) $0.00306 = 3.06 \times 10^{-3}$

(8) $0.0000005 = 5 \times 10^{-7}$

E. An expression with an exponent of zero is equal to 1.

(1) $a^0 = 1$ *(2)* $10^0 = 1$ *(3)* $(3 \times 10)^0 = 1$ *(4)* $7 \times 10^0 = 7$ *(5)* $8.2 \times 10^0 = 8.2$

F. A factor may be transferred from the numerator to the denominator of a fraction, or vice versa, by changing the sign of the exponent.

(1) $10^{-4} = \dfrac{1}{10^4}$ *(2)* $5 \times 10^{-3} = \dfrac{5}{10^3}$ *(3)* $\dfrac{7}{10^{-2}} = 7 \times 10^2$ *(4)* $-5a^{-2} = -\dfrac{5}{a^2}$

G. The meaning of the fractional exponent is illustrated by the following.

(1) $10^{2/3} = \sqrt[3]{10^2}$ *(2)* $10^{3/2} = \sqrt{10^3}$ *(3)* $10^{1/2} = \sqrt{10}$ *(4)* $4^{3/2} = \sqrt{4^3} = \sqrt{64} = 8$

H.   *(1)* $(10^3)^2 = 10^{3 \times 2} = 10^6$ *(2)* $(10^{-2})^3 = 10^{-2 \times 3} = 10^{-6}$ *(3)* $(a^3)^{-2} = a^{-6}$

I. To extract the square root, divide the exponent by 2. If the exponent is an odd number it should be increased or decreased by 1, and the coefficient adjusted accordingly. To extract the cube root, divide the exponent by 3. The coefficients are treated independently.

(1) $\sqrt{90,000} = \sqrt{9 \times 10^4} = 3 \times 10^2$

(2) $\sqrt{3.6 \times 10^7} = \sqrt{36 \times 10^6} = 6 \times 10^3$

(3) $\sqrt{4.9 \times 10^{-5}} = \sqrt{49 \times 10^{-6}} = 7 \times 10^{-3}$

(4) $\sqrt[3]{1.25 \times 10^8} = \sqrt[3]{125 \times 10^6} = 5 \times 10^2$

J. Multiplication and division of numbers expressed as powers of ten.

(1) $8000 \times 2500 = (8 \times 10^3)(2.5 \times 10^3) = 20 \times 10^6 = 2 \times 10^7$ or $20{,}000{,}000$

(2) $\dfrac{48{,}000{,}000}{1200} = \dfrac{48 \times 10^6}{12 \times 10^2} = 4 \times 10^{6-2} = 4 \times 10^4$ or $40{,}000$

(3) $\dfrac{0.0078}{120} = \dfrac{7.8 \times 10^{-3}}{1.2 \times 10^2} = 6.5 \times 10^{-5}$ or 0.000065

(4) $(4 \times 10^{-3})(5 \times 10^4)^2 = (4 \times 10^{-3})(5^2 \times 10^8) = 4 \times 5^2 \times 10^{-3+8} = 100 \times 10^5 = 1 \times 10^7$

(5) $\dfrac{(6{,}000{,}000)(0.00004)^4}{(800)^2(0.0002)^3} = \dfrac{(6 \times 10^6)(4 \times 10^{-5})^4}{(8 \times 10^2)^2(2 \times 10^{-4})^3} = \dfrac{6 \times 4^4}{8^2 \times 2^3} \times \dfrac{10^6 \times 10^{-20}}{10^4 \times 10^{-12}}$

$= \dfrac{6 \times 256}{64 \times 8} \times \dfrac{10^{6-20}}{10^{4-12}} = 3 \times \dfrac{10^{-14}}{10^{-8}} = 3 \times 10^{-6}$

(6) $(\sqrt{4.0 \times 10^{-6}})(\sqrt{8.1 \times 10^3})(\sqrt{0.0016}) = (\sqrt{4.0 \times 10^{-6}})(\sqrt{81 \times 10^2})(\sqrt{16 \times 10^{-4}})$

$= (2 \times 10^{-3})(9 \times 10^1)(4 \times 10^{-2}) = 72 \times 10^{-4} = 7.2 \times 10^{-3}$ or 0.0072

(7) $(\sqrt[3]{6.4 \times 10^{-2}})(\sqrt[3]{27{,}000})(\sqrt[3]{2.16 \times 10^{-4}}) = (\sqrt[3]{64 \times 10^{-3}})(\sqrt[3]{27 \times 10^3})(\sqrt[3]{216 \times 10^{-6}})$

$= (4 \times 10^{-1})(3 \times 10^1)(6 \times 10^{-2}) = 72 \times 10^{-2}$ or 0.72

EXERCISES

1. Express the following in powers of 10.

(1) 320	(7) 0.000002	*Ans.* (1) 3.2×10^2	(7) 2×10^{-6}
(2) 32,600	(8) 0.000706	(2) 3.26×10^4	(8) 7.06×10^{-4}
(3) 1006	(9) $\sqrt{640{,}000}$	(3) 1.006×10^3	(9) 8.0×10^2
(4) 36,000,000	(10) $\sqrt{0.000081}$	(4) 3.6×10^7	(10) 9.0×10^{-3}
(5) 0.831	(11) $\sqrt[3]{8{,}000{,}000}$	(5) 8.31×10^{-1}	(11) 2×10^2
(6) 0.03	(12) $\sqrt[3]{0.000027}$	(6) 3×10^{-2}	(12) 3×10^{-2}

2. Evaluate the following and express the results in powers of 10.

(1) 1500×260

(2) $220 \times 35{,}000$

(3) $40 \div 20{,}000$

(4) $82{,}800 \div 0.12$

(5) $\dfrac{1.728 \times 17.28}{0.0001728}$

(6) $\dfrac{(16{,}000)(0.0002)(1.2)}{(2000)(0.006)(0.00032)}$

(7) $\dfrac{0.004 \times 32{,}000 \times 0.6}{6400 \times 3000 \times 0.08}$

(8) $(\sqrt{14{,}400})(\sqrt{0.000025})$

(9) $(\sqrt[3]{2.7 \times 10^7})(\sqrt[3]{1.25 \times 10^{-4}})$

(10) $(1 \times 10^{-3})(2 \times 10^5)^2$

(11) $\dfrac{(3 \times 10^2)^3(2 \times 10^{-5})^2}{3.6 \times 10^{-8}}$

(12) $8(2 \times 10^{-2})^{-3}$

Ans. (1) 3.9×10^5

(2) 7.7×10^6

(3) 2×10^{-3}

(4) 6.9×10^5

(5) 1.728×10^5

(6) 1×10^3

(7) 5×10^{-5}

(8) 6.0×10^{-1}

(9) 1.5×10^1

(10) 4×10^7

(11) 3×10^5

(12) 1×10^6

Logarithms

DEFINITION OF TERMS.

The logarithm of a number is the exponent, or power, of a given base that is required to produce that number. For example, since $1000 = 10^3$, $100 = 10^2$, $10 = 10^1$, $1 = 10^0$, then the logarithms of 1000, 100, 10, 1, to the base 10 are respectively 3, 2, 1, 0.

The system of logarithms whose base is 10 (called the common or Briggsian system) may be used in all numerical computations.

It is obvious that $10^{1.5377}$ will give some number greater than 10 (which is 10^1) but smaller than 100 (10^2). Actually, $10^{1.5377} = 34.49$; hence $\log 34.49 = 1.5377$. The digit before the decimal point is the **characteristic** of the log, and the decimal fraction part is the **mantissa** of the log. In the above example, the characteristic is 1 and the mantissa is .5377.

The mantissa of the log of a number is found in tables, printed without the decimal point. Each mantissa in the tables is understood to have a decimal point preceding it, and the mantissa is always considered positive.

THE CHARACTERISTIC.

The characteristic is determined by inspection from the number itself according to the following rules.

(*1*) For a number greater than 1, the characteristic is positive and is one **less** than the number of digits before the decimal point. For example:

Number	5297	348	900	34.8	60	4.764	3
Characteristic	3	2	2	1	1	0	0

(*2*) For a number less than 1, the characteristic is negative and is one **more** than the number of zeros immediately following the decimal point. The negative sign of the characteristic is written in either of these two ways: (*a*) above the characteristic, as $\bar{1}$, $\bar{2}$, and so on; (*b*) as $9. -10$, $8. -10$, and so on. Thus the characteristic of the logarithm of 0.3485 is $\bar{1}$, or $9. -10$; of the logarithm of 0.0513 is $\bar{2}$, or $8. -10$.

TO FIND THE LOGARITHM OF A NUMBER by use of tables of logarithms in the Appendix.

Suppose it is required to find the complete log of the number 728. In the table of logarithms in the Appendix glance down the N column to 72, then horizontally to the right to column 8 and note the entry 8621 which is the required mantissa. Since the characteristic is 2, $\log 728 = 2.8621$. (This means that $728 = 10^{2.8621}$.)

The mantissa for log 72.8, for log 7.28, for log 0.728, for log 0.0728, etc., is .8621, but the characteristics differ. Thus:

$\log 728$	$= 2.8621$	$\log 0.728$	$= \bar{1}.8621$ or	$9.8621 - 10$
$\log 72.8$	$= 1.8621$	$\log 0.0728$	$= \bar{2}.8621$ or	$8.8621 - 10$
$\log 7.28$	$= 0.8621$	$\log 0.00728$	$= \bar{3}.8621$ or	$7.8621 - 10$

To find log 46.38: Glance down the N column to 46, then horizontally to column 3 and note the mantissa 6656. Moving farther to the right along the same line, the digit 7 is found under column 8 of Proportional Parts. The required mantissa is $.6656 + .0007 = .6663$. Since the characteristic is 1, $\log 46.38 = 1.6663$.

The mantissa for log 4638, for log 463.8, for log 46.38, etc., is .6663, but the characteristics differ. Thus:

$\log 4638$	$= 3.6663$	$\log 0.4638$	$= \bar{1}.6663$ or	$9.6663 - 10$
$\log 463.8$	$= 2.6663$	$\log 0.04638$	$= \bar{2}.6663$ or	$8.6663 - 10$
$\log 46.38$	$= 1.6663$	$\log 0.004638$	$= \bar{3}.6663$ or	$7.6663 - 10$
$\log 4.638$	$= 0.6663$	$\log 0.0004638$	$= \bar{4}.6663$ or	$6.6663 - 10$

Exercises. Find the logarithms of the following numbers.

(1) 454	(6) 0.621	*Ans.* (1) 2.6571	(6) $\overline{1}.7931$	or	$9.7931-10$
(2) 5280	(7) 0.9463	(2) 3.7226	(7) $\overline{1}.9760$	or	$9.9760-10$
(3) 96,500	(8) 0.0353	(3) 4.9845	(8) $\overline{2}.5478$	or	$8.5478-10$
(4) 30.48	(9) 0.0022	(4) 1.4840	(9) $\overline{3}.3424$	or	$7.3424-10$
(5) 1.057	(10) 0.0002645	(5) 0.0241	(10) $\overline{4}.4224$	or	$6.4224-10$

ANTILOGARITHMS.

The antilogarithm is the number corresponding to a given logarithm. "The antilog of 3" means "the number whose log is 3"; that number is obviously 1000.

Suppose it is required to find the antilog of 2.6747, i.e. the number whose log is 2.6747. The characteristic is 2 and the mantissa is .6747. Using the table of Antilogarithms in the Appendix, locate 67 in the first column, then move horizontally to column 4 and note the digits 4721. Moving farther to the right along the same line, the entry 8 is found under column 7 of Proportional Parts. Adding 8 to 4721 gives 4729. Since the characteristic is 2, there are three digits to the left of the decimal point. Hence 472.9 is the required number.

Similarly, the antilog of 1.6747 is 47.29; the antilog of 0.6747 is 4.729; the antilog of $9.6747-10$ is 0.4729; etc.

Exercises. Find the numbers corresponding to the following logarithms.

(1) 3.1568	(6) 0.9142	*Ans.* (1) 1435		(6) 8.208
(2) 1.6934	(7) 0.0008	(2) 49.37		(7) 1.002
(3) 5.6934	(8) $9.7507-10$ or $\overline{1}.7507$	(3) 4.937×10^5		(8) 0.5632
(4) 2.5000	(9) $8.0034-10$ or $\overline{2}.0034$	(4) 316.2		(9) 0.01008
(5) 2.0436	(10) $7.2006-10$ or $\overline{3}.2006$	(5) 110.6		(10) 0.001587

BASIC PRINCIPLES OF LOGARITHMS.

Since logarithms are exponents, all properties of exponents are also properties of logarithms.

(A) The logarithm of the product of two numbers is the sum of their logarithms.

$$\log ab = \log a + \log b \qquad \log(5280\times48) = \log 5280 + \log 48$$

(B) The logarithm of the quotient of two numbers is the logarithm of the numerator minus the logarithm of the denominator.

$$\log\frac{a}{b} = \log a - \log b \qquad \log\frac{536}{24.5} = \log 536 - \log 24.5$$

(C) The log of the nth power of a number is n times the log of the number.

$$\log a^n = n\log a \qquad \log(4.28)^3 = 3\log 4.28$$

(D) The log of the nth root of a number is the log of the number divided by n.

$$\log\sqrt[n]{a} = \frac{1}{n}\log a \qquad \log\sqrt{32} = \frac{1}{2}\log 32 \qquad \log\sqrt[3]{792} = \frac{1}{3}\log 792$$

ILLUSTRATIONS OF THE USE OF LOGARITHMS.

1. Find the value of $487\times2.45\times0.0387$.

Let $x = 487\times2.45\times0.0387$.

$\log x = \log 487 + \log 2.45 + \log 0.0387$
$\qquad = 1.6644$

$\quad x = $ antilog $1.6644 = 46.17$ or 46.2

$\log 487 \quad = 2.6875$
$\log 2.45 \quad = 0.3892$
$\log 0.0387 = \underline{8.5877-10}$ (add)
$\qquad \log x = 11.6644-10$
$\qquad$ or $\quad 1.6644$

2. Find $x = \dfrac{136.3}{65.38}$.

$\log x = \log 136.3 - \log 65.38 = 0.3191$

$\quad x = $ antilog $0.3191 = 2.084$

$\log 136.3 = 2.1345$
$\log 65.38 = \underline{1.8154}$ (subtract)
$\qquad \log x = 0.3191$

3. Find $x = \dfrac{1}{22.4}$.

$\log x = \log 1 - \log 22.4 = 8.6498 - 10$

$x = \text{antilog } 8.6498 - 10$

$= 0.04465 \text{ or } 0.0446 \text{ (three significant figures)}$

$\begin{aligned}
\log 1 &= 0 = 10.0000 - 10 \\
\log 22.4 &= \underline{1.3502} \quad \text{(subtract)} \\
\log x &= 8.6498 - 10
\end{aligned}$

Adding or subtracting $10.0000 - 10$, $20.0000 - 20$, etc., from any logarithm does not change its value.

4. Find $x = \dfrac{17.5 \times 1.92}{0.283 \times 0.0314}$.

$\log x = (\log 17.5 + \log 1.92) - (\log 0.283 + \log 0.0314)$

$\begin{aligned}
\log 17.5 &= 1.2430 \\
\log 1.92 &= \underline{0.2833} \quad \text{(add)} \\
& 1.5263 \text{ or } 11.5263 - 10
\end{aligned}$
$\qquad\begin{aligned}
\log 0.283 &= 9.4518 - 10 \\
\log 0.0314 &= \underline{8.4969 - 10} \quad \text{(add)} \\
& 17.9487 - 20 \text{ or } 7.9487 - 10
\end{aligned}$

$\begin{aligned}
\log 17.5 + \log 1.92 &= 11.5263 - 10 \\
\log 0.283 + \log 0.0314 &= \underline{7.9487 - 10} \quad \text{(subtract)} \\
\log x &= 3.5776 \\
x &= \text{antilog } 3.5776 = 3781 \text{ or } 3780 \text{ or } 3.78 \times 10^3
\end{aligned}$

5. Find $x = (6.138)^3$.

$\log x = 3(\log 6.138) = 3(0.7881) = 2.3643$

$x = \text{antilog } 2.3643 = 231.4$

6. Find $x = \sqrt{7514}$ or $(7514)^{1/2}$.

$\log x = \tfrac{1}{2}(\log 7514) = \tfrac{1}{2}(3.8758) = 1.9379$

$x = \text{antilog } 1.9379 = 86.68$

7. Find $x = \sqrt[3]{0.0592}$ or $(0.0592)^{1/3}$.

$\log x = \tfrac{1}{3}\log 0.0592 = \tfrac{1}{3}(8.7723 - 10) = \tfrac{1}{3}(28.7723 - 30) = 9.5908 - 10$

$x = \text{antilog } 9.5908 - 10 = 0.3897 \text{ or } 0.390 \text{ (three significant figures)}$

8. Find $x = \sqrt{(152)^3}$.

$\log x = \tfrac{1}{2}(3 \log 152) = \tfrac{1}{2}(3 \times 2.1818) = \tfrac{1}{2}(6.5454) = 3.2727$

$x = \text{antilog } 3.2727 = 1874 \text{ or } 1870 \text{ or } 1.87 \times 10^3 \text{ (three significant figures)}$

9. Find $(6.8 \times 10^{-4})^3$ or $(6.8)^3 \times 10^{-12}$.

$\log (6.8)^3 = 3(\log 6.8) = 3(0.8325) = 2.4975$

$(6.8)^3 = \text{antilog } 2.4975 = 314.5 \text{ or } 310 \text{ or } 3.1 \times 10^2 \text{ (two significant figures)}$

Then $(6.8 \times 10^{-4})^3 = 3.1 \times 10^2 \times 10^{-12} = 3.1 \times 10^{-10}$

10. Find $\sqrt{8.31 \times 10^{-11}}$ or $\sqrt{83.1 \times 10^{-12}}$ or $\sqrt{83.1} \times 10^{-6}$.

$\log \sqrt{83.1} = \tfrac{1}{2}(\log 83.1) = \tfrac{1}{2}(1.9196) = 0.9598$

$\sqrt{83.1} = \text{antilog } 0.9598 = 9.116 \text{ or } 9.12$

Then $\sqrt{8.31 \times 10^{-11}} = 9.12 \times 10^{-6}$

EXERCISES

Evaluate each of the following, using logarithms.

(1) 28.32×0.08254

(2) $573 \times 6.96 \times 0.00481$

(3) $\dfrac{79.28}{63.57}$

(4) $\dfrac{65.38}{225.2}$

(5) $\dfrac{1}{239}$

(6) $\dfrac{0.572 \times 31.8}{96.2}$

(7) $47.5 \times \dfrac{779}{760} \times \dfrac{273}{300}$

(8) $(8.642)^2$

(9) $(0.08642)^2$

(10) $(11.72)^3$

(11) $(0.0523)^3$

(12) $\sqrt{9463}$

(13) $\sqrt{946.3}$

(14) $\sqrt{0.00661}$

(15) $\sqrt[3]{1.79}$

(16) $\sqrt[4]{0.182}$

(17) $\sqrt{643} \times (1.91)^3$

(18) $(8.73 \times 10^{-2})(7.49 \times 10^{8})$

(19) $(3.8 \times 10^{-5})^2 (1.9 \times 10^{-5})$

(20) $\dfrac{8.5 \times 10^{-45}}{1.6 \times 10^{-22}}$

(21) $\sqrt{2.54 \times 10^{6}}$

(22) $\sqrt{9.44 \times 10^{5}}$

(23) $\sqrt{7.2 \times 10^{-13}}$

(24) $\sqrt[3]{7.3 \times 10^{-14}}$

(25) $\sqrt{\dfrac{(1.1 \times 10^{-23})(6.8 \times 10^{-2})}{1.4 \times 10^{-24}}}$

(26) $2.04 \log 97.2$

(27) $37 \log 0.0298$

(28) $6.30 \log (2.95 \times 10^{3})$

(29) $8.09 \log (5.68 \times 10^{-16})$

(30) $2^{0.714}$

Ans.

(1) 2.337

(2) 19.2

(3) 1.247

(4) 0.2902

(5) 0.00418

(6) 0.189

(7) 44.3

(8) 74.67

(9) 0.007467

(10) 1611

(11) 0.000143

(12) 97.27

(13) 30.76

(14) 0.0813

(15) 1.21

(16) 0.653

(17) 177

(18) 6.54×10^{5}

(19) 2.7×10^{-14}

(20) 5.3×10^{-23}

(21) 1.59×10^{3}

(22) 9.72×10^{2}

(23) 8.5×10^{-7}

(24) 4.2×10^{-5}

(25) 0.73

(26) 4.05

(27) -56

(28) 21.9

(29) -123.3

(30) 1.64

Appendix E

Units and Conversion Factors

Length

1 kilometer (km) = 1000 meters   1 inch (in.) = 2.540 cm

1 meter (m) = 100 centimeters   1 foot (ft) = 30.48 cm

1 centimeter (cm) = 10^{-2} m   1 mile (mi) = 1.609 km

1 millimeter (mm) = 10^{-3} m   1 mil = 10^{-3} in.

1 micron (μ) = 10^{-6} m   1 centimeter = 0.3937 in.

1 millimicron (mμ) = 10^{-9} m   1 meter = 39.37 in.

1 angstrom (A) = 10^{-10} m   1 kilometer = 0.6214 mile

Area

1 square meter (m^2) = 10.76 ft^2 1 square mile (mi^2) = 640 acres

1 square foot (ft^2) = 929 cm^2 1 acre = 43,560 ft^2

Volume

1 liter (l) = 1000.027 cm^3 = 1000 milliliters (ml) = 1.057 qt = 61.02 in^3 = 0.03532 ft^3

1 cubic meter (m^3) = 1000 l = 35.32 ft^3

1 cubic foot (ft^3) = 7.481 U.S. gal = 0.02832 m^3 = 28.32 l

1 U.S. gallon (gal) = 231 in^3 = 3.785 l

Mass

1 kilogram (kg) = 0.06852 slug;   1 slug = 14.59 kg

Speed

1 km/hr = 0.2778 m/sec = 0.6214 mi/hr = 0.9113 ft/sec

1 mi/hr = 1.467 ft/sec = 1.609 km/hr = 0.4470 m/sec

Density

1 g/cm^3 = 10^3 kg/m^3 = 1.940 slug/ft^3

1 slug/ft^3 = 515.4 kg/m^3 = 0.5154 g/cm^3

Weight density   1 lb/ft^3 = 16.02 kg-wt/m^3 = 0.01602 g-wt/cm^3

Force

1 newton (nt) = 10^5 dynes = 0.1020 kg wt = 0.2248 lb

1 pound (lb) = 4.448 nt = 0.4536 kg wt = 32.17 poundals

1 kilogram weight (kg wt) = 2.205 lb = 9.807 nt

1 U.S. short ton = 2000 lb;   1 long ton = 2240 lb;   1 metric ton = 2205 lb

Energy

1 joule = 1 nt-m = 10^7 ergs = 0.2389 cal = 0.7376 ft-lb = 9.481×10^{-4} Btu

1 calorie (cal) = 4.186 joules = 3.087 ft-lb = 3.968×10^{-3} Btu

1 Btu = 252 cal = 1055 joules = 778 ft-lb = 0.293 watt-hr

1 foot-pound (ft-lb) = 1.356 joules = 0.3239 cal = 1.285×10^{-3} Btu

1 electron-volt (ev) = 1.602×10^{-19} joule

1 kilowatt-hour (kw-hr) = 3.60×10^6 joules = 860.0 kcal = 3413 Btu

Power

1 watt = 1 joule/sec = 10^7 ergs/sec = 0.2389 cal/sec

1 horsepower (hp) = 550 ft-lb/sec = 33,000 ft-lb/min = 745.7 watts

1 kilowatt (kw) = 1.341 hp = 737.6 ft-lb/sec = 0.9483 Btu/sec

Pressure

1 nt/m^2 = 10 dynes/cm^2 = 9.869×10^{-6} atmosphere = 2.089×10^{-2} lb/ft^2

1 lb/in^2 = 6895 nt/m^2 = 5.171 cm mercury = 27.68 in. water

1 atmosphere (atm) = 76 cm mercury = 406.8 in. water = 14.70 lb/in^2

                 = 1.013×10^5 nt/m^2 = 1.013×10^6 dynes/cm^2 = 1013 millibars

Important Physical Constants

Speed of light in free space .... c = 2.9979×10^8 m/sec

Acceleration due to gravity (normal) .... g = 9.807 m/sec^2

Gravitational constant .... G = 6.670×10^{-11} nt-m^2/kg^2

Density of water (maximum).....................   = 0.999972 g/cm^3

Density of mercury (STP).......................   = 13.595 g/cm^3

Standard atmosphere ....   = 1.0132×10^5 nt/m^2

Volume of ideal gas at STP ....   = 22.421 cm^3 per mole

Avogadro number .... N_O = 6.025×10^{23} particles per mole

Universal gas constant .... R = 8.3166 joules/mole-^{O}K

Ice point ....   = 273.15^OK

Mechanical equivalent of heat .... J = 4.1855 joules/cal

Stefan-Boltzmann constant .... σ = 5.6686×10^{-8} watt/m^2-^{O}K^4

Planck constant .... h = 6.6252×10^{-34} joule-sec

Faraday .... F = 9.6520×10^4 coulombs

Electronic charge.............................. e = 1.6021×10^{-19} coulomb

Electron-volt.................................. ev   = 1.6021×10^{-19} joule

Ratio of electron charge to mass................ e/m_e = 1.7589×10^{11} coulomb/kg

Electron rest mass ....   = 9.1086×10^{-31} kg

Proton rest mass ....   = 1.6724×10^{-27} kg

Neutron rest mass ....   = 1.6747×10^{-27} kg

Alpha particle rest mass.......................   = 6.6434×10^{-27} kg

Atomic mass unit (1/16 mass of O^{16}) .... amu   = 1.6597×10^{-27} kg

Atomic mass of natural oxygen on physical scale ....   = 16.0044

$\dfrac{\text{Atomic mass on physical scale}}{\text{Atomic mass on chemical scale}}$ ....   = $\dfrac{16.0044}{16}$ = 1.00027

Rest energy of 1 amu..........................   = 931.16 Mev

THE GREEK ALPHABET											
A	α	Alpha	H	η	Eta	N	ν	Nu	T	τ	Tau
B	β	Beta	Θ	θ	Theta	Ξ	ξ	Xi	Υ	υ	Upsilon
Γ	γ	Gamma	I	ι	Iota	O	o	Omicron	Φ	ϕ	Phi
Δ	δ	Delta	K	κ	Kappa	Π	π	Pi	X	χ	Chi
E	ϵ	Epsilon	Λ	λ	Lambda	P	ρ	Rho	Ψ	ψ	Psi
Z	ζ	Zeta	M	μ	Mu	Σ	σ	Sigma	Ω	ω	Omega

Conversion of Electrical Units

Quantity	Symbol	Practical unit (mks)	Electrostatic unit (esu)	Electromagnetic unit (emu)
Mass	m	1 kilogram	1000 g	1000 g
Length	l	1 meter	100 cm	100 cm
Time	t	1 second	1 sec	1 sec
Force	F	1 newton	10^5 dynes	10^5 dynes
Energy	W	1 joule	10^7 ergs	10^7 ergs
Power	P	1 watt	10^7 ergs/sec	10^7 ergs/sec
Charge	q	1 coulomb	3×10^9 statcoul	10^{-1} abcoul
Current	I	1 ampere	3×10^9 statamp	10^{-1} abamp
Potential difference, emf	$V, \mathcal{E}$	1 volt	1/300 statvolt	10^8 abvolts
Electric intensity	E	1 volt/meter	$1/3 \times 10^{-4}$ statvolt/cm	10^6 abvolts/cm
Capacitance	C	1 farad	9×10^{11} statfarads	10^{-9} abfarad
Resistance	R	1 ohm	$1/9 \times 10^{-11}$ statohm	10^9 abohms
Permittivity of a vacuum	ϵ_O	$\dfrac{1}{36\pi \times 10^9} \dfrac{\text{coul}^2}{\text{nt-m}^2}$		
Permeability of a vacuum	μ_O	$\dfrac{4\pi}{10^7} \dfrac{\text{weber}}{\text{amp-m}}$		
Magnetic flux	Φ	1 weber		10^8 maxwells
Magnetic induction	B	1 weber/m^2		10^4 gauss
Magnetic field intensity	H	1 amp-turn/m		$4\pi \times 10^{-3}$ oersted
Inductance	L, M	1 henry	$1/9 \times 10^{-11}$ stathenry	10^9 abhenrys

FOUR-PLACE LOGARITHMS

N	0	1	2	3	4	5	6	7	8	9	Proportional Parts 1 2 3 4 5 6 7 8 9
10	0000	0043	0086	0128	0170	0212	0253	0294	0334	0374	4 8 12 17 21 25 29 33 37
11	0414	0453	0492	0531	0569	0607	0645	0682	0719	0755	4 8 11 15 19 23 26 30 34
12	0792	0828	0864	0899	0934	0969	1004	1038	1072	1106	3 7 10 14 17 21 24 28 31
13	1139	1173	1206	1239	1271	1303	1335	1367	1399	1430	3 6 10 13 16 19 23 26 29
14	1461	1492	1523	1553	1584	1614	1644	1673	1703	1732	3 6 9 12 15 18 21 24 27
15	1761	1790	1818	1847	1875	1903	1931	1959	1987	2014	3 6 8 11 14 17 20 22 25
16	2041	2068	2095	2122	2148	2175	2201	2227	2253	2279	3 5 8 11 13 16 18 21 24
17	2304	2330	2355	2380	2405	2430	2455	2480	2504	2529	2 5 7 10 12 15 17 20 22
18	2553	2577	2601	2625	2648	2672	2695	2718	2742	2765	2 5 7 9 12 14 16 19 21
19	2788	2810	2833	2856	2878	2900	2923	2945	2967	2989	2 4 7 9 11 13 16 18 20
20	3010	3032	3054	3075	3096	3118	3139	3160	3181	3201	2 4 6 8 11 13 15 17 19
21	3222	3243	3263	3284	3304	3324	3345	3365	3385	3404	2 4 6 8 10 12 14 16 18
22	3424	3444	3464	3483	3502	3522	3541	3560	3579	3598	2 4 6 8 10 12 14 15 17
23	3617	3636	3655	3674	3692	3711	3729	3747	3766	3784	2 4 6 7 9 11 13 15 17
24	3802	3820	3838	3856	3874	3892	3909	3927	3945	3962	2 4 5 7 9 11 12 14 16
25	3979	3997	4014	4031	4048	4065	4082	4099	4116	4133	2 3 5 7 9 10 12 14 15
26	4150	4166	4183	4200	4216	4232	4249	4265	4281	4298	2 3 5 7 8 10 11 13 15
27	4314	4330	4346	4362	4378	4393	4409	4425	4440	4456	2 3 5 6 8 9 11 13 14
28	4472	4487	4502	4518	4533	4548	4564	4579	4594	4609	2 3 5 6 8 9 11 12 14
29	4624	4639	4654	4669	4683	4698	4713	4728	4742	4757	1 3 4 6 7 9 10 12 13
30	4771	4786	4800	4814	4829	4843	4857	4871	4886	4900	1 3 4 6 7 9 10 11 13
31	4914	4928	4942	4955	4969	4983	4997	5011	5024	5038	1 3 4 6 7 8 10 11 12
32	5051	5065	5079	5092	5105	5119	5132	5145	5159	5172	1 3 4 5 7 8 9 11 12
33	5185	5198	5211	5224	5237	5250	5263	5276	5289	5302	1 3 4 5 6 8 9 10 12
34	5315	5328	5340	5353	5366	5378	5391	5403	5416	5428	1 3 4 5 6 8 9 10 11
35	5441	5453	5465	5478	5490	5502	5514	5527	5539	5551	1 2 4 5 6 7 9 10 11
36	5563	5575	5587	5599	5611	5623	5635	5647	5658	5670	1 2 4 5 6 7 8 10 11
37	5682	5694	5705	5717	5729	5740	5752	5763	5775	5786	1 2 3 5 6 7 8 9 10
38	5798	5809	5821	5832	5843	5855	5866	5877	5888	5899	1 2 3 5 6 7 8 9 10
39	5911	5922	5933	5944	5955	5966	5977	5988	5999	6010	1 2 3 4 5 7 8 9 10
40	6021	6031	6042	6053	6064	6075	6085	6096	6107	6117	1 2 3 4 5 6 8 9 10
41	6128	6138	6149	6160	6170	6180	6191	6201	6212	6222	1 2 3 4 5 6 7 8 9
42	6232	6243	6253	6263	6274	6284	6294	6304	6314	6325	1 2 3 4 5 6 7 8 9
43	6335	6345	6355	6365	6375	6385	6395	6405	6415	6425	1 2 3 4 5 6 7 8 9
44	6435	6444	6454	6464	6474	6484	6493	6503	6513	6522	1 2 3 4 5 6 7 8 9
45	6532	6542	6551	6561	6571	6580	6590	6599	6609	6618	1 2 3 4 5 6 7 8 9
46	6628	6637	6646	6656	6665	6675	6684	6693	6702	6712	1 2 3 4 5 6 7 7 8
47	6721	6730	6739	6749	6758	6767	6776	6785	6794	6803	1 2 3 4 5 5 6 7 8
48	6812	6821	6830	6839	6848	6857	6866	6875	6884	6893	1 2 3 4 4 5 6 7 8
49	6902	6911	6920	6928	6937	6946	6955	6964	6972	6981	1 2 3 4 4 5 6 7 8
50	6990	6998	7007	7016	7024	7033	7042	7050	7059	7067	1 2 3 3 4 5 6 7 8
51	7076	7084	7093	7101	7110	7118	7126	7135	7143	7152	1 2 3 3 4 5 6 7 8
52	7160	7168	7177	7185	7193	7202	7210	7218	7226	7235	1 2 2 3 4 5 6 7 7
53	7243	7251	7259	7267	7275	7284	7292	7300	7308	7316	1 2 2 3 4 5 6 6 7
54	7324	7332	7340	7348	7356	7364	7372	7380	7388	7396	1 2 2 3 4 5 6 6 7
N	0	1	2	3	4	5	6	7	8	9	1 2 3 4 5 6 7 8 9

FOUR-PLACE LOGARITHMS

N	0	1	2	3	4	5	6	7	8	9	Proportional Parts 1	2	3	4	5	6	7	8	9
55	7404	7412	7419	7427	7435	7443	7451	7459	7466	7474	1	2	2	3	4	5	5	6	7
56	7482	7490	7497	7505	7513	7520	7528	7536	7543	7551	1	2	2	3	4	5	5	6	7
57	7559	7566	7574	7582	7589	7597	7604	7612	7619	7627	1	2	2	3	4	5	5	6	7
58	7634	7642	7649	7657	7664	7672	7679	7686	7694	7701	1	1	2	3	4	4	5	6	7
59	7709	7716	7723	7731	7738	7745	7752	7760	7767	7774	1	1	2	3	4	4	5	6	7
60	7782	7789	7796	7803	7810	7818	7825	7832	7839	7846	1	1	2	3	4	4	5	6	6
61	7853	7860	7868	7875	7882	7889	7896	7903	7910	7917	1	1	2	3	4	4	5	6	6
62	7924	7931	7938	7945	7952	7959	7966	7973	7980	7987	1	1	2	3	4	4	5	6	6
63	7993	8000	8007	8014	8021	8028	8035	8041	8048	8055	1	1	2	3	3	4	5	6	6
64	8062	8069	8075	8082	8089	8096	8102	8109	8116	8122	1	1	2	3	3	4	5	5	6
65	8129	8136	8142	8149	8156	8162	8169	8176	8182	8189	1	1	2	3	3	4	5	5	6
66	8195	8202	8209	8215	8222	8228	8235	8241	8248	8254	1	1	2	3	3	4	5	5	6
67	8261	8267	8274	8280	8287	8293	8299	8306	8312	8319	1	1	2	3	3	4	5	5	6
68	8325	8331	8338	8344	8351	8357	8363	8370	8376	8382	1	1	2	3	3	4	4	5	6
69	8388	8395	8401	8407	8414	8420	8426	8432	8439	8445	1	1	2	2	3	4	4	5	6
70	8451	8457	8463	8470	8476	8482	8488	8494	8500	8506	1	1	2	2	3	4	4	5	6
71	8513	8519	8525	8531	8537	8543	8549	8555	8561	8567	1	1	2	2	3	4	4	5	5
72	8573	8579	8585	8591	8597	8603	8609	8615	8621	8627	1	1	2	2	3	4	4	5	5
73	8633	8639	8645	8651	8657	8663	8669	8675	8681	8686	1	1	2	2	3	4	4	5	5
74	8692	8698	8704	8710	8716	8722	8727	8733	8739	8745	1	1	2	2	3	4	4	5	5
75	8751	8756	8762	8768	8774	8779	8785	8791	8797	8802	1	1	2	2	3	4	5	5	
76	8808	8814	8820	8825	8831	8837	8842	8848	8854	8859	1	1	2	2	3	3	4	5	5
77	8865	8871	8876	8882	8887	8893	8899	8904	8910	8915	1	1	2	2	3	3	4	5	5
78	8921	8927	8932	8938	8943	8949	8954	8960	8965	8971	1	1	2	2	3	3	4	4	5
79	8976	8982	8987	8993	8998	9004	9009	9015	9020	9025	1	1	2	2	3	3	4	4	5
80	9031	9036	9042	9047	9053	9058	9063	9069	9074	9079	1	1	2	2	3	3	4	4	5
81	9085	9090	9096	9101	9106	9112	9117	9122	9128	9133	1	1	2	2	3	3	4	4	5
82	9138	9143	9149	9154	9159	9165	9170	9175	9180	9186	1	1	2	2	3	3	4	4	5
83	9191	9196	9201	9206	9212	9217	9222	9227	9232	9238	1	1	2	2	3	3	4	4	5
84	9243	9248	9253	9258	9263	9269	9274	9279	9284	9289	1	1	2	2	3	3	4	4	5
85	9294	9299	9304	9309	9315	9320	9325	9330	9335	9340	1	1	2	2	3	3	4	4	5
86	9345	9350	9355	9360	9365	9370	9375	9380	9385	9390	1	1	2	2	3	3	4	4	5
87	9395	9400	9405	9410	9415	9420	9425	9430	9435	9440	0	1	1	2	2	3	3	4	4
88	9445	9450	9455	9460	9465	9469	9474	9479	9484	9489	0	1	1	2	2	3	3	4	4
89	9494	9499	9504	9509	9513	9518	9523	9528	9533	9538	0	1	1	2	2	3	3	4	4
90	9542	9547	9552	9557	9562	9566	9571	9576	9581	9586	0	1	1	2	2	3	3	4	4
91	9590	9595	9600	9605	9609	9614	9619	9624	9628	9633	0	1	1	2	2	3	3	4	4
92	9638	9643	9647	9652	9657	9661	9666	9671	9675	9680	0	1	1	2	2	3	3	4	4
93	9685	9689	9694	9699	9703	9708	9713	9717	9722	9727	0	1	1	2	2	3	3	4	4
94	9731	9736	9741	9745	9750	9754	9759	9763	9768	9773	0	1	1	2	2	3	3	4	4
95	9777	9782	9786	9791	9795	9800	9805	9809	9814	9818	0	1	1	2	2	3	3	4	4
96	9823	9827	9832	9836	9841	9845	9850	9854	9859	9863	0	1	1	2	2	3	3	4	4
97	9868	9872	9877	9881	9886	9890	9894	9899	9903	9908	0	1	1	2	2	3	3	4	4
98	9912	9917	9921	9926	9930	9934	9939	9943	9948	9952	0	1	1	2	2	3	3	4	4
99	9956	9961	9965	9969	9974	9978	9983	9987	9991	9996	0	1	1	2	2	3	3	3	4
N	0	1	2	3	4	5	6	7	8	9	1	2	3	4	5	6	7	8	9

ANTILOGARITHMS

	0	1	2	3	4	5	6	7	8	9	Proportional Parts 1 2 3 4 5 6 7 8 9
.00	1000	1002	1005	1007	1009	1012	1014	1016	1019	1021	0 0 1 1 1 1 2 2 2
.01	1023	1026	1028	1030	1033	1035	1038	1040	1042	1045	0 0 1 1 1 1 2 2 2
.02	1047	1050	1052	1054	1057	1059	1062	1064	1067	1069	0 0 1 1 1 1 2 2 2
.03	1072	1074	1076	1079	1081	1084	1086	1089	1091	1094	0 0 1 1 1 1 2 2 2
.04	1096	1099	1102	1104	1107	1109	1112	1114	1117	1119	0 1 1 1 1 2 2 2 2
.05	1122	1125	1127	1130	1132	1135	1138	1140	1143	1146	0 1 1 1 1 2 2 2 2
.06	1148	1151	1153	1156	1159	1161	1164	1167	1169	1172	0 1 1 1 1 2 2 2 2
.07	1175	1178	1180	1183	1186	1189	1191	1194	1197	1199	0 1 1 1 1 2 2 2 2
.08	1202	1205	1208	1211	1213	1216	1219	1222	1225	1227	0 1 1 1 1 2 2 2 3
.09	1230	1233	1236	1239	1242	1245	1247	1250	1253	1256	0 1 1 1 1 2 2 2 3
.10	1259	1262	1265	1268	1271	1274	1276	1279	1282	1285	0 1 1 1 1 2 2 2 3
.11	1288	1291	1294	1297	1300	1303	1306	1309	1312	1315	0 1 1 1 2 2 2 2 3
.12	1318	1321	1324	1327	1330	1334	1337	1340	1343	1346	0 1 1 1 2 2 2 2 3
.13	1349	1352	1355	1358	1361	1365	1368	1371	1374	1377	0 1 1 1 2 2 2 3 3
.14	1380	1384	1387	1390	1393	1396	1400	1403	1406	1409	0 1 1 1 2 2 2 3 3
.15	1413	1416	1419	1422	1426	1429	1432	1435	1439	1442	0 1 1 1 2 2 2 3 3
.16	1445	1449	1452	1455	1459	1462	1466	1469	1472	1476	0 1 1 1 2 2 2 3 3
.17	1479	1483	1486	1489	1493	1496	1500	1503	1507	1510	0 1 1 1 2 2 2 3 3
.18	1514	1517	1521	1524	1528	1531	1535	1538	1542	1545	0 1 1 1 2 2 2 3 3
.19	1549	1552	1556	1560	1563	1567	1570	1574	1578	1581	0 1 1 1 2 2 3 3 3
.20	1585	1589	1592	1596	1600	1603	1607	1611	1614	1618	0 1 1 1 2 2 3 3 3
.21	1622	1626	1629	1633	1637	1641	1644	1648	1652	1656	0 1 1 2 2 2 3 3 3
.22	1660	1663	1667	1671	1675	1679	1683	1687	1690	1694	0 1 1 2 2 2 3 3 3
.23	1698	1702	1706	1710	1714	1718	1722	1726	1730	1734	0 1 1 2 2 2 3 3 4
.24	1738	1742	1746	1750	1754	1758	1762	1766	1770	1774	0 1 1 2 2 2 3 3 4
.25	1778	1782	1786	1791	1795	1799	1803	1807	1811	1816	0 1 1 2 2 2 3 3 4
.26	1820	1824	1828	1832	1837	1841	1845	1849	1854	1858	0 1 1 2 2 3 3 3 4
.27	1862	1866	1871	1875	1879	1884	1888	1892	1897	1901	0 1 1 2 2 3 3 3 4
.28	1905	1910	1914	1919	1923	1928	1932	1936	1941	1945	0 1 1 2 2 3 3 4 4
.29	1950	1954	1959	1963	1968	1972	1977	1982	1986	1991	0 1 1 2 2 3 3 4 4
.30	1995	2000	2004	2009	2014	2018	2023	2028	2032	2037	0 1 1 2 2 3 3 4 4
.31	2042	2046	2051	2056	2061	2065	2070	2075	2080	2084	0 1 1 2 2 3 3 4 4
.32	2089	2094	2099	2104	2109	2113	2118	2123	2128	2133	0 1 1 2 2 3 3 4 4
.33	2138	2143	2148	2153	2158	2163	2168	2173	2178	2183	0 1 1 2 2 3 3 4 4
.34	2188	2193	2198	2203	2208	2213	2218	2223	2228	2234	1 1 2 2 3 3 4 4 5
.35	2239	2244	2249	2254	2259	2265	2270	2275	2280	2286	1 1 2 2 3 3 4 4 5
.36	2291	2296	2301	2307	2312	2317	2323	2328	2333	2339	1 1 2 2 3 3 4 4 5
.37	2344	2350	2355	2360	2366	2371	2377	2382	2388	2393	1 1 2 2 3 3 4 4 5
.38	2399	2404	2410	2415	2421	2427	2432	2438	2443	2449	1 1 2 2 3 3 4 4 5
.39	2455	2460	2466	2472	2477	2483	2489	2495	2500	2506	1 1 2 2 3 3 4 5 5
.40	2512	2518	2523	2529	2535	2541	2547	2553	2559	2564	1 1 2 2 3 4 4 5 5
.41	2570	2576	2582	2588	2594	2600	2606	2612	2618	2624	1 1 2 2 3 4 4 5 5
.42	2630	2636	2642	2649	2655	2661	2667	2673	2679	2685	1 1 2 2 3 4 4 5 6
.43	2692	2698	2704	2710	2716	2723	2729	2735	2742	2748	1 1 2 3 3 4 4 5 6
.44	2754	2761	2767	2773	2780	2786	2793	2799	2805	2812	1 1 2 3 3 4 4 5 6
.45	2818	2825	2831	2838	2844	2851	2858	2864	2871	2877	1 1 2 3 3 4 5 5 6
.46	2884	2891	2897	2904	2911	2917	2924	2931	2938	2944	1 1 2 3 3 4 5 5 6
.47	2951	2958	2965	2972	2979	2985	2992	2999	3006	3013	1 1 2 3 3 4 5 5 6
.48	3020	3027	3034	3041	3048	3055	3062	3069	3076	3083	1 1 2 3 4 4 5 6 6
.49	3090	3097	3105	3112	3119	3126	3133	3141	3148	3155	1 1 2 3 4 4 5 6 6
	0	1	2	3	4	5	6	7	8	9	1 2 3 4 5 6 7 8 9

264

ANTILOGARITHMS

	0	1	2	3	4		5	6	7	8	9		Proportional Parts 1 2 3 4 5 6 7 8 9
.50	3162	3170	3177	3184	3192		3199	3206	3214	3221	3228		1 1 2 3 4 4 5 6 7
.51	3236	3243	3251	3258	3266		3273	3281	3289	3296	3304		1 2 2 3 4 5 5 6 7
.52	3311	3319	3327	3334	3342		3350	3357	3365	3373	3381		1 2 2 3 4 5 5 6 7
.53	3388	3396	3404	3412	3420		3428	3436	3443	3451	3459		1 2 2 3 4 5 6 6 7
.54	3467	3475	3483	3491	3499		3508	3516	3524	3532	3540		1 2 2 3 4 5 6 6 7
.55	3548	3556	3565	3573	3581		3589	3597	3606	3614	3622		1 2 2 3 4 5 6 7 7
.56	3631	3639	3648	3656	3664		3673	3681	3690	3698	3707		1 2 3 3 4 5 6 7 8
.57	3715	3724	3733	3741	3750		3758	3767	3776	3784	3793		1 2 3 3 4 5 6 7 8
.58	3802	3811	3819	3828	3837		3846	3855	3864	3873	3882		1 2 3 4 4 5 6 7 8
.59	3890	3899	3908	3917	3926		3936	3945	3954	3963	3972		1 2 3 4 5 5 6 7 8
.60	3981	3990	3999	4009	4018		4027	4036	4046	4055	4064		1 2 3 4 5 6 6 7 8
.61	4074	4083	4093	4102	4111		4121	4130	4140	4150	4159		1 2 3 4 5 6 7 8 9
.62	4169	4178	4188	4198	4207		4217	4227	4236	4246	4256		1 2 3 4 5 6 7 8 9
.63	4266	4276	4285	4295	4305		4315	4325	4335	4345	4355		1 2 3 4 5 6 7 8 9
.64	4365	4375	4385	4395	4406		4416	4426	4436	4446	4457		1 2 3 4 5 6 7 8 9
.65	4467	4477	4487	4498	4508		4519	4529	4539	4550	4560		1 2 3 4 5 6 7 8 9
.66	4571	4581	4592	4603	4613		4624	4634	4645	4656	4667		1 2 3 4 5 6 7 9 10
.67	4677	4688	4699	4710	4721		4732	4742	4753	4764	4775		1 2 3 4 5 7 8 9 10
.68	4786	4797	4808	4819	4831		4842	4853	4864	4875	4887		1 2 3 4 6 7 8 9 10
.69	4898	4909	4920	4932	4943		4955	4966	4977	4989	5000		1 2 3 5 6 7 8 9 10
.70	5012	5023	5035	5047	5058		5070	5082	5093	5105	5117		1 2 4 5 6 7 8 9 11
.71	5129	5140	5152	5164	5176		5188	5200	5212	5224	5236		1 2 4 5 6 7 8 10 11
.72	5248	5260	5272	5284	5297		5309	5321	5333	5346	5358		1 2 4 5 6 7 9 10 11
.73	5370	5383	5395	5408	5420		5433	5445	5458	5470	5483		1 3 4 5 6 8 9 10 11
.74	5495	5508	5521	5534	5546		5559	5572	5585	5598	5610		1 3 4 5 6 8 9 10 12
.75	5623	5636	5649	5662	5675		5689	5702	5715	5728	5741		1 3 4 5 7 8 9 10 12
.76	5754	5768	5781	5794	5808		5821	5834	5848	5861	5875		1 3 4 5 7 8 9 11 12
.77	5888	5902	5916	5929	5943		5957	5970	5984	5998	6012		1 3 4 5 7 8 10 11 12
.78	6026	6039	6053	6067	6081		6095	6109	6124	6138	6152		1 3 4 6 7 8 10 11 13
.79	6166	6180	6194	6209	6223		6237	6252	6266	6281	6295		1 3 4 6 7 9 10 11 13
.80	6310	6324	6339	6353	6368		6383	6397	6412	6427	6442		1 3 4 6 7 9 10 12 13
.81	6457	6471	6486	6501	6516		6531	6546	6561	6577	6592		2 3 5 6 8 9 11 12 14
.82	6607	6622	6637	6653	6668		6683	6699	6714	6730	6745		2 3 5 6 8 9 11 12 14
.83	6761	6776	6792	6808	6823		6839	6855	6871	6887	6902		2 3 5 6 8 9 11 13 14
.84	6918	6934	6950	6966	6982		6998	7015	7031	7047	7063		2 3 5 6 8 10 11 13 15
.85	7079	7096	7112	7129	7145		7161	7178	7194	7211	7228		2 3 5 7 8 10 12 13 15
.86	7244	7261	7278	7295	7311		7328	7345	7362	7379	7396		2 3 5 7 8 10 12 13 15
.87	7413	7430	7447	7464	7482		7499	7516	7534	7551	7568		2 3 5 7 9 10 12 14 16
.88	7586	7603	7621	7638	7656		7674	7691	7709	7727	7745		2 4 5 7 9 11 12 14 16
.89	7762	7780	7798	7816	7834		7852	7870	7889	7907	7925		2 4 5 7 9 11 13 14 16
.90	7943	7962	7980	7998	8017		8035	8054	8072	8091	8110		2 4 6 7 9 11 13 15 17
.91	8128	8147	8166	8185	8204		8222	8241	8260	8279	8299		2 4 6 8 9 11 13 15 17
.92	8318	8337	8356	8375	8395		8414	8433	8453	8472	8492		2 4 6 8 10 12 14 15 17
.93	8511	8531	8551	8570	8590		8610	8630	8650	8670	8690		2 4 6 8 10 12 14 16 18
.94	8710	8730	8750	8770	8790		8810	8831	8851	8872	8892		2 4 6 8 10 12 14 16 18
.95	8913	8933	8954	8974	8995		9016	9036	9057	9078	9099		2 4 6 8 10 12 15 17 19
.96	9120	9141	9162	9183	9204		9226	9247	9268	9290	9311		2 4 6 8 11 13 15 17 19
.97	9333	9354	9376	9397	9419		9441	9462	9484	9506	9528		2 4 7 9 11 13 15 17 20
.98	9550	9572	9594	9616	9638		9661	9683	9705	9727	9750		2 4 7 9 11 13 16 18 20
.99	9772	9795	9817	9840	9863		9886	9908	9931	9954	9977		2 5 7 9 11 14 16 18 20
	0	1	2	3	4		5	6	7	8	9		1 2 3 4 5 6 7 8 9

NATURAL TRIGONOMETRIC FUNCTIONS

Angle	Sine	Cosine	Tangent	Angle	Sine	Cosine	Tangent
1°	.0175	.9998	.0175	46°	.7193	.6947	1.0355
2°	.0349	.9994	.0349	47°	.7314	.6820	1.0724
3°	.0523	.9986	.0524	48°	.7431	.6691	1.1106
4°	.0698	.9976	.0699	49°	.7547	.6561	1.1504
5°	.0872	.9962	.0875	50°	.7660	.6428	1.1918
6°	.1045	.9945	.1051	51°	.7771	.6293	1.2349
7°	.1219	.9925	.1228	52°	.7880	.6157	1.2799
8°	.1392	.9903	.1405	53°	.7986	.6018	1.3270
9°	.1564	.9877	.1584	54°	.8090	.5878	1.3764
10°	.1736	.9848	.1763	55°	.8192	.5736	1.4281
11°	.1908	.9816	.1944	56°	.8290	.5592	1.4826
12°	.2079	.9781	.2126	57°	.8387	.5446	1.5399
13°	.2250	.9744	.2309	58°	.8480	.5299	1.6003
14°	.2419	.9703	.2493	59°	.8572	.5150	1.6643
15°	.2588	.9659	.2679	60°	.8660	.5000	1.7321
16°	.2756	.9613	.2867	61°	.8746	.4848	1.8040
17°	.2924	.9563	.3057	62°	.8829	.4695	1.8807
18°	.3090	.9511	.3249	63°	.8910	.4540	1.9626
19°	.3256	.9455	.3443	64°	.8988	.4384	2.0503
20°	.3420	.9397	.3640	65°	.9063	.4226	2.1445
21°	.3584	.9336	.3839	66°	.9135	.4067	2.2460
22°	.3746	.9272	.4040	67°	.9205	.3907	2.3559
23°	.3907	.9205	.4245	68°	.9272	.3746	2.4751
24°	.4067	.9135	.4452	69°	.9336	.3584	2.6051
25°	.4226	.9063	.4663	70°	.9397	.3420	2.7475
26°	.4384	.8988	.4877	71°	.9455	.3256	2.9042
27°	.4540	.8910	.5095	72°	.9511	.3090	3.0777
28°	.4695	.8829	.5317	73°	.9563	.2924	3.2709
29°	.4848	.8746	.5543	74°	.9613	.2756	3.4874
30°	.5000	.8660	.5774	75°	.9659	.2588	3.7321
31°	.5150	.8572	.6009	76°	.9703	.2419	4.0108
32°	.5299	.8480	.6249	77°	.9744	.2250	4.3315
33°	.5446	.8387	.6494	78°	.9781	.2079	4.7046
34°	.5592	.8290	.6745	79°	.9816	.1908	5.1446
35°	.5736	.8192	.7002	80°	.9848	.1736	5.6713
36°	.5878	.8090	.7265	81°	.9877	.1564	6.3138
37°	.6018	.7986	.7536	82°	.9903	.1392	7.1154
38°	.6157	.7880	.7813	83°	.9925	.1219	8.1443
39°	.6293	.7771	.8098	84°	.9945	.1045	9.5144
40°	.6428	.7660	.8391	85°	.9962	.0872	11.4301
41°	.6561	.7547	.8693	86°	.9976	.0698	14.3007
42°	.6691	.7431	.9004	87°	.9986	.0523	19.0811
43°	.6820	.7314	.9325	88°	.9994	.0349	28.6363
44°	.6947	.7193	.9657	89°	.9998	.0175	57.2900
45°	.7071	.7071	1.0000	90°	1.0000	.0000	

Index

SCHAUM'S OUTLINE SERIES